The Gender of Critical Theory

The Gender of Critical Theory

On the Experiential Grounds of Critique

LOIS McNAY

OXFORD
UNIVERSITY PRESS

UNIVERSITY PRESS

Great Clarendon Street, Oxford, OX2 6DP,
United Kingdom

Oxford University Press is a department of the University of Oxford.
It furthers the University's objective of excellence in research, scholarship,
and education by publishing worldwide. Oxford is a registered trade mark of
Oxford University Press in the UK and in certain other countries

© Lois McNay 2022

The moral rights of the author have been asserted

First Edition published in 2022

Impression: 2

All rights reserved. No part of this publication may be reproduced, stored in
a retrieval system, or transmitted, in any form or by any means, without the
prior permission in writing of Oxford University Press, or as expressly permitted
by law, by licence or under terms agreed with the appropriate reprographics
rights organization. Enquiries concerning reproduction outside the scope of the
above should be sent to the Rights Department, Oxford University Press, at the
address above

You must not circulate this work in any other form
and you must impose this same condition on any acquirer

Published in the United States of America by Oxford University Press
198 Madison Avenue, New York, NY 10016, United States of America

British Library Cataloguing in Publication Data

Data available

Library of Congress Control Number: 2021950189

ISBN 978–0–19–885774–7 (hbk.)
ISBN 978–0–19–885775–4 (pbk.)

DOI: 10.1093/oso/9780198857747.001.0001

Printed and bound by
CPI Group (UK) Ltd, Croydon, CR0 4YY

Links to third party websites are provided by Oxford in good faith and
for information only. Oxford disclaims any responsibility for the materials
contained in any third party website referenced in this work.

Acknowledgements

A shorter version of Chapter 2 first appeared as 'The Limits of Justification: Critique, Disclosure and Reflexivity', *European Journal of Political Theory*, 19 (1), 2016: 26–46. A shorter version of Chapter 3 first appeared as 'Social Freedom in the Family: Reflections on Care, Gender and Inequality', *Critical Horizons*, 16 (2), 2015: 170–86. A shorter version of Chapter 4 first appeared as 'The Politics of Exemplarity: Ferrara on the Disclosure of New Political Worlds', *Philosophy and Social Criticism*, 45 (2), 2019: 127–45.

I am grateful to the Principal and Fellows of Somerville College and to the Department of Politics and International Relations at Oxford University for granting me the year of sabbatical leave (2019–20) which enabled me to write the bulk of the manuscript. From 2018 to 2020 I held the post of Professor 2 in Political Theory at the Centre for Gender Research, University Oslo. The conversations that I had with staff and students during this time were instrumental in helping me clarify ideas for this book. I am indebted above all to Helene Aarseth for nominating me for the post, for the stimulating discussions I had with her about my work and for the care and generosity with which she hosted my visits to Oslo. The book has been immeasurably improved by implementing, as best I could, the insightful and constructive suggestions made by the anonymous readers of the original proposal and manuscript. Whether they know it or not, conversations (mostly brief and in passing) with Robin Celikates, Maeve Cooke, Murray Hunt, Nikos Papastergiadis, and Sophie Smith have been invaluable in allowing me to improve my thoughts on various matters. I thank Murray and my children, Maisie, Freddie, and Solomon for their enduring support and for providing distraction and fun—especially welcome as much of the book was written during lockdown.

Contents

Introduction	1
1. Unmasking Power: Experience, Gender, and Oppression	23
2. Experience at the Limits of Justification	62
3. Recognition and Progress in the Family	93
4. The Politics of Disclosure	124
5. Critique and the 'Merely Experienced'	156
6. The Incompatibility of Formalism and Negativism	191
Conclusion: Theorizing from Experience	225
Bibliography	243
Index	257

Introduction

Frankfurt School critical theorists typically set their style of normative thought apart from competing approaches by emphasizing its practical emancipatory credentials. Unlike speculative types of normative theory beginning from reflection on abstract principles and ideals, critical theory is rooted in analysis of social reality and specifically the multifarious inequalities and oppressive dynamics that, in its view, are inherent to capitalist societies. Unmasking critique's direct focus on existing oppressions is held to endow it with a practical political relevance that is missing in hypothetical normative theories which, if they address issues of power at all, tend to do so only secondarily in a derivative fashion. Unmasking critique further shores up its claim to practical emancipatory relevance by maintaining that not only does it confront asymmetries of power head on but also, in doing so, it aligns itself explicitly with the perspective and interests of oppressed groups. The critique of power is conducted not from a top-down, institutional view but instead from a bottom-up view anchored in everyday instances of suffering and misery which are taken as symptoms of deeper societal wrongs. As Iris Marion Young puts it: 'normative reflection arises from hearing a cry of suffering or distress or feeling distress oneself' (1990: 5). It is this responsiveness to real-world suffering that is the bedrock of the claim that Frankfurt School critique is of direct practical relevance to subordinated groups. For, in making explicit occluded connections between lived suffering and underlying structures of oppression, critique endeavours to help subordinated groups understand the causes of their misery better and contribute constructively to their struggles for emancipation. Negative experience is not just the animating object of inquiry, for it is also the subjects who undergo such experiences who are themselves the principal addressees of critique.

Given the defining primacy accorded to this nested set of arguments about negative experience, the critique of power and practical emancipation, this book asks why it is that Frankfurt School thinkers seemingly have so little of substance to say about real-world dynamics of oppression. This is not a startlingly new observation; other commentators have similarly remarked on the lack of sustained attention paid to major axes of oppression. Class oppression, a topic which one might imagine would be of overriding concern given the Frankfurt School's intellectual roots in Marxism, has been downplayed if not abandoned altogether (Thompson 2017). Issues of racial oppression have received virtually no attention whatsoever (Mills 2017a). Likewise, reliance on a deeply Eurocentric account of modernity and reason means that Frankfurt School theory also seems to lack an appropriate conceptual framework with which to address matters of colonial and postcolonial oppression (Allen 2016). Gender oppression—the concern of this book—does not fare much better. As a fundamental principle that organizes hierarchies of power in all societal realms, gender would seem, on the face of it, to be of paramount concern for unmasking critique. Yet, with a few notable exceptions, Frankfurt School theorists treat issues of gender oppression in a manner that is cursory and simplistic. When the topic is discussed at all, it is done so in a superficial way that construes gender as only bearing on personal relations between men and women in the family. Such epiphenomenal analyses show little understanding of gender as a structural force that systematically determines distributions of wealth and resources, shapes employment and labour practices, defines access to legal rights, tracks dynamics of violence, and so on. In short, the failure of Frankfurt School thinkers to address major fault-lines of oppression in any kind of concrete detail ultimately throws into doubt the practical emancipatory relevance that they declare gives unmasking critique a critical edge over other types of political philosophy.

What then explains this striking discontinuity between the Frankfurt School's description of its theoretical enterprise as a radical critique of power grounded in the lived reality of suffering, and the paucity of substantive sociological insights that it actually offers into enduring dynamics of oppression in capitalist societies? I answer this question by pointing, like several others, to the foundational normative turn taken by Frankfurt School thinkers over the last few decades, and the deep and unresolved ambivalence that this seems to have set in motion in relation to the status that the category of negative experience should play in unmasking critique. For while they ostensibly accord it an animating role and speak of the origins of theory in experiences of 'pain and repression', they also express with increasing frequency deep reservations about the stymying effect that too heavy a reliance on the idea of lived experience has on critique. These worries are typically articulated in terms of what is held to be the inherently partisan, unreliable, and particularistic nature of direct, lived experience and the problems of subjectivism, relativism, and so forth that this potentially presents for critique. By binding itself too tightly to the particularity of lived suffering, critique places in jeopardy its aim to produce wider, systematic knowledge about oppression and risks becoming merely localized complaint. These concerns have thus given rise to a discernible if subtle downplaying on the part of Frankfurt School theorists of the experiential grounds of unmasking critique.

Unsurprisingly, given the monumental influence that it has had on the intellectual direction of the Frankfurt School in the last few decades, it is in the work of Habermas that the origins of this retreat from experience can be located. From the mid-1960s onwards, his worries about the parochializing entailments that the category of experience may have for critique led him to concentrate on the corrective issue of context-transcending foundations. His well-known post-metaphysical solution to the problem of foundations is to identify a single principle that, although internal to social life, can be said to be so fundamentally determining of existence that it provides critique with an independent or 'quasi-transcendental' stance from which to evaluate plural life-worlds. Habermas's recasting of foundations as 'intra-mundane transcendence' seems to overcome worries about critique's wider diagnostic and normative relevance, since it furnishes a theoretical perspective not limited to any single experiential constellation. At the same time, the derivation of a foundational principle from social praxis remains consistent with the Frankfurt's School's commitment to sociologically grounded normative theorizing and responsiveness to lived suffering. There is no denying the galvanizing effect that Habermas's foundational turn has had on Frankfurt School critical theory. His thought has singlehandedly shifted the Frankfurt School's intellectual centre of gravity almost in its entirety towards metatheoretical reflection on issues of normative grounds, validity, and justification. In contrast to the rather despairing diagnoses of mass society in which first-generation critical theory was based, much of the Frankfurt School energy is nowadays devoted to metatheoretical issues of foundation and debate over the most effective 'rational universal' in which to ground critique. Is recognition more existentially capacious than communication? Does justification have greater deontological rigour than recognition? In what measure is participatory parity a more accurate measure of the complexities of power and oppression than either principles of recognition or justification? And so on. Of course, Frankfurt School thinkers still, in principle, insist on the importance of rooting emancipatory critique in the lived reality of oppression or, to paraphrase Rainer Forst, power must remain the first question of justice. But there is no doubt that real-world concerns about power and negative experience have lost much of their animating force and become of secondary theoretical significance, that is, they have become issues that tend to be tacked on, in some cases rather cursorily, only after second-order considerations about normative foundations have been completed. Indeed, it is my argument that the foundational turn has initiated a mode of theorizing that is more incompatible than Frankfurt School thinkers are willing to acknowledge with the kind of practical emancipatory critique of oppression that they claim to be engaged in.

This book's central contention is that the Frankfurt School's preoccupation with context transcendence has given rise to a 'paradigm-led' mode of theorizing that, because it is not sufficiently responsive to lived experience, undermines an effective diagnosis of oppression. The rationale of paradigm-led theory is to produce a comprehensive diagnosis of society that interprets all relations according to an underlying foundational principle. Paradigm-led critique is then both monist—the origins of social relations lie in a single, constitutive principle of communication, recognition, justification, and so on—and totalizing in accordance with the left-Hegelian desire to theorize capitalist society in its entirety. The problem with paradigm-led theorizing is that, when it is decoupled from an experientially grounded critique of power, it results in an account of oppression that is simplified and schematic. Indeed, the extent to which second-order debates about the respective merits of assorted founding principles have come to dominate recent Frankfurt School thought suggests that the main concern of paradigm-led theory is more to affirm the integrity and authority of a given monist framework than it is to develop an adequate critique of power. This self-referential concern with validating the integrity of a particular paradigm over its effectiveness as diagnosis of power has limiting effects on all three dimensions of unmasking critique: explanatory, normative, and epistemic.

First, in terms of social explanation, mono-causal or 'single lens' diagnoses, which focus on the origins of power rather than on its specific distributions and the experiential spaces to which it gives rise, do not adequately capture the complex nature of oppression. This mono-causal simplification is most obvious, as I go on to show, with regard to the Frankfurt School's failure to theorize intersectionality in even its most basic sense of the differential shaping of women's lives by intersecting vectors of race, class, and gender. Instead, where they do address issues of gender, Frankfurt School theorists rely on generic, sociologically underspecified archetypes of the family that ignore the significant disparities in experience and life chances that arise from the place families occupy in structures of race, class, and gender. Not only do these decontextualized accounts ignore differences between families but they are also narrowly focused on interpersonal dynamics between men and women at the expense of considering impersonal dynamics of subordination, that is, the socio-structural forces that routinely produce gendered vulnerabilities. In short, it seems to follow that if oppressions are intersectional and complex, then accordingly any explanation of them should be differentiated and multidimensional not mono-causal.

Second, given the interconnectedness posited by the Frankfurt School thinkers between fact and norm, the diagnostic shortcomings of paradigm-led theory inevitably give rise to corresponding limitations in normative responses to determinate issues of oppression. Monist normative solutions are, at best, tangential to the identification and correction of complex inequalities and dynamics of power. For instance, the treatment of gendered care work as an essentially ethical matter of recognition is vague and underdetermined in comparison with detailed feminist work on local and global economies of care.

Third, paradigm-led theory sits uneasily with the Frankfurt's School's explicit commitment to theoretical inquiry that is of practical relevance to oppressed groups in their struggles for emancipation. This commitment to practical theorizing goes beyond that of simply making experiences of oppression the principal theme or object of concern for inquiry, for it also means that disempowered groups themselves are the intended recipients or addressees of theory. This has implications for the practice of theoretical reasoning itself which, in line with the

Frankfurt School's hermeneutic premises, is in any case never a purely disinterested, scholastic activity, but situated in the field of inquiry itself and therefore necessarily responsive to the needs and demands of the groups it studies. The usual way in which this responsiveness is conceived is as the situated, dialogical, and reflexive nature of critical reasoning. As participant observer, the theorist unavoidably has a practical-ethical relation with those she studies and therefore grants them a role in the process of knowledge production that is more active than the one conventionally granted by objectifying explanatory theory. According to this dialogical dynamic, the legitimacy of critical theory does not rest solely on its internal characteristics of coherence, objective accuracy, and so on—although of course these qualities are of paramount importance—but also in the degree to which it captures the lived reality of oppressed groups themselves. The validity of unmasking critique partly depends on its acceptance or verification by the subjects whose situation it addresses. If critique is to meet this acceptability requirement, it needs to be responsive to and make sense of unfamiliar experiential life-worlds in a way that is not estranging but makes sense to the groups involved. In addition, given that unmasking critique addresses groups who are already disempowered, dialogism might be reasonably held to include an epistemic responsibility on the part of the theorist to avoid forms of didacticism and prescription that are unnecessarily alienating to them and might symbolically compound their vulnerability. In other words, reflexivity is the necessary correlate of dialogism. In the light of their encounter with vulnerable others, the theorist needs to be willing to be self-critical, to scrutinize their own intellectual practice and presumptions and, if needs be, modify them.

The problem with paradigm-led theorizing is that it undermines the enactment of these praxeological qualities of dialogism and reflexivity. The ambivalence that Frankfurt School thinkers hold about the epistemic value of lived experience to the critique of oppression means that they end up according it a circumscribed and passive role in the process of knowledge production. This problematization and containment of experience constrains the receptivity to difference and critical mutuality that defines dialogical reasoning, and replaces these features with an epistemic hierarchy that accords interpretative authority to the theoretical perspective, qua interpretative paradigm. The over-problematization of the experiential perspective as inherently partial and unreliable is accompanied by an under-problematization of the theoretical perspective as itself situated and therefore potentially marked by uninterrogated biases. Paradigm-led theorizing thus blocks the capacity for reflexivity or self-criticism that is supposedly an 'indispensable' feature of emancipatory critique. The quasi-transcendental status bestowed by Frankfurt School thinkers on their foundational principles serves, in practice, to mute reflexivity by placing their paradigms outside of the hermeneutic circle, thus shielding them from thorough-going critical scrutiny. Ultimately then, the curtailment of dialogism and reflexivity creates a paradigm closure that is antithetical to the experientially responsive mode of theorizing which is a supposed hallmark of Frankfurt School critique.

I maintain that overcoming this disjunction between the Frankfurt School's definition of itself as unmasking critique rooted in negative experience and its actual paradigm-led theoretical practice cannot be overcome simply by importing into their work more relevant detail about concrete forms of oppression. For what is in question here is precisely the inherent logic of paradigm-led theorizing itself, the ways in which its monist, totalizing and hierarchizing tendencies minimize the significance of lived experience for critique and therefore also undercut an effective understanding of oppression. As a corrective to these tendencies, I propose instead the idea of theorizing from experience, an approach which affirms the pivotal importance of the lived reality of those directly affected to an unmasking critique oppression. Its animating premise is that far from undermining critical theory's wider, diagnostic relevance, lived experience is indispensable to adequate theoretical understanding of the complex dynamics of oppression and therefore compatible with, not destructive of, context-transcending critique. Indeed, theorizing from experience is more consistent than paradigm-led theory with the political and ethical entailments of the asserted practical emancipatory nature of critique. If a defining feature of critical theory, vis-à-vis other types of normative theory, is that it directly addresses the concerns of oppressed groups and aims to make a practical contribution to their empowerment, then it follows that it ought to presumptively treat their experiences and accounts of the world as epistemically valuable. To do otherwise, that is to presume in advance that these experiences are inherently flawed and problematic, is inconsistent with the ethical, political, and theoretical commitments of emancipatory critique. In fact, it would be tantamount to retreating to exactly the top-down model of knowledge production as an abstracted, objectifying process that critical theorists explicitly reject. But, despite professing its practical emancipatory allegiance, this is in fact where paradigm-led theorizing ends up, in so far as it subtly disparages direct experiences of oppression and downplays their epistemic value relative to the superior insight of the theorist/theoretical framework in producing knowledge about oppression. In a fundamental sense, then, theorizing from experience is more consistent with the Frankfurt School's emancipatory tenets, because it is rooted not in an implicit hierarchy of theory over experience, but in an assumption of epistemic equality where credibility is granted to the experiences of oppressed groups in the process of knowledge production.

By drawing on the work of feminists and other radical thinkers, I show how the idea of theorizing from experience does not reduce critique to a parochial form of disclosure devoid of wider explanatory and normative impact. Rather it gives rise to a different understanding of context-transcending critique not, as Frankfurt School thinkers see it, as a totalizing interpretative framework into which all social problems can be fed but as a dialogical process of reasoning across perspectives.

Context transcendence is the critical and evaluative insight, or expansion of immanent perspectives, generated by bringing differing experiential and theoretical worldviews to bear on each other in the process of inquiry. This is not to dismiss out of hand concerns about subjectivism, particularism, relativism, and related problems that Frankfurt School theorists see as arising from uncritical deferral to experience and that have driven their quest for context-transcending foundations.[1] But though such concerns are legitimate and raise problems potential in any process of cross-perspectival reasoning, Frankfurt School theorists tend to overstate them and to attribute them aprioristically to one side only of the theory–experience dynamic. Put differently, their propensity to over-problematize the experiential perspective leads to its essentialization as inherently particularistic and parochial and therefore a hindrance to critique. However, my argument is that when experience is de-essentialized and understood in relation to social location and distributions of power, then the role that it plays in an unmasking critique of oppression becomes correspondingly more significant and less one-sidedly problematic. The correlate of the Frankfurt School's over-problematization of experience is an under-problematization of its own theoretical perspective, qua monist paradigm, that is, critique does not live up to its professed tenet of reflexivity by leaving its interpretative authority unquestioned. The theoretical worldview certainly has a crucial part to play in overcoming blindspots and errors in the first-hand worldview, but, contra paradigm-led thought, it does not automatically have a monopoly on this improving and authenticating role. For, direct subjective experience may be similarly instrumental in exposing shortcomings and errors in theoretical frameworks, in prompting the theorist to think differently and therefore in expanding horizons of understanding. On this alternative view, explanatory and normative insight is generated not by the comprehensive interpretative stance of the paradigm alone, but by the movement of thought itself between experiential and theoretical, subjective, and objective, personal and transpersonal worldviews. Context-transcending insight is, in short, internal to the process of dialogical reasoning where the mutual irreducibility and alienness of each perspective serves as the basis to interrogate and transcend the limitations of the other.

In contrast then to the synthesizing tendencies of paradigm-led theory where social relations are traced back to a constitutive source, theorizing from experience

---

[1] More generally, there are related interpretative difficulties connected to verstehen and appropriate methods for accessing the subjective experiences of others. How it is possible to understand someone else, to take their experiences seriously without, as Merleau Ponty puts it 'sacrificing him to our logic or it to him' (1964: 115). These issues lie at the heart of sociological understanding and are widely debated. While relevant to the experientially approach proposed here, it is beyond the scope of this book to address such methodological issues. Instead, focus is on the entailments that lived experience has for political theory.

works inductively from heterogenous life-worlds to crystallize a wider, multivalent or intersectional account of power. The point of advertence to experience is not to uncritically affirm it as the original truth of oppression, but to render critique alive to latent, unrecognized, or emergent dynamics of power that often fall below the threshold of public visibility. Responsiveness to direct subjective experience is, in short, indispensable in sustaining critique's diagnostic capacity, its ability to throw into question the seeming givenness of the social world and identify dimensions of power that may be insidious and indirect including those at work within thought itself. This has implications for the three main functions of critique. First, explanatory force is not equated with a grand theory into which all social problems can be subsumed but with a problem-led, abductive approach that systematically follows determinate lines of thought in order to clarify and resolve the conceptual and normative issues that surround a concrete social issue. This type of abductive analysis is a defining, but now seemingly forgotten, characteristic of Frankfurt School critique, namely, an open, relational and multidimensional mode of theorizing that aims to establish illuminating connections between phenomenal and structural levels of social reality. Second, the wider emancipatory import of critique does not depend on normativity being constructed around an unchanging constitutive core. Instead, theorizing from experience finds normative outcomes immanent in concrete situations and focuses on elucidating a plurality of emancipatory practices rather than formulating a single, overarching theory of emancipation. Finally, theorizing from experience enacts dialogical and reflexive reasoning based in the assumption of the methodological equality of the theoretical and experiential perspectives rather than, as is the case with paradigm-led critical theory, the tacit privilege of the former over the latter.

Although the source of paradigm-led theorizing can be traced to Habermas's thought, his work is not the primary focus of concern here. There is already a huge secondary literature on Habermas, so instead of going over well-known ground again, the focus of this book is on some of his successors in the third and fourth generations of the Frankfurt School. Although deeply influenced by Habermas's work, these succeeding generations of theorists have an acute awareness of some of the more obvious limitations of this thought, including its questionable responsiveness to the lived reality of those disempowered groups with whom it is supposedly most concerned. In different ways, the thinkers considered here explicitly develop their own paradigms in part as antidotes to this much commented upon 'chasm' between the highly rationalistic terms in which Habermas construes communicative ethics and the actual experiences of oppression that it is supposed to capture. Yet, I show how, in the end, each of these thinkers fails to make good on their intention precisely because of their unquestioned adherence to certain tenets of paradigm-led theorizing and, especially, Habermas's strong version of context transcendence that opposes theory to experience, rather than dialogically linking them.

Feminism and Critical Theory

This, in a nutshell, is the argument of the book. By underscoring the importance of an experiential basis to critique, I aim to open up renewed grounds for a revitalized engagement between feminism and Frankfurt School critical theory. But, in the light of what has been said so far about paradigm-led theory, the reader might be forgiven for wondering why feminists concerned with advancing a critique of gender oppression should bother engaging with the thought of the Frankfurt School. In fact, the lack of relevance the latter has for feminist concerns arguably points to the converse; that it perhaps should be members of the Frankfurt School who need to pay more attention to feminist theory so as to improve their own rather undeveloped accounts of gender oppression. Unsurprisingly, then, a number of feminist theorists are sceptical about the intellectual resources that the Frankfurt School has to offer and view it, not without justification, as 'anachronistic rather than still fecund post-Marxist thought' (Brown 2006: 2). On Wendy Brown's account, for instance, Anglo-American feminist theory has become intellectually and politically domesticated precisely in the measure that it has drawn on Habermas's discourse ethics to the exclusion of other more radical thinkers. Feminist theorists of a Habermasian stripe have, in her view, abandoned radical political ambitions 'to overthrow relations of domination' and have settled instead for quietist projects of 'resistance, reform, or resignification on the one hand, and normative political theory abstracted from conditions for its realization, on the other' (Brown 2006: 2). Removing the epithet 'dead', feminists might agree with Stuart Jeffries's provocative observation that 'perhaps, after all, we can dismiss the Frankfurt School as just another bunch of dead white men whose writings have little to say to us now?'[2]

I agree with many of these reservations and, indeed, one of my aims here is to highlight the shortcomings of contemporary Frankfurt School critique, viz. an account of gender oppression, by reading it through the work of feminists situated within areas of critical political theory that are more broadly defined. Nonetheless, despite initial unpromising appearances, I also maintain that Frankfurt School thought does in fact have useful intellectual resources to offer feminists—resources that are arguably not found in such a specific combination in other types of political theory—and that these come, by and large, from the pragmatist threads of the tradition that have been somewhat side-lined by the foundational turn of recent years. Certainly, Frankfurt School thinkers frequently emphasize affinities with pragmatist philosophy in so far as critique's interest in negative

---

[2] Stuart Jeffries 'The Effect of the Whip: The Frankfurt School and the Oppression of Women' at https://www.versobooks.com/blogs/2846-the-effect-of-the-whip-the-frankfurt-school-and-the-oppression-of-women.

experience implies an agent-centred, contextually indexed approach. In practice, however, these affinities are often difficult to discern given the schematizing and socially deracinating tendencies of paradigm-led theory. I argue, however, that it is in the work of certain prominent feminist theorists associated with the Frankfurt School that we can find an alternative, more emphatically pragmatist version of critical theory. Thinkers such as Amy Allen, Seyla Benhabib, Angela Davis, Nancy Fraser, and Iris Marion Young have successfully elaborated neopragmatist outlooks that place the experiences of women and other disempowered groups at the centre of an unmasking critique of power. These differing experientially grounded modes of inquiry suggest an intellectual path for critical theory other than the paradigm-led one it is currently following. Evidently, the pronounced pragmatist orientation of this work is attributable in part to the connections these thinkers have to feminism as a transnational, political movement. Even if academic feminism's roots in political praxis are more highly mediated and therefore weaker than they were in the 1960s and 1970s, it nonetheless often retains a stronger awareness of activist grass-roots concerns than much political theorizing that comes from the heart of the academy. A long-standing priority for transnational feminist politics has been to formulate a systematic critique of gender oppression, in its global operations, while, at the same time, remaining responsive to women's experiences across cultures, those of poor and oppressed women in the global South. This practical activist concern with advancing an effective critique of gender oppression across what are often deep socio-cultural barriers has given rise to related debates within feminist theory, the themes of which are by now familiar. How to conceptualize experience without falling into an unreflective phenomenalism? How to develop explanatory and normative abstractions that illuminate rather than obfuscate gender oppression in its global complexity? How best to articulate justified judgements about gender inequity that avoid ethnocentric moralism on the one side and cultural relativism on the other? How to cultivate modes of reasoning and epistemic dispositions that are genuinely receptive to the voices of others? And so on. In reflecting on these matters, feminist theorists of all stripes, including those allied with the Frankfurt School, have been especially motivated to question conventional organizing assumptions of inquiry, notably, overly dichotomous oppositions of universality and particularity, transcendence, and immanence and attendant ideas of anonymity, neutrality, detachment, impartiality, objectivity. In place of such false antitheses, they have developed pluralized modes of theorizing that connect the particularities of women's lived experience to a wider critique of gender subordination. In short, rather than starting with abstract questions about normative foundations, feminist thinkers begin with praxeological questions about how theory, as situated inquiry, may best respond to the experiences of the women it addresses. Feminists do not ask how 'emancipatory political practice can be theoretically defined and defended', rather they ask 'what theory must look like if it is to speak to practical concerns.... [it]requires...grounding in the immediacy and plurality of life experiences' (Leonard 1990: 213. My parenthesis).

It is against this backdrop of practical concerns that Frankfurt School feminist thinkers have eschewed paradigm-led theory and developed instead experientially grounded and pluralized modes of critical inquiry. In contrast to the totalizing, monist frameworks of their male counterparts, I argue that their approach broadly exemplifies what Iris Marion Young describes as 'theorising with practical intent', that is, a mode of thinking that aims not 'to develop systematic theories that can account for everything in a particular field' but rather follows a line of 'to solve particular conceptual or normative problems that arise from a practical context' (Young 1997: 5). Within this loose unity of theorizing with practical intent, common themes and approaches emerge. First, with respect to the diagnosis of power, feminist theorists reject single-lens or monist social explanations which occlude gender oppression in favour of 'problem led', multidimensional analyses. In the view of Fraser and others, it is not possible to advance a comprehensive critique of capitalism without recognizing the myriad ways in which it is fundamentally dependent on gendered relations of care and women's reproductive labour. To this end, feminist critical theorists deploy a distinctively expansive account of power, a non-economistic materialism that is familiar from the work of the first-generation Frankfurt thinkers and that combines political economy, psychoanalysis, sociology, aesthetics, and philosophy. This open theoretical matrix yields a rich account of social power that penetrates 'language, the psyche, sexuality, aesthetics, reason, and thought itself' (Brown 2006: 3). Feminist critical theory uses this enlarged account of social power as the basis for imaginative and wide-ranging analyses of gender subordination. In particular, it enables them to elicit connections, in a distinctively non-reductive fashion, between the micro and macro levels of social experience, linking studies of concrete phenomena to 'large objects of inquiry', that is, underlying socio-economic structures (Fraser and Nicholson 1990). This open abductive approach to theorizing is reflected in, for example, the essays of Iris Marion Young which range from her celebrated phenomenological studies of female embodiment to more abstract work on conceptualizing gender inequality as the practico-inert or a social connection theory of responsibility and justice (Young 1997, 2005). Nancy Fraser's early essays display a similar interest in problem-led, inductive theorizing where detailed sociological and ethnographic studies are used to elucidate latent socio-structural dynamics of oppression. For example, her essay on needs interpretation (2013) shows how the differing responses of black and white teenage mothers to professional therapeutic interventions sheds light on latent dynamics of racialized, normalizing social control.

Second, the feminist concern with practical political judgement has meant that these critical theorists have developed evaluative models that differ markedly in certain key respects from the normative monism of paradigm-led theory. Prima facie, the Frankfurt School's reconstructive approach to value is seemingly more compatible with feminist theoretical aims than approaches that categorically separate diagnostic from normative aims.[3] Of paramount importance for feminism is, of course, the question of how to construct normative responses to gender oppression that are coherent and systematic but, at the same time, avoid simplistic alignment with Western values and interests. As Khader reminds us, 'Westerners often assume that what is universally valuable for women just is (an idealized form of) the Western way of life. In many theoretical discussions, this peculiar narrow and ethnocentric variant of universalism is what is meant by universalism' (Khader 2019: 4). Immanent critique's method of deriving normative responses from existing practices and struggles seems therefore an appropriate way of responding to this concern about contextual specificity. But, unlike other Frankfurt School thinkers who organize these normative responses around a single generative principle, feminists critical theorists have concentrated on developing pluralized, non-teleological ideas of evaluative reasoning that are sensitive to the context of power and particularly to the situation of disempowered groups. In seeking to overcome gender oppression, they hold that it is politically more effective to devise multiple, situationally specific normative responses than a single grandiose account of emancipation. To this end, some feminists have proffered revised versions of Habermas's discourse ethics because they deem its intersubjective redefinition of rationality to be especially responsive to differences of power and experience. The most well-known exponent of this approach is Seyla Benhabib (1992) who has rectified the excessive cognitivism of Habermasian discourse ethics by, inter alia, expanding moral reasoning to include not just the impartial stance of the General Other but the situated, ethical stance of the Concrete Other.[4] Even with such revisions, however, there are lingering doubts about whether modified versions of discourse ethics are sufficiently responsive to deep difference, given their rootedness in an idea of communicative reason that

---

[3] The ethics-first approach of liberal political thought is problematic for feminist theory in the light of the latent bias of seemingly impartial ideals and abstract universals. While other types of critical theory have developed compelling critiques of power, often from a Foucauldian perspective, they tend to be unconcerned by normative questions of justification and validity. There are undoubted strengths to this *laissez-faire* approach, but it leaves unanswered normative issues that need to be resolved in order to conceive emancipatory critique outside of the parameters of moral universalism. Questions such as how to formulate justifiable criticisms of oppressive gendered practices while retaining sensitivity to different life-worlds.

[4] In this regard, Brown's criticism of the domesticating political effects of Habermas's discourse ethics on feminism is a little off target because it fails to consider how pivotal it has been in ousting monological conceptions of pure reason from the centre of political theory. The idea of universal pragmatics has resonated strongly with feminists who do not find such a comprehensive working through of intersubjectivity and dialogical rationality in other traditions of political theory. A monological conception of reason still informs liberal political theory, by and large, even if it is presented as the highly stylized, constrained dialogism of public deliberation under ideal circumstances. The post-structural tradition of critical theory certainly places greater stress on the relational nature of social being, but it tends to develop its insights largely in terms of linguistic and other symbolic structures rather than as a pragmatic reasoning across perspectives.

many regard as culturally biased and implicitly exclusionary (e.g., Allen 2016; McNay 2009).

In keeping with the book's focus on post-Habermasian theory, it is not this body of work that is of prime concern here (partly also because there is already an extensive literature on feminist Habermasians) but the work of other feminist critical theorists such as Fraser, Jaeggi, and Young (1996) who have broken more decisively with the communicative paradigm. These thinkers reject unifying, teleological normative strategies and, instead of relying on the rules of rational discourse or similar constitutive universals, develop pluralized approaches to normativity based in analysis of determinate instances of oppression. Justice, as Iris Marion Young puts it, must be defined negatively through the specification of injustice and, accordingly, feminist critical theorists seek to elicit felt but unrealized possibilities inherent in the lived experience of oppression. In their eyes, a virtue of such a negativist approach is that it represents an apt way of responding to the criticisms made by non-Western feminists of closed universals and monist, overly unifying ideas of emancipation. As Khader puts it 'many western values, even ones that have helped erode sexist oppression in the West, can contribute to sexist oppression in other contexts and bear no conceptual relationship to its absence' (2019: 4). Naturally, feminist critical theorists take negativist critique in different directions according to where they fall on the Kantian–Hegelian axis that defines the contemporary Frankfurt School. These differences notwithstanding, however, they share a broad conception of emancipatory critique that is less fixated on monist models of justification and validity, and more concerned with solving concrete problems of subordination, with the ongoing expansion of evaluative and political horizons and with exploring the implications that women's lived experience has for normative theorizing.

In developing multivalent approaches to normative reasoning that are sensitive to the context of power and, particularly, to the encounter with vulnerable or disempowered groups, this body of feminist work exemplifies more consistently than paradigm-led theory the idea of critique's practical emancipatory standing. Feminists appear to take more seriously the consequent epistemological responsibility for the theorist to reason in a manner that is genuinely open to other, alien viewpoints (dialogism) and sensitive to the way that theorizing itself may compound discrepancies of power between the subject and object of knowledge (reflexivity). Such meta-level critical awareness about the status of their own theoretical stance helps feminist critical theorists to trace the connections between their normative position and those of their interlocutors, and thereby potentially enhances understanding of shared political goals. In short, by stepping beyond the parameters of paradigm-led thought, it is my contention that the feminist theorists of the Frankfurt School are more successful than many of their contemporaries in thinking through what it means for unmasking critique to be guided by the experiences, practical concerns, and interests of oppressed groups.

Beyond Frankfurt School Feminism

The idea of theorizing from experience presented here is indebted to feminist critical theory and draws productively on many of its insights and concepts. Yet, for all that feminist thinkers have done to realign Frankfurt School critical theory with practical issues of power, gender, and experience, it is my view that some of them nonetheless retain a lingering attachment to certain aspects of paradigm-led theorizing. I examine how these residues manifest themselves in the work of Nancy Fraser and Rahel Jaeggi as an unresolved ambivalence about the status that experiential understanding should have in the process of knowledge production. I argue that both overstate the parochializing effects that experiential understanding may have on critique and, as a result, remain attached to those aspects of paradigm-led theorizing that accord singular interpretative authority to the theorical worldview over the experiential one. This implicit epistemic hierarchy sits uneasily with their professed pragmatist leanings and respective attempts to further inquiry that is supposed to be sensitive to the context of power, dialogical, and reflexive in nature.

Thus, in order to conceive the theory–experience relation in terms that are more compatible with practical emancipatory critique, I draw on feminist thought outside of the Frankfurt School including, inter alia, the work of black and postcolonial feminist theorists, feminist epistemologists, and standpoint theorists. While these theorists share many of the aims expressed in the Frankfurt School's idea of unmasking critique, they diverge in a significant respect, namely they do not assume a priori that experiential knowledge is inherently unreliable and particularistic and, therefore, somehow stymying of critique. Instead, they proceed on the presumption that the first-hand experiences of disempowered groups are not just a reliable source of insight into oppression but an indispensable one and therefore also of pivotal importance in validating unmasking critique. In their view, people who are oppressed know it, and it is precisely the first-hand nature of this knowledge that renders it deeper and more revealing in certain crucial respects than a removed theoretical perspective. This constructive view is animated by an anti-essentialist understanding of experience—a relational phenomenology so to speak—that situates it in relation to social location and what it may reveal about the structural workings of power and oppression. The irony of feminist critical theory is that while it is deeply committed to anti-essentialist inquiry, its implicit disparagement of lived experience rests on naturalizing assumptions about its insuperable particularity. Theorizing inductively from experience in the manner of other feminist theorists serves to demonstrate that, while not incorrigible, a given experiential constellation is equally not inevitably particularistic; when it is located on socio-structural fault lines, it may be the source of unique insight into the underlying reproductive logic of society, qua disclosing critique. As feminist standpoint theorists have repeated many times in response to criticisms of uncritical phenomenalism, if an epistemic privilege accrues to direct experience it is not absolute but relative to social location and power.

By avoiding the preemptive problematization of lived experience as inherently unreliable and partial, these alternative feminist theories demonstrate another way of enacting the reflexivity and dialogism to which Frankfurt School theory is also committed to but fails to fully enact. The relativization of experience to power enables feminists to break down a cluster of analogous oppositions that arise from an over-schematic division between theory and experience—those of generality versus particularity, objectivism versus subjectivism, transcendence versus immanence, and so forth. This destabilization of over-drawn oppositions in turn facilitates a more egalitarian and dialogical configuration of knowledge production described by Patricia Hill Collins as the call and response structure that is an essential feature of African-American culture (Collins 2000: 280). It is this body of feminist work that informs my construal of context transcendence as a dialogical process of cross-perspectival reasoning where the theoretical and experiential perspectives have equal epistemic credibility. The contention that unmasking critique should proceed on the assumption of epistemic equality does not reductively imply that the experiential perspective is infallible nor that there aren't considerable differences and asymmetries between it and the theoretical worldview. It implies rather that limitations in either worldview—experiential or theoretical—need to be dealt with, as they arise, in the process of cross-perspectival reasoning itself. As much as theory is capable of overcoming limitations in an experiential point of view, so the reverse is also potentially the case. Each perspective functions relative to the other as a productive outside position that may prompt interlocutors to critically reflect on their own immanent interpretive position. Context-transcending insight is immanent within the dialogical process and not, as the Frankfurt School one-sidedly sees it, the definitive worldview afforded by a totalizing, monist paradigm. Instead of subsuming diverse social phenomena against the rubric of an unchanging constitutive principle, enlarged understanding comes from the way actors utilize the various resources—norms, meanings, and practices—that are present within specific contexts to address problematic social reality. In short, context transcendence is less about producing a comprehensive interpretation of society according to a given paradigm and more about working towards the gradual and continuous expansion of immanent critical perspectives in the ongoing political conversation about overcoming oppression.

In my attempt to bring the insights of black feminist theorists and other philosophers of race and postcolonialism to bear on the work of Frankfurt School thinkers, a key transitional figure is Angela Davis. Her work has a foothold in both theoretical camps, so to speak, although it is mostly overlooked by one of them. Davis was taught by both Adorno and Marcuse, explicitly traces her intellectual inspiration to the 'emancipatory promise of the German philosophical tradition' and has produced pioneering critical analyses of, among other things female slavery, black women blues singers, and the prison–industrial complex.[5] Yet despite this prodigious and ground-breaking output, her work is almost entirely absent from standard overviews and commentaries on Frankfurt School critical theory. In many respects, Davis's work bears the same intellectual hallmarks as the work other feminist theorists associated with the Frankfurt School, especially that of Nancy Fraser. Both are materialist thinkers, in a distinctively expansive sense, but do not subscribe to the idea that power can satisfactorily be explained by tracing its origins back to a single source. Their work demonstrates that critique may have general explanatory relevance without taking the form of diagnostic monism. Davis's analyses of the prison–industrial complex or female chattel slavery, for instance, exemplify a problem-led, abductive mode of theorizing that uses the specific experiences of those subject to these violent, disciplinary regimes to elucidate racialized dynamics of exploitation and domination that underpin capitalism. The multidimensional critique of power resonates with Fraser's recent work on neoliberal expropriation but, arguably, Davis is more mindful of the primary place that the experiences of oppressed groups occupy in a materialist diagnosis of social power. Fraser's work has become increasingly removed from the phenomenal realm of everyday experience as she has concentrated on 'thinking big' and mapping the contours of global capitalism. In contrast, Davis's work retains an unfailing sense of the specificity of experience and also its centrality to an intersectional account of power and oppression. Her study (1998a) of women's blues singers in the early twentieth century, for instance, epitomizes this experientially grounded approach, interweaving attentiveness to the thick texture of concrete life-worlds with explanation of subtending structural forces. It aims to recover a forgotten moment of empowerment for black women where blues songs were instrumental in articulating a newly sexualized and explicitly working-class female consciousness. At the same time, it also underscores the fragility of such counterhegemonic identity formation by situating it in the wider context of the racism and patriarchal norms of feminine conformity that prevailed at the time. The ceaseless movement of Davis's thought between micro and macro levels of sociality, is similarly exemplified in her essay on Afro Images (1998c) which moves from description of her own feelings of estrangement at seeing images of herself appropriated for alien political ends, to reflection on the commodification of race and the importance of combatting this through the creation of political counter-memories. The centrality of experiential

---

[5] For accounts of Davis's life and work see J. James (1989) Introduction; Arnold Farr (2018) and S. Jeffries, The Effect of the Whip: the Frankfurt School and the Oppression of Women https://www.versobooks.com/blogs/2846-the-effect-of-the-whip-the-frankfurt-school-and-the-oppression-of-women.

understanding to Davis's theorizing extends to the normative dimensions of critique. Whereas Fraser, and to a lesser extent Young in her final work, elaborate models of normativity that are, for radical democrats, rather too close to the liberal problem space of justice, Davis has a more variegated and pragmatic understanding of critique's normative effects. The ideas of validity and adjudication that dominate Fraser's participatory parity paradigm are nowhere in evidence because, for Davis, critique has the dialogical function of mediator that reflects 'the voices and agency' of disadvantaged groups and discloses the felt but unspoken political potential latent in a certain moment. The normative force of Davis's critique is motivated less by a concern to impose a definitive interpretative framework on indeterminate social reality so much as the effort, always unfinished, to keep theory rooted in the lived reality of struggle with the aim of clarifying possibilities for social transformation. In short, Davis's work is an instance of what Frankfurt school critique might have looked like if it had not taken its foundational turn and diverged so far from its declared starting point in experiences of pain and suffering.

Disclosing the 'Alienated Familiar'

By identifying the nascent but at present under-utilized resources in the Frankfurt School tradition that resonate powerfully with feminist concerns about gender, I aim to re-open an important conversation between the two theoretical strands and to sketch the outline of a distinctive (non-Habermasian) feminist critical theory. In the broadest sense, the idea of theorizing from experience proposed here is aligned with an understanding of normative critique as disclosure. Disclosure involves construing the world in such a way as to render it unfamiliar and, in seeing it afresh, to open new vistas of understanding and political practice. Its normativity resides in the imaginative and rhetorical impact of its reconfigured vision of the world and the potential contribution that this makes to wider political practices of emancipatory world-building. Of course, much has already been written about the disclosive function of critique often in reaction to Habermas's narrowing of political expression to a hyper-rational core and consequent marginalization of its rhetorical, imaginative, and figurative dimensions. In the eyes of many, this exaggerated cognitivism leaves critical theory stranded in an arid proceduralism that casts much practical political speech and protest, especially that which comes from below, as peripheral or 'irrational' simply because it is not straightforwardly amenable to formal reconstruction. Effective political reasoning, in the eyes of many, ought not to be reduced to such narrow parameters because, as Kompridis puts it, 'the plurality of voices in which reason speaks is not subsumable by or reducible to any procedural unity of reason...any conception of reason that cannot recognise the activity of disclosing the world anew as one of reason's own... is blind and self-alienating' (Kompridis 2006: 86). This stringent rationalism potentially gives rise to a gulf between Habermasian discourse ethics and those individuals it supposedly addressees who, for reasons of disempowerment, might be unable to transpose their complex experiential reality into the formal terms required.

In response, Habermasians argue that its proponents mystify disclosure as an ineffable act of revelation which, in so far as it defies rational reconstruction, cannot be democratically accountable: 'telling a story or adducing an exemplar is not an alternative to advancing a reason' (Fraser 1997b: 173). This riposte is certainly not without force especially as it refers to certain Heideggerian propensities to construe disclosive thought in vague, overblown terms as the reimagining of temporal possibilities or discovery of 'another voice of reason' and so on (e.g., Bohman 1994; Kompridis 2012, 369–81). In place of this idea of disclosure as a gestalt switch or emergence of a startling new truth, I conceive of it in more mundane, practical terms, as the ongoing attempt to keep lived experiences of oppression at the centre of unmasking critique. Disclosure in this sense is the recalling of experiences and things about the world that, although commonly known on an everyday level, are frequently forgotten, or discounted by official, elite, and hegemonic forms of knowledge. To capture disclosure in this ordinary, deflated sense, I adapt Charles Mills's felicitous phrase the 'alienated familiar'. Mills uses the phrase to denote experiences that stand outside of hegemonic views of the world not because they are entirely alien to it but because, if included, they threaten to 'redraw the map of what was thought to be explored territory' (1998: 28). Experiences of oppression—the lived realities of sexism, racism, poverty, and other social vulnerabilities—might be usefully understood through this idea of the 'alienated familiar' because, despite their social ubiquity, they are frequently downplayed, trivialized, or ignored in mainstream thought, including much mainstream political theory. There are many possible reasons for this; ideological delusion, political hostility, the indifference of privilege, intellectual orthodoxy, willed ignorance, unconscious bias, and so on. Regardless of the cause, the effect of this omission is to naturalize and sediment certain worldviews which, despite their partiality, are somehow accepted as definitive and orthodox. It is not after all that we don't know that society is structured according to hierarchies of race, gender, class, and so on; even so, hegemonic knowledges often fail to register awareness of these entrenched asymmetries lest their settled vision of reality is unsettled. Critique as disclosure then is less about revealing startling new truths about the world so much as the more mundane, always unfinished task of bringing the alienated familiar, qua lived experiences of oppression, back into view in order to gradually improve on established frameworks of understanding. This capacity to see something that was previously ignored as relevant, is crucial if unmasking critique is to live up to its claims of responding to lived experiences of oppression and practically contributing to emancipatory social struggles.

Outline of the Book

The objective of the first chapter is to establish the centrality of direct experiential understanding to an unmasking critique of oppression. It argues that attentiveness to the lived experience of oppressed groups is a necessary theoretical and political entailment of the Frankfurt School's claim that unmasking critique aims to make a practical contribution to their struggles for emancipation. Not only does Frankfurt School theory fail to attend to the lived reality of oppressed groups, but it is also marked by a distinct retreat from experience because of the supposed parochializing effects it is held to have on critique. To offset such parochialism, Frankfurt school theorists have concentrated on issues of normative foundation and context transcendence. This foundational turn has given rise to a mode of 'paradigm-led theorizing' that prevents Frankfurt School theorists developing an adequate diagnosis of oppression, exemplified here in their tokenistic treatment of gender oppression. Paradigm-led theorizing also prevents them from realizing the dialogical and reflexive aspects of their theoretical practice, qua practical emancipatory thought. This chapters proposes a model of experience-led theorizing as an alternative to paradigm-led thought and draws on other types of radical theory, notably black feminist theory, to illustrate what this entails. Relativizing lived experience to power allows it to be recast as an indispensable source of knowledge for unmasking critique. It also serves to reconfigure context transcendence in dialogical terms as the insight that comes from reasoning across theoretical and experiential perspectives rather than, *pace* the Frankfurt School, the definitive viewpoint afforded by a monist paradigm.

The argument of the opening chapter sets out the general evaluative framework from which subsequent, more detailed examination of paradigm-led theorizing in the work of individual Frankfurt School thinkers proceeds. Chapter 2 focuses on the work of Rainer Forst and his justification-theoretic paradigm. I argue in relation to issues of gender that the capacity of justification critique to unmask oppression is limited by its reliance on a tendentious concept of noumenal power. Noumenal power obscures the complexities of oppression at both the level of its lived reality and the level of intersecting vectors of power. The normative reach of justification critique is also stymied by its failure to consider sufficiently how the latent workings of power in the actual conversation about justice may subvert the formal equality of a right to justification. In neglecting to address how the abstract principle of mutually owed justifications would operate in a real-world context of power disparities between interlocutors, justification critique fails to enact the reflexivity that Forst claims is an indispensable feature of emancipatory theory.

Chapter 3 considers the implications that Axel Honneth's recent work on recognition and progress have for an account of gender oppression. On the face of it, Honneth's neoHegelian recognition model is more compatible than the neoKantian model of justification with feminist concerns about gender in so far as it accords a foundational role to the family and intimate relations in sustaining social justice. I argue, however, that this affinity is undercut by the distorting effects that Honneth's teleology of progress has on his understanding of gendered asymmetries of power in the family and other social realms. The inherent bias of recognition monism towards identifying progressive tendencies in the life-world underestimates the persistence of those negative dynamics that are instrumental to the continuing subordination of women. Descriptive shortcomings in recognition monism's diagnosis of gender oppression have limiting effects on resulting normative proposals which are both undetermined and somewhat tangential to the correction of entrenched hierarchies of power. I illustrate these limitations by comparing Honneth's rather naïve idea of care as ethical mutuality with the more developed work of feminists on, among other things, economies of care.

The fourth chapter considers the work of Italian critical theorist Alessandro Ferrara on exemplarity that forms part of his broader attempt to place a notion of disclosure at the heart of democratic reasoning. Ferrara argues that 'at its best' political thought should have the capacity to animate the democratic imagination by disclosing, through exemplary instances, new political possibilities for thought and action. I argue that Ferrara's notion of exemplarity provides important conceptual resources for a regrounding of critical theory in the type of experientially based disclosing critique that has, post Habermas, been marginalized. Exemplary universalism suggests a way of reasoning inductively from concrete particularity that is normatively more inclusive of the voices of the marginalized and disempowered than procedural universalism. Moreover, contra Habermas, Ferrara makes the important argument that, far from being an unstable process of meaning creation, exemplary disclosure has a systematic internal rationale that renders it amenable to practical inter-subjective validation. The critical promise of Ferrara's idea of exemplarity is ultimately unfulfilled, however, because of the way he grounds its disclosive effects in the speculative, context-transcending construct of *sensus communis* understood as a matrix of precultural intuitions about human flourishing. This unifying abstraction works against sensitivity to context and forecloses consideration of how enduring inequalities of race, gender, and class may prevent groups converging around shared ideals of flourishing. Drawing on critical race theorists such as Angela Davis, I propose a repoliticized understanding of exemplary disclosure that locates its normative impact in the dynamics of concrete struggles against oppression rather than in a socially weightless abstraction. This politicized notion of exemplarity is consistent with a reconfigured idea of context transcendence as the outcome of reasoning across perspectives.

The fifth and sixth chapters shift in focus to reflect on the work of feminist thinkers in the Frankfurt School and the important ways in which it has broken from the dominant tendencies of paradigm-led critical theory. Chapter 5 examines Nancy Fraser's influential writing which, in contrast to the tokenistic approaches of her peers, has been instrumental in moving gender concerns to the heart of critical theory of oppression. In so doing, she has formulated an innovative multidimensional typology of power which, unlike mono-categorial paradigms, is capable of explain intersectional dynamics of oppression. Likewise, her model of justice as participatory parity rests on a pluralized, 'neo-pragmatist' account of normative reasoning that finds emancipatory responses embedded in concrete situations and hence resonates with the work of other feminist theorists on gender inequality in a global context. However, as ground-breaking as it has been in foregrounding issues of gender oppression and developing a non-monist approach to critique, Fraser's work is arguably limited by a residual attachment to certain aspects of paradigm-led theorizing. This is evident in the way she downgrades the value of an experiential perspective for critique and consequently fails to fully think through epistemological implications of reasoning dialogically with disempowered interlocutors. Instead, working largely within the normative space of justification, Fraser tends to accord a questionable adjudicative authority to the theoretical perspective over the experiential one in assessing the validity of injustice claims. This epistemic hierarchy is inconsistent with her contention that the participatory parity paradigm embodies dialogical and reflexive reasoning. It also confines the normative function of emancipatory critique to the unduly narrow one of adjudication.

The final chapter explores Rahel Jaeggi's work on ethical forms of life and the central place it affords to criticism of regressive constellations of experience or blocked social relations. In developing her distinctive, negativist approach to critique, Jaeggi breaks with several Habermasian orthodoxies that dominate Frankfurt School theory, especially the preoccupation with monist foundations and the normative rush to judgement. Her pragmatist emphasis on problem solving and learning suggests that normatively efficacious critique consists in devising situationally specific strategies of empowerment rather than a single, all-encompassing theory of emancipation. I show, however, that the promise of Jaeggi's negativist ethics is not fully realized because of the way context transcendence is thematized through a 'formal' account of progress as rational continuity derived from Hegel. Jaeggi justifies this formalist approach on the grounds that it allows her to bring an acute sense of historicity back into critique and, accordingly, her version of progress is deflated, open, and multifactorial. Even with these modifications, however, I argue that the formal idea of progress has troubling dehistoricizing effects in so far as its evaluative criteria of rational continuity undermine the very attentiveness to experiential particularity that is required for the critique of *lebensform*. In principle, it would be possible for Jaeggi to mitigate this tension between the negativist and formalist aspects of critique by conceiving of context transcendence in dialogical terms that align more closely than the abstracted idea of progress with the declared pragmatist orientation of her thought. On this alternative view, context transcendence comes not come from measuring life-worlds against the abstract yardstick of progress, but rather is enabled by the way actors utilize the various resources—norms, meanings, and practices—that are present within a given form of life to expand their immanent perspective. Jaeggi forecloses such an option, however, by dismissing experientially grounded critique as parochial standpoint theory. This tendentious assumption is mistaken and means that, lacking experiential content, Jaeggi's ethical critique remains stranded in a hollow formalism unable to adequately diagnose blocked relations of power.

In the Conclusion I pull together the various threads of the idea of theorizing from experience by specifying its entailments for an unmasking critique of oppression. Critique, on this view, is premised on a dialogical account of context transcendence, works with a relational account of experience, uses an abductive, problem-led method of inquiry, and takes an experientially negativist approach to normativity.

1
Unmasking Power
Experience, Gender, and Oppression

Introduction

This chapter sets out the book's core argument, namely, that an interpretative account of experience—direct subjective experience—ought to be a central element of a critical theory that takes its goal to be the unmasking of oppression. Frankfurt School critical theory understands itself in precisely these terms, as an unmasking critique of power which is animated by the practical concerns and lived experiences of oppressed groups. This practical emancipatory orientation is supposed to be a hallmark of the critical theory approach. Unlike objectifying modes of political theory, critical theorists claim to directly address those oppressed groups who are the subjects of inquiry and aim thereby to make a practical contribution to their struggles for freedom. This chapter questions the declared practical emancipatory status of critique on the grounds that Frankfurt School thinkers fail to live up to this claim, that is, they do not in fact accord sufficient weight to the experiences of disempowered groups in the process of knowledge production. This is because they fear that critique's wider emancipatory relevance—its context transcending force—is undermined by anchoring itself too deeply within specific constellations of experience. First-hand experiences of oppression are deemed, for various reasons, to be too particularistic and unreliable to make anything more than a limited epistemic contribution to an unmasking critique of power. As a result, there has been a discernible retreat from experience in the work of Frankfurt School theorists over the last few decades. I contend that the motives for this retreat are overstated and partially misguided and that the lack of attention paid to the experiences of oppressed groups undermines the Frankfurt School's critique of power in key respects. I illustrate my argument by focussing on gender oppression and trace how the one-dimensional and tokenistic treatment that the topic receives in the hands of Frankfurt School theorists is a consequence of their failure to attend to the experiential complexities of women's experience. Ultimately, it is this reluctance of Frankfurt School theorists to attribute more weight to the direct experiences of oppressed groups that undermines their assertion to be producing knowledge that has practical emancipatory relevance.

The Frankfurt School's retreat from experience has been propelled by the preoccupation, inherited from Habermas, with issues of normative foundation

The Gender of Critical Theory: On the Experiential Grounds of Critique. Lois McNay, Oxford University Press.
© Lois McNay 2022. DOI: 10.1093/oso/9780198857747.003.0002

and context transcendence. There is no doubt that this foundational turn has been intellectually fruitful, but it has also led to the rise of a distinctive mode of analysis which I call paradigm-led theorizing, and which is based in an overly dichotomized understanding of the relation between critical transcendence and experiential immanence. The propensity of paradigm-led theories to monist and totalizing forms of social diagnosis blunts responsiveness to the complexity of lived experiences of oppression and consequently constrains the critique of power. As well as limiting social explanation, paradigm-led theory also gives rise to normative diagnoses that are tangential and underdetermined and therefore of questionable use to practical thought about emancipation. Finally, paradigm-led theory undercuts the epistemic features of dialogism and reflexivity that Frankfurt School theorists regard as defining of situated emancipatory critique. In so far as they hold that a political-ethical connection exists between critique and its addressees, qua oppressed groups, so accordingly there arises a responsibility on the theorist to reason in a manner that is sensitive to the context of power and is dialogical and self-critical (reflexive) in nature. Yet, the ability of Frankfurt School theorists to concretely enact these other-regarding epistemic features is undermined by the way they subtly but persistently disparage experiential understanding, and consequently invest their own theoretical paradigms with a one-sided interpretative authority.

As an alternative to paradigm-led thought, I propose a model of experience-led theorizing and draw on feminist theory—in particular black feminist thought and feminist critical theories of postcolonialism and race—to exemplify what this entails. I maintain that while the Frankfurt School's worries about the particularistic, subjectivist and relativist entailments of direct experiential understanding are not without foundation, they are exaggerated and also naturalized by the way in which they resort to an overplayed dichotomy of transcendence and immanence. In contrast, in as much as feminist theory routinely unpacks such debilitating dichotomies, it concretely exemplifies how, far from being a purely particularistic source of knowledge, direct experiential understanding is indispensable to a critical theory of oppression. When the category of experience is denaturalized and relativized to social location, it becomes clear how it may reveal aspects to power that are not necessarily visible to an external, theoretical perspective, particularly when it comes to understanding the impact of intersecting vectors of power on everyday life. I maintain then, that feminist theory provides the resources for conceiving of systematic social explanation, not as a stylized but closed grand theory, but instead as a problem-led, open process of abductive theorizing from experience. Likewise, the normative import of critique does not depend on the adoption of a monist evaluative perspective, qua paradigm-led critical theory, but instead finds normative responses immanent within concrete situations. Rather than devising a single, grand theory of emancipation, it focusses instead on clarifying a multiplicity of situationally specific practices of empowerment. Finally, theorizing from experience enacts a dialogical and reflexive approach to reasoning that assumes the methodological equality of the theoretical and experiential perspectives rather than, *pace* paradigm-led theory, the tacit privilege of the former over the latter. This leads to a pragmatically reconceived idea of context transcendence as potential insight that is internal to the dialogical process of thinking across perspectives, rather than as the externally imposed authority of the theoretical paradigm.

Experience and Unmasking Critique

Despite its roots in the left–Hegelian intellectual tradition, Frankfurt School critical theory has more frequently been aligned in recent years by various observers with liberal democratic theory, given the interest shown by some of its most high-profile members in a certain set of normative justice concerns. It hardly needs saying that this shift has been catalyzed in large part by Habermas and the increased emphasis in his writing, from *Knowledge and Human Interests* onwards, on a Kantian rather than Hegelian interpretation of critical theory, perhaps best exemplified in his exchange with Rawls (e.g., Kompridis 2006: 25ff). This neoKantian turn notwithstanding, Frankfurt School theorists emphatically reject any such alignment with liberal theory and, in keeping with their Marxist intellectual heritage, insist on the radical democratic entailments of their thinking about social justice. In their eyes, what secures the radical democratic credentials of critique is its practical emancipatory orientation. Unlike idealizing political theories, critical theory has a distinctive commitment to normative thinking that tackles issues of injustice and oppression head on, and is therefore of practical use to those groups most directly affected. From Horkheimer onwards, Frankfurt School thinkers have long expressed scepticism about normative theory that sidelines the examination of existing injustices to first abstractly define ideal moral principles and then work downwards to real-world problems. Frankfurt School thinkers maintain that such speculative or 'traditional' theory fails to complete the move from ideals to actuality and remains stranded in abstract and self-referential reflection that has little practical relevance to existing social problems. By subsuming facts about the world under preconstituted, all-inclusive principles, traditional theory generates thin 'covering-law' models of morality that have little traction in dealing with the thick complexities of real-world normative dilemmas (Urban-Walker 1992). Not only does the assimilation of complex experiential realities to the stylized rules of knowledge efface socio-historical particularity, but it may also introduce an unexamined bias towards the status quo into normative theorizing which mistakes its own privilege and scholasticism for impartiality and objectivity (Horkheimer 1975: 193–4). The most troubling aspect of traditional theory's 'hypostatization of Logos as reality' is the way in which it systematically downplays the deep inequalities of power that are inherent to capitalist societies by construing them as anomalies (Horkheimer 1975: 198). If inequalities of power are considered at all they are done so only as a secondary matter of application, that is, in a stylized and derivative fashion as a 'surprising abnormality' from the norm of justice, as Judith Shklar famously described it (1990: 17). The occlusion of power belies any possible claim on theory's part to practical, action-guiding relevance given, as Charles Mills put it, 'little or nothing will be said on actual historic oppression and its legacy in the present, or current ongoing oppression, though these may be gestured at in a vague or promissory way' (Mills 2005: 168). Accordingly, then, in contrast to the speculative top-down approach of traditional theory, critical theory asserts its practical emancipatory credentials by emphasizing its rootedness in a sociological critique of existing injustices; as Rainer Forst puts it, 'the first question of justice' must be 'the question of power' (Forst 2011: 37).

Frankfurt School theorists further shore up their claim to practical-emancipatory relevance by maintaining that not only does unmasking critique confront asymmetries of power head on but also, in doing so, it aligns itself explicitly with the perspectives and interests of oppressed groups. The critique of power is conducted not from a top-down, institutional view but instead from a bottom-up view anchored in everyday instances of suffering and misery. Unmasking critique takes these everyday forms of misery and unhappiness—'lived suffering'—as symptoms of a deeper disorder inherent to capitalist social structures (Geuss 1981: 90). Given that suffering and other negative experiences are an unavoidable part of the human condition, not all manifestations are necessarily indicative of underlying social disorder or pathology. Of significance rather are only those types of suffering that can be shown to be the avoidable outcome of the workings of power and the contingent organization of social relations—social suffering to use Bourdieu's term. Although widespread, these negative experiences are often ignored, trivialized, even denied, and thus rendered socially invisible. This suppression is an effect of capitalism's intrinsic tendency to conceal its exploitative nature by fostering convictions and practices that distract attention from the 'real character of... social conditions' (Honneth 2004: 343–44). Discourses of, say, individual merit or market freedom serve to naturalize socially created inequities as normal and inevitable, as the consequence of individual failing rather than societal organization. The normalization of inequality generates in turn 'silence' and 'apathy' on issues that should otherwise be matters of urgent public concern (Honneth 2004: 343–44). Through ideology critique, critical theory aims to shatter these distorting cognitive façades and show how seemingly random and unconnected experiences of suffering are in fact subjective manifestations of a systematically inegalitarian and alienating mode of societal organization. It is by anchoring its critique of oppression in analysis of negative experiences that critical theory acquires its 'recognizable face' as radical political thought (Wiggershaus 1994: 657).

Despite the frequency with which Frankfurt School theorists allude to the existential grounds of unmasking critique, it is not at all self-evident what they mean when they invoke the category of negative experience. There are considerable differences between, for instance, the way Adorno conceives of suffering as 'objectivity that weighs upon the subject', Honneth's phenomenology of misrecognition, and Habermas's idea of rationally redeemable injurious experience (Adorno 1974: 17). These conceptual differences are overlaid by the different weight that individual critical theorists attribute to the category of experience in the overall process of knowledge production. For some, such as Adorno, experience remains the fundamental touchstone around which theoretical knowledge circulates and ceaselessly seeks to ground and reground itself. For others, of a more Habermasian stripe, experience may well be the necessary starting point of critique, but it is only that, a starting point, and should not be allowed to constrain autonomous theoretical understanding of society; as Nancy Fraser puts it, 'critical theory doesn't give participants in social struggles the last word, but it does give them the first word' (Fraser and Jaeggi 2018: 124). These differences between Frankfurt School theorists on the role that suffering plays in critique are partly symptomatic of conceptual indeterminacies in conceiving the category of experience more generally, how it can be constructed as the object of inquiry in a variety of ways; through large-scale statistical analysis, ethnographic and other qualitative approaches, historical and genealogical research, symbolic representations, and so on. Each way of construing experience has its own distinctive theoretical strengths which will yield differing insights germane to whatever the broader aims of a given social inquiry happen to be. Yet, regardless of these conceptual and methodological variations, I maintain that there is one particular way of construing experience that is indispensable for critical theory if it is to be consistent with its declared practical emancipatory import, and that is an interpretative understanding of subjective experience. Naturally, this inevitably raises methodological questions of *verstehen*, of the most effective way the theorist should go about interpretatively capturing lived experiences of oppression. Despite their salience, it is not my intention to engage with issues of sociological method here, partly because they have already been extensively discussed by social theorists. Rather, my argument bears on critical political theory and centres on the claim that attentiveness to the lived experiences of oppressed groups is a necessary entailment of the historicized and radical conception of inquiry to which Frankfurt School thinkers cleave. Given their general aim of unmasking oppression, the subjective experiences of oppressed groups—their lived reality and understanding of the world—must necessarily have special significance for unmasking critique. Indeed, as I argue throughout this book, to fail to attend to the lived reality of oppressed groups or to subtly undercut and minimize the role their experiences play in the process of knowledge production, is to be inconsistent with the basic premises—theoretical and political—that animate unmasking critique and its assertion to have radically emancipatory import.

On the face of it, it may not be immediately clear why the lived experience of oppressed groups should be so pivotal for critique given that Frankfurt School theorists treat suffering as merely a 'symptom' of a deeper socio-structural malaise. As a 'symptom', it is not the thick texture of lived social reality per se that is necessarily of primary interest to critical theorists, so much as the underlying systemic tendencies of power that it signals. Indeed, if all that critical theorists sought to do was produce an objective account of the wrongs of capitalist society, there would seem to be no compelling reason why special prominence should be placed on lived experience as part of a systematic sociological account of power and oppression. Direct subjective experience may certainly make a valuable contribution to a general understanding of how oppression operates on the ground, so to speak, but it would be simply one among several relevant sources of data upon which the theorist could draw. Indeed, given the inevitably limited and fallible nature of direct experience—that individuals aren't always fully cognizant of the real causes of their misery—it would seem to be foolish for the theorist to base a critical account of power too heavily upon first-hand accounts over other transpersonal sources of information. But, by its own lights, critical theory is not conventional theory and aims to do more than offer an objectively accurate account of oppression. For it also makes the ambitious claims that in clarifying the causes of their suffering, critique is of direct concrete help to oppressed groups in seeking to improve their situation and also that, as a situated practice also implicated in the field of inquiry, it has a distinctive ethical-political relation with its addressees. Frankfurt School theory, as Geuss puts it 'is not just a theory about some objects different from itself, it is also a theory about social theories, how they arise, how they can be applied, and the conditions under which they can be acceptable' (Geuss 1981: 79). Put differently, members of oppressed groups should be able to recognize in some way their own experiential reality in a theory that claims to speak not only on their behalf but also directly to them. In seeking to capture this experiential reality, critical theory aims to expand subjects' understanding of the hidden causes of their suffering, enable them to decide where their true interests lie, and practically motivate them to mobilize for their own emancipation. Thus, as Geuss puts it: 'critical theory must be expressed in a form comprehensible to the agents addressed, and which allows them to recognize it as a description of their own situation and use it as a guide for action' (Geuss 1981: 85) As practical, emancipatory theory, then, unmasking critique depends in several crucial ways on the assent and verification of the agents to whom it is addressed. This 'hermeneutic requirement' (Habermas) implies that as the primary addressees of critique, oppressed groups, their experiences and understanding of the world, play a foundational role in the process of knowledge production. Indeed, to do otherwise, to fail to accord lived experience sufficient credibility, would be to lapse into the type of objectifying abstract reflection unconnected to its field of inquiry—theoretic rather than praxeological theory—which critical theory explicitly rejects.

In short, interpretative understanding of experience is indispensable to Frankfurt School theory because it is a logical entailment of the practical emancipatory terms in which the object, aims, and method of unmasking critique are conceived. To be clear, this is not to recommend an uncritical phenomenalism and assert that direct subjective experience provides, on its own, a comprehensive or incontestable account of oppression. It is however to argue that advertence to lived experience is a vital and necessary condition of critique which claims to unmask real-world dynamics of oppression, to speak directly to the political interests of those groups most affected and, in doing so, to inform and empower them. Given these defining tenets, it would be highly problematic for practically engaged theory to independently label situations oppressive without the input of those groups directly involved. As Herbert Kogler puts it: 'subjects may not have the adequate conceptual tools to thematize how power relations actually function, yet, to be evaluated by the interpreter as oppression, the subjects' assessment and experience of them as oppressive is indispensable' (Kogler 1996: 262).

Beyond this general political-ethical imperative, the importance of interpretative understanding of experience to an account of oppression can be further elaborated in relation to the explanatory, normative, and methodological features of critical theory. First, with regard to the diagnosis of oppression, the experiences of directly affected groups have a uniquely valuable role to play in revealing aspects of power not necessarily visible from the external, and often privileged, vantage point of the theorist. As bel hooks puts it:

> there is a particular knowledge that comes from suffering. It is a way of knowing that is often expressed through the body, what it knows, what has been deeply inscribed on it through experience. This complexity of experience can rarely be voiced and named from a distance. It is a privileged location, even as it is not the only or even always the most important location from which one can know.
> (hooks 1991: 182–3)

The irreplaceable nature of experiential knowledge does not of course obviate the importance of measuring asymmetries of power against a range of experience-distant and objective indices, but the latter, on their own sufficient, do not constitute sufficient grounds for a comprehensive account of oppression. It is also vital to consider those subjective and lived dimensions of oppression that pertain to the way in which individuals are subjected to power often via the subtle manipulation of bodies and meanings. By virtue of their insidiousness, such forms of symbolic violence are often 'invisible' to an external observer even as they are all too apparent to those who are its direct targets. They include dynamics of stigmatization, de-authorization, hermeneutic marginalization, unconscious bias, and so on. These dynamics of oppression are not only difficult for outsiders to discern but may also be difficult for those who endure them to convey to others, because they are frequently lived in a chaotic and diffuse manner that is often hard to pin down. Oppressive experiences are, as Charles Mills puts it 'full of structured heterogeneities and discontinuities' and therefore may appear 'alien' and not fully expressible within the terms of established frames of theoretical understanding (Mills 1998: 27). Likewise, emergent or previously unnoticed dimensions of subjugation may be hard to identify if they fall outside the scope of established diagnostic frameworks. These semi-suppressed harms can often only be given wider visibility and brought to the attention of the theorist by those groups who are directly affected by them. In short, without an appreciation of the subjective reality of oppression, objective accounts of power may miss embodied, unthematized aspects of its operations, and therefore be incomplete, inappropriate, or outdated.

Second, experiential understanding is crucial to the way that critical theory formulates determinate normative responses to oppression. In keeping with their rejection of Kantian ideas of pure reason and transcendence, critical theorists do not conceive of normativity in the form of a priori, independent ideals. Nor, in keeping with their hermeneutic premise of the historicity of thought, do they subscribe to *dirigiste* ideas of the political philosopher as a 'secular priest' who alone devises the impartial rules and principles intended to guide the negotiation of concrete social dilemmas. According to the logic of immanent critique, the theorist does not stand outside or above the reality she describes but forms part of it as participant-observer. Instead of prescribing the right course of action from a lofty vantage point, the theorist's role is to help elucidate the values and norms that are already embodied in an incomplete form in the practices, beliefs, and struggles of social life, 'to clarify the wishes and struggles of an/the age', as Fraser puts it in her famous paraphrase of Marx. By reconstructing these immanent normative resources, critical theory establishes the evaluative perspective on which to base its criticism of unjust society and practical proposals for emancipatory change. It follows from this reconstructive approach that these immanent normative resources must be drawn in large part from those individuals most directly affected by oppressive social dynamics. These experiences form the basis upon which the theorist articulates a 'normative grammar' of struggle and emancipation that has greater practical traction than purely abstract models of democratic agency (e.g., Arruzza, Bhattacharya, and Fraser 2019). Indeed, the experiences of those directly involved may be an invaluable way of improving on shortfalls in purely theoretical understanding in so far as they reveal discontinuities between so-called action-guiding principles and practical reality. Normative proposals that seem to be uncontentious from the theorist's point of view may in fact be misaligned with the lived reality of the groups whom they are intended to help and thus turn out to be insufficient, counter-productive, or inappropriate. For example, preempting current debates on white normativity, bell hooks argues that experiences of racial oppression render black women reluctant to endorse normative strategies, advocated by white feminists, that are founded in ideas of shared vulnerability and victimhood. Instead, precisely because of their overwhelmingly disadvantaged social status, black women have often preferred to mobilize around emancipatory strategies based on solidarity and empowerment:

> women who are exploited and oppressed daily cannot afford to relinquish the belief that they exercise some measure of control, however relative, over their lives. They cannot afford to see themselves solely as "victims" because their survival depends on continued exercise of whatever personal powers they possess. It would be psychologically demoralizing for these women to bond with other women on the basis of shared victimization. They bond with other women on the basis of shared strength and resources. (hooks 2000: 46)

Interpretative understanding of experience is vital then to developing normative repertoires that are attuned to the lived reality of disempowered groups and potentially richer than some models prescribed by political theorists. In bringing to light certain felt realities, it may reveal obstacles that disempowered groups face in enacting certain moral demands and thereby throw into doubt received ideas of moral agency (e.g., Herzog and Zacka 2019). Again, this is exemplified in the work of black feminist theorists who, based on their political experience, reject the arguments of liberal feminists such as Martha Nussbaum that anger, while an understandable reaction to chronic oppression, is not a productive one because it may alienate others. Audre Lorde (1981), Marilyn Frye (1983a), Macalaster Bell (2009), and Barbara Ransby (2015) are among the many who maintain that, on the contrary, 'black rage' needs to be reclaimed as a weapon of social justice. It may function as a politically energizing force that motivates collective movement for change and allows oppressed groups to bear witness to injustice and track an 'important moral truth'. As Barbara Ransby says of Black Lives Matter: 'it is precisely this notion of collective, unapologetic black rage that has been the catalyst for the new movement condemning police violence against black people' (2015: 32). Phenomenological patterns of anger—those areas in which women and marginal groups are 'allowed' to express anger and those in which they are not—in some respects correspond to distributions of power and therefore provide insight into oppression; as Bell says, 'anger provides a distinct form of knowledge about oppression that those who lack these emotions do not have access to' (Bell 2009, also Frye 1983a: 94). Not only does the liberal feminist insistence on withholding anger fail to adequately engage with the existential and emotional realities of oppression, but it also misrepresents its own position of privilege and disengagement as a normative virtue. It fails to recognize that, although well intentioned, its call for emotional self-restraint may delegitimate the lived reality of disempowered groups and constitute a further affective burden on them.

Finally, attentiveness to the experiences of oppressed groups is an indispensable dimension of critique in so far as it is logically entailed in the Frankfurt School's own definition of theoretical inquiry as a situated, praxeological intellectual practice. Put negatively, to fail to attend to these experiences would be for critique to contradict its own fundamental tenets about the nature of inquiry. On this view of immanent critique, then, the position of the theorist in relation to the object of inquiry is, as we have seen, akin to that of a participant observer, or, as Habermas famously put it, 'in a process of Enlightenment, there can only be participants' (Habermas 1973: 40). The practical implication of the theorist in the field of study gives rise, inter alia, to the idea that critique is necessarily dialogical and reflexive in nature. Dialogical in the sense that the theorist, qua participant-observer, necessarily has a practical, ethical relation with those that she studies and grants them an enhanced, that is active, role in the process of knowledge production. This enhanced role includes not just one of data input, providing the empirical content of the theory, but also an active role in the process by which knowledge is verified or legitimated. The legitimacy of critical theory does not rest exclusively on its internal characteristics of coherence, objective accuracy, and so on—although of course these are of paramount importance—but also on its acceptance by the subjects whose situation it addresses. If critical theory is to meet this acceptability requirement, it needs to be responsive to and make sense of unfamiliar experiential life-worlds in a way that is relevant to the groups involved and to which they assent. Given that unmasking critique concentrates on groups who are particularly disadvantaged, dialogism might also be reasonably held to include an epistemic responsibility on the part of the theorist to avoid the type of top-down intellectual prescription that is potentially alienating and may symbolically compound their vulnerability. Enacting this epistemic responsibility may involve, inter alia, the relinquishment of objectifying, potentially estranging, forms of inquiry which grant sole interpretative authority to the theorist or theoretical framework over other perspectives. This is not to say that the process of knowledge production should swing the other way and give oppressed groups the final word on matters of the veracity and legitimacy of critique. Instead, the validity of critique is established through a dialogical, practical process of verification rather than through formal criteria of justificatory acceptability that are specified in advance by the theorist and may disadvantage disempowered interlocutors. Dialogical knowledge production implies a process of reasoning across perspectives where neither position—the experiential or theoretical one—is accorded automatic epistemic privilege over the other. Instead, reasoning takes place from within social perspectives, operating 'across the range of possible practical perspectives that knowledgeable and reflective social agents are capable of taking up and employing practically in their social activity' (Bohman 2001: 105). Knowledge production is based on a cooperative, fallibilistic dynamic that runs between the inquirer and subject of inquiry where the latter is explicitly or implicitly asked to 'practically verify' the interpretation that is being offered, or reject it or present an alternative interpretation (Bohman 2001: 223–4).

The dialogical dimension of critique is closely connected to its reflexive dimension. Reflexivity or critical self-awareness is, as Frankfurt School thinkers are at pains to point out, a defining characteristic of theory that is critical rather than traditional in nature. It emanates from the hermeneutic presupposition of critique's own situatedness and that therefore it may carry within itself certain unconscious assumptions, gaps, or biases that limit its diagnostic capacity. To exercise reflexivity involves theory's attempt to scrutinize itself vis-à-vis its own social location and to interrogate as many of these latent presuppositions and biases as possible. As Rainer Forst puts it: 'a theory can only count as critical and radical in the extent to which it understands itself as an activity that reflects back on itself and its own blind spots and exclusions in a self-critical manner' (Forst 2011: 8). The capacity for critical self-scrutiny may be built into the structure of inquiry in various ways—for example through collective authorship, working across disciplinary boundaries and so forth—but it is important to recognize that the prompt for critical self-examination is not always reliably generated from within theory itself. Indeed, given the increasingly specialized conditions of academic production and path-dependency, political theory may be prone to self-referentiality, intellectual solipsism, and other kinds of naturalizing scholastic fallacies. 'White normativity', for instance, exemplifies such scholastic self-enclosure in so far as theory fails to recognize that what it takes to be a position of analytical neutrality may in fact be one of social privilege (e.g., Akin 2019). Awareness of one's own positionality, qua unscrutinized presuppositions, may be prompted when, what are assumed to be inclusive and neutral concepts and approaches, are applied to discrepant or 'alien' life-worlds and found to be inadequate in some respect or another. Discrepant experiences may therefore be important external triggers for critique's self-scrutiny in a way that is not necessarily generated from within theory itself. In so far as they don't fit easily into prevailing interpretative frameworks, alien experiences may deliver an 'ontological shock' that prompts the theorist to consider shortcomings in their approach. Although granted this presupposes an openness to context on the part of theory, that is not always the case. Bridging this potential gap between dominant ways of viewing the world and unthematized, unfamiliar experiences may require the responsive critic to scrutinize their own presuppositions, concepts, and epistemic norms and be willing, in principle, to revise and rethink them in the light of 'other' experiences. Bourdieu describes this process as the objectification of the objectifying subject or effort to dispossess 'the knowing subject of the privilege it normally grants itself' (Bourdieu 2000: 10).

Of course, if for whatever reason, theory lacks the responsiveness to experience necessary for critical self-awareness, it may be unable to identify disjunctions between itself and the 'anomalous' life-world it examines. In such cases, the unchanging validity of the interpretative paradigm will be upheld. But the hope for a truly critical theory is that the effort of coming to terms with unfamiliar constellations of experience that may challenge preestablished explanatory frameworks may also prompt reassessment of the basic terms of inquiry. As Oksala puts it:

> we must listen especially to those whose experiences have been marginalized and whose voices have been silenced, not because they are in possession of some authentic truth about reality revealed only through suffering or oppression, but simply because their perspective is different from ours. It might therefore reveal some contradictions and alternative presuppositions that are not available to us and that therefore might shake the invisible privileges built into our own perspective. (Oksala 2016: 52)

After all, to be more than a merely tokenistic gesture, reflexivity requires more than formal acknowledgement of alterity, of seemingly alien modes of being. It requires an effort to respond as fully as possible to other perspectives and experiences and to consider fully the destabilizing implications that these may have for a previously settled interpretative framework. In short, in so far as they remain neglected, trivialized, or only partially understood within dominant paradigms, the experiences of subordinate groups may shed light on the dynamics of power that are always implicit in the operation of reason, and therefore on what the theorist might need to do to mitigate potentially exclusionary effects of their intellectual practice.

In conclusion then, according to the Frankfurt School's own definition of what is required for theory to have practical emancipatory impact, interpretative understanding of the experiences of oppressed groups is evidently pivotal to unmasking critique. Attentiveness to these experiences undergirds the claim that critical theory has greater political efficacy and real-world traction than comparable types of normative theory. These experiences may play an important informative role for critique, deepening the diagnosis of oppression with regard to explaining its subjective effects on individuals, and also ensuring that normative responses are sufficiently attuned to the context of power. As the main recipients of critique, disempowered groups also play a central role in producing and legitimating knowledge about oppression, a process that Frankfurt School theorists explicitly define as a dialogical and reflexive process. Indeed, the special importance that the lived experience of oppressed groups has for emancipatory critique is frequently acknowledged by Frankfurt School theorists. Adorno claims that the 'need to lend a voice to suffering is a condition of all truth' (Adorno 1974:

17–18). Habermas states that critical theory 'has its origin in the experience of pain and repression' (Habermas 1971: 283). Honneth (2007) asserts the importance of grounding critique in a phenomenology of injustice and social suffering. Iris Marion Young declares that critique emanates from hearing a cry of suffering or distress. Nancy Fraser stipulates that critical theory must work from an account of 'how differently situated agents understand themselves' in order to clarify the 'grammar of social struggle' and possibilities for social change (Fraser and Jaeggi 2018: 123). Forst maintains that a critical theory of justice is ignited by 'concrete experiences of...powerlessness and social exclusion' (Forst 2007: 121). Rahel Jaeggi claims that critique is guided by its awareness of blocked, negative constellations of experience. And so on. Certainly, the primacy accorded to the experiential perspective is not absolute; care must be taken to avoid its hypostatization as the unquestionable ends of theory. But, with this caveat in mind, it seems that critical theory should accord a central place to interpretative understanding of experience if it is to be consistent with its own self-understanding as historicized inquiry that directly addresses oppressed groups.

Context Transcendence and the Retreat from Experience

Yet, despite the apparent prima facie centrality of experiential understanding to unmasking critique, an unresolved ambivalence about the category runs throughout the work of Frankfurt School theorists. For as much as they declare the origin of theory in experiences of pain and repression, there is also in their writing a noticeable, if subtle, down-playing of the significance of experiential understanding for critique. This down-playing is partly motivated by legitimate concerns about the status of experience within theory and the attendant problems it brings with it such as subjectivism, parochialism, and relativism. But it is my view that these concerns are not only over-stated but have also been instrumental in initiating a one-sided and limiting preoccupation with normative foundations and context transcendence. Limiting because the 'paradigm-led' theorizing to which it gives rise is incompatible with critical theory's prima facie commitment to a mode of practical and dialogical inquiry that responds directly to the experiences and concerns of oppressed groups.

Worries about the status that experiential understanding should occupy in political theory are of course not limited to the Frankfurt School, but have long run through social and political thought more generally. Feminism in particular, and perhaps because of its strong links to practical politics, has 'swung like a pendulum' in its assessment of the status that the category of experience should occupy in theory (see Oksala 2016: ch. 2). Concerns typically centre on a cluster of issues—subjectivism, particularism, and relativism—that seem to be unavoidable consequences of too narrow and uncritical a focus on direct subjective experience.

If it aspires to be more than thick ethnocentric description, theory needs to be careful not to confine itself to the faithful recording of negative and marginalized experiences for, after all, 'normative arguments are not settled with thick descriptions any more than they are with statistical distributions' (Herzog and Zacka 2019: 19). It would be misguided for the theorist to take direct experience as an incontrovertible indicator of injustice and oppression given the limitations of any determinate perspective vis-à-vis a comprehensive account of social power. Even more so because, as the ideology critique of the early Frankfurt School made abundantly clear, the experiential point of view is likely to be prone to delusion and cognitive distortions that render it an unreliable guide for a systematic diagnosis of power (see Geuss 1981: 80–5). Even in cases where the direct experience gives valuable insight into the workings of power, the inevitable narrowness and particularity of this insight centred on a single life-world means that it need not necessarily have wider explanatory and normative significance. What is true for one group's experience of the world, may not hold for others and, if taken as gospel, this lack of generalizability undermines the general emancipatory force of critique. Too strict an adherence to a specific narrative of suffering threatens to reduce critique to mere complaint, and a systematic account of power to an arbitrary and partisan intervention on the part of the disadvantaged. In short, experiential disclosure may well be the cornerstone of critical theory's distinctive method, but it has worrisome implications in so far as its particularizing focus seems to deprive critique of trans-contextual relevance and validity.

Such concerns about the limiting effects of experiential understanding on critique have been instrumental in propelling the turn by Frankfurt School members to prioritize issues of context transcendence and normative foundations. As is well known, it is Habermas's work on universal pragmatics that, above all, has been the driver of this foundational turn for, as Geuss observes, from the mid-1960s 'he seems to have been frightened by the spectre of relativism and retreated into a kind of transcendentalism' (1981: 64). This foundational turn has accentuated worries about the parochializing effects of negative experience on critique and prompted subsequent generations of Frankfurt School thinkers to place limits on the role that experiential understanding plays in knowledge production. While it is acknowledged that experiential disclosure may shed valuable light on certain aspects of oppression, it is also felt that these insights need to be carefully tested and verified by being inserted into an objective, 'experience-distant' theoretical framework. For the purposes of systematic evaluation, critique must refer to 'something' that transcends immediate circumstances and that allows it to place a given experiential constellation in a comparative social and normative context. Evidently, the Frankfurt School's rejection of metaphysical notions of transcendence means that this 'something' cannot be construed in conventional Kantian terms as an independent foundation or free-standing warrant of some kind or another. Habermas's famous and influential response to this dilemma has been to immanentize transcendental foundations. A 'quasi-transcendental' foundation is established for critique through the identification of a principle which, although internal to social life, provides a trans-contextual evaluative stance by virtue of its constitutive nature. For Habermas, along with thinkers such as Benhabib, this constitutive principle is communication (universal pragmatics); for Honneth, it is recognition; for Forst justification; for Ferrara judgement (qua *sensus communis*); for Fraser participatory parity, and so on. The claim is that these intra-mundane universals furnish an independent yardstick against which a multiplicity of negative experiences can be systematically examined, compared, and assessed. At the same time, because they are rooted in social reality, these thin 'non-foundational foundations' do not blunt attentiveness to the varied patterns of power and experience that are the primary focus of unmasking critique.

There is no doubt that the recasting of context-transcending foundations in thin, postmetaphysical terms has been immensely productive for the Frankfurt School. It seems, on the face of it, to overcome worries about critique's wider diagnostic and normative relevance while remaining consistent with the historicizing premises of critical theory. But, at the same time, it has initiated a wholesale shift of critical theory's intellectual centre of gravity towards issues of normative foundation and transcendence, a shift that has not been welcomed by those who think it undermines other fundamental aspects of Frankfurt School critique. Indeed, Habermas himself admits that he finds quasi-transcendentalism the most difficult idea of all those in his work to defend, even though he regards it as indispensable in preventing the slide of critical theory into relativism and irrationalism (see Aboulafia 2002). Controversy around quasi-transcendental foundations has been prodigious, and centred in large part on the ways in which they may not be as thin and inclusive as they initially seem, but in fact harbour assumptions, biases, and blindspots that call into question their supposed neutrality and 'universal' status (e.g., Allen 2016; Mills 2017a). Broadly in agreement with this line of criticism, I maintain that the main cost of the Frankfurt School's foundational turn has been to undermine the experientially grounded critique of oppression that is supposedly a hallmark of emancipatory critical theory.

To be clear, the difficulty lies not with the idea of context transcendence itself, but rather with the strong monist and totalizing terms in which Frankfurt School theorists construe it. As the ability to distance oneself from the immediacy of any given situation in order to form critical judgements, to interpose an evaluative space between subject and world, context transcendence is a necessary feature of all thought including even the most radical forms of contextualism. Without this critical-evaluative space, inquiry would be swamped by the manifold flux of being, unable to discriminate between relevant and irrelevant empirical data. Yet, although it is a necessary condition of thought, context transcendence is also an ambiguous concept, one that could even be described as essentially contested.

Disagreement arises over the scope and historicity of critique, that is, over the kind of assumptions that it is necessary to make to authorize a theory's claim to trans-contextual validity. How far in space and time is validity understood to hold? What kind of social and cultural differences is context-transcending judgement capable of bridging? How diverse and inclusive are the notions of reason and rationality that underpin it? How strictly can the notion of universal validity be adhered to without lapsing into dogmatism, idealism, or some similar untenable assertion of unconditionality? And so on. Of the many possible responses to these questions, Frankfurt School thinkers, under Habermas's influence, have opted for a formulation of context transcendence in terms often so strong and unconditional that, in the eyes of many, it cannot but stand in tension with the historicizing premises of their thought. Consider for example Habermas's defence of the transcending force of communicative rationality: 'The transcendent moment of *universal* validity bursts every provinciality asunder...the validity claimed for propositions and norms transcends spaces and times, *"blots out" space and time'* (Habermas 1985: 322–3). According to Richard Rorty, this grandiose construal of context-independent validity implicitly invokes ideas of unconditionality that directly contradict the hermeneutic premises of immanent critique, namely, that all thought, critique included, is situated (Rorty 2000: 1–10). Even commentators more sympathetic than Rorty such as Thomas McCarthy maintain that the Habermasian notion of context transcendence is conceived in such unrestricted terms that it operates in a fashion closer to the idealized, free-floating foundations that critical theorists ostensibly reject: 'reason, truth, and justice...while no longer pretending to a God's-eye point of view, retain something of their critical force' (1990: 367). Accordingly, it is my contention that the Frankfurt School predilection for a particularly emphatic interpretation of context transcendence has given rise to a mode of paradigm-led theorizing that stands in tension with the experientially grounded critique of power. Moreover, there are ways of conceiving context transcendence that do not necessarily push critique back into radical contextualism but that are more compatible with the responsiveness to experience that defines emancipatory critique. But, by and large, Frankfurt School theorists have eschewed such a route and opted instead for a mode of paradigm-led thinking whose main concern is the self-referential one of maintaining its monist interpretative authority.

What do I mean by paradigm-led theorizing? It has several distinguishing features including, first, the adoption of uni-categorial or monist explanation. Context-transcending critique is conducted within the 'master' term of a given paradigm—whether that be communication, justification, or recognition—and all types of power are treated as variables that flow from this single constitutive source. The problem with such monist interpretations is that they simplify power relations and misdiagnose the experiences of oppressed groups. Rather than crystallizing an intersectional account of oppression by inductively working outwards from experience, monist explanations tie experience to a foundational logic, thereby effacing its complexity. If the commonplace observation that patterns of oppression are complex and multidimensional is correct, then it seems to follow that unmasking critique accordingly needs to mobilize differentiated, multivalent diagnostic frameworks, not monist ones. Differently put, the insistence on mono-categorical explanations speaks to a one-sided preoccupation with maintaining the authority of the interpretative paradigm over its adequacy as a critical account of oppression or, as Bourdieu puts it, the 'reality of the model' comes to prevail over the 'model of reality' (Bourdieu 1990b: 48). The preoccupation of critical theorists with the integrity of the paradigm explains why, even as they proclaim an animating concern with unmasking oppression, they in fact have surprisingly little of substance to say about most major forms of oppression. Unsurprisingly, given the imbrication of fact and norm, the inability of paradigm-led theory to yield anything other than stylized, broadbrush accounts of power has ramifications for the evaluative aspects of critique. The monist normative responses of Frankfurt School theorists to problems of oppression are often so general and underdetermined that it is hard to see how they practically contribute to the transformation of entrenched relations of power.

Problems of mono-categorical or single lens analysis are compounded by a second, related feature of paradigm-led theorizing, namely that it is totalizing. Following on from their historical commitment to 'grand theory', Frankfurt School theorists associate explanatory force with a comprehensive interpretative framework capable of diagnosing all social problems. But the problem with grand, covering theories is that they often result in vague and over-stylized diagnoses that lack diagnostic relevance to the concrete particulars of social experience. Bourdieu describes this social weightlessness as the 'artistocratism of that totalizing critique which retained all the features of grand theory, no doubt out of a concern not to dirty its hands in the kitchen of empirical research' (Bourdieu 1990b: 30; Bourdieu and Waquant 1992: 192–3). Given the emptiness of grand theories, vis-à-vis a determinate account of oppression, it may be that critique's explanatory force is enhanced by substituting a totalizing approach centred on origins with a problem-led one focussed on the patterns and particularities of negative experience. As Maeve Cooke puts it:

> the complexity of contemporary social orders and their multiple and multifaceted interdependencies raises the question of whether grand explanations are still possible today (if, indeed, they ever were). It could be argued that a more fruitful line of enquiry for contemporary critical theories is to endeavour to explain the ways in which dominating power is distributed and reproduced in a particular social order, leaving aside the question of the origins of such power. (Cooke 2006: 198)

A third feature of paradigm-led theorizing is that it implicitly rests on a hierarchy of theory over experience which undermines its claims to be a dialogical mode of inquiry. The difficulty, in a nutshell, is that the epistemic authority granted to the critical paradigm in determining questions of validity is sits uneasily with other claims to be engaged in a process of cross-perspectival reasoning with the subjects of enquiry. Critique partly accrues this determining authority to itself by over-problematizing the epistemic status of the experiential perspective relative to the theoretical one. In various ways, the former is subtly but disparagingly construed as inherently particularistic, parochial, and unreliable. The myopia of direct experience can only be satisfactorily corrected from the superior trans-perspectival vantage point of the paradigm. To some degree, this low-level disparagement of the experiential perspective is the legacy of the work of first-generation critical theorists—notably Adorno and Horkheimer's *Dialectic of Enlightenment*—whose reliance on an overstated and bleak account of ideological pacification effectively denied individuals the capacity for autonomous thought and action. On their elitist vision, high-art and critical theory are the only remaining positions from which the alienated reality of social existence can be adequately exposed; they are, in other words, the privileged vehicles of emancipatory insight. Thanks to Habermas's intersubjective turn, subsequent generations of critical theorists have moved away from this despairing mass cultural pessimism and overstated account of ideological delusion. However, the questionable privileging of critique as sole locus of emancipatory insight persists in a residual form. It lingers implicitly in the exaggerated problematization of the experiential perspective as inherently flawed and bounded—an 'epistemic prison' as Bohman puts it—which serves to neutralize it as a reliable source of knowledge. It lingers too in a corresponding under-problematization of the paradigm as situated theory, the effect of which is to decontest its singular interpretative authority.

The problematization of experience is troubling not because the concerns raised aren't legitimate but because they are exaggerated and reifying. Rather than regard them as contingent and circumstantially caused, Frankfurt School thinkers tend to present these limitations as inevitable, as flaws that are inherent to the perspective of those who are oppressed. There are undoubted difficulties with relying too heavily on first-hand experience in the construction of knowledge, for it may well be distorted, unclear, or misguided in some significant sense or another. But these limitations are not intrinsic to the experiential perspective per se, nor can they be assumed in advance as paradigm-led theorizing tends to do. Rather these flaws are the outcomes of hierarchical circumstances and uneven distributions of power and therefore, as contingent effects, they should be addressable and potentially corrigible through the mechanism of dialogic reasoning itself. What also gets forgotten in critique's too hasty disparagement of experience, is that those directly involved may be able to reveal things about power that are not necessarily visible from an external (theoretical) standpoint. Paradigm-led theorizing, however, tends to routinely underestimate the knowledge and insights of ordinary actors. Instead, it proceeds on the latent assumption of the inherently flawed nature of the experiential perspective, the validity of whose insights is a matter to be determined by the theoretical framework alone.

In the light of the validating role implicitly assumed by critique, it follows that the idea of dialogical reasoning is of a constrained nature. Dialogism is not conceived as reasoning across perspective between interlocutors on the same epistemic plane. Instead, knowledge production is structured around a hierarchy of theory over experience, where the views of subjects directly involved are akin to passive data fed into a pre-given paradigm. Correspondingly, the critical perspective, qua paradigm, is attributed an epistemic 'super-vision' or 'synthetic consciousness' understood as the capacity to transcend situatedness and to reconstruct the totality of social relations (Kogler 1997: 159–60). By being able to transcend epistemic boundedness in a way that dominated subjects are not, the theorist is in a position to assess the validity of the latter's inevitably partial insights and whether they genuinely 'merit' the title of injustice of not (Fraser and Honneth 2003: 205). But this one-sided transcendence is in tension with the historicizing premises of immanent critique; the idea of holistic super-vision appears to be a 'methodological fiction' that obscures the situatedness of the theorist and their implication within the hermeneutic interpretative circle. As Kogler puts it: 'given the interpretative situatedness of the political theorist, it is not clear on what basis [he or she] can claim a "higher objectivity" superior to that of the reflexive agents that use their conceptual and critical faculties to synthesize the social world from their point of view' (1997: 161). Above all this constrained, hierarchized dialogism is in tension with the claim that critique is immanently connected to the practical concerns of disempowered groups. For, rather than being internally connected, the perspectives of the subject and object of inquiry are external to each other and related not dialogically but by a unidirectional dynamic whereby theory stands over and validates experience.

Arising from constrained dialogism is the fourth feature of paradigm-led theorizing which is its insufficient self-awareness or reflexivity. Critical theory's over-problematization of experience is accompanied by a corresponding failure to be sufficiently mindful of potential epistemic limitations in the scholastic stance. This is not to fall into a romantic anti-intellectualism that privileges direct subjective experience while under-appreciating the independent epistemic contribution of the theoretical perspective. It would be reductive in the extreme to discount the ways in which a distanced explanatory perspective acts as an essential complement and corrective to the immediacy of the experiential stance. In drawing together wider sources of information, the transpersonal theoretical viewpoint is an invaluable counterweight in dialogical inquiry to the epistemic constraints of first-hand experience. It often identifies more precisely the causal dynamics that connect seemingly isolated or purely personal experiences to deeper social structures. To question the privilege of the theoretical perspective, then, is not to undermine its intrinsic epistemic value per se in dialogical knowledge production. Rather it is intended here to direct attention to the ways that critique itself is unavoidably shaped by a particular social location, and therefore may suffer from its own type of intellectual particularism and bias. Theoretical knowledge rests on a distinctive type of scholastic withdrawal from the world and, to some extent, it is the features of this withdrawal that determine the kind of thinking that is made possible. To fail to examine the nature and implications of this withdrawal is therefore to naturalize theoretical knowledge as somehow neutral and unbounded, to elide its decentred, transpersonal stance of critique with objectivity per se. The theoretical worldview might be limited, for example, by the importation of unnoticed scholastic assumptions into sociological description which can be the basis for misunderstanding. For example, where the leisurely tempo of the observer's perspective is projected onto a situation effacing the urgency felt by those directly involved and thus resulting in misinterpretation. As Bourdieu observes:

> as soon as we observe the social world, we introduce in our perception of it a bias due to the fact that, to study it, to describe it, to talk about it, we must retire from it more or less completely. This *theoreticist* or *intellectualist* bias consists in forgetting to inscribe in the theory we build of the social world the fact that it is the product of a theoretical gaze, a 'contemplative eye'.
> (Bourdieu and Wacquant 1992: 69, note 17)

In principle, it is by building into itself the capacity for reflexive self-scrutiny that critical theory guards against such potential scholastic bias and intellectual solipsism. Yet, as much as they stress the situatedness of critique and its inevitable implication within its own field of inquiry, Frankfurt School theorists often fail, in practice, to subject their paradigms to precisely the kind of critical scrutiny that this entails. On the face of it, reflexivity implies that all aspects of a theory should be open to examination and alteration in the light of disconfirmation from a changing social context. But, in fact, reflexive self-scrutiny is frequently curtailed by the 'quasi-transcendent' status that Frankfurt School thinkers bestow on their chosen constitutive principle that effectively shields their paradigms from extensive examination. Everything is up for questioning, critically speaking, except it seems for the paradigm's governing principle, which remains beyond contention as an appropriate explanation of social power. In so far as this paradigm closure undermines reflexivity, it jeopardizes one of the essential features that betoken critique's responsiveness to context, especially the experiences of oppressed groups.

In short, paradigm-led theorizing sits uneasily with the historicized premises of immanent critique. Regardless of their stated epistemic aims, Frankfurt School theorists finish by reproducing a model of knowledge production that is closer to conventional, objectifying accounts than it is to a dialogic and reflexive method of inquiry. Rather than playing an active role in the production and verification of knowledge about oppression, the subjects of inquiry (disempowered groups) are reduced to passive recipients of an externally bestowed, superior knowledge where: 'inquirers independently discover the best explanation using the available comprehensive theory;... then persuasively communicate its critical consequences to participants who may have false beliefs about their practices' (Bohman 2005). It is this tendency to attribute interpretative authority to the critical paradigm alone that explains why commentators have repeatedly criticized Frankfurt School theory for an 'epistemic authoritarianism' that stands in marked contrast to its emancipatory political objectives (Cooke 2006; also Celikates 2018b). In short, by defaulting to a top-heavy, paradigm-led model of knowledge production, critical theory fails to comply with its own hermeneutic requirement.

Reconfiguring Context Transcendence

Frankfurt School theorists typically respond to such criticisms by insisting that, if critique is to retain minimal trans-contextual normative force and avoid relativism, it needs to be grounded in a rational universal. Habermas expresses this, as we have seen, in terms of a perspective that, by virtue of its constitutive nature, bursts asunder every other provincial worldview. His conviction is echoed by other Frankfurt School thinkers. Honneth stipulates that, without a universal core, context transcendence becomes merely the outcome of 'contingent conflict situations', its meaning dissipated through historicization to little more than 'unfulfilled, and to that extent transcending, social ideals and goals... still to be found within social reality at a particular time' (Fraser and Honneth 2003: 244). Critique's wider emancipatory impact depends therefore on an unchanging core or 'normative potential that emerges in every new social reality because it is so tightly fused to the structure of human interests' (Fraser and Honneth 2003: 244). Echoing this, Forst insists that his principle of justification captures the essence of practical reason and is therefore independent of all conceptions of the good. Likewise, Jaeggi describes her idea of progress as a 'free-standing-determinate' principle that rises above other contextually indexed modes of thought.

This widespread anxiety about the contingency and parochialism of contextually indexed theory and the attempt to find a definitive standpoint is not only inconsistent with the Frankfurt's School's idea of situated rationality but also rests on a questionable zero-sum logic. Is it really the case that without an unchanging core, critique lacks trans-contextual relevance and systematicity and is plunged back into a mere parochialism and standpoint relativism? If, by their own lights, all thought, critique included, is situated, it seems contradictory for critical theorists to maintain that, even so, there exists a single, nonprovincial standpoint that effectively stands outside space and time and provides an independent vantage point from which all other local forms of knowledge can be assessed? More consistent with their idea of immanent critique would be a weaker, less absolutist formulation of context transcendence, in perhaps genealogical, hermeneutic, or pragmatist terms, as insight that comes not from some putatively unchanging principle but from bringing unfamiliar worldviews to bear on each other such that existing immanent horizons of understanding are enhanced and expanded. As Rorty puts it: 'the only thing that can transcend a social practice is another social practice, just as the only thing that can transcend a present audience is a future audience. Similarly, the only thing that can transcend a discursive strategy is another discursive strategy' (2000: 7). The assertion of an invariant, ahistorical core to critique implicitly invokes schematic and analogically linked antitheses of universalism versus particularism, transcendence versus immanence, objectivity versus subjectivity, theory versus experience, and so on. In Nancy Fraser's well-known phrase, these are false antitheses in so far as the very problems of particularism, subjectivism, relativism, and so forth are, if not created, at least considerably magnified by the absolutized, ahistorical terms in which Frankfurt School thinkers construe the problem of context transcendence. As Albrecht Wellmer puts it, relativism is a problem produced by a 'philosophy of the absolute'. If the angle of vision is changed, then the problem of relativism disappears (Wellmer 1991: 180).

To all intents and purposes, quasi-transcendence operates in a way that is practically indistinguishable from the metaphysical notions of transcendence that Frankfurt theorists ostensibly reject. The correlate of such strong universalism is the dismissal of direct experience as mere particularism—an assumption that is undermining of emancipatory critique. In this light, it would be more productive to unhitch critique from these strongly formulated, ahistorical foundations and reconceptualize context transcendence in terms more compatible with historicized inquiry. Instead of fidelity to a single-lens paradigm, context transcendence might be thought of as a potential inherent within dialogical inquiry itself, an effect of the process of thinking across perspectives. Explanatory and normative insight are outcomes generated by the movement of thought itself between the experiential and theoretical (the subjective and objective, personal and transpersonal) stances, where the mutual irreducibility and alienness of each perspective serves as the basis from which to interrogate and transcend the limitations of the other. The theoretical worldview has a crucial part to play in overcoming blindspots and errors in the first-hand worldview, but, contra paradigm-led thought, it does not have an unquestioned monopoly on this improving and authenticating role. For, direct subjective experience may be similarly instrumental in exposing shortcomings and errors in theoretical frameworks and expanding horizons of understanding. Context transcendence as the interpretative authority of the comprehensive paradigm is thereby replaced with a pragmatically reconfigured notion of context transcendence as internal to the process of thinking across perspectives. This dialogically reworked notion is akin, for instance, to Sandra Harding's (1992) 'strong objectivity' or Haraway's (1988) 'positioned objectivity' where the multiperspectival character of knowledge is regarded as an epistemic strength rather than as a weakness to be overcome by the single vision of the transcending paradigm.

As cross-perspectival reasoning, context-transcending critique is focussed less narrowly on determining validity or the fact of the matter—although of course such issues are still relevant—and instead more broadly on a political process of sustaining openness to others and expanding horizons of understanding (see Bohman 2001: 100). Questions of validity are not unimportant, but criteria for assessing the legitimacy of knowledge are contextualized rather than formal and are to be decided upon by participants themselves, not given in advance by a paradigm. Validity is about assessing the adequacy of given interpretations of the world according to the resources immanent in a given socio-political context, and not according to preselected, unchanging, monological criteria. Reconfiguring validity as practical verification in this way avoids, on the one hand, the problematic abstracting tendencies of context-free Kantian procedures which are often less neutral than appears. On the other hand, however, practical verification cannot be dismissed as merely arbitrary relativism where any subjective worldview is held to be as plausible as any other. The sheer contingency of radical contextualism is replaced by a relational approach that, through cross-perspectival reasoning, assesses the adequacy of competing interpretations of the world against various sociological and political criteria with an ultimate view to the working through of concrete problems. Moreover, practical verification of a worldview is not accomplished once and for all as certain justificatory scenarios teleologically oriented to the goal of universal consent suggest. Rather verification is an inescapably iterative, historical process in as much as it forms part of ongoing political struggles against injustice. If interpretative schemas or worldviews—theoretical or experiential—are developed in response to objective conditions as a way for individuals make sense of their situation, it follows that if objective conditions change, then the worldview may also become redundant or anachronistic in some way. Hence practical justification is necessarily a continuing political process.

The reconfiguration of context transcendence and validity in dialogical and praxeological terms is, on the face of it, more compatible than paradigm-led formulations with critical theory's claim to be of practical, emancipatory relevance to oppressed groups. Based on a methodological presumption of equality between the theoretical and experiential worldviews, it instantiates a more expansive dialogism that allows for greater input from oppressed groups in emancipatory knowledge production. Differently put, it is compatible with what I call theorizing from experience. Contrary to the fears of Frankfurt School members, theorizing from experience need not inevitably drag critique into a merely subjectivist, particularistic, and relativist stance. Indeed, these difficulties are the result of an essentialized view of experience as inherently particularistic which is yet another consequence of reliance on over-played dichotomies of universality and particularity, transcendence and immanence, objectivism and subjectivism. Accordingly, as I will show in the next section, an anti-essentialist account of experience conceived in relation to social location and power is a crucial underpinning of a dialogically reconfigured idea of context transcendence. Conceived in these relational terms, experience becomes a reliable basis from which to theorize in so far as it can reveal important, suppressed aspects of power that are not necessarily visible from other standpoints and that enhance critical social understanding.

Feminist Theorizing from Experience

When it comes to reconceiving experience as a reliable basis from which to theorize, members of the Frankfurt School could learn from the other types of radical theory that are more closely connected to identity politics movements. Although one of the aims of this type of theory is to recover the experiences of oppressed groups, it hardly results in the dead-end of parochial, subjectivist, and relativist knowledge that Frankfurt School thinkers fear. Rather these other theories use experience as the basis from which to inductively develop a structural account of the workings of power. Black feminist thought is a paradigm of this type of theorizing from experience. In the view of black feminist theorists, it is especially important to take the first-hand experience of black women as a 'criterion of credibility' for knowledge claims, if theory about oppression is not to talk over the heads of its addressees and have a practical emancipatory effect. Indeed, given the ways in which the views of black women and other disempowered groups are routinely ignored, discredited, and marginalized in formal as well as everyday modes of thought, it would be ethically and politically inconsistent for unmasking critique to aprioristically assume what Nancy Fraser describes as the 'notorious unreliability' of lived experience (see Chapter 5). In contrast to the subtly disparaging stance often taken by Frankfurt School members, black feminist theorists hold that problems with connecting theory to experience tend to arise not so much from giving unquestioning credence to the latter, but rather from the tendencies of the former to solipsism and over-rationalization. Theory's connection to experience is often so highly mediated through what Adorno memorably labelled as 'estranging enigmas of thought' that it risks become unmoored from the social reality it supposedly addresses, and stranded in its own rarefied constructs. Similarly, preempting recent work on white normativity, black feminist theorists have long pointed out that the tendency to dismiss the testimony and experiences of marginalized groups as partial and restricted, is a propensity of dominant groups who fail to recognize the ways in which they naturalize their own 'particular' stance as theoretical holism. Writing about white solipsism's 'masquerade' as universal philosophy, Joy James comments: 'the thoughts of "outsiders" are reduced to descriptions of a part (of humanity or subhumanity) rather than analyses of a whole (humanity)... teaching about the lives of black activist women, for example, is viewed as a descent to the particular from the "universal norm" (white, male, monied)' (James 2013: 5).

Resisting the elision of experience with particularism, black feminist theorists maintain that there are certain collective experiences which, by virtue of being located at the intersection of key vectors of power, offer important insights into the structural dynamics of oppression. As Angela Davis puts it: 'there is something in the nature of racism's role in this society that permits those who have come up through the ranks of struggles against racism to have a clearer comprehension of the totality of oppression in this society' (Bhavnani and Davis 1989: 72). This presumption of the credibility of experience does not mean, however, that an apodictic epistemic privilege is imputed to it; indeed black feminist theorists have repeatedly rejected such essentializing gestures: 'there is no essential or archetypal Black woman whose experiences stand as normal, normative and thereby authentic' (Collins 2000: 32). Instead, experience is de-essentialized by being conceptualized in relation to changing socio-structural configurations of power. It is less of a static, homogeneous existential category than a historicized one that is internally differentiated by 'specific political economies' (Collins 2000: 22). Black women, as individuals, certainly have experiences and biographical trajectories that vary from each other but, as a group, they are connected by recurring patterns of experience that arise from their shared social location—vis-à-vis structures of class, race, and gender—that expose them to similar obstacles and challenges. These recurring experiential patterns may, in turn, form the basis of a distinctive consciousness about their position in the world and society more generally. This consciousness is not, however, automatically guaranteed, it is a political achievement:

> while common experiences may predispose Black women to develop a distinctive group consciousness, they guarantee neither that such a consciousness will develop among all women nor that it will be articulated as such by the group. As historical conditions change, so do the links among the types of experiences black women will have and any ensuing consciousness concerning those experiences. (Collins 2000: 28)

Epistemic insight into oppression does not spring naturally from unmediated lived reality, but is actively constructed through the political reflection upon certain commonalities of experience relative to social advantage and the 'self-validation' that often occurs in disempowered groups. There is nothing given or incorrigible about the experiential standpoint, it is always 'unfinished' (Collins 2000: 290).

Nonetheless, the relativization of direct subjective experience in relation to social location allows black feminist theorists to treat it as a 'reliable source of knowledge' and 'central criterion' for theorizing without falling into uncritical phenomenalism (Collins 2000: 11). At some level, people who are oppressed know it, and it is precisely the first-hand nature of this knowledge that renders it more revealing in important respects than removed perspectives of privilege: 'those individuals who have lived through the experiences about which they claim to be experts are more believable and credible than those who have merely read or thought about such experiences' (Collins 2000: 276; also Narayan 1988). This insight is positional not essential; it comes precisely from the dislocation that certain groups experience vis-à-vis structures of power and advantage. Speaking of the black feminist academic, Collins famously calls this dislocated perspective the standpoint of the 'outsider within' and explicitly locates it within a long sociological tradition that attributes critical insight to marginal and disadvantaged social positions. By aligning this perspective with analogous notions such as Simmel's idea of the stranger, Merton's idea of the outsider, or Bourdieu's notion of the lucidity of the excluded, Collins implicitly rebuts the criticism of standpoint essentialism that is repetitively levelled at radical feminist theory. The very position of social exclusion, of being marginalized from social sources of power, makes certain intersecting dynamics of oppression more visible to subordinate groups than they are to dominant groups in a different position. Perceptive capacity is not unstructured, but the potential result of occupying a certain pivotal location, viz. the 'simultaneity of oppression' (Smith 1999: xxxii). Black women, as Collins describes it: 'have a clearer view of oppression than other groups who occupy more contradictory positions vis-à-vis white male power—unlike white women, they have no illusions that their whiteness will negate female subordination, and, unlike black men, they cannot use a questionable appeal to manhood to neutralise the stigma of being black' (Collins 1986: 19).

By dismantling overplayed dichotomies of experiential particularism versus theoretical holism, black feminist theory provides an alternative model of methodical critique that breaks the link between systematicity and a totalizing monist paradigm. Instead of the paradigm-led goal of all-encompassing social theory, black feminist thought uses an abductive, experientially based line of reasoning to systematically work through clusters of conceptual and normative issues that pertain to a concrete problem. Being indexed to context and experience in this way need not reduce critique to mere local thought, or weaken its normative rigour, so much as open it up to diagnosing oppression that is more flexible and multidimensional than monist interpretation. The implications that theorizing from experience has for the diagnostic, normative, and epistemic functions of critique will now be considered in more detail in relation to feminist work on gender oppression.

Power and Abductive Theorizing

In terms of explaining oppression, experience-led theory works outwards from concrete problems towards general conclusions about power, and not, in a paradigm-led fashion, downwards from a constitutive principle towards social reality. This kind of experientially based inductive theorizing that imaginatively establishes connections between experiences and social structures yields an account of power that is more flexible and multidimensional than monist paradigms where power is tied to an original source. Black and postcolonial feminist theorists have been in the forefront of arguing that such single-lens diagnoses of power are too simplistic to capture the complexities of intersectional oppression, gender or otherwise and consequently, have developed alternative, problem-led models of social inquiry. In her recent work, for example, Collins discusses the idea of abductive analysis by which she means a mode of inquiry that extrapolates its analytical toolkit a posteriori from a common object of inquiry, instead of positing fixed theories or methods in advance. As she describes it: 'an abductive approach does not decide on the front end which social theory is the best and then try to fit others into its framework. Instead all social theories are in play and come into dialogue with one another... in relation to their common object of investigation. Such theories do not compete for dominance in trying to be the best fit for explaining the topic' (2019: 147). The theoretical toolkit may change over time as inquiry works recursively back and forth between theory and findings. Abductive analysis is, in short, an innovative, multidimensional and fallibilist approach to social critique: 'building questions from what we sense to true from our partial perspectives, pausing to develop a "theory" or explanation of the social world around us, then testing that explanation through lived experience or by seeking out alternative explanations that in turn change our initial partial perspectives' (Collins 2019: 148–9; see also Strydom 2011: 155–60).

To some extent, intersectionality itself can be seen as a critical lens that has emanated from a problem-based abductive approach in so far as an under-theorized cluster of experiences—those of black women and other marginalized groups—has propelled the development of an expanded account of power. Kimberley Crenshaw (1991) famously formulated the notion as a way of explaining how African-American women were routinely subjected to racial and gender discrimination that went unrecognized and unaddressed because of the compartmentalized structure of the legal system. Put simply, gender discrimination was legally recognized, but only as it affected white women; likewise, racial discrimination was recognized but only as it affected black men. Crenshaw's goal was not to assert the intrinsic authenticity or incontrovertible truth of black women's experiences, but to use them as the basis on which to shed light on the intersectional operations of race, class, and gender, to draw a link as she puts it between 'structural convergence and political marginality' (Guidroz and Berger 2009: 65). By linking the experiences of a particular group to deeper formations of power, she improved on the existing monocausal explanations of women's oppression as patriarchy that prevailed in feminism at the time. As a multidimensional account of power, intersectionality brings together different zones of social reality in a non-reductive explanation. On a horizontal level, it moves between qualitatively different vectors of power and, on a vertical level, weaves back and forth, between experiential constellations and socio-structural explanation.

This abductive mode of analysis is amply exemplified in the work of other feminist theorists of race and postcolonialism. So, for example, Angela Davis's research on the experiences of female slaves is intended not only to retrieve lost historical material (although this is undoubtedly an important task in itself) but also to insert an under-theorized dimension of gendered power and violence into extant accounts of chattel slavery (Davis 1981, 1998b). In exposing the ways that female slaves were regarded as labouring bodies, first, and women, second, her pioneering work dispelled the myth that they were better treated than their male counterparts but rather bore the 'terrible burden of equality' in oppression (1981: 19). Drawing on historical records of slave testimony, Davis demonstrates how the rape of women slaves was less an expression of the sexual urges of their male owners and more a brutal and deliberate strategy of domination that presaged its similar use in the twentieth century as a weapon of mass political terrorism (1981: 23). Likewise, her studies of the prison–industrial complex enact a mode of experientially rooted analysis that, at the same time, does not lack materialist rigour and wider explanatory impact (see James 1989: part 1). Starting from the direct experiences that a disproportionate number of African-Americans have of imprisonment, she works outwards to a sophisticated critique of supermax prisons as having abandoned any attempt at rehabilitation and hence having become little more than 'dumping grounds and ways of avoiding social problems'. Extrapolating partly from her own experience of prison as well as those of the prisoners in her case-studies, she introduces a much-needed gendered dimension to the analysis of the penal system that, inter alia, shines a light on the unacknowledged violence frequently perpetrated against women prisoners by warders, doctors, and the police (Davis 2012: 33). Moving outwards, she shows how the penal system of forced labour (the slavery of prison) contributes to global patterns of labour exploitation, unemployment, and the pauperization of the working class more generally. In short, by weaving back and forth between concrete life-worlds and underlying structural forces, between the micro and macro levels, she systematically builds up a nuanced and far-reaching analysis of the way in which democracy is underpinned and enabled by a pervasive system of racialized carceral power. Contra Frankfurt School fears, there is little of the parochial, then, in the way Davis proceeds from analysis of specific experiential constellations outwards to expose the gendered, racialized modes of domination that are integral to the accumulation of capitalist wealth.

Intersectionality is hardly a new concept; it is widely taken to be a standard feature of any account of structural oppression, gender or otherwise. In spite of this, it remains almost entirely untheorized in monist critical theories. This absence is evidently bound up with the Frankfurt School's failure to consider racial inequality and its imbrication in other dimensions of oppression (e.g., Mills 2017a; Outlaw 2005). More generally, single-lens diagnostic frameworks are ill-suited to capturing the intricacies of intersectional dynamics of power. So for instance, gender oppression is described in generalized, uni-directional terms as stemming at base from, say, the misrecognition of women's social role (*pace* Honneth) or, from the acceptance of patriarchal justifications (*pace* Forst), or the colonization of the life-world (*pace* Habermas). As we see in subsequent chapters, absent cross-cutting dynamics of race, class, etc., these diagnoses are too vague and stylized to have much explanatory bite and, in some cases, simply misdiagnose what is really going on in terms of the logic of gender oppression. Their generic analyses seem to be oblivious to the significant differences in experience and life chances that exist between women depending on their positioning within structures of class and race. This effectively renders black women's social experience invisible, by disregarding the way in which their oppression is tied not just to unpaid domestic labour but also to the role they have historically played in labour markets. Broadbrush ideas of misrecognition, for instance, are orthogonal to explanations of how the structure of black family life has been shaped by the position of super-exploitation that black women have historically occupied in the labour market, which sees them segregated in low-paid, care, and service sectors of the economy (Collins 2000: 29ff; Threadcraft 2016). Likewise, explanations such as that offered by Forst, where gender oppression is causally related to widespread social acceptance of patriarchal narratives, is both reductive and ignores the complexities of black women's subordination where racialized norms have historically placed them in a tangential position vis-à-vis male-defined ideas of femininity (Collins 2000: 76–106). Problems with an insufficiently differentiated account of power are compounded by the left–Hegelian tendency to analytically separate social spheres from each other, and hence obscure the ways in which they interact with each systematically perpetuating cycle of gendered vulnerability. The separation of social spheres means that Frankfurt School thinkers typically work with a superficial and sociologically anachronistic account of gender as a matter that pertains primarily to interpersonal relations between men and women in the family. By confining gender issues to the sphere of intimacy, they fail to appreciate its importance as a fundamental principle of societal organization, a structural logic that pervasively and systematically organizes behaviour across all social realms.

The disregard of intersectional power dynamics is arguably a considerable flaw in a theory that declares itself to be an unmasking account of oppression. The specificities of black women's subordination challenge the accuracy of socially deracinated analyses of the family (and labour) and hence throw into question more generally the supposed comprehensiveness of monist interpretative paradigms. Put differently, explanatory power does not seem to be straightforwardly co-extensive with totalizing critique, because when sociological concepts are used without regard to experiential specificity, the dangers of omission and distortion increase. Frankfurt School theorists might respond that this failure to conceptualize the simultaneity of oppression can be easily surmounted by introducing the relevant empirical details into their explanatory models. But the problem is not merely one of sociological under-specification, but rather pertains to the explanatory rationale of the paradigm itself, where all types of oppression are treated as variables that flow from a single constitutive source. In so far as intersectionality denotes a complex social reality, where power relations overlap, are discontinuous or contradictory, it is not clear how the idea could be straightforwardly integrated into Frankfurt School critique in its current paradigm-led instantiation. It seems that an altogether different approach to social theoretical understanding seems to be required; not expanded monism, but one which moves dialectically between structural and phenomenal levels in order to explain how axes of power interact in varying ways to create heterogeneous experiential worlds and life trajectories.

In sum, as any number of feminist problem-led analyses demonstrate, critique's systematic explanatory force is not automatically jeopardized when the Frankfurt School's elision of systematicity with monism is resisted. The well-documented feminist suspicion of universalizing thought does not entail a 'simple-minded opposition to *all generalizations*' rather only to those that obfuscate the embodied reality of being oppressed (Narayan 2000: 97). It entails, in other words, a commitment to discriminating between deficient, that is falsely homogenizing, abstractions and politically useful types of abstraction, the latter being those that shed light on rather than obscure oppression. Abstractions such as patriarchy and white supremacy are useful because they capture 'the essentials of the situation of women and nonwhites, not abstract away from them'(Mills 2005: 173). In disclosing this experiential reality, they go beyond mere, localized description since they may be generative of new categories and principles that expand understanding of different kinds of subordination.

As Uma Narayan explains: 'the claim that virtually every community is structured by relationships of gender that comprise specific forms of social, sexual, and economic subjection of women seems a generalization that is politically useful; it also leaves room for attention to differences and particularities of context with respect to the predicaments of different groups of women' (Narayan 2000: 97).

The goal of systematic critique on this view is not the development of a comprehensive framework according to which all social problems can be evaluated, but the more modest one of gradual improvement and expansion of social understanding.

Normativity

In light of the Frankfurt School's view of the inherence of fact and norm, it is unsurprising that the explanatory shortcomings of paradigm-led theory give rise to related normative limitations. When social relations and practices are misdescribed, it follows that attendant normative proposals risk being tangential to the correction of oppressive gendered dynamics. As Stephen Leonard explains: 'an interest in emancipation can lead to real emancipation only if it is grounded in an accurate understanding of how social and political practices, knowledge and self-identity come to be structured' (Leonard 1990: 232–3). It follows from the complex nature of intersectional oppressions that proposals devised to mitigate them should be formulated in a way that is attentive to the context of power and therefore should be similarly multidimensional in nature. Such an approach is foreclosed in paradigm-led theory because the organization of normativity around an invariant core tends to produce emancipatory proposals that are tangential and undetermined. It may also verge on ethnocentrism in so far as the definition of human interests may be culturally biased (e.g., Allen 2016). Even were it possible to define fundamental interests in a sufficiently nonexclusionary way, their practical emancipatory force would be questionable since, of necessity, they must be defined in terms so thin as to be unlikely to produce determinate outcomes.

This underdetermination is evident in neoKantian critical theories—such as those of Habermas, Forst, and, to a lesser extent, Fraser—where the deontological bracketing of ethical concerns means that they are often unable to deal with the thick social issues pertaining to gender oppression (see Chapters 2 and 5). Beyond providing general moral orientation, formal proceduralism often lacks the responsiveness to context that is necessary to give it practical traction in dealing with real-world normative dilemmas of gender (see Woolf 2019: 15). Moreover, in the eyes of feminists and other pragmatic thinkers, the neoKantian focus on matters of justification and validity can seem to be an overly narrow and, at times, uncomfortably adjudicative way of construing the space of normativity. For instance, procedures of rational justification can be insufficiently attentive to the epistemic obstacles they present to disempowered groups and therefore may have the unintended consequence of silencing those who most need to be heard. Even with the proviso of equality between interlocutors, the demand that individuals redeem their claims according to preestablished criteria can all too easily appear to be an imposition by dominant groups of their own privileged mode of reasoning, one which places them in a position of judgement over vulnerable others. NeoHegelian critical theories suffer from not dissimilar problems of underdetermination because they are also drawn so broadly. The propensity to explain social relations at the level of constitutive dynamics of social being (e.g., recognition/ misrecognition or progress) produces ethical responses so generalized that they seem ineffectual in tackling entrenched dynamics of oppression. So, for example, recognition monism's depiction of care as a primary ethical bond not only naturalizes women's domestic labour in the family but also neglects the complicated social reality of 'care work' as undervalued, poorly paid, and carried out in the main by black, working-class, and migrant women. Given the term's inherent lack of specificity, it is not clear what enhanced recognition would entail as a normatively effective attempt to correct the stark inequalities that shape current economies of care. Likewise, with regard to gender justice in the family, recognition models tend to overemphasize certain internal 'democratizing' tendencies towards greater equality between men and women, while downplaying negative tendencies such as undiminishing levels of domestic violence, women's 'double shift', rising levels of deprivation, and child poverty. The endemic nature of these problems suggests that normative responses to gender oppression might need to be more targeted, distributive in nature, and radical in scope than the personalist model of ethical mutuality allows.

Instead of organizing normativity around a constitutive principle, then, emancipatory responses are more effectively derived from analysis of specific problems and contexts of power. A problem-led inductive approach to normative reasoning is more congruent with critical theory's claim to speak directly to the concrete concerns of the oppressed than its current attempt to construct all-encompassing paradigms of justice, progress, and so on. Emancipatory critique would focus instead on examining constellations of experiences, in their particularity, as a way of eliciting determinate responses to a given situation. This is, after all, the guiding premise of immanent critique that normative solutions are already embedded, as felt but unrealized possibilities, in existing social practices. As Adorno famously put it: 'the false, once determinately known and precisely expressed, is already an index of what is right and better' (1998: 288). On this experientially grounded view, it is not the responsibility of critique alone to formulate normatively appropriate responses to social problems, but rather to work out what these might involve in dialogue with those directly involved. By giving expression to counter-hegemonic forms of agency and 'resistant knowledges projects' of oppressed groups, this immanent, dialogic method yields a normative repertoire that is more varied than paradigm-led theory (Collins 2019: 88). For, as we saw earlier, marginalized women often develop strategies of resistance that vary considerably from those adopted by privileged white feminists who are often too 'enamoured' with theories of domination and victimhood to think about empowerment. Precisely because of their greater vulnerability, marginalized women focus on devising bottom-up strategies of collective empowerment and resistance such as the 'power of disbelief', 'refusal to accept definitions of oneself put forward by the powerful', and so on (Threadcraft 2019: 651–2). In a broader sense, the normativity that is at play here is that of practical wisdom and strategy that leans less towards legislative outcomes than the development of everyday practices of empowerment. In line with this, theorizing from experience yields an 'orientational' normativity whose evaluative standards are melioristic, revisable, and aimed at improving the practical reality of subordinated groups.

Even though it is tied not to an invariant core but to specific experiential constellations, critique is not left moving inconsequentially from the evaluation of one 'contingent conflict situation' to another as Frankfurt School theorists fear. Feminist theorists have long attempted to transcend such a schematic and debilitating opposition of universalism to relativism, and have shown instead that attentiveness to social particularity does not amount to mere arbitrariness but can be compatible with systematic moral reasoning. Such contextually indexed approaches do not automatically foreclose first-order universal commitments, but they are operationalized in a manner that is dialogical and reflexive rather than being imposed through a paradigm the authority of which is assumed in advance (e.g., Ackerly 2008; Khader 2019). Teresa Tobin and Alison Jaggar (2013), for instance, have argued that in encounters characterized by deep disparities of power between interlocutors, contextually indexed modes of normative reasoning and justification are more likely than principle-led modes to have efficacious political outcomes. They concretize their claims through a case study that compares two differing ways of evaluating the practice of female genital cutting (FGC) among Maasai communities in Kenya. Both approaches endorse the use of universal human rights as the correct moral standard against which FGC is held to be an instance of systematic violence against women, one that has resulted from historically entrenched relations of male domination and female subordination. There is considerable difference, however, in the way that each approach justifies and applies the standard to the circumstances in question. One justificatory approach pivots on the deductive application of a universal moral standard (DAU) to the particular case in order to demonstrate to doubters—that is, cultural relativists—that FGC does indeed constitute a violation of women's human rights. The other practice of moral justification—empirically informed reflective equilibrium (EIRE)—also draws on women's human rights as a universal standard to identify 'morally suspicious' gendered practices, but interprets the standard in the light of relevant contextual details. Rather than assume violation in advance, EIRE aims to establish whether this is the case in the concrete instance concerned and, if so, to generate a comprehensive, i.e., multiperspectival account of the injurious practices. While neither approach is culturally relativist on the matter of FGC and each supports the efforts of governments and other agencies to eliminate the practice, Tobin and Jaggar argue that the DAU approach is less effective than

EIRE because of its alienating effects. It seeks to prohibit FGC by appealing to a single settled moral standard of women's humans right that it then applies, in a blanket fashion, to all variants of the practice wherever it occurs.[1] Regardless of its admirable intention to protect vulnerable women, the unnuanced and top-down application of human rights discourse is often seen by the indigenous Maasai groups as an abusive imposition of Western power that alienates them. Particularly alienating is the way in which decontextualized appeals to universal rights as a priori fixed and settled seems to implicitly lay the blame for such practices in 'unenlightened' Maasai culture, and ignores the part played by British colonial rule in shaping the patriarchal norms and modes of economic and political disempowerment that render the Maasai women vulnerable to FGM in the first place. In other words, in appealing to supposedly transcendent norms, DAU ignores the West's historical complicity in enabling the gendered violence it condemns and, by displacing blame onto the Maasai, creates hostility and resistance to eradication attempts which are perceived as yet another act of unwarranted colonial intervention. In contrast, Tobin and Jaggar argue that, by virtue of its responsiveness to context, the EIRE approach is practically more effective because, rather than assuming a culturally neutral description of FGM in advance, it suspends automatic initial judgement of the moral wrongness of a specific practice. For, as they put it, 'even if physical descriptions of these practices may be similar, their symbolic and cultural meanings vary widely. The "it" being described is not assimilated to practices all over the world' (Tobin and Jaggar 2013: 427). Instead, the EIRE approach takes a bottom-up, inferential approach which turns on salient contextual and historical details rather than fixed moral norms. It attempts to build up a comprehensive 'horizontal web' of inferences' which, inter alia, acknowledges the specificity of the intervenor's own interpretation of women's human rights as well as endeavouring to make space for the 'perspective of those who have the most at stake in the issue under scrutiny and who are the most epistemically disadvantaged' (Tobin and Jaggar 2013: 433). The aim of EIRE approaches is to assist efforts at eradication of FGM by involving the Maasai women themselves, and by developing a comprehensive account of the abuses they have suffered that, importantly, includes those abuses perpetrated by British colonial rule.

Differently put, Tobin and Jaggar's study of immanent normative reasoning challenges the assertion made by Frankfurt School thinkers that, without an invariant emancipatory core, critique lacks wider moral relevance. In this respect, their study is indicative of a larger corpus of feminist theory that demonstrates how 'principled' or meta-normative contextualism need not leave critique 'mired

---

[1] For instance, practices of symbolic genital nicking and 'circumcision with words' are less damaging than cutting and may perhaps be used as a substitute in place of blanket prohibition. See Tobin and Jaggar 2013: 427, 434.

in a substantive or first-order moral-political relativism' (Allen 2016: 34). It is possible to believe that certain standards and norms ought to be universally applied while at the same time accepting that, at a second order level, this belief can only ever be justified in a contextually indexed and recursive fashion. Justification in this second-order sense amounts, as Cooke puts it: 'to a willingness to engage with the question of the context-transcending validity of the deep-seated, normative intuitions and expectations to which she [the theorist] appeals in her critical diagnoses and emancipatory projections' (Cooke 2006: 71). To claim to have identified in advance a universal emancipatory core, qua monist paradigm, is epistemically and politically counterproductive in so far as it may be perceived by vulnerable interlocutors as an unilateral imposition by dominant groups and therefore antithetical to their concerns. Attempts to circumvent this problem need not imply the foregoing of universal normative standards so much as the importance of utilizing them in a manner that is sensitive to context, dialogical and reflexive. Of course, there are significant respects in which Frankfurt School critical theory is not assimilable to DAU approaches, not least that it does not endorse 'predemocratic' modes of normative reasoning that downwardly apply pregiven moral ideals to specific cases. Despite this, there is nonetheless a methodological parallel with DAU in as much as paradigm-led critique applies monological frameworks in an insufficiently reflexive and dialogic fashion. While eschewing direct normative prescription, Frankfurt School theorists nonetheless shield their monist paradigms from critical scrutiny by maintaining that, as expressions of fundamental human interests, their presumptive authority is beyond contestation. In so far as context-transcending validity is assumed rather than worked towards, paradigm-led theory inescapably retains a kernel of 'epistemological and ethical authoritarianism' that is ultimately not that dissimilar to the idealizing moral approaches of which they are critical (Cooke 2006: 70). In contrast, feminist critique shows how context-transcending standards are themselves a matter for negotiation and agreement and therefore must be invoked in a way that attends to local circumstances and especially the perspectives and experiences of vulnerable groups. The normative aim of feminist critique in this sense is not the blanket validation or denunciation of discrete cultural practices, but the deepening of systematic understanding of the commonalities and differences in gendered practices across cultures. To locate, for instance, specific patterns of gender violence and vulnerability as elements of broader 'constellations' of social practice 'such that similar occurrences would share some elements, but not necessarily all or even the same elements in each case' (Freyenhagen 2013: 152; see also Narayan 2000: 98). So, for example, instead of condemning honour killings as a retrograde practice peculiar to non-Western societies, feminist critique interprets the phenomenon as a specific expression of the violence against women that is endemic in all cultures and societies. The normative effects of such dialogic interpretative effort reside in the way that establishing connections between seemingly disconnected phenomena deepens knowledge of gender oppression, and opens up new grounds for solidaristic political action and the empowerment of vulnerable women at both local and transnational levels.

Thinking Across Perspectives

Many feminists would regard their theoretical work as subject to the same hermeneutic requirement that defines Frankfurt School critical theory; if critique aims to be of practical emancipatory use in unmasking (gender) oppression, it should address the concerns and experiences of those (women) directly affected. But, unlike Frankfurt School theory, feminists have arguably been more successful at developing the dialogical and reflexive modes of reasoning that are logically implied by this requirement. In theorizing from experience, feminist thinkers have stressed the importance of grounding inquiry in an assumption of the epistemic equality between interlocutors (e.g., Harding 1992; Collins 2000: 279–81). Epistemic or methodological equality does not deny differences and asymmetries between interlocutors and their respective grasps of a given situation, but rather holds that these should not be presumed in advance. To presuppose the flawed and partial nature of direct subjective experience, as Frankfurt theorists tend to do, is to remain within an external and hierarchized first/third person dialogism. 'I' the theorist observes 'you', the other, and improves on your partial perspective by presenting you with a comprehensive account of your real interests. In dialogical reasoning, however, the inter-subjective second-person perspective of the 'you' inherent within the situated encounter comes to the fore and mediates the otherwise mutually externalized perspectives of subject and object of inquiry. Inquiry comprises a dialogical relationship between two 'you's, the theorist and the subject of inquiry. This has various ramifications for inquiry, including that, problems and limitations in cross-perspectival reasoning need to be dealt with on an ad hoc basis as they arise in the process of dialogical reasoning itself. In place of general theories of justificatory acceptability, prescribed usually by the theorist, the validity of understanding is established as part of a cooperative enterprise between the interpreter and interpreted. As much as theory is capable of overcoming limitations in an experiential point of view, so the reverse is also potentially the case. Each perspective functions as a relative and productive outside position to the other that may prompt interlocutors to critically reflect on their interpretive positions and schema more clearly. In this process, the subjects of inquiry are treated as active participants in the process of knowledge production rather than as passive sources of data. When it is understood in terms of conversation across perspectives, a different rationale for critique emerges; it is less a question of determining whose interpretation is best but rather what critique can do in staking out new sites of interaction and new political possibilities.

Assumption of epistemic equality is therefore a methodological prerequisite for emancipatory theory rather than a route into uncritical subjectivism. It affords an understanding of the dialogical structure of inquiry that is more expansive than the Frankfurt School's rather qualified one, where the final interpretative authority attributed to the theoretical paradigm implicitly devalues the epistemic contribution of those subjects directly involved.

This idea that the production of context-transcending knowledge is less about the application of a definitive theoretical paradigm and more about reasoning across perspectives animates black feminist theory. Collins describes this dialogism as the 'call-and-response discourse mode' which is fundamental to the assessment of knowledge claims and requires the 'active participation of all individuals' (2000: 280). Echoing this, Davis describes the essential function of critique not as validating authority but as a mediator of dialogue, a unifying cognitive medium that brings disparate perspectives together in the process of knowledge production. She presents the idea of theory as mediator as part of a general description of how her research into the US penal system led to her adoption of an abolitionist political stance. Interviews with women inmates were integral to this research and centred on their experiences of imprisonment and ideas about possible alternatives to incarceration. A widely articulated view was that prisons had abandoned any kind of rehabilitative effort, if they had ever had one, and were now purely punitive institutions that in crucial respects compounded the social problems they were supposed to redress. The prisoners felt strongly that incarceration should only ever be a last resort after other re-educative alternatives have failed. On Davis's account, the inmates' views were influential in persuading her to step outside of established intellectual frameworks of retribution versus restitution and to advocate instead for the decarceration of women prisoners convicted of nonviolent offences. The process by which she crystallizes her political position is essentially an interactive one, a 'bridge-building' dialogue: 'our goal is to formulate alternatives to incarceration that substantively reflect the voices and agency of a variety of imprisoned women. We wish to open up channels for their involvement in the current debates around alternatives to incarceration, while not denying our own role as mediators and interpreters and our own political positioning in these debates' (Davis 1998e: 71). The aim of critique in this mediating role is as much to give voice to marginalized groups and bear witness to their experiences as it is to formulate progressive alternatives to dysfunctional and unjust social situations.

Davis's work is illustrative of dialogical reasoning that takes place from within social perspectives, operating across 'the range of possible practical perspectives that knowledgeable and reflective social agents are capable of taking up and employing practically in their social activity' (Bohman 2001: 105). Similar ideas of theory as mediator rather than adjudicator are widely endorsed by other feminists and radical theorists and serve as a reminder that if critique is to have practical relevance to existing struggles, it must take seriously the experiences and viewpoints of those directly involved. Starting from experiences rather than paradigms also serves as a reminder that critical theory may have normative functions other than that of furnishing a monist, grand theory of emancipation. These functions may involve giving voice to marginalized others, mediation, bearing witness to suffering, advocacy, clarifying felt but inchoate political possibilities, contributing to world-building activism, and so on. These various functions can be loosely gathered under the general label of critique as disclosure. Disclosure not in the dramatic sense of sudden radical insight, a gestalt switch where a startling new truth emerges. But disclosure in the more mundane sense of recalling things about the world that, although widely known in a diffuse, everyday sense, are often, discounted, downplayed, or disregarded by official knowledges for reasons of ideological bias, political indifference, intellectual solipsism, and other cognitive rigidities. Mills, as we saw earlier, calls this type of disavowed knowledge the 'alienated familiar', understood as marginalized experiences and perspectives that are routinely disregarded in hegemonic knowledge production processes. The work done by black feminist and other radical theorists on reconstruing critique around these marginalized perspectives might be thus regarded as bringing the alienated familiar back into view. By attending to the experiences of subordinated groups, disclosive critique in this practical sense aims to redescribe the world according to these suppressed, alienated aspects and thereby dislodge and improve on settled frameworks of social understanding. Disclosure in this sense is not a one-off revelation but an ongoing critical effort to maintain the openness of thought to its context and to sustain its capacity to see the relevance of things that may not initially appear to be important or have conventionally been dismissed as insignificant. The capacity to see something previously ignored as relevant, qua marginal experiences, is crucial if thought is to develop and to overcome its own internal blindspots and rigidities.

Conclusion

Even those theorists of the Frankfurt School with the most developed neoKantian sensibilities acknowledge the significance that disclosing thought has for a critical theory of oppression. If it weren't for the ability to see the world in a new way, to see the significance of hitherto suppressed or ignored aspects of existence for social understanding, then unmasking critique would quickly reify and lose practical political relevance. But this in principle acknowledgement of the importance of disclosure seems to have little concrete impact on the Frankfurt School's current theoretical practice, which is directed by the ambition to produce monocausal, self-referential, and totalizing social theories. The ensuing shortcomings in their diagnosis of gender oppression are symptomatic of the way in which, more generally, paradigm-led theory is inconsistent with its basic intellectual tenets about the situated nature of rationality and its inevitable co-implication with those subjects whose plight is their primary object of concern. Theorizing from experience unsettles some of the presumptions that underpins paradigm-led thought, notably the idea that if critique is not monist and totalizing, it cannot avoid lapsing into anything other than particularistic complaint and relativist reasoning. The force of experientially grounded critique comes not from conformity to a monist paradigm but from utilizing an imaginative, abductive mode of inquiry that systematically works through the conceptual and normative issues surrounding a determinate problem. It derives normative responses from the particularities of lived experiences of oppression and these take the form of multiple, experimental practices of empowerment rather than a single, grand theory of emancipation. Finally, theorizing from experience enacts the dialogism and reflexivity that are supposedly defining features of emancipatory critique, but are undermined by the privilege that Frankfurt School theorists accord their own paradigms over direct experience in determining what really counts as oppression or not. In place of the authority of the paradigm, it hinges on a more modest idea of the distinctive contribution that theory can make, as one among many interlocutors, to ongoing political conversations about injustice. This contribution consists in refining existing understanding of oppression, with reference to the lived reality of those directly affected, and in exploring possibilities for progressive social transformation. Understood in these terms, an explicitly political dimension is reintroduced into critical theorizing, a dimension that is seemingly crucial in validating the claim to be of emancipatory relevance to disempowered groups, but a dimension that seems to have been half-forgotten by Frankfurt School theorists in their limiting preoccupation with metatheoretical issues of normative foundation and justification.

2
Experience at the Limits of Justification

Introduction

Like other leading thinkers of the Frankfurt School, Rainer Forst frequently affirms the radical democratic credentials of critical theory over comparable types of normative political thought. Critical theory is animated not by abstract normative matters but by real-world experiences of suffering and injustice which are the cue for its radical critique of existing social relations. Power, Forst says, is the 'first question' of justice, and normative theory lacks practical emancipatory force unless accompanied by a developed critical theory of oppression. The primacy Forst attributes to power is not limited to sociological criticism but extends to the practice of theorizing itself for, as situated inquiry, critique must endeavour to guard against intellectually reifying tendencies that might dull its responsiveness to real-world circumstances of injustice. Practical emancipatory critique is necessarily reflexive; it must build into itself the capacity to critically scrutinize its own conceptual limitations and blindspots in response to feedback from the social environment and especially from those disempowered groups whose plight it addresses. These interrelated concerns of power and reflexivity are indispensable to critical theory; ensuring its radical democratic credentials while, at the same time, guarding against the predemocratic, prescriptive tendencies that Forst finds so problematic in mainstream ideal theorizing.

Yet, despite endorsing familiar premises of the Frankfurt School's idea of immanent critique, Forst's work diverges from that of his peers in a crucial respect, namely, his demurral from the idea of grounding critique in intramundane or 'quasi-transcendental' foundations. In his view, strategies of intramundane transcendence do not furnish critique with normative foundations that are sufficiently robust and independent to support truly emancipatory claims. Historical immanentism pays a 'huge price', as he puts it, in its failure to recognize that, to be fully warranted, radical critique must necessarily transcend the normative horizon of its time. Accordingly, Forst finds such autonomous grounds in the principle of justification which he maintains represents the transcendental core of practical reason. He insists however that, although free-standing, the principle of justification does not fall prey to the 'metaphysical slumber' that afflicts the transcendent ideals of analytical political philosophy. Its thin, discursive nature means that justification critique is capable of reconciling strong transcendental foundations with the diagnostic and reflexive qualities that are necessary to radical immanent critique.

In this chapter, I argue that Forst's 'practical transcendentalism' is a contradictory and self-undermining enterprise that starkly embodies limitations of paradigm-led theorizing. Contradictory, because Forst is unable to establish an immanent connection between justification as a transcendental principle and as tool of critical social analysis and, as a result, his paradigm vacillates between the two inconsequently. Self-undermining, because this disconnection between norm and social criticism incapacitates his declared emancipatory objective of a disclosing critique of power. Forst attempts to connect the transcendental and practical aspects of justification critique through his idiosyncratic understanding of power as a noumenal force. This concept is ineffective as an instrument of social critique, however, because its exaggerated cognitivism forecloses explanations of the way in which structural oppression is entrenched and naturalized through material, embodied dynamics of power that have little to do with reason. Noumenal power's core rationale of the acceptance of reasons is simply too superficial and stylized a device to explain complex processes of social subordination. This is evident in Forst's reductive understanding of the way in which gender oppression is secured through a supposedly widespread acceptance of patriarchal narratives. These shortcomings in the diagnosis of power have entailments for normative relevance of justification critique. Its normative scope is stymied by the failure to acknowledge how power dynamics latent in actual conversations about justice may subvert formally equal relations of justification and make it difficult for certain individuals to be taken seriously as democratic interlocutors. This lack of sensitivity to the context of power in turn undermines the critical self-awareness or reflexivity that is, by Forst's own lights, an indispensable feature of emancipatory critique. This lack of reflexivity is evident in the failure of justification monism to consider how certain types of epistemic injustice may be mitigated only by advancing beyond the abstract formula of mutually owed justification and tackling head on asymmetries of power inherent in the reasoning process itself. Ultimately, then, the degree to which justification critique can be considered to have successfully realized its practically emancipatory aims is moot.

Immanent and Transcendent Foundations

In accordance with the basic tenets of Frankfurt School critical theory, Forst maintains that if normative thought is to have practical political import, it must be rooted in the critique of power or what he describes as a 'sociologically informed, conceptually clear critique of domination' (Forst, 2020: 324). Attentiveness to the context of power includes not only critique's object of inquiry, namely, existing social injustice, but also critique itself which, as a situated reasoning practice, is practically implicated within its own field of inquiry. In line with other Frankfurt School theorists, then, Forst insists that it is precisely the awareness that critical theory has of itself as situated, self-reflexive inquiry whose first concern is power that sets it apart from conventional normative reasoning: 'transcendental reflection merely tries to reconstruct the necessary principles of making sense, in our context the principles of valid norms. A critical conception of reason, being situated and historically informed, is aware that such principles often lead to reifications and exclusions of those who don't "fit in"' (Forst 2020: 327). Yet despite cleaving to familiar Frankfurt School tenets about emancipatory reasoning, Forst's work diverges from that of his peers in one key respect and that is on the issue of the normative foundations of critique. For in Forst's view, the stratagem of intra-mundane transcendence that has been adopted from Habermas onwards is not a strong enough safeguard of critique's normative force. The grounding of critique in principles that are constitutive but internal to social life is insufficient to establish the truly impartial foundation from which emancipatory claims ought to be justified. Absent such independent, unconditional standards, critique, in Forst's eyes, is reduced to an unsystematic, parochial and relativist mode of thought where 'we would just replace one form of justification with another more to our liking' (Allen, Forst, and Haugard 2014: 11).

The attempts of other Frankfurt School theorists to derive a 'rational universal' from social ontology are flawed, in Forst's view, because they are either too procedurally thin to have binding moral force or too biased to serve as a non-partisan foundation for critique. In respect of proceduralism, the difficulty with Habermas's communicative ethics is that it is founded in a discursive process so formal that it can demonstrate only *how* individuals should justify moral claims but not *why* they ought to do this, in terms of a corresponding moral duty. There is a 'normative gap between the pragmatically derived and hence weak transcendental "must" of discourse ethics and the stronger, normatively justified "must" that he [Habermas] holds to be crucial for a binding political theory of justice and its essential components, such as a theory of human rights' (Forst 2007: 59. My parenthesis). In respect of unexamined bias, the problem with Honneth's recognition paradigm is that, because it generalizes a thick ethical good, qua substantive anthropology of self-realization, it lacks sufficient impartiality to act as the basis for inclusive political structures. As complex and open as a formal theory of the good or flourishing life might seem, it will inevitably fail to encompass the plurality of possible ethical ways of life and will therefore yoke respect for persons as 'ends in themselves' to 'particular ends or ways of pursuing ends that are supposed to characterise a good life' (Forst 2007: 118). A comprehensive theory of social justice can only do justice to the good, 'the less it rests on particular conceptions of the good' (2007: 118.). To avoid these twin dangers of formalism and relativism and ensure its irrefutable emancipatory force, critique must be based in a 'non-arbitrary way' in principles and standards that transcend particular contexts and that, in so far as they are genuinely independent, all subjects can recognize as morally binding (Forst 2020: 324).

In contrast to the socially reconstructive method of Habermas and Honneth, Forst establishes autonomous moral grounds for critique—what he terms a *'fundamentum inconcussum'*—through a constructivist method that reflects on the essential nature of practical reason. According to him, if we reconstruct what it means to reason practically, then we discern at the very heart of the process, a shared basic practice of justification. In answering fundamental questions such as 'what should I do?' or 'why did I believe that a certain course of action was permissible or necessary?', the individual is required to 'provide reasons that can justify actions according to criteria that are valid in a moral context' (Forst 2007:15). Valid criteria in this sense of moral justification are not subject relative but inter-subjective in nature; the point of justification is not to explain actions as the most rational way of realizing personal ends and goals, but rather to provide reasons for actions that others, who are morally affected, cannot reasonably refuse. Practical reason is, at its core, 'the ability to answer a moral question with a morally justifiable answer that can be supported intersubjectively. It is reasonably justified if no moral reasons speak against it '(2007: 15). This inter-subjective formulation highlights a further defining feature of reasonable justification that, for a normative claim to be accepted as valid, it must meet the criteria of *reciprocity* and *generality*. Reciprocity is defined in terms of content—'no one may refuse the particular demands of others that one raises for oneself'—and reasons—'no one may simply assume that others have the same values and interests as oneself or make recourse to "higher truths"' that are not shared' (2007: 6). Generality means that 'reasons for generally valid basic norms must be sharable by all those affected', that is they must not exclude the objections of anyone affected (2007: 6). The criteria of general and reciprocal justification generate a binding normative force that is stronger, according to Forst, than comparable ideas of de facto accord, like-mindedness, or assent that rest on weaker notions of moral reasoning as intersubjective acceptability or agent neutrality. At the same time, by making the regulative principle of deliberation that which cannot be reasonably rejected rather than the demanding notion of consensus, Forst's model overcomes a problem with the Habermasian one, namely, it shows us how a claim can be justified even if agreement cannot be achieved. Moreover, by accommodating a degree of disagreement in this way, justification critique is arguably better able to deal with the 'diversity of evaluative approaches' that should characterize truly inclusive deliberation. Forst maintains that the principle of justification is unconditional in so far as it is not dependent on any prior notion of the good or other extraneous social criterion. Moral constructivism reveals justification to be the essence of practical reason; there is no other entity that can be appealed to beyond reason because reason constitutes its own grounds, as he puts it: 'there are no external derivations" that can trump the construction' (2007: 7). This autonomy establishes that 'moral persons have a fundamental *right to justification* and corresponding unconditional *duty to justify* morally relevant actions' (2007: 21).

Forst argues that the a priori of justification establishes incontestable normative foundations for a binding concept of justice: 'moral constructivism form[s] the normative core of *political* constructivism' (2007: 6). Justification is a basic moral right in the sense that all humans have the right not to be subjected to norms and institutions that cannot be adequately justified. The first task of justice is accordingly to guarantee a 'basic structure of justification', that is, one in which all affected subjects have an irrevocable right to collectively deliberate and decide about the institutions that they are to live under and veto any arrangements that cannot be reciprocally and generally justified to her. The basic structure of justification is not intended to provide a complete blueprint for a fair society, but rather to establish the 'minimally' just conditions and principles upon which further discussion about a 'maximally' just society can be realized. In succeeding discussions about maximal justice, the criteria of general and reciprocal justification provide the independent standards for judging whether particular social arrangements have legitimate foundations or not. The criteria provide a morally rigorous 'normative grammar' that 'works like a filter to sort out justifiable from unjustifiable claims, one that opens up and at the same time restricts the possibility of justice claims' (Forst 2011: 113).

Disclosure and Reflexivity

While the a priori of justification certainly appears to provide a way out of what are taken to be the relativist dilemmas of immanent critique, it does seem to have shifted Forst's thinking some distance from the power-first approach to normative reasoning that he endorses and that typifies the Frankfurt School approach. Indeed, his insistence on the necessity of transcendental foundations seems to have moved Forst so far from the recognizable terrain of unmasking critique that a number of commentators hold that the justification paradigm is closer to the political reasoning famously described by Bernard Williams as an ethics-first approach (see Allen 2014: 83; Bajaj and Rossi 2020: 127; Olson 2014: 100). On this view, Forst's attempt to transcendentalize the justification principle replicates the ideological errors of ideal theory which reifies contingent social practices as free-floating universal principles (e.g., Tully 2011). Certainly the influence of Rawls is evident in this aspect of Forst's thought, but he nonetheless emphatically rejects comparisons with 'ideal theory' arguing that justification critique offers an approach to social justice that is far more radical because it proceeds not from preestablished principles but from 'everyday experiences of injustice' and the voices of real world 'participants' (2007: 210). Transcendental foundations notwithstanding, justification monism is catalysed, like all critical theory, by the practical concern with diagnosing real-world distributions of power and exposing domination, qua 'norms that cannot be adequately justified' . Power must be the 'first question' of justice and 'a critical theory of (in)justice has to be above all a critique of the existing *relations of justification*' (2011: 120). It is not that ideal theorists are uninterested in how moral principles might bear on unwarranted social hierarchies, but for them, this is an extrinsic and secondary matter of 'application' whereas, for Forst, the critique of power lies at the very heart of normative reasoning. Emancipatory political thought is most politically effective when it disrupts settled norms and assumptions through the unmasking of injustices: 'every theory of justice requires a complex theory of injustice, not just as a normative account, but also in the form of a social analysis' (Forst 2011: 114).

It is not only through an unmasking critique of power that justification monism safeguards its radical democratic credentials but also through its recursive structure which permits it give a paramount place to the voices of ordinary citizens in normative reasoning. A particularly troubling aspect of ideal theory, for Forst, are the 'predemocratic', prescriptive tendencies that flow from its method of antecedently justifying principles of justice. Antecedent justification has the practical effect, albeit unintended, of undermining democratic sovereignty by reducing it to the medium for executing pregiven moral principles rather than treating it as the autonomous political body that actively determines the content of a just social structure (2007: 106–10). By deploying a constructivist method that is 'discursive' rather than 'metaphysical' in nature, Forst believes that he avoids the difficulties that arise from such a problematic imposition of 'teleological values'. Other than 'a certain conception of the person and particular criteria of reasonable practical justification', everything else in his justification paradigm is determined by the discursive practice itself (2007: 111). Discursive thinness enables justification monism to avoid the stylized and tacitly normalizing concept of 'reasonable' deliberators that prevails in idealized scenarios and instead open itself to the heterogeneity of views held by deliberators in the real world. It affords space, above all, to disempowered and marginalized groups, allowing them to challenge the status quo and to dispute settled notions of justice, affectedness, and subjection and revise it when appropriate (2014: 178). In this way, justification critique engenders genuine democratic self-determination because it is not the political philosopher but citizens themselves who autonomously determine the normative content of justice (2011: 8). Contra Rawls, the conversation about justice can never be finished; if it is to retain emancipatory relevance it must be ceaselessly taken up and given renewed meaning by each successive generation and constituency to whom it pertains. The radical political bite of justification critique is vested in the way it positions all individuals, not just idealized representatives, as co-authors of the fundamental norms that guide society and replaces passive, 'principle-interpreting' accounts of justice with an emancipatory 'principle-generating' account (2007: 184).

The final way in which Forst asserts the radical democratic standing of justification critique is by drawing attention to its inherent reflexivity, that is, its ability to withstand theoretical bias and conceptual reification by building into itself a heightened capacity for critical self-scrutiny. In this respect he follows a well-established line of argument that Frankfurt School critical theory is superior to other types of normative political thought precisely because of this amplified awareness of its own potential limitations and willingness to correct them. These self-distancing qualities, qua awareness of the inter-implication of reason and power, are even more vital when dealing with disempowered subjects. Forst underscores the importance of reflexivity by reiterating Kant's well-known formulation of the 'critique of critique' that is, that no aspect of social practice should be immune from critical scrutiny, including critique itself. Immanent grounds may be normatively insufficient for emancipatory critique, but it is just as unsatisfactory to resort to notions of 'otherworldly transcendence' to fill this foundational gap. This would be to fall into a 'metaphysical slumber' which ignores thought's own social preconditions: 'no social critic, no matter how radical, is not also an immanent critic' (Forst 2011). A theory can only count as critical and radical, in Forst's eyes, in the extent to which it understands itself as 'an activity that reflects back on itself and its own blind spots and exclusions in a self-critical manner' (2011: 8). Embodying a principle that is simultaneously transcendent and immanent, justification critique does precisely this by moving constantly between the two poles using the perspective of the one to interrogate and overcome limitations of the other.

As 'practical transcendental' critique, justification monism seems, on the face of it, to cover all bases. It displays the deontological rigour that comes from unconditional foundations in practical reason while, at the same time, it possesses the characteristics crucial to ensure practical emancipatory force, namely, grounding in a sociological critique of power, normative inclusivity, and reflexivity. In anticipation of the argument to come, however, a preliminary question about reflexivity comes to the fore and bears on how it is precisely that Forst sustains a meaningful internal connection between justification as an ahistorical principle and as a contextually sensitive critique. How exhaustive can critique's reflection upon its own presumptions, blindspots and potential exclusions be if its animating core is construed in such strongly transcendent terms that it floats free of all parochial configurations of power? If the principle of justification is a universal constant, then, by definition, there must be a limit to the extent to which it is open to critical evaluation and reappraisal, should it be found to be less inclusive or diagnostically insightful vis-à-vis analysis of concrete social relations. In short, by removing the justificatory essence of critique from the hermeneutic circle, Forst appears to drastically curtail the scope of the supposedly 'indispensable' tenet of reflexivity and 'critique of critique'. This question, then, about how Forst goes about reconciling strong transcendental foundations with sensitivity to the context of power without thereby lapsing into performative contradiction or aporia goes to the heart of his critical endeavour.

Forst's response to the question is to deploy the idea of noumenal power as the pivotal analytic category that mediates any potential tension between justification understood as an unconditional foundation and as tool of social diagnosis. Noumenal power is the point at which it becomes clear how the reflexive capacities of critique converge with its disclosing, or unmasking function. For it is the unmasking of suppressed, negative aspects of social experience—as Adorno puts it, the 'cross-grained, opaque, unassimilated material'—that frequently serves as the catalyst for critical self-scrutiny (Adorno 1974: 151). Reflexivity entails the capacity to respond as fully as possible to these things that 'don't fit in', qua marginalized or suppressed constellations of experience, and to acknowledge where necessary the destabilizing implications that they may have for previously settled views of the world. As the diagnostic category through which these non-identical elements of social life are brought into light, noumenal power initiates potential questioning not only of the assumed legitimacy of established social orders but also of the adequacy of a given interpretative framework. It is, in other words, the main prompt for scrutiny of the justification paradigm and how well it is fulfilling its radical critical aims. However, as I argue in the next section, whether the idea of noumenal power engenders this type of critical awareness is questionable. As a tool of social diagnosis, noumenal power is inadequate since it does not so much capture the complexities of oppression as simplify them by aligning them with the linguistic logic of justification. Its explanatory rationale that social relations are secured through justificatory narratives that rest on the 'acceptance of reasons' results in a reductive account of power clearly evident in Forst's handling of issues of gender oppression. In so far as noumenal power is oriented less to explaining distributions of power and more to validating a questionably linguistified model of reality, it speaks to an attendant failure on Forst's part to submit justification monism to reflexive critical scrutiny.

Noumenal Power

Power is the first question of justice and in order to understand it, Forst claims, it is first necessary to understand justification. Accordingly, he proposes that social relations be conceptualized as orders or relations of justification. Conceptualizing society in this way as multiple, overlapping orders of justification, allows radical critique to focus on evaluating the legitimacy of accepted rationalizations for existing hierarchies and, conversely, exposing the *lack* of valid justificatory practices for hierarchies that are misleadingly deemed to be natural and inevitable.

The objective is an exhaustive analysis of 'all those more or less institutionalized social relations and structures which...are marked by forms of exclusion, by privileges and domination' (2011: 8). The correlate of Forst's linguistic construal of sociality is his idea that power is essentially a noumenal, discursive, cognitive or intellectual force—he uses the terms interchangeably—that operates through control over the 'space of reasons' (2011: 9). Power is the capacity of some individuals to get others to think or do something they would otherwise not have thought or done, it is the ability to 'determine the limits of what can be said and thought and...of what is accepted and acceptable, of what is justified' (2011: 103). Power is emphatically not a matter of strength or will, nor a material state of affairs, but one of convictions and beliefs: 'to be a subject of power is to be moved by reasons that others have given me and that motivate me to think or act in a certain way intended by the reason giver' (2015: 112). This cognitivist construal does not mean that the reasons given for a particular state of affairs need to be fully justified and coherent—they may be false or misleading and used to uphold relations of oppression, subordination, and inequality. But, in essence, even in cases of extreme social disparity, power always acts upon cognitively motivated subjects and rests on the recognition and 'acceptance' of reasons (2015: 116ff.).

If 'power is what goes on in the head', then an issue that immediately confronts Forst's is how to explain types of power that take hold through material constraints, whose modus operandi is not manipulation of consciousness and acceptance of reasons but the brute shaping of socio-structural and embodied conditions of existence. It is not just that these types of material power do not operative in a cognitive mode, but that they are arguably prior to and enabling of noumenal power in so far as they constitute the social conditions in which specific reasons and justifications become intelligible in the first place. Evidently there are various ways of conceptualizing these material forces including, notably, ideas of disciplinary embodiment, theorized by Foucault, Bourdieu, and others, which provide compelling explanations of why it is that inequalities of race, gender, sexuality, and class persist in affluent, formally equal democracies. Of particular significance is how, on these accounts, inequalities are held to endure not because individuals buy into justifications (good or bad) of conventional social roles, but rather because of insidious processes of internalization where objective asymmetries of power are realized in embodied form as a cluster of naturalized, subjective dispositions (e.g., habitus). In terms of gender, the living through of these normalizing tendencies anchors wider social inequalities in everyday practices and renders women (and men) complicit with their own subordination. Thus, at a rational level, individuals may be conscious of the limitations of conventional gender norms but, at the level of emotional and psycho-sexual dispositions, they may be nonetheless unconsciously invested in their continuing subjection in the sense captured by Butler's notion of 'passionate attachments' (Butler 1997b). This kind of embodied power appears to have little to do with justification because it operates below the radar of rational acceptance through the moulding of corporeal being so that it practically aligns with the tendencies of the world and hence upholds the status quo.

Forst insists, however, that ideas of disciplinary bio-power do not seriously challenge his concept because, ultimately, to be efficacious all types of power necessarily possess a noumenal essence: 'material means...only serve their function if they are seen as reason giving' (2014: 180–1). Thus, the material power of money can only be properly explained, according to Forst, with reference to its noumenal effects for 'money only motivates those who see its use as justified and who have aims which make money necessary' (2014: 180–1). If people do not recognize the justification for money, then it ceasesb to have power over their behaviour and lives. The plausibility of such an argument is thrown into doubt, however, when we consider the simple fact that, regardless of whether individuals recognize the use of money as 'justified' or not, its absence imposes significant and often harmful constraints on their life chances, qua lack of material resources. Analogously, hegemonic gender norms would not cease to have a myriad of detrimental effects on women's daily lives if they chose—as they frequently do—not to recognize the force of patriarchal arguments used to justify them. Nonetheless, Forst maintains that a reading of Foucault's notion of disciplinary embodiment as a process that bypasses reason is misleading in that it rests on a 'super-Cartesian' separation of the symbolic from the material realm with what he regards as the untenable implication that there exists a corporeal reality 'beyond justification' (2015: 123). Indeed, according to Forst, Foucault's idea of regimes of truth lends itself to his cognitively grounded idea of noumenal power (2015: 122). If this parallel holds at all, it does so only in a very narrow sense and one which expediently disregards Foucault's Nietzschean impulse to use the idea of regimes of truth to discredit precisely those notions of justification, validity, and reason that Forst wants to retrieve.

Setting aside the credibility of Forst's cognitivist interpretation of Foucault, the diagnostic reach of power as the acceptance of reasons is further compromised if we think about the materiality of power on a macro rather than micro scale, that is, as the economic and social forces that routinely reproduce structural oppression. Take the case of gender, most feminists concur that women's subordination in advanced democracies is caused in large part by impersonal structural dynamics rather than by personalized modes of masculine domination (e.g., Cudd 2006; hooks 2000, Young 1990: 39–64). Gender subordination no longer relies, in any significant sense, on patriarchal justifications (although they undoubtedly persist), but rather on entrenched systemic dynamics that disadvantage women regardless of whether they accept conventional norms or not. Susan Okin famously described this impersonal mode of subordination as 'a cycle of socially caused and distinctly asymmetric vulnerability by marriage' denoting the combined effects of a skewed domestic division of labour, especially as it relates to child rearing, interacting with the operations of a gender-segregated labour market and insufficient state protection for women and disadvantaged groups (Okin 1989: 4). This impersonal cycle affects all women, even those who are unmarried and childless, rendering them vulnerable to economic exploitation, political and social marginalization, and poverty (Young 2009: 228). Forst concedes that such 'subjectless' cyclical modes of oppression challenge his cognitivist formulation of power in the way that they appear to function on a level entirely unconnected to the agent-centred one of the acceptance of reasons. He insists nonetheless that social structures do still depend upon noumenal power but that, in this impersonal mode, it takes hold of individuals through the mechanism of narrative inculcation rather than that of interpersonal influence. Moreover, noumenal power in this structural sense is defined very broadly, including not just direct appeals to reason but unconscious socialization processes, false narratives, ideological distortions, emotional investments and so on. On his account, imperfect social structures are often accepted because it is felt that nothing else is available; acquiescence is generated by naturalizing narratives that make a particular order seem inevitable and thereby socialize individuals into a conformist 'frame of mind' (2015: 120). Gender inequality persists because, although the figure of the patriarch may no longer be omnipresent in Western democracies, patriarchal narratives continue to exert an enduring influence over women who conform to its rules for 'reasons of love, admiration, self-interest, convention, religious upbringing, fear, or despair' (2015: 126).

There is no doubt that sexist beliefs thrive in social life, but it is tendentious to suggest, as Forst does, that women's subordination persists primarily because of the widespread acceptance of patriarchal narratives and not because of structurally generated asymmetries of power and resources. By disregarding background 'structures of constraint' (Folbre 1994) and cleaving instead to such a simplistic explanation of gender oppression, Forst does not seem to have advanced significantly beyond his original agent-centred account of power. Rather he seems to have simply scaled up his cognitivist model of power to explain structural forces in terms of a collective subject or macro-agency. As a routinely reproduced feature of 'advanced' democracies, gender subordination has little to do with the acceptance of false narratives so much as a structural lack of opportunities. Poor women, for instance are frequently placed in situations where they have few options and where these options may be organized to provide few gains, often even to be 'no win'. In such situations, the only rational course is often for women to accept low-paid domestic and sex-work as well as shoulder unpaid responsibilities (e.g., Jaggar 2014: 34). Likewise, there is considerable sociological evidence to suggest that nowadays, many women and men do not unthinkingly buy into traditional 'narratives' of gender; they see marriage and parenting in terms of a shared partnership rather than fixed roles and have expectations of equal treatment in education and work. Yet, despite these expectations, gender inequality persists, suggesting that a convincing explanation lies not in the enduring noumenal force of patriarchal narratives but rather in intersecting structural dynamics that have a determining effect on women's life chances regardless of what they might believe. The persistence of labour markets that systematically disadvantage women combined with lack of state attention to domestic work and child-care mean that even couples who hold egalitarian values are often compelled to adopt an inegalitarian gender division of labour against their best intentions. Given the economic status quo, it often makes sense to choose to develop the husband's professional skills rather than the wife's because, in most cases, this ensures greater financial security (Young 2009: 228). In short, it is not because of justificatory narratives that gender oppressions persist but because of the overlapping systemic tendencies which auto-poetically reproduce them. As Amy Allen puts it 'systemic relations of dominance and subordination... are probably always connected to... hegemonic narratives of justification—but this does not mean that they are inculcated in individuals through or by means of... such justifications or even that they are recognized by their targets as reasons to act in a certain way (Allen, Forst, and Haugaard 2014: 18–19).

If, on the one hand, Forst overextends the idea of noumenal power by subsuming heterogeneous social logics under the unifying rubric of the acceptance of reasons, on the other, he somewhat arbitrarily truncates its diagnostic scope by excluding some vectors of power. This is evident in his treatment of the issue of violence which is disconnected from the concept of noumenal power and thereby placed beyond the remit of justification critique. This is a curious omission for critique whose stated aim is the unmasking of oppression, given that systematic forms of sexualized, racial, homophobic, and transphobic violence and hatred are endemic societal features that reveal much about the hierarchical relations that produce, sustain, and normalize them. Violence against women is pervasive, routinely manifesting itself in intimate/familial relations across all societies; moreover, it shows no signs of diminishing even in states where levels of democratization and formal equality are higher. Theorists such as Iris Marion Young explicitly name systemic violence as one of the key vectors of gender subordination. But she also points out that justice theorists are often silent about violence, not because they deny that it is a moral wrong, but because they fail to appreciate its systemic character, treating it instead as an individual failing: 'what makes violence a phenomenon of social injustice, and not merely an individual moral wrong, is its systematic character, its existence as a social practice' (Young 1990: 62). Noumenal power provides few conceptual resources for understanding either the persistence of violence nor what it might reveal, as a pervasive social practice, about patriarchal and racialized norms. The voluntarist emphasis on power's agential dimensions does not easily accommodate relevant explanatory ideas of structural and symbolic violence. The pronounced cognitivist bias of noumenal power imposes a conceptual hiatus between the phenomenon of violence and the wider social context of masculine domination. Following Arendt, Forst maintains that violence is the opposite of power because the agency of the victim, qua the capacity to accept reasons, is negated by the perpetrator of violence: the autonomous subject becomes mere object. The erasure of agency is of course an undeniable effect of violence but this brute fact, on its own, does little to develop understanding of how, in a domestic context, violence does not so much represent the end of patriarchal power but rather one of its symptoms. To better understand violence, it needs to be situated in the matrix of social forces that engender and tacitly legitimate it rather than being taken out of the field of social intelligibility. When the category in its entirety is dismissed as the undifferentiated other of power, then its varying causes and societal significance remain untheorized. Why, for example, are some types of violence pathologized or spectacularized, and others routinely ignored? (e.g., Threadcraft 2017). The answer to such questions lies partly in being able to unravel the matrix of racial and gendered relations in which violence is situated. Given that it is a pervasive feature of intimate relations, male violence must be connected to the larger societal context of masculine (and racialized) 'scripts' of entitlement, aggression, and independence, on the one side, and feminine scripts of dependence, passivity, sacrifice, and duty to care on the other (Hirschmann 2002: 128). It is truistic to say with Forst that sexual or racial violence is beyond the scope of reasonable justification for this does not explain why it arises, how it might be a revealing pathological symptom of tolerated but injurious social relations, and what might be done to prevent it.

In replying to his critics, Forst frequently repeats the claim that his concept of power is not a normative one: 'as much as my account of power fits my normative conception of justice ... it is *not* a normative account' (2020: 319). He insists that it is, in essence, 'a conceptual and descriptive theory' that 'mediates between the empirical and the normative levels' and yields a 'neutral' notion of power that can be subsequently elaborated into positive ideas of empowerment or negative ones of 'domination, oppression, or exploitation' (2020: 319). Given the arbitrary way in which violence and types of social hatred are either sanitized or relegated to a zone of critical unintelligibility because they lack a 'cognitive core', this assertion of noumenal power's descriptive neutrality is doubtful. More generally, it seems that an overly normativized account of sociality seems to be an inescapable feature of this type of paradigm-led theorizing that insists on tracing all relations of power back to a single constitutive source. Dynamics of oppression, marginalization, domination, expropriation, exploitation, violence, and so on are pushed into the background by being filtered through the monist lens of justification. As Crenshaw observes, 'single axis' diagnoses end up marginalizing the oppressed, albeit inadvertently, in so far as they are unable to capture the nonlinear, multi-causal dynamics which typify subordination. Crenshaw (1991) is of course referring to the experiences of African-American women and how analyses that do not consider intersectionality are unable to account for their particular vulnerability to violence. But, *mutatis mutandis*, her conclusion can be said to apply equally to justification monism. To adequately grasp oppression, top-down generic diagnoses need to be replaced by bottom-up, contextually sensitive ones that begin by addressing the 'needs and problems of the most disadvantaged' and work outward from these experiences to crystallize an account of power (Crenshaw 1989: 167).

In sum, Forst's contention that it is only when we understand justification that we understand power is open to question. He maintains that 'an important test of the realism of the theory of noumenal power is whether it can explain the power of "structures"' (Forst 2015: 118). In the light of the above criticisms, however, he seems to have failed this test. The orientation of social critique around a logic of justification in fact initiates a discursive reduction upwards where relations of power that do not operate according to a one-dimensional linguistic rationale are occluded. Rather than develop the type of multidimensional analysis that a systemic critique of oppression seems to require, Forst vacillates, in an unsettled fashion, between 'expansive' and restricted ideas of noumenal power (2020: 301). With the expansive conception, Forst attempts to offset potential blindspots by stating that justificatory power does not work only through the recognition of reasons but encompasses broader noncognitive socializing dynamics: 'recognition can be the recognition of a good reason but also of a threat, it can be a matter of accepting a lie as truth or of accepting an ideological justification and thereby succumbing to delusion' (2020: 319). In so far as such a catch-all list of phenomena is sociologically under-specified, it gives the impression that the couplet noumenal power–acceptance of reasons is an overly expansive device, devoid of much diagnostic purchase. Indeed, its explanatory capaciousness does not seem to be so very different from monolithic conceptions of ideology that use notions of false consciousness and delusion as a kind of enveloping social glue and thereby efface the complexity of practice as well as the manifold reasons why individuals resist or acquiesce to social arrangements. At other points, Forst backtracks from an expansive notion of noumenal power to endorse a narrower, agent-centred definition where: 'to be a subject of power is to be moved by reasons that others have given me and that motivate me to think or act in a certain way intended by the reason-giver' (Forst 2015: 112). This hyper-rationalist notion is critically limited when it comes to explaining complex dynamics of embodiment, structural causation, and other material forces. This vacillation between inclusive and restricted concepts remains unresolved and forestalls the development of the differentiated, multidimensional account of power necessary for effective analysis of oppression.

The explanatory limitations of noumenal power are symptomatic of a deeper problem with justification monism, namely its failure to sustain a dialectical connection between immanent and transcendent perspectives, or what Forst describes as a 'synthetic theory of justification that unites empirical uses...with normative uses' (2018: 296). Such a synthesis is undermined by the paradigm's overall propensity to prioritize, rather than interconnect, the transcendent, normative sense of justification over its contextualized, critical sense. As we will see in the next section, this implicit hierarchy means that insufficient attention is given to the ways in which justificatory processes are always historically situated and, therefore, must inevitably confront discrepancies of power between interlocutors. Forst justifies this lack of attention to the context of power by claiming that it leads to 'historical immanentism' and the abandonment of normative standards (2020: 328). But, as we will see, as well as being a false antithesis, this need not be the case when justificatory processes are detranscendentalized, pluralized, and rendered more responsive to disempowered groups.

Justification: Ideal and Actual

Aside from its grounding in analysis of existing injustices, the radical political import of justification critique is supposedly underwritten by its recursive structure. Unlike teleological models of deliberation, the recursive or reiterative quality of justification critique renders it sensitive to the perspectives of ordinary citizens especially those not normally included in the conversation about justice. In this respect, Forst follows an argument similar to the one mounted by Cavell against Rawls, namely, that the conversation about justice can never be brought to a close. Rawls maintains that it falls on those who object to the principles of justice arrived at in the original position, to show how they have injurious or unjust consequences. In Cavell's view, however, the idealized conditions of Rawlsian deliberation ignore the latent 'context of violence' in which contracts are made and which inevitably excludes some people, usually the most disempowered, from the very outset of the conversation about justice. As Cavell puts it: 'What if there is a cry of justice that expresses a sense not of having *lost* out in an equal yet fair struggle, but having from the start been *left* out' (Cavell 1990: xxxvii). Deprivation of a voice in deliberation about justice is not the deliberate work of 'the scoundrel' but the unintended effect of 'the moral consensus itself' and it is for this reason that the conversation must always be kept open. Justification monism's recursive structure is animated by a similar concern; it has an explicitly maieutic function intended to bring to the fore unnoticed forms of social suffering and injustice as and when they arise. Justice as justification is ignited by 'the claims of individuals themselves' and bestows paramount importance on 'their concrete experiences of... political powerlessness and social exclusion' (2007: 121).

As Forst well knows, however, it is one thing to assert the abstract existence of a recursive right to justification but another entirely to ensure that it will be universally and substantively implemented in actual conversations about justice. It may well be that, in the idealized space of practical reason, where subjects are disembodied justificatory agents, they do indeed understand themselves as 'reasonable, autonomous and moral beings who must be able to account for their actions to one another' (2007: 22). But, in the situated deliberative encounter, individuals frequently do not live up to this formally ascribed responsibility, often failing to treat each other as morally reasonable and autonomous beings. Latent dynamics of power and authority may subvert formally equal relations, making it far more difficult for certain individuals and groups to be taken seriously as justificatory agents than others. Testament to this is the burgeoning literature on epistemic injustice and the many ways in which, despite outward appearance of discursive equality, individuals are implicitly denied credibility by, inter alia, not being granted deliberative 'uptake', being smothered, silenced, and stigmatized (e.g., Dotson 2011; Fricker 2009). In important respects, black feminist theory preempted many of these thematic concerns, and has long pointed out the myriad forms of epistemic injustice that disproportionately affect subordinate groups, discounting, trivializing, and ignoring their voices. History too shows how, because of processes of symbolic and epistemic de-authorization, marginalized political groups (suffragettes, civil rights activists, environmental campaigners) have struggled to be taken seriously as democratic interlocutors, even when obeying the rules of the deliberative game, and have often had to resort to 'coercive' forms of civil action for their demands to be heard (e.g., Medearis 2004; Stears 2010).

Naturally, Forst is aware of this problematic gap between formal and actual justificatory equality, but nonetheless his drift towards transcendentalism threatens to have damaging implications for the real-world emancipatory relevance of his theory. If what he deems to be the universal practice of justification turn outs in practice to be a socio-culturally specific form of reasoning, then it is likely to be less inclusive then he presumes. The exclusionary effects of this type of discursive universalism takes effect not through the direct imposition of Western ideals but through the naturalization of the linguistic and epistemic habits of dominant groups. In the cross-cultural context, for instance, ideas of reasonable justification may reflect the depersonalized sensibility and linguistic habitus of Western elites which, if not wholly inaccessible to less privileged, nonWestern groups may nonetheless be estranging and hence implicitly limiting and exclusionary. Such latent status quo bias is a much noted difficulty with Habermas's communicative ethics, because of the way it reduces speech acts to their supposedly rational core, with the consequence that disempowered groups may find themselves unable to participate fully in deliberation about justice. For instance, the lived reality of certain injustices may be confusing, inchoate, or fragmenting and hence are difficult to reconstruct in the formally rational terms that Habermasian validation requires (e.g., Honneth 2007). These experiences are therefore de facto excluded from consideration in discourse ethics regardless of its formally inclusive structure. If Forst is to avoid similar difficulties, a lot depends on the mechanisms and standards he puts in place to mediate between the asserted transcendental right to justification and its concrete enactment in situated forms of speech and rationality.

It is the thinness of Forst's discursive constructivism that provides one possible way of circumventing latent status quo bias because, unlike the Habermasian model, it does not impose any kind of condition upon the manner of the justificatory process or its content. The definition of what counts as 'reasonable' justification is left entirely open and must be determined by participants in debate according to the demands of their specific context: 'only reason—constantly reflecting on what counts as reasonable and whether that is deserved—can provide a solution here' (Allen, Forst, and Haugaard 2014: 21). The very parsimony of justificatory monism is what creates 'evaluative pluralism' and a space for disempowered and marginal groups to be heard, thus enabling Forst to rebut criticisms of ethnocentrism and other types of status quo bias. Indeed he makes the counter-charge that it is, in fact, those who level such criticisms who are more likely to be guilty of ethnocentrism in so far as they reify cultural difference as an insuperable barrier to understanding, and thereby deny the 'other's' capacity for justification: ' [they] homogenize non-Western societies as frameworks in which no radical critique asking for new or better reasons was either possible or legitimate' (Allen, Forst, and Haugaard 2014: 21). It is imperative, in Forst's view, to cut through misleading appearances of unbridgeable difference in the cross-cultural encounter in order to discern an underlying commonality, namely, the way in which heterogenous claims are motivated by the same, unifying demand for justification.

Yet Forst's claim that it is the inherent thinness of justification that ensures its responsiveness to context and the 'normative reality' of marginalized groups, is questionable on several counts. First, justification critique doesn't really explore the question of how asymmetries of power between democratic interlocutors might be dealt with so much as displace them, unaddressed, from the hypothetical scenario to that of the actual conversation. As a radical democrat, Forst argues rightly that it is citizens themselves who ought to determine the parameters of real-world justification rather than the theorist who 'predemocratically' prescribes them in advance. But given that, of the number of power differentials that may exist between interlocutors, many are relatively predictable in that they track established hierarchies of gender, race, and class, and it would seem that some preliminary thought might be given at least to how these asymmetries might be offset. In fact, Forst gives little indication as to the kind of safeguards that might be put in place in concrete deliberations to prevent powerful citizens from defining 'reasonable' justification in a way that continues to favour their interests over those of the less powerful. Since hierarchized difference and inequality are ubiquitous features of social life, it would be reasonable to hope that a model of moral reasoning that claims to possess real-world, emancipatory traction ought to try to address some of their comparatively foreseeable epistemic effects head on rather than derivatively and, possibly, not all. As Jaggar and Toibin put it:

> in existing contexts of diversity and inequality, it is unlikely to be rational to rely on moral-reasoning strategies that fail to build in safeguards against repression and abuse, even though such safeguards will never be infallible. Moral reasoning that ignores systematic cultural and social variations in moral points of view is likely to permit or even legitimate the repression of 'nonmainstream' moral perspectives and vocabularies and to fail to facilitate the emergence of new ones.
> (Jaggar and Toibin 2013: 399)

Instead of engaging with how systemic power relations might impact on justification critique, Forst relies, like Rawls, on the term 'reasonable' to do a considerable amount of tacit work in manufacturing an implicit consensus around justificatory norms and thereby papering over the deep differences that exist between citizens. The duty to justify oneself, that is to render one's position congruent with acceptable norms, presumes too readily that there always exists a set of commonly held values of univocal relevance for all cases of injustice. Establishing a set of shared, univocally relevant public criteria might be a more fraught process than abstract models of reasonable justification acknowledge when it comes to actual circumstances of deep social division (e.g., Dawson 2006). Moreover, there are no guarantees that these norms will be used appropriately. There are good reasons why, to groups who stand outside the mainstream, the demand to justify oneself may appear inappropriate or even disciplinary in nature. Describing the way a culture of justification operates in the discipline of philosophy to marginalize its black female members, Kristie Dotson argues that 'most disciplinary practitioners feel as if they are judge and jury over "appropriate" professional conduct and production, while never recognizing the demand to acknowledge the ways prevalent social and political structures of empowerment and disempowerment influence their judgment' (Dotson 2012: 1). Likewise, Salamon (2009) contends that the apparently reasonable request to justify one's position can mask privilege and serve as a subtle form of gatekeeping that works against nonorthodoxy, diversity, and change. In a real-world context, the demand for justification cannot be assumed to be inherently uncontroversial; it could represent a latent exertion of power on the part of dominant groups described by Berenstain (2016) as epistemic exploitation. Here, privileged interlocutors require marginalized individuals to explain their experiences while preemptively doubting the credibility of marginalized individuals' testimony. The doubts raised by privileged groups principally stem from their own faulty presuppositions, misunderstandings, and ignorance of a particular situation but these are presented nonetheless as reasonable objections. Rather than acknowledge their ignorance and exercise forbearance and willingness to learn from others, they instead disguise these shortcomings by positioning themselves as first among epistemic peers and assuming a default attitude of scepticism towards oppressed groups. As a result, the latter are caught in a double bind where they are required to explain themselves in the terms prescribed by others (and will be criticized if they decline to accept the reasonable demand) while knowing that their explanations will be discounted for relatively spurious reasons.

In the light of such arguments, it behoves radical democrats who accord justification a central place in the space of moral reasoning to interrogate more carefully the social conditions of inequality that make the request appear less reasonable to some groups than it does to others. Responding to such concerns, Forst maintains that to reduce the term reasonable to 'a contingent set of norms with which powerful groups in a society can live' is a positivist move that reduces reason to a descriptive term, thereby disregarding the 'the validity claim we necessarily make when we call something "reasonable"' (2020: 322). But the circularity of his response begs the question of whether, given systematic social inequalities, a common notion of 'reasonable' justification can be presumed to be unproblematically shared by interlocutors. It avoids considering the possibility that criteria determining validity may tacitly favour dominant groups by deploying 'sliding scales of reasonableness to dogmatically defend a preferred set of justificatory constraints' (McGuire 2016: 118).

The second respect in which the neutrality of justification critique is questionable relates to the 'criteria' of general and reciprocal acceptability that Forst employs to distinguish normatively justifiable from unjustifiable claims. As he puts it: 'with the help of the criteria of reciprocity and generality, it is possible to say that there are good, not reasonably rejectable, reasons for an action, which a reasonable person should have accounted for—and be reproached for failing to do so' (Forst 2007: 24).

These criteria are not as uncontentious as Forst seems to think in so far as they may hinder the inclusion of marginal and oppressed voices in the conversation about justice. For all that the experiences of oppressed groups are held by Forst to ignite the justificatory scenario, they can be rationally redeemed only by passing the threshold of general and reciprocal acceptability applied to all participants in the conversation: 'experiences of disrespect and exclusion need to be transformed into generally and reciprocally justifiable claims to legal, political or social respect and inclusion' (Forst 1999: 157–8). The testimony and experiences of marginal groups cannot stand as they are, so to speak, in their particularity but must be converted into an uncontroversial discursive form so that interlocutors may not reasonably withhold assent. The difficulties inherent in what is presented as an essentially smooth process of discursive alteration should not be underestimated. Given that experiences of injustice are often marked by 'structured heterogeneities and discontinuities' it is not clear that the conversion of inchoate and disempowering lived realities into standardized, generally acceptable criteria would be that straightforward (Mills 1998: 28). It may be uncontentious in the frictionless, symmetrical world of the ideal conversation, to claim that all perspectives, those of privileged and suffering interlocutors alike, ought to be redeemed according to the same neutral criteria. But if the normal situation of democratic debate is one of struggle, then it is unlikely that many injustices could in fact pass the justificatory threshold of reasons that all can accept, precisely because of the different experiential realities and background interests at play. Some justice claims cannot be formulated in criteria that all can accept precisely because they directly confront social advantage and challenge the status quo in a way that may discomfort dominant groups; as Young puts it: 'some claims of justice are not likely to express an interest all can share, because they are claims that actions should be taken to reduce the privilege some people are perceived to have' (Young 2000: 116).

The struggle and disagreement that characterize democratic debate goes all the way down to include not just the topic at hand, but also the quality of the reasoning process itself and what counts as a good reason: 'such general notions cannot be set aside from deliberation to serve as neutral arbiters of deep conflict but are themselves subjects for deliberation' (2009: 264).Indeed, some critics, argue that the idea of 'reasons that all can accept' (RACAs) frequently adduced by Forst and other deliberative theorists as a seemingly neutral method of harmonizing debate is in fact an 'illusory hope' (Bohman and Richardson 2009: 254). Bohman and Richardson contend, for instance, that is in fact difficult to arrive at a workable interpretation of the 'can accept' component of the RACA formula in either empirical or normative senses. The empirical sense of the 'can accept' is too vague and underspecified to capture the heterogenous, often arbitrary dynamics through which real-world agreements are reached. In cases where interlocutors have managed to agree, the idea of acceptance operates only retrospectively as a post-hoc description of that fact but not prospectively as a reliable guide for deliberation. In a normative sense, RACAs are also redundant in so far as their apparent unifying effects turn out to be the result of the constitutive commitments that underlie them but are not fully articulated—ideas of, say, 'reasonableness' or moral generalizability versus ethical specificity.[1] Were deliberative theorists to be more candid about the unifying effects brought about by their reliance on tacit normative standards, it would follow that their claims about RACAs as 'neutral' arbiters of debate would not be sustainable. In fact, neither as a descriptive nor counterfactual model of deliberation, does the mediating device reveal much about 'how actual deliberators would choose among RACAs in

---

[1] See, for instance, Bohman and Richardson's description of how Rawls's idea of the reasonable is tacitly generative of consensus: 'Rawls's principle of legitimacy does not ask us to survey the diverse commitments of the many actually existing reasonable people from their own perspective, in order to filter out any reason that any one of them could not accept. Rather, it effectively asks us to determine, more abstractly and in general, whether a given reason is consistent with the constitutive commitments of reasonableness, which are the same for each person' (2009: 260).

common cases of conflict' (Bohman and Richardson 2009: 264) Nor do they help to improve cases where deliberation is clearly defective and agreement is the result of 'biases' within the deliberating group, or tacit 'framing effects'. Arguably then, in the context of asymmetries of power between speakers, bias, and so on, the quality of deliberation is more likely to be improved not by appeals to neutral criteria but by making the process more heterogenous and open rather than less so, that is, by 'doing without' RACAs altogether.

Forst tries to smooth over such discrepancies between ideal and actual scenarios of justification through the circular argument that real-world situations of injustice must always be answered through the counterfactual thought experiment that, under ideal epistemic conditions, democratic citizens would not find them justifiable. For example, he maintains that, on his definition of justification, it would not be possible for gay individuals to be denied an equal right to marriage because this would involve relying on 'thick' religious and traditional notions of the meaning of marriage that are deeply contested and therefore reciprocally nongeneralizable (2011: 113). But this overlooks the fact that, beyond the hypothetical scenario of justification, the right to marriage for gays continues to be highly disputed on precisely these terms even where it has been legally recognized by the state. In predetermining the outcome of the justificatory process in this way, Forst seems to tacitly draw on substantive, but unarticulated principles of equality, freedom, tolerance, solidarity, and so on, in a manner that he explicitly rejects in his criticism of the predemocratic nature of antecedent justification. Indeed, it is precisely on these grounds of the 'performative contradiction' of paternalistically lapsing into an antecedent moral wisdom of the type he explicitly rejects that Habermas criticizes Forst (Habermas 2011: 296).[2] In short, Forst appears to want to have his cake and eat it too; asserting, on the one hand, that the conversation about justice is always situated, that there can never by a perspective outside of it, but, repeatedly affirming, on the other, the moral priority of an ideal perspective over a situated one.

The Burdens of Justification

Differently put, the justification paradigm fails to reflexively enact the dialectic of transcendence and immanence that Forst regards as a defining feature of

[2] 'Rainer Forst assumes that the founding fathers and mothers are intrinsically moral persons. *As such* they feel committed to human rights and bring these *morally justified* rights into their constitution-making practice in order to implement them as civil rights and to establish the process of democratic legislation, among other things. In this way, however, the liberal priority of human rights would be translated into the paternalism of an assembly of morally pre-programmed founders who cannot proceed democratically because the system of rights and the democratic procedure first established along with this system would be a function of their antecedent moral wisdom that they bring to bear prior to any political deliberations.'

emancipatory critique. If it turns out that the criteria of general and reciprocal acceptability do disadvantage disempowered interlocutors in the conversation about justice then, on his own definition of reflexivity, it follows that Forst might need to think more carefully about how to amend the formal process of justification to render it more inclusive. But such critical self-reflection is repeatedly foreclosed by the way he insistently prioritizes abstract procedures over situated encounters. So, for example, issues of interpretative incommensurability and testimonial injustice are foreclosed because of Forst's reliance on an undifferentiated notion of affectability which holds that 'in moral contexts the community of justification may not be arbitrarily restricted, but rather must include all those affected by actions or norms in morally relevant ways' (2007: 214). The blanket use of the term 'moral relevance' does not make sufficient allowance, however, for the deep discrepancies that may exist between individuals in terms of 'intensity of affectability' where a given state of affairs may have a more prolonged and harmful impact upon some individuals than on others. Individuals who have suffered directly from chronic or severe injustice may justifiably feel that a greater urgency and moral weight attaches itself to their view than to those of citizens less directly affected, and that this should somehow be acknowledged in deliberation. From this perspective, Forst's stipulation that all groups, regardless of experiential discrepancies, must meet the unchanging threshold of justificatory acceptability may constitute a supervening form of epistemic or hermeneutical injustice that compounds the original injustice.

The practical enactment of concern for others might require us on occasions to consider whether, with certain cases of injustice, it is in fact appropriate to insist on reciprocally acceptable justifiability: 'affectability brings with it an excess over rational justifiability' (Fritsch 2015: 813). This is the view of Adorno, for instance, who is sceptical about the possibility of establishing discursive foundations for morality because he believes that our moral responses rest largely on immediate, quasi-intuitive reactions to suffering. It is an 'outrage', in his view, to demand that we justify our response to the evil of Auschwitz when it is our spontaneous reactions to the event that should be our normative guide. We instinctively recognize oppression when we see it and grounding morality in a priori theories and principles is neither desirable or necessary, since it entangles us in an infinite chain of argument (Freyenhagen 2013: 198–9). Adorno famously prefers a negativist construal of morality, namely, that our normative responses to possible injustices should be directed not by comprehensive principles of the good or the right but by concrete knowledge of social suffering and other 'bads' and what might be done practically to overcome them.

It is not necessary to endorse a negativism as austere as Adorno's to recognize that in certain cases there may be deep disconnection between the lived reality of suffering, on the one side, and the demand, on the other, that experiences be vindicated according to pregiven criteria, no matter how seemingly thin. There are some cases of suffering, where the assumed reversibility of perspectives that underpins the demand for justification is inappropriate. Echoing Adorno, Laurence Thomas argues:

> If one encountered a Holocaust survivor, it would be moral hubris of the worst sort—unless one is also such a survivor—to assume that by way of rational imaginative role-taking...that one could even begin to grasp the depth of that person's experiences—the hurts, pains, and anxieties of that individual's life. There is not enough good will in the world to make it possible for persons (who are not Holocaust survivors) to put themselves imaginatively in the mind of a Holocaust survivor, to do so simply as an act of ratiocination.   (Thomas 1998: 360)

In the context of such experiential disparities, especially when they are reinforced by power hierarchies, the demand for justification may sometimes be misplaced and burdensome by way of a normative response. The paradox of equal treatment for all is that sometimes the perspective of what is equally good for all be abandoned temporarily for the sake of its other perspective, that of singular-oriented treatment (e.g., Fritsch 2015: 810). Thomas, for instance, interprets orientation to singularity as entailing the cultivation of virtues of deference and humility especially towards persons in 'diminished social categories'. Deference involves learning to listen properly to the other's experiences as the first step in a longer, more difficult process of learning from and bearing witness to their pain. Learning through listening is not easy because it involves rendering oneself open to another's concern and 'letting another's pain reconstitute one so much that one comes to have a new set of sensibilities' (Thomas 1998: 377). In principle, Forst recognizes the significance of such ethical dilemmas when, for instance, he invokes Levinas's argument that moral law derives its authority from 'the face' or singular presence of the other. Yet rather than exploring in a concerted fashion the ways in which normative receptivity to the vulnerable subject of injustice may be practically enacted, he just categorically contents that empathy generates amoral results. His conclusion is that, if there is a role for empathy in the encounter with vulnerable others, it can only be the 'reasonable empathy' generated by the criterion of justification (2014: 176–7). Setting aside the uninterrogated work that the term 'reasonable' does in this context, it is an open question whether formal justificatory procedures do in fact have the capacity to spontaneously engender the sensitivity and related practical dispositions necessary to ensure genuine uptake of the claims of vulnerable and suffering others, rather than reaffirming the deontological sufficiency of the abstract model of justification. Rather than reaffirming the deontological sufficiency of justification, reflexivity here seems to require that Forst pay greater attention to the patterns of epistemic deauthorization that typically skew deliberative exchanges between unequal interlocutors and adapt his paradigm accordingly.

In short, by cleaving to the abstract formula of mutually owed justifications, Forst is in danger of doing what he explicitly denies, namely, treating 'injustice as a "surprising abnormality" from the norm of justice' (Sklar 1990: 17). If a theory of normative validity is to provide a viable internal point of justification for oppressed groups, then it must seemingly be more responsive than justification monism to the effects of social position on epistemic and linguistic capacity. Forst claims in response to such criticisms that excessive reliance on immanent criteria means succumbing to 'historical relativism' and relinquishing the 'robust' standards of justification that ensure genuinely emancipatory critique. As he puts it: 'without a principle of justification there can be no self-reflexivity, no grounded critique and no critical theory, only an arbitrary affirmation of "that which doesn't fit in"' (Forst 2020: 324). If we don't accept Forst's all-or-nothing logic, however, it is possible to see that sensitivity to the context of power need not necessarily involve the wholesale abandonment of an emancipatory critical perspective so much as the adoption of a more thoroughly detranscendentalized one. Such an approach might involve, for example, the demotion of justification from its position as governing principle or 'moral command centre' of a unified paradigm to being one of several normative approaches to be adopted according to what the context requires. Feminists and other philosophers interested in a developing more open and varied approaches to normativity have argued that the generalized, monist paradigms that philosophers recognize as moral theories are not necessarily distinguished by their scope so much as the kind of systematic organization they impose on a field. The normative problem space is organized according to a 'theoretical-juridical model' that takes a deductive and cognitivist approach to morality: 'It is assumed that morality is essentially knowledge; that moral knowledge is essentially "theoretical", of an explicitly stateable, highly general and systematically unified type; and that this pure, properly moral knowledge, when brought to bear on incidental, "nonmoral" information about a situation at hand, serves to tell us what to do' (Urban Walker1992: 28). Critics of this model of 'justified judging' argue, inter alia, that it is elitist, has an 'authoritarian subtext', and an ethos of 'managerial privilege'. The claimed universal reach of the judgement model is also thrown into question by pointing to its limited real-world bearing on a narrow sub-set of normative dilemmas. For these thinkers, what is required for a comprehensive and inclusive approach to social justice is not greater abstraction and uniformity of judgement but a more varied ethical repertoire where justificatory practices represent one of a multiplicity of normative responses. These responses are prompted by the particular circumstances of injustice itself, and might include bearing witness, giving voice to pain, disclosure, affirmation, building solidaristic relations, and so forth. Emancipatory insight is not foregone with the development of such pluralized approaches, as Forst fears, but it would undoubtedly take a different form from the authoritative, action-guiding verdicts that are the supposed outcome of justification monism. Instead, by linking normative thought more tightly to social context, insight emerges from a dynamic of 'mutual adjustment and understanding'. Context transcendence not as knowledge that comes from applying the correct justificatory framework but as the expanded horizons generated by reasoning across perspectives in a dialogic and inclusive fashion.

Correlative to the deflated role accorded to justification in normative critique is the less teleological nature of the justificatory process itself. Of course, Forst's model of justification is not strongly teleological, but nonetheless the criteria of general and reciprocal assent impose a certain direction and outcome to deliberation which is more limiting than it appears. Instead of being oriented towards universally acceptable validation, justification might then be oriented towards what Azamova (2012) calls 'giving reasons for having reasons'. Justification, on this alternative account, would be to start from personal experience and the narration of how one has come to one's view and reasons that prompted one to form it. Instead of imposing a threshold of acceptability, it would allow disadvantaged subjects to explain their experiences in their own terms, and thereby hopefully generate enhanced understanding of their normative stance as well as shedding light on connections and commonalities with the position of others. In line with this construal of justification as 'progressive and mutual moral accounting', the merit of a given claim is verified against contextually relevant norms rather than those of universal acceptability (Urban Walker 1992: 32). Practical verification draws on a variety of yardsticks and methodologies relevant to a given situation, deploying them in a way that is as much about keeping a political dialogue going as it is about reaching a final evaluative position. Formal criteria of legitimacy are replaced by those such as what a particular experiential constellation might reveal about distributions of power; how it might enrich understanding and disrupt settled preconceptions; how it might promote dialogue and enhance solidarity and hold out new emancipatory possibilities, and so on. Unlike justification monism, the aim of practical verification is not to assimilate singular experiences under univocally relevant principles, but rather to contribute to political problem-solving understood not in the once and for all sense of definitive judgement, but in the ongoing sense of what Dotson calls a 'culture of praxis'. This type of praxeological reasoning does not dispense with justification entirely, but nor does it accord it a determining role in normativity: 'it is at once useful for some projects and irrelevant to others' (see Dotson 2012: 26).

A detranscendentalized account of justification recalibrates the burden of the conversation about justice so that it falls more heavily on privileged rather than on vulnerable interlocutors. Although the duty to justify oneself applies to all subjects, privileged and vulnerable alike, a common criticism is that it is often more onerous for the latter groups to comply with, and doing so potentially compounds their disempowered status. Instead of focusing one-sidedly on the formal vindication of suffering and injustice and, consequently, tacitly limiting how vulnerable groups can appear to others, it may be more equalizing to make greater demands of privileged interlocutors in the democratic conversation along the lines of cultivating moral deference, and learning to listen properly to what vulnerable others tell us about their experiences. It might involve assuming an attitude of 'presumptive generosity' (Connolly 2004), cultivating an ethos of 'epistemic responsibility' (Fricker 2009), a dispositional 'caring to know' (Dalmiya 2016), or the deliberative virtue of civility (Bohman and Richardson 2009) and any number of other similar ideas. These proposals aim, in various ways, at dislodging the cognitive and discursive habits of dominant groups which are often generalized as impartial justificatory procedures and generate hermeneutically marginalizing effects for subordinate groups. Evidently, the cultivation of relevant phronetic sensibilities is not a straightforward task, but might involve such measures as renunciation of fixed principles of interpretation, willingness to render oneself vulnerable to others, embracing rather than smoothing over experiential disruption and complexity, and the use of imagination and sympathy in interactions with others rather than fixed categorizations (Medina 2012: 112ff). In short, challenging epistemic 'metablindness' and 'metainsensitivity' to injustice and oppression seems to require the development of communicative and interpretative virtues quite different to the reasonable empathy of Forst's justificatory process.

Reconciliation or Vacillation?

It is difficult to demur from a hypothetical principle that accords the right to justification to all affected but, on closer inspection, it seems to be such a socially weightless notion that its precise relevance to the correction of actual injustices is unclear. At best, the syntax of justification is what Nancy Fraser terms a 'circuitous route' to dealing with unwarranted disparities of power between individuals that may be more effectively dealt with by a direct focus on the nature of the specific injustice in question (see Fraser 2008 and Chapter 5). In the end, Forst's inability to advance beyond a one-dimensional formulation of justification speaks to the contradictory nature of his enterprise, where instead of establishing an internal connection between critical and ideal perspectives, between immanence and transcendence, he vacillates inconsequently between the two in a manner that is ultimately self- undermining. No sooner does he establish the universal status of justification as the core of practical reason, then he appears to backtrack from this by stating repeatedly that there can be no truly objective perspective, that all reasoning is situated and perspectival. But when faced with challenges from the perspective of social practice, he prioritizes the a priori of justification over a contextually embedded response.

The undermining effects of this vacillation permeate Forst's work and are evident, for example, in the uncertain status of the criteria of reciprocity and generality. Neither first-order moral principles or socially derived norms, they lack determinate content and are unsatisfactory from both ideal and critical stances. Hence, for the ideal theorist concerned with grounding justice in independent foundations, the criteria are insufficient because they are not substantive moral principles. As we have seen, this thinness is a deliberate strategy on Forst's part because he wishes to avoid making metaphysical claims and replicating the predemocratic error of ideal theory. Any normative content the criteria possess must necessarily come to them from the outside, from the deliberations of citizens in a given justificatory scenario. But this thinness inevitably weakens the unconditional moral force that Forst wishes to confer on justification critique. Consequently the criteria are vulnerable to such criticisms from ideal theorists as they are tautologous (generality implies reciprocity), too vague (a more precise idea of all affected principle needs to be worked out), or require supplementing with other criteria (such as that of priority), to render them normatively effective (e.g., Caney 2014; Muller 2013). To preempt such criticisms, Forst implicitly draws on thick norms of tolerance, solidarity, freedom, and so on, to demonstrate the criteria's supposed moral rigour. However, as we have seen, this covert paternalism violates the premise that it is citizens who are the rightful authors of democratic principles, not the theorist.

From the opposing perspective of the critical theorist concerned with immanent social critique and power, the criteria are just as empty but in the different sense of being abstractions that repress awareness of their social conditions of possibility. According to Honneth, for instance, the criteria would be devoid of normative bite if they did not implicitly presuppose that 'social norms and corresponding roles already exist and determine the elements of justification' (Honneth 2011: 416). In his view, Forst is only able to establish justification as the universal core of practical reason by fictitiously bracketing off the social context in which dialogue always takes place and which gives it substantive content. Context does not simply constitute the post-hoc setting to transcendental practice but rather is its necessary precondition. It is only ever in a given social context that the criteria of justification make sense, for in considering whether particular social relations are just or not, individuals invariably encounter each other as situated beings who draw on their accumulated knowledge of social roles, norms, and practices to make such judgements.

In the end, this vacillation between critical and ideal perspectives throws into question the supposed moral and analytical force of the justification paradigm. Perhaps, even more significantly, this methodological indecision undermines the very capacity for reflexive self-scrutiny that Forst regards as an indispensable feature of emancipatory critique, preventing its lapse into metaphysical slumber, on the one side, and parochial relativism, on the other. The effect of according justification a transcendental status is to immunize it against systematic critical scrutiny, since an invariant principle, *eo ipso*, cannot be subject to extensive revision. There are several grounds, however, on which we might want to subject the justification principle to precisely such critical scrutiny, particularly when it comes to its status as the supposed essence of practical reason. Questionable from a historical perspective, for instance, is Forst's insistence that all political struggles can be interpreted as expressions of a supervening demand for justification regardless of the actual terms in which their concrete demands are framed. Jeffrey Flynn points out, for instance, that when Muslim women around the world struggle against patriarchy in Islam, they may be asking for equal treatment as Muslims on the basis of an alternative interpretation of their rights and duties in the Qur'an, but whether this can be construed in the strong terms as a claim about their moral right to justification is moot: 'It does not seem to be the case that whenever people demand reasons from others or even when they demand that they no longer be ignored, that they necessarily enter into a kind of dynamic that implicates a moral right to justification' (Flynn 2015: 801). It might very well be possible to agree with Forst that what distinguishes certain struggles as properly political rather than merely personal or existential is that they are undergirded by a claim, of some sort or another, to democratic universality. It is open to question, however, whether this claim is most appropriately conceptualized as an assertion of the right to justification or instead as an assertion of the right to equality or freedom, as Rancière (1999) and Honneth (2014a) respectively hold, or in negative terms as a right not to suffer injustice and domination. Certainly, these latter formulations seem to be politically more germane and better able to capture the urgency and outrage that motivate struggles for social justice than the abstract, rather bloodless idea of justification.

Even by Forst's own lights, that is, according to his initial constructivist scenario, it is doubtful whether justification emerges as the fundamental characteristic of practical reasoning rather than some other inter-subjective principle of, say, dialogue, or recognition. After all, the reason that the need to justify one's position arises in the first place is as a response to the demand emanating from an 'other' who has already been recognized as a partner in dialogue. If reason was not already presumed to be dialogical there would be no duty to justify oneself in a general, reciprocally acceptable fashion. Forst asserts the inter-subjective nature of reason but fails to pursue the potentially subversive implications that this concession has on the supposedly foundational status of the justification principle. If it is dialogue with the other that precedes and creates the demand for justification, then, as Honneth points out, recognition must be the more fundamental principle: 'mutual recognition always precedes discourse, and the mutual ascription of normative capacities...always precedes justification' (Honneth 2011: 416). Indeed, according to Honneth, the antecedence of recognition emerges 'unnoticed' in Forst's work—for example, in his frequent reference to practical 'contexts' of justification—and, as such, does a lot of unacknowledged work to make the idea of justification operable. Similarly, Muller concludes from Forst's presumption of the intersubjective nature of practical reason that there is a 'deeper root of justice' and more fundamental right than that of justification, namely, the right to participate in dialogue. It is only in the context of a right to participate in dialogue that a subsequent right to justification makes sense: 'dialogue does not take place because there is a need of justification, but the other way round, there is a need of justification because reason is, in its own dynamic and inner life, dialogical' (Muller 2013: 1057). Pointing to these criticisms is not necessarily intended to endorse the contention that recognition is in fact the more fundamental principle, but rather to draw attention to the way in which the conferral of a transcendental status on justification prevents Forst from effectively implementing the type of reflexive self-scrutiny that he regards as indispensable for emancipatory critique. Once the principle of justification is up and running, so to speak, little attempt is made to revisit and revise it in the light of possible shortcomings vis-à-vis the treatment of concrete instances of injustice. Rather, in line with paradigm-led thinking, its interpretative priority is relentlessly reaffirmed.

In the end, Forst's vacillation is perhaps inevitable in so far as his Janus-faced objectives of establishing independent moral grounds for critique, on the one side, and of developing a penetrating critical theory of injustice, on the other, are perhaps more contradictory than he is prepared to acknowledge. In so far as these objectives cannot be fully reconciled—or at least not in the monist form that Forst intends—they represent what Adorno calls torn halves which, when brought together, do not add up to a unified whole (Adorno 1974: 123). A solution to Forst's difficulties, given his stated allegiance to Frankfurt School critique, would be to let go of the transcendental side of his project and construe the right to justification as a contingent historical achievement, albeit a significant one akin to what other critical theorists term an immanent universal. Instead, by overemphasizing the autonomy of morality, Forst severs the links between universalism as a contingent achievement and the social institutions and practices that are required to sustain it (e.g., Benhabib 2015: 784).

Historicizing the principle of justification in the way suggested here would enhance its responsiveness to context and reflexivity but it would undoubtedly mean giving up on a certain type of strong universalism. But, contra Forst, it doesn't follow that, by detranscendentalizing its governing principle, critique automatically forgoes trans-contextual explanatory and evaluative force. Indeed, this is perhaps the real underlying difficulty with Forst's work, namely, the misleading presumption that if critique cannot find incontestable foundations and a way out of the hermeneutic circle, it must inevitably fall prey to a parochial relativism. This false antithesis between transcendence and immanence forecloses exploration of the complicated middle ground where there are better and worse interpretations of the world and a variety of methodological indices, standards of evidence, and conceptual logics with which to test any given theory's respective explanatory and normative merits. Forst fails to see, in other words, that the dilemma of transcendence versus immanence that haunts him is in fact one of his own making, for, it is the 'ideal of impartiality' itself that 'generates a dichotomy between universal and particular' (Young 1990: 97). Accepting the situated nature of reason would mean, however, that the validity of critique's diagnoses and proposals will always be a matter for argumentation and justification without resort to a transcendental guarantee. Critique must be 'guided by a concern for an answer that is right in a context transcending sense and that proceeds in a historicist, comparative, open-ended, and concrete way' (Cooke 2006: 70). The attempt to dehistoricize the justification principle forecloses what many would regard as the essential strength of an effective critical theory, namely, a dialogical, contextually sensitive, and cumulative style of political reasoning. Moreover, Forst is arguably mistaken in thinking that, by deriving justification from the constructivist method of 'moral invention', his paradigm is freed from the hermeneutic circle and provides a definitive frame for questions of social justice. He is mistaken because, as Michael Walzer reminds us, there are always an infinite number of possible 'inventions', and every invention inevitably requires interpretation (1987: 26).

Conclusion

While the emphasis placed on free-standing foundations sets Forst's work apart from that of his Frankfurt School peers, in other respects, it typifies, in peculiarly intensified form, some of the central difficulties with paradigm-led critique. The central problem is the deep tension that exists between the Frankfurt School's situated and practical conception of critique, on the one side, and attempts to establish its context-transcending grounds in totalizing and monist terms, on the other. According to their left–Hegelian logic, the tension between context dependence and context transcendence cannot ever be fully resolved, in so far as it is an insuperable but enabling condition of all rationality. Rather, critique aims to move between the two poles in an open and productive a fashion as possible. However, the construal of context-transcending foundations in monist, ahistorical terms halts this to-and-fro and pushes critique towards the type of unquestioned evaluative authority that it supposedly rejects. These abstracting tendencies are especially pronounced in Forst's justification monism because of the way he eschews the Frankfurt School's usual method of normative reconstruction, and grounds critique instead in constructivist speculation on practical reason. The idealizing effects of this constructivist method on his thought brings justification critique far closer than he is perhaps prepared to acknowledge to the types of analytical political philosophy that he rejects. Reliance on a decontextualized notion of justification makes it difficult for him to work backwards to the social world, and establish the unmasking account of power and oppression that he believes should be the first concern of a theory of justice. Given this, the practical emancipatory force of critique might well be enhanced by replacing the monist totalizing paradigm of justification with experientially grounded, problem-led modes of theorizing about social justice.

3
Recognition and Progress in the Family

Introduction

On the face of it, neoHegelian critical theory of the type represented in Axel Honneth's work on recognition seems to be more responsive to issues of gender oppression than neoKantian types such as Forst's. The pivotal ethical significance that Hegelians typically accord to the family enables them to place an intensified emphasis on gendered issues of intimacy, care, and reproductive labour in a critical social theory. A sociology of recognition is a much-needed corrective to mainstream political theory's default setting of the public–private distinction which, in so far as it naturalizes the family and shields it from political scrutiny, also obscures gender subordination. Updated to contemporary life, the sociology of recognition allows Honneth to construe the family, and intimate relations more generally, as a foundational sphere of social freedom and, accordingly, to give renewed explanatory significance to key feminist concerns with relations of care and the gender division of labour. This resonance between Honneth's thought and feminism is reinforced further by the interpretative methodology which propels recognition critique and accords a key role to the lived suffering of subordinated groups in guiding unmasking critique. The weight that Honneth gives to this phenomenology of injustice contrasts with the tokenistic treatment that direct subjective experience seems to receive in the hands of other Frankfurt School thinkers. It also induces Honneth to reject deontological models of normativity because, in his view, the 'groundless circularity' of Kantianism is insufficiently attentive to widespread but unthematized forms of social suffering and misery. Honneth shares a preference with many feminist theorists for normative theorizing that is more strongly indexed to context and inductive in nature.

But the promise of a fruitful overlap between Honneth's sociology of recognition and feminism, vis-à-vis integrating a fuller account of women's subordination in unmasking critique, remains largely unfulfilled. It is thwarted, I argue, by Honneth's recognition monism and ahistorical conception of context-transcending critique which give rise to diagnostic and normative limitations in an account of gender oppression. Evidently, many of the problems with his critique of gender, and power more generally, have already been extensively discussed by feminist theorists in the Frankfurt School, most notably Nancy Fraser in her exchange with Honneth in *Redistribution or Recognition?* Rather than go over well-trodden ground, the focus of this chapter is on Honneth's recent work, where he has explicitly tried to overcome some of these limitations by introducing a more developed sense of historicity and social specificity into the recognition paradigm. Honneth makes this historicizing move by shifting the normative centre of gravity of his recognition paradigm from ontological claims about self-realization to the idea of progress. The idea of progress is held to improve on recognition in that it provides a context-transcending vantage point from which forms of social misrecognition can be criticized but which, at the same time, avoids the possibility of cultural bias in having to substantively specify what successful self-realization or recognition might involve. In terms of an account of gender relations, I argue that the shift to ostensibly thinner normative foundations is largely unsuccessful, because of the way Honneth deploys a narrative of progressive social development that is so selective and idealized that it skews immanent critique. These skewing effects are palpable in Honneth's social theory of the family as the steady democratization of love where diagnosis of intimate relations is one-sidedly focussed on latent ethical potential and ignores distorting asymmetries of power. In so far as he underestimates the persistence of negative dynamics internal to the family, as well as the part it plays in reproducing gender subordination in its cyclical interaction with other social institutions, Honneth's normative response to related gender harms is underspecified and vague. This is evident in the way that complex socio-structural relations of gendered care work are reduced to an interpersonal dynamic of ethical mutuality. Honneth defends this ethical reduction by arguing that it is integral to his 'selective' method of normative reconstruction which, absent a guiding notion of progress, would be condemned to arbitrary contextual analysis. Using feminist work on the family and care as a critical counterpoint, I question Honneth's contention and argue, inter alia, that it rests on precisely the exaggerated dichotomy of universalism versus relativism that is a typical feature of paradigm-led critical theory. Moreover, Honneth's reliance on a metanarrative of progress undermines his stated commitment to derive normative principles not from over the heads of the people that critique addresses but directly from their experiences and expectations.

Recognizing Gender

While, in principle, Frankfurt School theorists freely acknowledge that the family is a foundational institution of the life-world, in practice few of them study it in any sociological detail as part of an unmasking of critical theory. Axel Honneth's work bucks the trend in this respect in so far as it assigns a central role to the family and intimate relations in understanding ethical social life. His Hegelian treatment of the family as a primary site of social freedom contrasts with the tokenistic way it is more usually construed by androcentric democratic theories as a mere background institution of the life-world. Consequently, Honneth's thought productively crosses over with analogous arguments made by feminists of various stripes about the fundamental moral and political significance of the undervalued care work carried out mostly by women, in and beyond the family. Intimate bonds of mutual responsibility and care form the ethical bedrock on which other democratic virtues are founded, and the family should therefore be demarginalized and given a central place in any account of social justice. It is not just that Honneth's recognition theory and feminism share an intellectual focus on family life and relations of care, for they also have potentially fruitful points of methodological overlap. Honneth's explicit enshrining of an interpretative phenomenology of injustice at the heart of his recognition paradigm chimes with an analogous orientation in feminist theory to recover, explore, and revalorize the neglected experiences of women. Moreover, Honneth's preference for normative reasoning as a socially reconstructive endeavour instead of 'the groundless circularity' of moral constructivism (*pace* Forst for example) converges with a feminist preference for non-ideal, relational modes of political theorizing over idealizing, monological modes (e.g., Schwartzman 2006). Many (although not all) feminists share with Honneth the insight that, if it is to have practical political relevance, normative thought is more effectively guided by the analysis of actual lived forms of injustice and suffering than by idealized and remote scenarios of justice and equality. Elizabeth Anderson describes this as feminism's non-ideal standpoint methodology, where theorists 'should start thinking from the injustices we encounter in our non-ideal, unjust world, and think about those problems from the perspective of those who are oppressed by that injustice' (Anderson 2009: 30).

On the face of it, then, there appear to be several theoretical avenues along which feminists might fruitfully take up the insights of recognition social theory in order to more firmly embed a systematic account of gender subordination at the heart of social and political thought. Yet, despite the promise of this convergence, feminists who draw on recognition critique in order to advance an analysis of gender subordination would first have to overcome fundamental difficulties, many of which stem from its foundation in a trans-historical anthropology of recognition or what I have called elsewhere an ontology of recognition (McNay 2009). Put bluntly, the grounding of social theory in an ontology of recognition has, I contend, deeply dehistoricizing effects on the critique of power. The psychological need for recognition is, in Honneth's view, not a contingent or culturally relative construct but an ahistorical constant and fundamental prerequisite of healthy human self-development. This ontogenetic premise drives Honneth's monist social theory which depicts the developmental dynamic of modern societies as driven by the progressive, although not unfaltering, instantiation of ever more inclusive and differentiated forms of recognition. Ontologized social theory has dehistoricizing entailments which unavoidably curtail sensitivity to socio-cultural variation and downplay power dynamics. For example, the depiction of care dynamics in the family as mutual relations of nurturance and esteem obscures its reality as highly gendered, undervalued, and sometimes exploitative work, and hence naturalizes women's subordination in the family. It mystifies the historically variable, hierarchical, and often exploitative organization of the family's internal gender relations as an ethical mutuality. As Nancy Fraser, one of Honneth's most trenchant critics, puts it: 'what Honneth calls affective care is actually women's labour, ideologically mystified and rendered invisible' (Fraser and Honneth 2003: 220). In short, recognition monism stands in tension with a disclosing critique of power and this has led to criticisms of Honneth's work as psychologically reductive, depoliticizing, and naïve in its understanding of power and conflict, especially with regard to an appreciation of recognition as a normalizing mode of social control (e.g., Owen and Van Den Brink 2007).

To his credit, Honneth has always been mindful of this tension between social theory and ontology but his efforts to mitigate it have in the main, been rather circular in nature. Resorting to a questionable form–content distinction, he maintains that although the desire for recognition is supposedly a universal 'need anchored in human nature', it only ever manifests itself in variable, socially distinctive practices (2002: 504). It is hard to see, however, how this circular logic is anything but self-cancelling; the claim to historical specificity is surely undermined by the positing of a self-same desire for recognition that remains untouched through the course of history and resurfaces, time and again, as the catalyst for social conflict and change. This historicized version of eternal recurrence seems to be a case of Honneth having his cake and eating it too. However, in his recent work, Honneth has once again revisited this troubling tension between historical openness and ontological closure, but his argument has changed tack in so far as it subtly displaces recognition as social theory's normative core. Honneth acknowledges that previously he had perhaps not thought through in sufficient detail whether the three principal domains of recognition (love, esteem, rights) should be conceptualized as 'constants of human nature' or as the result of 'historical processes' (Honneth 2002: 501). His renewed attempts, principally in *Freedom's Right*, to address this dilemma involve a general reorientation of the recognition paradigm around an intensified emphasis on its socially contingent and variable elements. On this historicized view, the recognition regimes of the life-world are explained not so much in terms of the externalization of a presocial need but instead as 'bundles of customs' whose significance is tied to the distinctive contribution they make to socialization processes in any given historical era and which change over time. The fact that love, for example, until recently was linked to issues of utility (securing ties of blood, land, and property) suggests that it is more productive to conceptualize this particular recognition order less as a socio-ontological given and more in terms of changing historical circumstance. The stress that Honneth now places on the historical variability of intimate relations in this sphere represents an especially significant shift in the light of his earlier claim that love did not have the potential for normative development, and that only the spheres of law and achievement were amenable to the possibility of progressive change (Honneth 1995: 176). He is thus able to revise his previous rather uncritical acceptance of Hegel's nuclear family model centred on mutual complementarity of husband and wife, to include families in nonheteronormative and 'blended' arrangements. Similarly, the stress formerly placed on generic psychological dynamics in his account of misrecognition is replaced by a focus on the 'social and experiential reality' of being recognized in certain determinate ways and not in others as part of a process of social interaction played out in the 'historically emergent *space of moral reasons*' (2002: 503). Misrecognition is no longer thematized as a free-floating psychological injury but as rooted in an historically specific 'moral' experience tied to the biased or misplaced evaluations that individuals make of each other; as Honneth describes it, the 'historically fuelled feeling that others unjustly fail to recognise certain aspects of who one is' (2002: 504).

Although historicizing recognition in this manner goes some way to mitigating the naturalizing effects of ontology upon social theory, it brings back for Honneth the potential problem of the context-transcending grounds of critique. Too emphatic an emphasis on historically specific analysis pushes critique dangerously close to cultural relativism. The problem is particularly acute for Honneth given the strong terms in which he interprets context transcendence, that is, as a normative principle that can identify social discontent 'independently of public recognition' (Fraser and Honneth 2003: 125).[1] To be genuinely emancipatory, critique must have an unchanging normative core that reemerges in every social struggle 'because it is so tightly fused to the structure of human interests' (Fraser and Honneth 2003: 244). Lacking such a normative core, context transcendence is relativized to immediate circumstances and becomes the mere local outcome of 'contingent conflict situations', its meaning dissipated to little more than 'unfulfilled, and to that extent transcending, social ideals and goals...still to be found within social reality at a particular time' (Fraser and Honneth 2003: 244). It follows that if, in his reworked theory, recognition relations are now to be understood as socially variable configurations of power then the trans-historical standards on which to judge whether they represent a contribution to human emancipation or not seem to recede. Ironically, for all its problems, Honneth's earlier psychosocial anthropology of recognition has the distinct advantage of allowing the comparative evaluation of concrete social arrangements according to whether they promote or block healthy self-realization. The displacement of this

---

[1] Cooke points out that in the original German version, Honneth's terminology has even stronger foundationalist implications since he uses the words 'all' and 'completely' which are omitted in the translation. Cooke 2006: 224n. 116.

evaluative criterion, qua ontology, exposes immanent critique to the value relativism of the radical contextualist where, any regime of recognition regime is as valid as any other given its essential contingency: 'the validity of the recognitional attitude... would depend exclusively on the normative givens of the form of life in question' (2002: 508). To avoid this dilemma Honneth has to find other nonsubstantive, nonontological grounds to ensure the evaluative bite of his newly historicized paradigm, and he finds this alternative rational universal in the idea of progress: 'I do not think we can do without a conception of progress if we are to avoid the relativism that would ordinarily accompany claims to the alterability of evaluative human qualities' (2002: 510).

The idea of progress is not a radically new departure for Honneth; it has always been present in his writing in a background sense linked to the influence of Hegel and to a lesser extent the functionalist sociology of Durkheim and Parsons on his thought. It is only with the historicizing turn of his later work, however, that it acquires an augmented normative status. Needless to say, along with the idea of progress come potential problems of teleology, determinism, historical finalism, and so forth, and hence Honneth strives to rid his version of such questionable metaphysical baggage in order to acknowledge more effectively the 'ineradicable element of historical revisability and openness' to societal development. He uses his weaker, postmetaphysical idea of the inevitability of progress to solve the problem of the context-transcending grounds of critique, steering a course between relativism and constructivist abstraction. On the one hand, without a progressive teleology, there is a risk of becoming enmeshed in a nihilist Foucauldian vision that, in so far as it understands any social order as the contingent outcome of a will to power, cannot find the normative resources in the reality it examines in which to ground immanent critique. On the other hand, the intra-mundane quality of the idea of progress renders redundant the grounding of critique in Kantian appeals to free-floating external moral standards. For, on Honneth's view, these moral standards can be identified within the direction of social development itself: the discernible expansion and democratization of the core institutions of social freedom attests to the fact of modernity's inevitable normative progress; it shows us that, as Honneth puts it: 'prevailing values are normatively superior to historically antecedent social ideals or "ultimate values"' (Honneth 2014a: 5). Belief in the inexorability of progress is, according to Honneth, 'an inevitable element of modernity's self-understanding', the result of a 'centuries long learning process'. Additionally, reflecting the immanent connection between unmasking critique and existing social values, 'historical-teleological thinking' must necessarily also be an integral element of Honneth's own method (2014a: 4, 18). Honneth is not unaware of possible pitfalls in this approach, most notably that the fact of modernity's progress is no reason to complacently endorse the current order. Rather, any existing social order is only ever an imperfect concrete embodiment of the general values and ideals latently expressed in its institutions and practices. To uncover this latent emancipatory potential, reconstructive critique must necessarily be selective in focus. Only some institutions and practices have the capacity to reveal the teleological unravelling of reason as progress, as he explains: 'In following the thread of the progressive realization of the original institutional promise of freedom, the historical material must be "gently" stylized so as to make this progressive development clear' (Honneth 2011: 221). Other institutions and practices, because of their regressive or dysfunctional nature, cannot shed light on the immanent logic of progress; Where the historical material 'persistently refuses to be teased into such a line' then the reconstructive endeavour must be 'broken off' (p. 221). In sum, it is the task of critique to reconstruct the 'moral surplus' imperfectly embodied in the institutions and practices of the life-world in order to use it as the normative perspective from which to measure the shortcomings of the existing social order and to press for emancipatory change.

These are, in brief, the basic steps that Honneth takes to recalibrate his social theory, ostensibly augmenting its receptivity to socio-historical variation, reducing its reliance on an ahistorical psychology of recognition but nonetheless avoiding contextualist continency. In the light of these aims, how successful is Honneth's substitution of an ontology of recognition with a teleology of progress as the normative core of critique? Despite continuing references to the 'invariant dependence' of human beings on the experience of recognition, to what extent does it enable him to engage in unmasking social critique that is alert to changing configurations of power and experience? By attaching it to a thin idea of progress rather than the substantive good of self-realization, does the recognition paradigm acquire greater analytical and normative scope vis-à-vis an account of social justice? Most importantly from the perspective of this book's concern with gender oppression, to what extent does Honneth's intensified stress on the historicity of recognition relations, especially in the sphere of love and family life, open up grounds for a renewed engagement with feminist critical theory? In what follows I cast doubt on the success of Honneth's move from ontology to teleology, viz. the practical emancipatory aims of critique, and this is because of the distorting effects that the narrative of inevitable moral progress has on a critical theory of oppression. At the heart of the problem is the declared selective nature of Honneth's reconstructive method and the questions that this raises with regard to those social phenomena deemed to be worthy of normative reconstruction and those that he disregards. Such interpretative issues about the scope and focus of societal analysis are not of course limited to Honneth's work alone but are inherent to the reconstructive method that typifies Frankfurt School critique. Given the situated nature of critique, such interpretative questions can never be entirely avoided either, but they can be partially pre-empted by rendering theory as open as possible to its social context and testing and retesting the relevance of ideas with reference to empirical reality. However, the type of paradigm-led theorizing encapsulated in recognition monism undercuts precisely the abductive and reflexive approach that might render critique receptive to context, and this ultimately has problematic implications for Honneth's social theory and, especially, his account of gender subordination. The priority given to interpreting society in terms of an immanent progressive rationality leads Honneth to underplay negative tendencies and contradictions by depicting them as historical residues that will wither away. This normative skewing is particularly evident in the story he tells of the development of gender relations within family life as a steady process of democratization driven by the gradual unfurling of dynamics of reciprocal empowerment and authorization. The idea of ethical mutuality underestimates the gendered asymmetries of power that persist within the family and the barriers posed by them to women's autonomous self-realization. Moreover, Honneth's idealized and sociologically undifferentiated account of the family ignores marked discrepancies in the life chances of its members according to subtending inequalities of gender, race, and class. By focussing on internal ethical dynamics in isolation from wider social forces, Honneth also disregards the pivotal role the family plays in the wider systemic cycle that routinely reproduces gendered vulnerabilities and oppression. Given such diagnostic shortcomings, it is not surprising to find that normative proposals couched in the terms of enhanced recognition are indeterminate and tangential to entrenched gender inequalities within and beyond the family.

Democratization of Love

As recognition recedes in significance as the normative driver of Honneth's thought, the value of autonomy or individual freedom comes to assume more prominence. In *Freedom's Right*, Honneth argues that freedom has been the preeminent concern animating most democratic social movements from the nineteenth century onwards. As the single metavalue under which other values and goods can be subsumed, the idea of freedom has had the greatest impact on the development of the theory and practice of modern democracy: 'our individual self-determination and our insistence that a social order be "just" are joined by an indissoluble bond, because our desire for justice is merely an expression of our subjective capacity for justification... individual self-determination... is not just some contingent human quality, but the essence of our practical-normative activity' (2014a: 17). Such is its normative centrality that the overarching developmental trajectory of modernity can be interpreted, in Hegelian fashion, as the gradual although not unfaltering, realization of the ideal in ever expanded form within social institutions. Freedom is the 'directional index' of moral progress in modern democracies, it is the main criterion by which to evaluate the emancipatory potential of any particular regime of recognition: 'every new evaluative quality whose confirmation through recognition increases a human subject's capacity for autonomy must be viewed as a progressive step in the historical process of cultural transformation' (2002: 510–11).

But though freedom has been the supreme galvanizing ideal of democratic thought and practice, in Honneth's view, it has been conceptualized historically, in a one-sided and incomplete manner, as a primarily negative and individualistic category. Their immediate intuitive appeal notwithstanding, negative theories of freedom have a number of well-known limitations, many of which boil down to the disproportionate emphasis placed on the absence of obvious external constraints, and corresponding neglect of less visible or internal types of constraint that may hinder self-knowledge and, hence, rational self-determination. For Honneth, reflexive or positive theories of freedom (e.g., Rousseau) represent an improvement on thin negative conceptions by offering thicker accounts of rational self-understanding and, hence, of what it means for an individual to be truly autonomous. But these positive conceptions are also limited because their primarily self-referential nature passes too swiftly over the intersubjective and material conditions—i.e., the relations of social freedom—that Honneth regards as necessary for individual autonomy to be fully instantiated. If conditions of social freedom are taken into account at all by reflexive conceptions, they are usually conceptualized, in weakly residual fashion, as the backdrop to an already established individual freedom rather than being conceived as prior to and constitutive of individual freedom itself. Drawing on both Hegel and Parsons, Honneth argues that social freedom is constitutive of individual freedom because subjects cannot experience themselves as truly free in the first place unless the objective conditions for the implementation of their autonomous aims already exist in external reality: 'our dealings with others, our social interaction, necessarily precedes the act of detachment captured in relations of negative or reflexive freedom' (2014a: 60). These objective conditions are understood by Honneth as a network of interpersonal and institutional relations of recognition; as he puts it: 'mutual recognition...refers to the reciprocal experience of seeing ourselves confirmed in the desires and aims of the other, because the other's existence represents a condition for fulfilling our own desires and aims. Once both subjects recognize...their own aims in the other, merely reflexive becomes intersubjective freedom' (2014a: 44–5). These variously institutionalized forms of social recognition provide the grounds, space and ultimate telos of self-realization. When individuals feel that their intentions and purposes are fully supported and appreciated in the social order then they will be more likely to pursue life courses and ends that are compatible with democratic virtues. They will align their aims and projects with those of other social actors and, crucially, willingly assume the obligations and duties required of them by their social roles instead of experiencing these as externally imposed and therefore unwanted burdens. In other words, autonomy is a social, relational, and intersubjective achievement.[2]

An advantage of conceptualizing autonomy as social freedom is that it yields an enlarged understanding of justice. The tendency of political philosophers to define freedom primarily as the moral and legal autonomy of the individual has obscured adequate appreciation of the extent to which it is preceded and sustained by the institutions of social freedom. In Honneth's view, once the foundational importance of this socio-institutional substrate is recognized, it shifts the centre of an account of justice from a distributive emphasis on the equitable allocation of basic individual rights and freedoms to a relational emphasis on guaranteeing that all members of society have the opportunity to participate fully in foundational regimes of recognition. In other words, the focus for justice is no longer solely on the principles and procedures of distribution but encompasses prior issues of 'the structure and quality of social relations of recognition' (Anderson and Honneth 2005: 144). Accordingly, in the social-theoretical section of *Freedom's Right*, Honneth concentrates on reconstructing these constitutive but overlooked practices of mutual recognition and complementary role obligation in the three core spheres of social praxis: personal relations, market interactions, and political life. Each sphere is structured around an implicit core ethical dynamic of 'reciprocal empowerment and authorisation' which is realized in its distinctive practice, set of norms, and personality type (Honneth 2014b: 819). In following a 'socially practised morality', any individual may appeal to the practice's governing norms, as part of a wider process of deliberation, to ensure a fairer and more reciprocal distribution of tasks and duties. This deliberative ethical practice brings about an ever-improving alignment of the freedom of individuals with willingness to assume the obligations and duties required of them in their social roles. As Honneth has it, it gradually eliminates '[the] gulf separating duty and inclination ... reason and sensibility' (2014b: 821). When individuals feel that their intentions and purposes are fully supported and appreciated in the social order, the more likely it is that they will be able to develop their personalities and aims in harmony with those of other actors, and experience their social duties as expressive of their inclinations and sensibilities, rather than as imposed, self-negating burdens. Honneth's fear is that, under the conditions of intense materialist individualism that characterize contemporary life, these prepolitical relations of social freedom are being steadily eroded. His hope is that a selective normative reconstruction of these neglected reserves of ethical praxis will remind us anew of their central significance in sustaining individual freedom and, consequently, force us to think harder about how to shore up these 'load-bearing' institutions against the atomizing pathologies and mis-developments set in train by neoliberal capitalism.

---

[2] There are interesting parallels here between Honneth's idea of social freedom and feminist work on relational autonomy. E.g. Mackenzie and Stoljar (2000). See also McNay 2016.

In keeping with his Hegelianism, Honneth regards intimate and familial relations of care and duty as the fullest expression of this ethical dynamic of 'reciprocal self-subjection', as the 'epitome of democratic virtues' and, consequently, as the primary grounds of social freedom (2014a: 175). The atomizing effects of neoliberal late-modernity notwithstanding, he offers a generally optimistic account of the evolution of familial and intimate relations in the postwar period as the 'democratization of love' characterized as the faltering but ultimately steady uncovering of the ethical mutuality that lies at their core. In the last fifty years of so, intimate relations have become institutionally decoupled from marriage and have attained an independent legitimacy. Same-sex relationships are the litmus test of this moral progress in so far as they are acquiring ever greater social acceptance culminating, in many countries, in the legal recognition of gay marriage. At the same time, the internal structure of the heterosexual family unit has undergone a corresponding liberalization, moving from a rigid nuclear model to embrace complicated and extended patterns of intimacy captured under the term 'patchwork' families. This diversification of the family structure has been accompanied by a dismantling of its traditional organization around fixed and complementary gender roles, giving way to more fluid notions of partnership and shared responsibility and this, in turn, has brought about an attenuation or 'levelling' of the gendered division of labour (2014a: 161). Fathers are less likely to be remote authority figures and more likely to play a greater part in their offsprings' upbringing, cooperating even after divorce. Conversely, the idea of the good mother is no longer limited to those women who stay at home, but now includes the 'career mother' (2014a: 159). Conventional patterns of parenting have also shifted from a basic rationale of instilling order and obedience to one of negotiation between parents and children. An interesting new dimension of modern family life is that, with increased life expectancy, there has been a 'temporal expansion of reciprocity' where older people have greater and prolonged involvement in the lives of their children and grandchildren, opening up new dimensions of care.

The democratization of the modern family has not been without setbacks and conflict, for example, the liberalization of its internal structure has been accompanied by rising divorce rates. Honneth also recognizes that, given power inequalities between its various members, intimate bonds are too fragile on their own to support justice within the family. To prevent interpersonal domination, family relations need to be securely nested within a wider protective legal framework of equal rights (Honneth 2007: 144–62; Young 2007: 203). Moreover, bonds of mutuality are also under threat from wider social mis-developments and pathological tendencies towards over-individuation. According to Honneth, many contemporary cultural forms (film, literature, and so on) attest to a growing purposelessness or emotional anomie where individuals find it increasingly difficult to form lasting attachments and emotional ties. Yet, despite the threats posed by anomic social tendencies, Honneth concludes that overall trends towards the democratization of family life and intimacy are historically inevitable; as he puts it: 'almost all empirical data indicates that this new ideal is inevitable, because the non-coercive power to assert a normative surplus exercises a permanent pressure that will sooner or later destroy any remains of traditional practices' (2014a: 164). Progress is inevitable because as the norms of familial intimacy are contested and revised over time there is a 'socialising feedback effect' which correspondingly alters the desires and expectations of participants and leads to the dropping away of 'ethically faded or withered norms' (2002: 823). This commitment to the idea of the inevitability of progress underpins the quasi-functionalist language of successful problem-solving that peppers *Freedom's Right*. When discussing gay marriage Honneth says: 'in the long term, the sources of the reasons used to justify excluding homosexual couples from the legal privileges of officially sanctioned marriage will dry up...' (2014a: 150). On the democratization of the family structure and the move away from fixed gender roles, he writes: 'this structural transformation has not been without complications and the usual delays which means that for a certain time we will have to expect the constant revival of the old role fixations. On the other hand, almost all empirical data indicates that this new ideal is inevitable... [it] will sooner or later destroy any remains of traditional practices' (2014a: 164. My parenthesis). Elsewhere: 'the modern family is currently on a path of normative development that allows it to train and practice democratic and cooperative forms of interaction better than ever before in its brief history' (2014: 174).

Purification of the Family

Honneth's sanguine depiction of evolving family life as a process of ethical purification and democratization is undoubtedly appealing. It goes some way in overcoming a gap in the existing literature on justice which disregards the pivotal normative role played by the family in sustaining wider social freedoms. The inculcation of dispositions to responsibility, role obligation, tolerance, and other essential citizen virtues is a process that should not be taken for granted and, therefore, in Honneth's view, any theory of justice should think seriously about how to maintain the right material circumstances in which the family may flourish. In this respect, there is a productive cross-over between Honneth's thought on this matter and the work of feminist ethicists of care, who have long argued that the family and its internal emotional bonds are not merely adjuncts to a theory of justice but rather should be one of its central features. Care, or rather its deficit, is one of the central problems facing both traditional and posttraditional societies. When it is unlinked from a romanticized maternal essentialism, and instead connected to issues of human finitude, vulnerability, and dependency, care is reconceived as a fundamental public good that should be distributed equitably around society. As thinkers such as Joan Tronto (2012), Diemut Bubeck (1995), and Eva Kittay (1999)have argued, an ethics of care perspective leads directly into issues of justice, such as how to avoid the exploitation of women as carers, how to address inequalities in meeting people's need for care, and how to promote an equal distribution of the burden of caring.

But while Honneth's thought contributes to plugging a gap in the literature on justice and care, the rosy depiction of changes within the family that this entails is disputable and lacks secure sociological foundations. As we know, his sociological reconstruction of the family is not intended to be descriptively exhaustive, but is rather necessarily selective in keeping with his normative aim of recovering the latent surplus validity immanent within its internal relations. Indeed, Honneth declares that he is acutely aware of the many inequalities that permeate family life, and hence his sanguine account represents nothing more than a 'gentle stylization' that is fully justified by his reconstructive normative aims. When seen from a feminist perspective on gender inequality, however, this 'gentle' stylization may in fact be suspected of having a stronger idealizing bias in so far as insufficient consideration is given to certain negative features that may be equally as defining of the way in which the family has developed over the last few decades. Honneth, as we recall, would justify the exclusion of such negative phenomena on the grounds of their ethical nonrepresentativeness, that they are residues of traditional practices that 'persistently refuse to be teased' into the narrative arc of progress. But from a feminist perspective, exclusion on such grounds is unwarranted because it results in a serious misdiagnosis of power and the lived realities of family life. Arguably, certain negative dynamics—to do with gendered asymmetries of power—are not incidental to core familial dynamics but are as fundamental as the progressive ones that Honneth's logic of ethical purification emphasizes. Certainly, Honneth doesn't entirely ignore these negative features, but his teleology of progress implies that, as remainders of traditional gender arrangements, they will fade away; they are anomalous deviations from the generally progressive developmental path followed by modern democracies. Given the persistent nature of gender inequalities in contemporary society and the role that the family plays in their reproduction, it would be reasonable to infer that these negative tendencies are not mere residues, but as fundamental to its internal dynamics as the progressive ones that Honneth focusses on. In short, the teleological narrative of the gradual purification of reason and withering of dysfunctional social characteristics has sanitizing and distorting effects on the critique of power.

Feminists might question, for example, the extent to which familial relations do in fact permit the progressive realization of women's autonomy, given that they are still so strongly anchored in heteronormative psycho-sexual dynamics and gendered division of labour, neither of which display many signs of diminishing. By depicting the family's essence as ethical mutuality, Honneth smooths away the contradictory lived reality it has for many women. Against the backdrop of enduring gender inequality, the 'reciprocal self-subjection' and 'deliberative autonomy' that supposedly animates family life is perhaps more accurately understood as hierarchical, nonreciprocal relations between men and women. If Honneth is to successfully avoid a charge of mystification, he needs to pay more attention, inter alia, to the fundamental ways in which intimate sex-affective dynamics underpin wider societal processes of gender socialization that maintain the 'soft domination' of male privilege (e.g., Friedman 2005). In an era when patriarchy is no longer functionally necessary for social reproduction, it is the internalization of a heteronormative 'sex/affective system' that is a key factor in sustaining male domination, and what Butler terms the 'passionate attachments' of subjects to their own gendered subordination. The endemic nature of domestic violence, for instance, can only really be properly understood in the context of a ubiquitous societal valorization of masculinity. There is a connection, albeit not a direct causal one, between male violence, on the one side and widespread social norms of male entitlement, aggression, and independence and female passivity, dependence, and duty to care on the other: 'the social constructions of romantic love, idealized masculinity, and women's social responsibility for men's emotional lives provide the discursive context for batterers' anger and frustration, remorse, appeals to sympathy, and shifting of blame' (Hirschmann 2002: 128). Moreover, violence and domestic abuse can hardly be classified as symptoms of fading, traditional gendered behaviours since, as ONS (Office for National Statistics) figures for the UK show, levels of both have risen steadily over the last few years and increased quite dramatically during the pandemic lockdowns.[3]

On Honneth's own account, the idea of justice as social rather than individual freedom necessarily shifts attention to the basic material conditions necessary to permit individuals to participate equally in social life. In principle, justice as social freedom requires full consideration of 'the ways in which a society's recognitional infrastructure can leave the autonomy of individuals unacceptably vulnerable' (Anderson and Honneth 2005: 142). But, in practice, he gives little consideration of the way extant relations of recognition are skewed by power such that, even within intimate relations, the autonomy and freedom of some groups is a more fragile and fraught affair than it is for others. Inquiry into the causes of vulnerabilities directly and indirectly associated with heteronormatively structured intimacy is truncated by the over-emphatic investment in a progressive account of modernity. Feminist critiques of intimacy and family life are not new, but bear rehearsing once again mainly to contest Honneth's skewed narrative of progress where negative features in the family are viewed as dysfunctions that will inevitably drop away with the gradual purification of socially instantiated ethical

---

[3] https://www.ons.gov.uk/peoplepopulationandcommunity/crimeandjustice/articles/domesticabuse duringthecoronaviruscovid19pandemicenglandandwales/november2020

practice. Indeed, an alternative feminist account of the development of the modern family might replace the story of ethical progress and democratization, for instance, with one of the succession of different eras of patriarchy: from the direct domination of paternal and then fraternal/husband forms to the indirect oppression of public patriarchy that typifies contemporary modernity (Ferguson 1997: 50–7).

This alternative feminist view of the family as a 'saturated site' of power relations might cast doubt on the sanitized depiction of the sex-affective triangle of father–mother–child as an ethical bond of care where duty and obligation are aligned with autonomous self- realization (Collins 2019: 235). Arguably, there is no such alignment, actual or potential, for the woman in this triad because the bonds that Honneth hopefully describes as 'reciprocal self-subjection' are in fact better understood as asymmetrical and nonreciprocal, creating a far more ambivalent and constraining emotional and practical reality. Compared to the father, a structural contradiction marks the mother's sex-affective interests in the family; the greater investment she is conventionally expected to make in emotional bonds with the child, while undoubtedly rewarding, also puts her in a self-sacrificing role with regard to other aspects of her self-realization. Moreover, the feminized nature of nurturing means that she is expected to attend to her husband's emotional needs in addition to those of the child. Consequently, the mother usually carries the burden of responsibility for the emotional welfare of the family as a whole, and places herself in the self-abnegating position of 'adjudicating actual and potential conflicts in the sex/affective family triangle' (Ferguson 1997: 47). Differently put, the alignment that Honneth posits between obligation and self-realization does not exist—and has historically has never done so—for the woman in the family. Rather, she is confronted with a dilemma where the more she conforms to feminized norms of care, the more likely it is that she narrows down possibilities for autonomous self-fulfilment. Contra Honneth's progressive narrative of ethical purification, these entrenched sexual and affective dynamics are not simply outmoded symbolic dysfunctions that will gradually wither away but are deep-rooted expressions of the 'compulsory' heteronormativity that ineluctably shapes all areas of social life.

This is not to deny that intimate relations may well exemplify important values of love, care, and sacrifice but rather to claim that these are at one and the same time inextricably bound up with gendered asymmetries of power that may well conflict with and undermine any putative ethical potential. Honneth's underestimation of negative tendencies endemic in the family as a social institution is symptomatic of a deeper problem with his method of normative reconstruction, namely that its idealizing tendencies place in jeopardy the very feature that, in his view, renders normative reconstruction a more robust way of theorizing about justice than moral constructivism, namely its descriptive proximity to social existence. Gendered power asymmetries seem to be historically hardwired into familial dynamics, and not, as Honneth's developmental model implies, alien, external forces that intrude upon an essential ethical mutuality but will eventually fade away. Honneth has criticized Habermas's colonization of the life-world thesis for precisely this problem of externalizing power with respect to the family and failing to recognize its immanent contradictions and hierarchies. Yet ironically, his own thesis of the inevitability of progress replicates this error and finishes in a similar romanticization of family life (Hartmann and Honneth 2006). Power doesn't just move from the outside inwards, but is inextricably intertwined in family dynamics, as evident for example, in negotiations over domestic finance, domestic violence, abuse, etc. As Nancy Fraser puts it: 'families...are sites of egocentric, strategic and instrumental calculation as well as sites of usually exploitative exchange of services, labour, cash, and sex—and, frequently, sites of coercion and violence' (Fraser 1989: 120). On this view, the family is inherently a patriarchal unit, although it may have changed its form over time. Indeed, arguably more than any other type of domination, masculine privilege is secured not through explicit discrimination and exclusion but through the naturalizing work of socialization within the family (Friedman 2005: 152; also Bourdieu 2001). In this light, there is not much evidence of the long-term democratizing tendencies that Honneth identifies where gender hierarchies and norms in the family structure will eventually dry up to reveal an egalitarian core of cooperative interaction.

Families and Gender Inequality

The idea of progress does not just over-ethicize dynamics within the family, but also separates the analysis of the family, as institution, from the wider social context. An effect of the analytical separation of the social spheres, inherited from Hegel, is to obscure the ways in which relations in the family are partly shaped by subtending structural inequalities. Were he to take this wider context into account, Honneth might find it more difficult than he does to treat the family as an undifferentiated ideal type and overlook the complex and divergent social realities that are created by cross-cutting forces of class, race, and gender. A picture of the family that was more sociologically differentiated would also complicate his univocal narrative of progress and democratization. Put bluntly, the relatively unmodified Hegelian sociology on which Honneth's social critique leans is outdated, and therefore an inadequate template through to which explain the realities of contemporary gender subordination within and beyond the family.

If, for example, women's position in the family is partly defined by gendered patterns of employment and distribution of material resources, then Honneth's assertion that the domestic gender division of labour is slowly being levelled out by an unstoppable democratizing tendency seems questionable. Honneth supports this claim about democratization by pointing to the increasing number of women entering the workforce which he argues necessitates a rebalancing of the burdens of care work on more egalitarian terms. There is much sociological evidence to show, however, that, while larger numbers of women than ever before have taken on work outside the home, their household duties have altered little. Several phrases have been coined to describe this double duty—the 'double day', 'second shift', or 'double burden' and there is a considerable sociological literature that attests to its persistence (Beaujot and Lieu 2005; Berk 1985; Hochschild 1989). There is certainly some evidence to support Honneth's claim that women and men, in certain types of households, are sharing tasks more equitably than before especially when both work outside of the home and have young children (Baxter, Hewitt, and Western 2005). However, across all families (in Western Europe and North America), women still carry out most of the unpaid work including housework, household management, child-care, and care of the elderly and other dependents, putting in anywhere between five to thirteen hours per week on these activities (Lee and Waite 2005). It is also worth noting that Honneth's depiction of women's greater presence in the workforce in the figure of the 'career mother' is somewhat misleading, since most women are employed not in the professions but in low-esteemed, part-time occupations, receiving on average 10 per cent less than their male counterparts for the same jobs. From the other side of the gender divide, Honneth also claims that fathers have greater involvement with their children's upbringing than they have done historically, especially post-divorce. Again, there is some evidence for this, but statistics show that the vast majority of single-parent families (86 per cent in the UK) are headed by women, suggesting that, while men retain some kind of contact with their children, it is still far from the levels that might be meaningfully considered as an even division of care work.[4] Furthermore, the increase in the number of single-parent families is connected to rising rates of poverty. From 1959 to 2009 the percentage of families headed by a single parent has tripled from 11 per cent to 33 per cent and these families are economically vulnerable because they only have one wage earner. Six out of ten poor adults are women and in 2019, 60% of poor children in the US lived in families headed by women.[5] In other words, gender inequality in the family is further reinforced by what sociologists identify as tendencies towards the feminization of poverty. Gender poverty levels deepen when the impact of race is taken into account. It is not just that there is little evidence for a thoroughgoing restructuring of gender roles in the family on more egalitarian lines but there are also indicators that other dimensions of gender subordination are intensifying. So

---

[4] Office for National Statistics 'Families and Households in the UK: 2019'.
[5] National Women's Law Center (2020) 'National Snapshot: Poverty Among Women and Families, 2020' https://nwlc.org/wp-content/uploads/2020/12/PovertySnapshot2020.pdf. Figures are similar in the UK. See Child Poverty Action Group (2021) 'Child Poverty Facts and Figures' https://cpag.org.uk/child-poverty/child-poverty-facts-and-figures.

for instance, studies in the UK suggest that levels of domestic violence against women and children in the family were on the increase, again accelerated by the pandemic.[6] Indeed, many experts fear that the actual rate of domestic violence is in fact far higher than official figures because of the widely acknowledged problem of underreporting where women only go to the police and other authorities after enduring, on average, thirty-five repeated assaults.[7]

Entrenched gender inequalities such as these are often compounded by the class inequalities that also have an impact on the family. Honneth is not oblivious to issues of class, discussing them elsewhere in his work—indeed he has famously criticized Habermas for sidelining the issue—but he does not bring this discussion to bear on his account of the family which is concentrated on generic internal dynamics of mutuality and care. To be sure, Honneth acknowledges that caring, solidaristic familial bonds are relatively fragile and need to be protected from the fragmenting forces of the commodified individualism that is rampant in neoliberal societies—a phenomenon he has described as organized self-realization. As he put it: 'Partly as a result of new forms of employment, which blur the lines between work and free time, and partly due to shifts in our self-understanding that place greater cultural value on mobility, members of society are increasingly unwilling to follow the normative rules that provide personal relationships with the required stability in the first place' (2014a: 152). This idea of anomic over-individuation is, however, only a partial diagnosis of possible threats to the cohesion of the family, because another consequence of the atomizing, marketized forces unleashed by neoliberalism is that they deepen existing economic inequalities and give rise to new types of social vulnerability. There is a mass of data to suggest that, with the dismantling of the welfare state, the implementation of 'flexible' work patterns, and the marketization of social relations, that inequalities of wealth are deepening in a way that hasn't been seen before in the postwar era of welfare. In the UK, for instance, overall levels of poverty have remained unchanged at 22 per cent or one in five of the adult population for the last fifteen years. Even before the catastrophic effects of the pandemic, there were, according to the Joseph Rowntree Trust (2021), rising levels of child and in-work poverty, increasing occurrences of destitution (50 per cent increase since 2007) and falling levels of income especially among the lowest paid sectors of the workforce. Moreover, the changing nature of work means that, in the unregulated conditions of the gig economy, it no longer provides a guarantee against poverty—hence, the rise in a new class of 'near poor' families. Child poverty is a good indicator of general levels of family poverty, and it is estimated by the Child Poverty Action Group (2021) that

---

[6] 'Everyone's Business: Improving the Police Response to Domestic Abuse'. HMIC 2014. See also *Violence Against Women: An EU-wide Survey*. 2014. ONS: 'Domestic Abuse Overview in England and Wales: November 2020'.

[7] Women's Aid 'Domestic Violence: A Hidden Crime' (2008).

currently 31 per cent of children (that is 4.3 million) in the UK live in poverty. 75% of children growing up in poverty in the UK live in families where at least one parent works. This growing social division (accentuated by the impact of Covid-19) can only be made worse with the general direction of much public policy, in the UK and Europe, towards the ever-increasing privatization of welfare.

There are two general points to be made in relation to deepening class inequality and rising levels of poverty. First, these intensifying inequalities complicate Honneth's progressive account of the development of modernity and, notably, of the steady democratization of the family. We might say instead that the reality is more fractured and polarized, that growing material inequality entails increasing divergences between the life chances of affluent and poorer families, and that the latter are often under great internal stress in the struggle to stay afloat. In short, one might question how feasible it is for Honneth to deploy a single ideal type of familial dynamics, instead of a sociologically differentiated model that reckons more fully with the location of families within a social structure marked by growing economic inequality. Second, it is not just that family life might be more fractured and stressful than Honneth acknowledges, but also that growing social division seems to be accompanied by an overall decline in levels of social solidarity and a corresponding rise of what Habermas famously termed 'familial privatism'. Individual family members may well be internally bound to each other by ties of empathetic mutuality, but it does not follow that they feel analogous outward-directed empathy or solidarity with other families and citizens. Inward-looking self-advancement of the family unit may trump outward-looking sentiments of commonality, tolerance, and duty to others. In other words, families do not only generate in their members the virtuous dispositions necessary to sustain social freedom but may also be key in inculcating the competitive and privatist orientation that is necessary for capitalist reproduction and that undermines wider feelings of social solidarity. Indeed, recent moral panics around economic migration, refugees, and welfare dependency, along with the rise in Western democracies of reactionary populist politics, suggest the relative success in influencing public opinion of a conservative narrative that identifies the causes of economic stagnation with overly generous public expenditure on the poor and excessive state economic regulation. As Joseph Schwartz puts it 'our society's inability to comprehend the emotional and financial stress that poor families confront in raising children indicates how weak the bonds of solidarity are' (Schwartz 2009: 41). It is naïve, at best for Honneth to depict the family as the primary breeding ground for solidaristic relations of social freedom while ignoring the role it also plays in sustaining intolerance and lack of care for external others, a phenomenon described by Norman Geras as the contract of mutual indifference (Geras 1999).

Drawing attention to the asymmetrical power relations within and between families in this way does not, on the face of it, deliver a fatal blow to Honneth's claims about the family as a site of social freedom. Once again Honneth could defend himself by adducing the avowedly selective nature of reconstructive normative critique; his depiction of the family must necessarily be stylized and omit certain regressive features to better focus attention on its latent but unrealized ethical content. The problem is, however, that if this reconstruction is idealized to the degree that it is descriptively far removed from the actuality of contemporary family life, then it risks losing the 'objective foothold in pre-theoretical practice' that Honneth regards as a distinguishing feature of critical theory. What sets critical theory apart from conventional forms of political thinking is precisely the quality of intra-mundane transcendence that 'its innermost core is dependent upon a quasi-sociological specification of an emancipatory interest in social reality itself' (Honneth 2007: 65). If, however, the reconstructed institution is normatively sanitized to the point that its connection to social reality is questionable, Honneth comes close to a position that he explicitly wants to avoid, namely, devising ethical principles that have a tenuous relevance to actual social practice. Were he to proffer a more complicated, less rosy picture of the development of the family in modernity along the lines sketched out above, then this may also imply that the project of securing social freedom might well be a more fraught, radical and, consequently, controversial process than Honneth's quasi-organic model of progress acknowledges. For instance, if we take seriously the idea that material deprivation presents a significant barrier to the realization of freedom in a growing number of poor and near-poor families, then this might imply extensive and drastic redistributive measures. Not only would this seem to require the boldness of vision and political will that currently seems to be lacking among political leaders in advanced democracies, but would also seem to necessitate a significant deviation from the neoliberal mentality of marketization that has dominated public policy-making, especially in the US and UK, unabated since the 1980s (McNay 2021). To garner legitimacy for such putative radical redistributive measures would also involve a proactive ideological engagement with public opinion to purge it of its current insular and regressive elements and engender instead a proactive commitment to inclusive public life and community. Similarly, the task of transforming the family from the principal domain in which the psycho-sexual investments that shore up soft male domination are inculcated to being a domain of social freedom would seem to require a restructuring of interpersonal gender relations far more extensive than anything Honneth's notion of ethical progress seems to allow.

Care and Social Justice

It would be possible, in principle, for Honneth to offset some of the shortcomings in his democratization narrative by reckoning more fully with the enduring asymmetries that shape family life and intimacy. Even so, efforts to correct the skewed emphasis on 'normative promise' with closer consideration of gendered power dynamics would, for some feminist critics, still be insufficient. On their view, the recognition paradigm, as a whole, is conceptually inappropriate because of its failure to grasp the functional centrality of gender subordination to the reproduction of capitalist social relations (e.g., Fraser 2014a). What the recognition-theoretic model understands primarily as a matter of unbalanced interpersonal relations in the private domestic sphere is, in fact, more adequately understood as impersonal socio-structural cycles that subordinate all women regardless of their personal circumstances. The androcentric tendency to conceive of gender as interpersonal relations in the private/domestic sphere, thereby obscuring its wider significance as a fundamental organizing principle of societal practice, has been widely noted in feminist criticisms of the public/private distinction. For all that Honneth would agree with these criticisms, there is a sense in which his reliance on an anachronistic Hegelian social theory has similarly obfuscating effects with regard to diagnosing the complexities of gender oppression. Explanations of gender narrowly focussed on the family unit are descriptively inadequate to grasp the 'enclosing structure of forces and barriers' that are characteristic of intersectional oppressions (Frye 1983b: 11).

Accordingly, what Honneth presents as generalized patterns of misrecognition and lack of sensitivity to women's needs in the sphere of intimacy is arguably better understood in socio-structural terms as systemically generated oppression. While psychological dynamics are certainly a factor in anchoring subordinating practices at an interpersonal level, most feminists agree that the persistence of gender inequalities in advanced democracies is, to a great extent, also the work of interlocking, impersonal systemic tendencies (e.g., Cudd 2006; Young 1990: ch. 2). The gendered division of labour, revolving around women's traditional responsibility for child-care, helps shape labour markets that disadvantage women resulting in unequal power in the marketplace which, in turn reinforces and exacerbates unequal power in the family. Not only does vulnerability in marriage increase over time as the gap between spouses' earnings widen, but it is also often dramatically worsened by divorce and separation which invariably brings a drop in women's living standards. The playing out of neoliberal capitalist tendencies on a global scale have only made systemic cycles of gender vulnerability more complex and intractable (e.g., Jaggar 2014). As Iris Marion Young puts it: 'all women, even unmarried women and even women who are not mothers, are made vulnerable to domination, exploitation, and deprivation by these structural processes, which pivot around the gendered division of labour in the family' (Young 2009: 225). By focussing primarily on the family's internal ethical bonds in isolation from other social structures, Honneth effectively renders these systematic structural dimensions of oppression invisible. For instance, his reconstruction of the deliberative ethical core of family life where individuals appeal to latent norms of mutual respect and care to ensure a reciprocal distribution of tasks and duties seems orthogonal to what practically determines the domestic division of labour, namely, the more general economic disadvantage of women. Given the entrenched nature of women's economic disadvantage, it seems that their autonomy in and beyond the family may be more effectively brought about not by enhancing ethical dynamics of mutuality and care but through measures that focus on redistributing material resources and breaking the systemic cycle of vulnerability. After all, modern societies frequently find ways of according a certain kind of social 'esteem' to wives and mothers but all too often, as Iris Marion Young remarks, 'feminists find these gestures hollow and demeaning, because the achievement principle continues to define what counts as a "real" contribution' (2007: 210). In the light of enduring material inequalities, it is arguably not more 'recognition' that women need—whatever that may mean—but greater economic independence and other forms of practical empowerment achieved through measures such as increasing wages, provision of affordable child-care, enhanced welfare support for single parent families and carers, extending educational and training opportunities, greater state intervention into private marital relations to provide security for victims of violence and abuse, and so on. Such corrective measures might of course have the indirect effect of enhancing ethical mutuality in the family, but their main focus has to be on breaking the structural cycle that generates gender vulnerability.

The diagnostic limitations with Honneth's personalist model of gender and power are most evident in his discussion of care as ethical mutuality. Whereas for Honneth, care and reproductive labour are matters to be dealt with in the frame of the family, for feminist critical theorists, such as Fraser, they need to be understood as the conditions of possibility of capitalist accumulation. Moreover, as structures of care are eroded and unbalanced by the fissiparous tendencies of global neoliberalism, they increasingly become pivotal sites of 'general crisis' and struggle (Fraser 2014b). The ramifications of the care deficit in Western societies extend beyond the gender division of labour in the domestic sphere to include structural inequalities of race and class as well as migration issues. The commercialization of care is something that Honneth does not address at all in his reconstruction of family dynamics and is a surprising omission given that it is a growing feature of contemporary family life (Hochschild 2000). Women's entry into the workforce, an increasing population of elderly persons, and the neoliberal privatization of types of social provision previously provided by the welfare state are among the factors that have led to this care deficit (e.g., Griffin-Cohen and Brodie 2007). It has been filled to a large extent by the migration of female workers from poorer countries that, while providing them with much-needed employment, also compounds certain patterns of gender and race inequality. Migrant labour is cheap, and this exerts a downward pressure on an area already characterized by low pay for its predominantly female workers. The privatized nature of many of these care solutions also creates further inequalities between rich care commanders and poor care providers and between those who can afford to pay for private care and those who are dependent on increasingly depleted state provision. Furthermore, the commodification of care is symptomatic of a wider process where market dynamics are penetrating ever deeper into intimate life, leading to what Hochschild has identified as a growing depersonalization of our intimate bonds (Hochschild 2012: 224). In sum, commercialized relations of care are creating new inequalities and systematic imbalances that traverse and exceed the ethical logic of recognition that Honneth uses to analyse dynamics within the family.

In terms of a corrective account of social justice, the complex nature of the care deficit and inequalities in its provision call for a range of multidimensional normative responses. Recognition monism is an inadequate basis from which to generate such responses given its sociological underdetermination and descriptive stylization. Diagnostic inadequacies are compounded by the elevated position Honneth accords to the metavalue of freedom as the governing moral dynamic of societal progress. Although he justifies this normative primacy on the grounds that freedom is a thin enough principle to encompass all other values, he in fact makes little attempt to think through what this imbrication might mean in a determinate sense, especially with regard to what other radical theorists would regard as the equally fundamental democratic principle of equality. Indeed, for leftist thinkers with a less pronounced Hegelian bias than Honneth, it may well seem more appropriate for an unmasking critique of oppression to be strongly anchored in the normative ideal of equality rather than freedom. As Alessandro Ferrara puts it, 'had "equality" been chosen, in lieu of freedom, a different narrative would have resulted (perhaps crude equality, reflexive equality and social equality), and the same if "justice" as such had been chosen' (Ferrara 2019: 638). Thus, despite Honneth's claim that every democratic community has a vital interest in creating the 'socio-economic relations under which all families can adopt the practices that are already institutionally available', his suggestions for a bolstering the grounds of social freedom are surprisingly vague.

If Honneth had attempted to conceive equality as the material conditions necessary for social freedom rather than as ethically nebulous ideas of reciprocity and mutuality, then arguably he might be able to devise a repertoire of normative responses more germane to overcoming inequalities of gender and care. For example, in contrast to the vague dynamics of mutual empowerment and support, feminists have thought in greater sociological detail about ways of enhancing the equitable distribution of the public good of care. They have concentrated on analysing the political economy of existing regimes of care and treated it not so much as an affective bond but as a cluster of diverse practices—'care work'—that is carried out largely by working-class and migrant women and that is undervalued, poorly paid, and maldistributed. Attentiveness to the particularity of gendered care dynamics has enabled them to generate a multiplicity of targeted normative proposals, such as, for example the redistribution of different elements of care work, provision of 'doulia rights', greater protection for migrant labour, not allowing market forces exclusively to adjust the pay of careworkers, and increased public spending on care facilities. Consider for example Nancy Fraser's (1997a) celebrated essay on reforming welfare so that it is organized around the nongendered notion of a universal care giver. Or, for example, the work of Lynch et al. (2009) on affective equality where they break down the frequently undifferentiated notion of care into its constituent elements to work out more precisely those aspects that can be delegated to others (to the state and through a reordered division of labour) in order to relieve the burden of unpaid care that falls mostly to women and compounds gender inequalities. The differentiation of care into its commodifiable and noncommodifiable elements (love work) speaks also to a broader understanding of care as not only a relation of nurturance but as also nonrelational reproductive labour (laundry, cooking, domestic labour). This fundamental, but often overlooked, aspect of care is obscured in the undifferentiated paradigm of interpersonal recognition and, as a result, Honneth is unable to discern the internal hierarchies of race and class that further distort the current gendered provision of care and that would inevitably need to be addressed in a reconstructive account of social justice (e.g., Tronto 2012: 7–10). A generous interpretation would say that Honneth's ethical model of familial relations does not necessarily preclude analysis of care in a materialist register and therefore could incorporate a more developed, intersectional understanding of reproductive labour and care economies. This may be so, in principle, but, in practice, it is hard to see how, given deep-seated problems of normative skewing and lack of determinacy, the ideas of recognition and progress could be given sufficient explanatory and normative purchase without abandoning altogether the monist, paradigm-led mode of theorizing to which Honneth seems wedded.

Progress and Agency

The problems arising from Honneth's over-ethicized account of care and gender are symptomatic of other difficulties with his underlying attempt to historicize recognition by attaching it to a narrative of progress. As we have seen, the idea of progress seems to be more compatible than naturalizing philosophical anthropology with an enhanced emphasis on the historical variability of recognition regimes. Be that as it may, it's historicizing effects are comparatively weak and result in an under-theorization of the contradictions, 'negative' tendencies, and asymmetries of power that characterize extant orders of recognition. This throws doubts on the appropriateness of the idea of progress as an instrument of normative reconstruction for unmasking critique. For, if its selective focus on surplus validity undermines the critique of power and leads to a questionable idealization of social life, this suggests that the narrative of irreversible progress should perhaps be tempered or pluralized in some way. By Honneth's own lights, unmasking critique is guided by suffering and other negative experiences, and, therefore, in order to realize this emancipatory aim, it might need to replace problematic teleological claims with evaluative analyses more closely indexed to particular social contexts and determinate instances of oppression. Honneth's view is, however, that the cost of relinquishing the narrative of progress is too great because it sacrifices the context-transcending perspective necessary for critical theory to have normative purchase. Indeed, in his view, it is not possible for normative critique to avoid the idea; even the most contextually attuned types of evaluative thought are implicitly motivated by the weak telos of progress: 'I see no appropriate tool to guide the direction of our emancipatory efforts and to equip us with the required confidence for those efforts, other than the attempt to find a line of progressive improvement in the past. This gives us the courage to continue our struggles, as it allows us to recognize that the struggles of the past have already borne fruit' (Honneth 2015: 222).

The difficulty here is not the idea of progress per se but the strong, zero-sum terms in which it is construed where, absent a teleological line of change, critique apparently finds itself unable to evaluate whether societal conditions have improved or not. In this sense, Honneth's idea of progress is intended as a 'post-metaphysical equivalent' to the Hegelian idea of the 'Logic of the concept' that in plainer terms denotes the determining force of ideas: 'that a certain class of the Spiritual [*Geistigen*]—namely, normative ideas—have the ability to shape and remodel social reality in accordance with their own content' (2015: 207). To offset the impression that he is simply reformulating Hegel's problematic idealism, Honneth maintains that normative ideas of progress and so forth only ever 'come to fruition' in social struggles. Once again, then, he is trying to square the circle by insisting on a normative core to critique which is both unchanging and ineluctably historical. Honneth's 'idealist consecration of social struggles' notwithstanding, it is hard to avoid the impression that real-world actors are little more than puppets of impersonal notions and forces, rather than themselves the concrete agents of change. With this idealist inversion of causality, politics itself disappears or, at least, is sublated onto the ethereal plane of reason; as Kempf observes: 'Honneth repeats Hegel's problematic deduction of political subjectivity from the intellectuality of the "idea", instead of empirically reconstructing the "idea" as resulting from the historical constitution of concrete and particular political subjectivities' (Kempf 2019: 264).

Honneth's version of progress is problematic, then, because, attached to a grandiose narrative of inevitability, it sanitizes and simplifies complex processes of historical change by attributing them to impersonal tendencies rather than concrete forces and agents. Fraught, uncertain, often violent dynamics of upheaval, resistance, and struggle are retroactively effaced by being subsumed under the unfurling logic of progress. Consider, for example, the depoliticizing effects of Honneth's presentation of gay marriage as an instance of an overarching, syncretic arc of the democratization of love. By being harnessed to this supervening rationale, decades of activism and political contention are obscured. For, while gay marriage undoubtedly represents significant progress for many activists, for others, it has a more questionable significance in so far as it is viewed as a normalizing form of recognition that tolerates gays as long as they conform to heterosexual norms (Warner 1999). Indeed, in general, Foucauldian issues of normalization are not really dealt with satisfactorily from within 'historical-teleological thinking' because the tendency to emphasize the progressive nature of achieved forms of recognition consequently underplays their potential disciplinary entailments. The ambivalence of what Foucault identified as the neoliberal government of individualization, namely, that the creation of new autonomies, qua recognition, is inevitably bound up with the emergence of new forms of dependency and subordination, is lost in Honneth's one-sided emphasis on the positive side only of this dialectic. Even though Honneth rightly stresses that we should not unproblematically endorse the existing social order, this is undermined by the conventionalist implications of the narrative of progress which overplay the significance of the recognition battles that have been won and underplay those that not only have still to be fought but also may well be fought in dramatically different, and as yet unknown, terms. In other words, the syncretic notion of social progress tacitly skews an account of emancipatory change towards known, pre-established routes, for example, freedom as the endless extension of recognition rights. But what Honneth does not reckon with sufficiently is the possibility that future struggles for emancipation may radically challenge established modes of recognition and political practice and recognition and take forms more disruptive, polemical, and violent than can currently be imagined.[8]

Differently put, submerged within the idealizing narrative of progress are unanswered questions about the perspective from which judgements about whether social conditions can be said to have normatively improved or not are made. From whose perspective is a specific historical event, struggle, or institutional practice deemed to represent progress? Which view prevails if what is taken as an uncontroversial indicator of social progress by some is in fact contested by others? After all, under conditions of social struggle, it is not uncommon to find that phenomena taken as indisputable evidence of progress from, say, the perspective of dominant groups vested in the status quo may seem questionable from

---

[8] Moreover, as thinkers such as Dipesh Chakrabarty (2000) and Amy Allen (2016) point out, when it is tied so closely to the development of modernity, the idea of the inevitability of progress has troubling colonial implications in so far as it seems to imply a view of the nonWest as immature and normatively underdeveloped.

the perspective of subordinate groups distant from centres of power and authority. These interpretative matters will be considered in more detail in Chapter 6, but here it suffices to note that they are foreclosed by Honneth's presumption of an already established consensus around the normative surplus supposedly expressed in social institutions and norms. Embedded in institutions and practices is a perpetually unfulfilled utopian potential that, when unearthed and utilized by a particular struggle for its own ends, serves also to reenergize a wider sense of common democratic purpose. The question raised by this unifying dynamic of retrieval and renewal is whether, in contemporary societies, such a unifying normative surplus can be held to latently subsist in institutions and practices, forming a rallying point for a myriad of struggles, or whether the reality of political struggle is far more fissiparous and fraught, centred as it is on deeply conflicting interpretations of our common world. In other words, political conflict goes all the way down; the idea of a normative surplus is itself a matter for debate and definition rather than foregone agreement. The degree to which Honneth sidesteps these interpretative questions is evident, in *Freedom's Right*, in his attempt to reconstruct the ethical logic immanent in the capitalist economy in order to demonstrate how it might be considered a sphere of social freedom. In the eyes of several commentators, this attribution of a latent normative rationale to market economies is highly tendentious, its plausibility only maintained by a dramatic underplaying of the exploitative, monetizing tendencies of capitalist accumulation. As Fazio and Ferrara put it: 'wouldn't it be more adequate to understand the capitalist market as a social field, dominated by permanent struggles among different normative views of liberty, but also among multiple power relations, material interests and functional restraints?' (Fazio and Ferrara 2019: 634). In the end, Honneth's reliance on a decontested, teleological idea of progress undermines his professed intention to avoid the Kantian error of developing normative principles 'over the heads and historically evolved claims of the people to which they are intended to apply' (2015: 206). For, from the perspective of groups exposed to capitalism's exploitative tendencies, Honneth's depiction of the market as a sphere of social freedom is arguably precisely the type of abstracted and estranging fiction that has little to do with their lived reality. Instead, as context-transcending perspective, the teleology of progress seems to be more compatible with a top-down and 'Whiggish' historical narrative rather than one rooted in suffering and social struggle (e.g., Celikates 2018b).

Such problems with the idea of progress do not necessarily imply its outright abandonment, but suggest that it be conceptualized neither as indisputable historical achievement nor as irreversible line of moral development but, in more modest terms, as the hope for change that is revealed contingently and unevenly in social struggle. In this weaker, anticipatory sense, progress is the aspiration towards the better that motivates political struggle or as Allen describes it, 'progress toward some kind of improvement or even away from some negative state of suffering or domination' (Von Redecker 2018: 158). Pragmatically minded critical theorists such as Allen would dispute the all-or-nothing logic adopted by Honneth where critique is thrown irretrievably into relativism if it does not adhere to a narrative of inexorable progress. These pragmatists might well maintain that it is possible to make evaluations on the basis of a limited, 'deflationary' notion of progress that acknowledges advances that have been made in certain areas, and according to certain standards currently regarded as important, but without having to subscribe to an overarching metanarrative or teleology. To return to gender concerns, it is clear that in the postwar period women's social position has improved in significant respects but less so in others, an unevenness which is all too apparent in the persistence of certain forms of subordination (widening pay gap and levels of poverty, unabating rates of domestic violence and abuse, sexualized commodification). Deflated notions of progress permit the acknowledgment of these uneven patterns, of the nonsynchronous and fragile nature of social improvement, better than unifying master narratives which are often, in practice, deployed to legitimate and obfuscate continuing forms of domination. Such ideological obfuscation is illustrated, for example, in Nancy Fraser's critique of the way in which neoliberal discourses acquire spurious legitimacy by co-opting feminist discourses of emancipation to further secure the exploitation of women through flexible labour practices (e.g., Fraser 2013c). Similarly, Mills's work on white ignorance exposes the way in which, in the US, 'progressive' liberal ideas of colour blindness—based on the false premise that racial equality has been achieved post-1964—serve to mask a deeply inegalitarian and racialized society. In so far as it substitutes the historical and socio-structural causes of racial inequality with the fiction of race-less equality of opportunity, colour blindness represents a cultivated 'refusal to recognise the long history of structural discrimination that has left whites with the differential resources they have today and all its consequent advantages in negotiating opportunity structures' (Mills 2017b: 63). The creation, by capitalism in its globalizing neoliberal phase, of new types of social vulnerability and precariousness—many of which disproportionately affect women and people of colour—suggests that progress is not straightforwardly cumulative or irreversible, as Honneth implies, but rather fragile, uneven, and discontinuous. Gaps between formal and substantive freedoms may be mitigated in some areas, but, given the pace and unplanned nature of social change, may perpetually resurface in other areas, in new, unforeseen guises.

In short, there is good reason to question the misleading antinomy between universalism and historicism set up by Honneth, and which obscures the possibility that critical-normative insights may arise from a number of hermeneutically informed perspectives including comparative, historical, and genealogical approaches and, for that matter, Honneth's own earlier phenomenology of social suffering. By dispensing with an overarching account of progress, immanent critique is not automatically condemned to undiscriminating relativism. Nor does accepting the premise that critique is always a situated practice necessarily relegate it to 'disorder and contingency'. There are evidently better and worse interpretations of the world, and their merits can be decided, inter alia, by debate on the relative explanatory force of one account over another. In short, immanent critique does not need a teleological idea of progress in order to aspire to generalized validity, clarity, internal rigour, systematic analysis, correspondence with facts, and so forth; as Foucault puts it: 'the work in question has its generality, its systematicity, its homogeneity, its stakes' (1984: 317).

The narrative of progress is justified by Honneth on the grounds not only of the context-transcending stance it affords critique but also its motivating force. If we did not think that progress—in both backward-and forward-looking dimensions as achievement and trajectory—was a possibility, we would not be motivated to criticize the social order in the first place. It is necessary to 'have in mind both the direction of progress through which those deficiencies in future could be overcome, and also the hope that the description of these inequalities will contribute to the efforts required for such progress' (Honneth 2015: 222). But given the rarefied and depoliticized terms in which Honneth's idea of progress is formulated, it is difficult see where its motivating force lies. Indeed, it might be descriptively more accurate to say that the motivation for political action is a negative one, coming from the moral outrage, anger, and pain felt at continuing injustice and suffering rather than from the positive idea of progress itself. What Margalit says about justice stands, *ceteris paribus*, for the idea of progress: 'it is not justice that brings us into normative politics, but injustice. Not equality but inequality. Not freedom but despotism and, more to the point...there is...more urgency to dealing with humiliation than to dealing with recognition and respect' (Honneth and Margalit 2001: 127). In this regard, Honneth's own earlier work on negativism is instructive. Following Adorno, Honneth holds that a commitment to negativity is the motivating methodological impulse of critique for it is the sensibility to suffering that enables us to question the world in the first place. By attending to negative experiences, it becomes possible to acquire understanding of the deeper systematic sources of inequality and subordination that render a given social order deficient (Honneth 2004: 338ff). Honneth discusses negativism mainly in connection with the social theoretical orientation of disclosing critique but, ultimately, he does not think that it can provide normative resources required to guide decisions about intervening in the world or justifying actions. It may tell us what is wrong with the world but ultimately it is a 'parasitical critical procedure' that needs to be supplemented with the transhistorical normative principles of progress and recognition (Honneth 2009: 48). But is it really the case that what Adorno calls unalleviated consciousness of negativity is so normatively insufficient? On the contrary, given the vagueness and orthogonality of the ethical solutions generated by the recognition–progress couplet, it may be that negativist analysis of determinate forms of suffering and inequality might in fact be a more fruitful way of orienting normative thought. On the negativist view, normative responses lie submerged within the particulars of suffering itself rather than in a questionable narrative of progress. As Adorno famously put it: 'the false, once determinately known and precisely expressed, is already an index of what is right and better' 1998: 288). Negativism then is not simply negation, empty refusal or nay-saying, but is determinate in that it 'delineates and animates a new set of positions for the subject; it is inventive and, in that sense, operates as a determinate negation' (Butler 2009: 792). This methodological focus on negative power relations often goes hand in hand with 'epistemic negativism'; it might not be possible to know what the good is prior to its realization in certain circumstances, but we do know what the bad is because it is instantiated in the world and confronts us in an immediate and visceral fashion (e.g., Freyenhagen 2013: 3–4). It is the avoidance or mitigation of the latter that helps to inform our judgements about how to practically orient ourselves with regard to others, that provides us with an 'orientational' normativity whose evaluative standards are derived from an attentiveness to the repressed particularity of existing forms of oppression and domination (Azamova 2012: 131). Such a negativist orientation is exemplified in the contextually indexed, but systematic evaluative reasoning that, as we saw earlier, undergirds feminist proposals about overcoming inequalities in the provision of care. Given the constraints that the idea of the inevitability of progress imposes on Honneth's thought, it might be this negativist orientation that is, in the end, the more productive normative route for unmasking critique in a world permeated by hierarchically ordered differences and worsening inequalities.

Conclusion

In their jointly authored introduction to *Redistribution or Recognition?*, Honneth concurs with Fraser in rejecting the view that 'casts "grand theory" as epistemologically unsound and politically depassé'. They maintain on the contrary that 'critique achieves both its theoretical warrant and its practical efficacy only by deploying normative concepts that are also informed by a structural understanding of contemporary society, one that can diagnose the tensions and contextualise the struggles of the present' (Fraser and Honneth 2003: 4).[9] In this chapter, however, I have cast doubt on the theoretical warrant and practical efficacy of Honneth's recognition paradigm, qua grand theory, at least with respect to its

---

[9] Elsewhere in the same work, Honneth seems to retreat from this endorsement of grand explanatory theory arguing that his 'attempt to reconstruct the recognition order of modern capitalist societies was not connected to any explanatory aims' (Fraser and Honneth 2003: 249). Rather it seems here he has the more 'modest' goal of revealing 'the moral "constraints"' underlying social interaction' and 'the normative principles that to a large extent structure communication processes from within' (pp. 249–50).

flawed diagnosis of gender subordination. The governing principle of progress distorts analysis of gendered asymmetries of power through a selective interpretation of institutions and practices in terms of their latent normative validity. The ensuing account of social life is over-ethicized; it misdiagnoses entrenched, sexualized hierarchies between men and women as historical residues that will wither away, and misrepresents the structural-functional dimensions of gender oppression as interpersonal mutuality. Unsurprisingly, given the immanent connection that Frankfurt School theorists posit between fact and norm, these shortcomings in Honneth's social explanation are mirrored in his normative proposals which are under-determined and orthogonal to the inegalitarian tendencies at play in gendered regimes of care and so on. Ironically, Honneth intends the idea of progress to be a historicizing device enabling the recognition paradigm to capture the specificity of social relations more adequately than when it was previously grounded in an a-historical ontology. In spite of these intentions, the idea of progress in fact has deeply dehistoricizing effects because of the way it is coupled to a teleological metanarrative that replaces concrete agents and struggles with an abstract logic of Hegelian reason. In the final analysis, Honneth's anti-Kantian intention to derive normative principles from below is undermined by the imposition of a contrived and over-inflated idea of progress. The device appears to be more reflective of a need to vindicate recognition monism as a totalizing interpretative paradigm than it is of a theoretically apt way of responding to the experiences and struggles of those individuals who are supposedly the primary addressees of emancipatory critique.

Honneth's defence of the metanarrative of progress on the grounds that, without it, critique would be unable to evaluate social developments as normative improvements, rests on a tendentious opposition between universalism and relativism. Such a defence is troubling because it is at odds with the Frankfurt School's idea of situated, immanent critique where evaluative judgements should only be arrived at in a fallibilistic and context-sensitive fashion and without recourse to a unilinear, overblown narrative of progress. Feminist work on care demonstrates how empowering normative outcomes might be reached following a problem-led and experientially grounded mode of theorizing that systematically works through the practical and normative concerns surrounding a given social issue. Ultimately, Honneth's defence of the metanarrative of progress hinges on a narrowly theoretic construal of context transcendence as fidelity to a monist paradigm, as the insight generated by applying the correct interpretative framework. The alignment that he originally envisaged between recognition theory and experiences of suffering and injustice is weakened and might be retrieved were he to conceive of context transcendence differently, as the insight created by reasoning across theoretical and experiential perspectives in a dialogic and inclusive fashion.

4
The Politics of Disclosure

Introduction

World-disclosing thought has typically occupied a place of pivotal importance in the Frankfurt School's conception of their emancipatory political project. Understood as the bringing forth of experiences of social suffering that, for ideological reasons have been hidden or unacknowledged, disclosure is regarded as crucial to unmasking critique of oppression. Yet, despite its centrality, there has been, over the last few years, a marked waning of interest in the part that disclosive thought plays in critique as Frankfurt School thinkers have shifted their focus to issues of justice, validity, and procedure. This shift has been fuelled to a large extent by Habermas's well-known criticism of disclosure as meaning creation that is essentially figurative and rhetorical in nature and therefore inherently unamenable to procedures of rational justification. Although Habermas's arguments have had a huge impact, for good reasons, his marginalization of disclosure from the core work of democratic politics is not without problems. Not least, it has been instrumental in ushering in the phase of paradigm-led thinking where, because of the concentration on a narrow subset of normative issues to do with validity and justification, Frankfurt School theorists have neglected to develop pluralized and imaginative modes of critical understanding that may be more receptive to the experiential realities of disempowered groups. No wonder, then, that the marginalization of disclosing critique has been singled out by several commentators as one of the main reasons why contemporary Frankfurt School critical theory seems to have lost its radical political bite and accommodated itself to a liberal justice agenda.

It is against the backdrop of this procedural turn, that the work of Italian critical theorist Alessandro Ferrara on exemplarity and disclosure is of significance. Ferrara argues that 'at its best' democratic thought should have the capacity to animate the imagination by disclosing new political worlds and hence new possibilities for thought and action. Exemplarity is the vehicle of this emancipatory imaginative capacity. The exemplar is a concrete instantiation in the present of how things could be in the future and therefore its unique and inspirational nature may play a fundamental part in galvanizing the will for democratic change. By reconstructing the process through which exemplars takes hold of the collective imagination, Ferrara develops an account of democratic reasoning that is more pluralized and inclusive than the procedural models of rationality that dominate not only critical theory but political theory more generally. Derived from a Kantian notion of reflective judgement, the normativity of the exemplar flows from keen appreciation of its singular, ground-breaking character and gives expression therefore to a 'universalism without principles'. When transferred to the political domain, exemplary universalism suggests a way of reasoning across contexts that is potentially more inclusive of deep socio-cultural differences than formalized rational procedures which often tacitly naturalize dominant, Western modes of expression. By reconciling deep difference with universalism in this way, exemplary reasoning seems better able to respond to the challenges faced by democracy in a 'hyper-pluralist' contemporary world. Ferrara also makes the important argument, against Habermas, that far from being an unstable process of meaning creation, exemplary disclosure has a systematic internal rationale that renders it amenable to inter-subjective validation although not in hyper-rationalist, procedural terms. Indeed, instead of being separate and implicitly subordinate to procedural justification, disclosure is a necessary precondition of the latter. This is so because the practical capacity to recognize the relevance of the new (changed circumstances, new facts, new interlocutors, etc.) is indispensable in preventing the rigidification of democratic deliberation and fostering the ethical openness to others that is a hallmark of genuinely emancipatory theory. In important respects then, Ferrara's idea of the imaginative force of exemplarity resonates with this book's argument about the importance of anchoring unmasking critique in a responsiveness to the experiences of disempowered and marginalized groups. For by attending to the lived reality of marginalized and disempowered groups—the 'experiences of victims' as Ferrara has it—political theory is afforded the capacity to break from settled worldviews where necessary, and also by drawing on these experiences to expand horizons of understanding and possibility.

I go on to argue, however, that the critical promise of the idea of exemplarity is foreclosed by the way Ferrara grounds it in the speculative construct of *sensus communis* defined as a set of non-naturalized, transcultural intuitions about human flourishing. I contend that this socially deracinated, syncretic abstraction blocks an adequate understanding of the hierarchized relations of power in which hyper-pluralist difference is inescapably embedded. In terms of the concerns of this book, *sensus communis* represents a particularly problematic mode of paradigm-led theorizing that cancels out the sensitivity to contextual particularity and difference which is precisely the very strength of exemplary universalism. This in turn leads to a questionably domesticated and depoliticized view of democratic reasoning that replaces disagreement and conflict with a fictitious social consensus. Ultimately, abstraction from the context of power undermines the emancipatory aims of critique in that rather than disclosing new political worlds and radical possibilities for thought, exemplarity reinforces a politically quietist narrative of progress. Drawing on critical race theory, I propose a repoliticized understanding of exemplarity that locates its disclosing force not in a socially weightless abstraction but in the actual dynamics of social struggle.

Rethinking Disclosure

In so far as the primary aim of Frankfurt School theory is, broadly construed, the unmasking of domination and oppression, it can be understood, in a fundamental sense, as disclosing critique. On this view, capitalist societies are organized in such a way as to ensure the systematic reproduction of societal relations that are unequal and oppressive and, more importantly, this exploitative character is routinely denied. Ideological denial takes the form of a panoply of naturalizing and mystifying discourses, beliefs, and practices that have 'the paradoxical quality of distracting one's attention from the very social conditions that structurally produce that system' (Honneth 2007: 30). Disclosing ideology critique penetrates these cognitive distortions in order to lay bare an underlying social reality that is pathological and alienating. Critique performs this unmasking function by shining a light on the many 'hidden' or suppressed forms of societal suffering that may be interpreted as symptoms of an inherently inegalitarian order. But disclosing critique also has a positive as well as negative function, for negative experiences not only are indicative of structural oppression but also may, in some cases, be important sources of counter-hegemonic normativity. The resistant knowledge and practices that subordinated groups develop to deal with oppressive circumstances reveal a surplus of meaning in social life—as Honneth would put it—that provides critique with alternative evaluative resources. Since Habermas's foundational turn, Frankfurt School theorists have tended to define normativity in relation to deep structures and principles that are claimed to be constitutive of social being. But, as we have seen, these monist definitions of normativity are often quite narrow, top-heavy, and insufficiently responsive to the array of concrete problems that confront oppressed groups on an everyday basis. Adopting a pragmatic, action-theoretic approach, other critical theorists, notably feminists, have therefore sought to expand critique's normative scope by drawing on the values and ideals expressed in the practices and struggles of these groups. It is these ordinary struggles and practices that drive the contestation and renewal of norms and values, the creation of new meaning, and ultimately wider processes of social transformation. This then is the positive disclosing function of critique; giving voice to marginalized groups, in the hope of fuelling an expanded critique of power and revealing unforeseen or neglected possibilities for change and progressive world-building.

Yet, despite the seeming centrality of disclosure to emancipatory critique, its theoretical significance for many Frankfurt School thinkers has markedly declined in recent years. It hardly needs stating that this diminished significance is, in large part, the effect of Habermas's influential arguments about what he regards as the inherently 'aesthetic' and therefore non-generalizable nature of disclosing critique. Habermas recognizes that world disclosure has a vital role to play in politics, broadly conceived, in so far as it challenges settled understanding of the world and invigorates the creation of alternative meanings. But, because disclosive insights are, in his view, essentially aesthetic in character, they are also essentially non-formalizable and are therefore peripheral to the core business of democratic reasoning. Based in the free play of the imagination, disclosure is an essentially expressive, figurative, and rhetorical activity and thus has limited relevance to practical problem-solving and systematic political argument. Habermas characterizes world disclosure as a 'poetic demiurge', an impersonal, haphazard force driven by 'the anonymous hurly-burly of the institutionalisation of ever new worlds from the imaginary dimension' (Habermas 1985: 330). Since it is governed by the mere contingency of innovation, disclosure is an 'abnormal' process whose validity cannot be established through the 'normal' processes of rational justification that govern democratic discourse. It is only these rational discourses 'specialized in questions of truth and justice' and indexed to 'inner-world learning processes' that possess substantive problem-solving capacities. Disclosure's lack of formal propositional content obfuscates its relation to the 'truth', ultimately rendering it democratically unaccountable.

Unquestionably, Habermas's concern about connections between meaning, validity, and argumentation is not without legitimate foundation, as is his wariness of overly romanticized Heideggerian notions of disclosure as epiphanic or gestalt revelation of some kind or another.[1] But his marginalization of disclosing critique, *tout court*, via an overdrawn portrayal of it as a haphazard and volatile process of meaning creation is questionable. His sequestration of disclosure to a narrowly defined category of aesthetics is tendentious, as is his assertion that its insights are inherently unamenable to any process of practical verification. Moreover, his stringent separations of critique from discourse, of disclosure from reason, have been instrumental in weakening what Frankfurt School thinkers regard as the fundamental connection between emancipatory critical theory and disempowered groups. As critics have pointed out, the fixation of discourse ethics on rational procedures of justification is ultimately too rigidly procedural to allow expression of many types of suffering and negative experience that merit inclusion in a broad account of social injustice. These lived experiences are often inchoate, opaque, and fragmented and, in so far as they confound the strict logic of validity, are often more aptly captured in symbolic, figurative, and

---

[1] Although as well as querying Habermas's blanket exclusion of disclosure from democratic reasoning, critics also cast doubt on the accuracy of his interpretation of Heidegger, e.g., Kompridis 2006: especially part II.

aesthetic modes of expression. Even once they have been articulated in this way, and acquired a degree of public visibility, such experiences may still resist easy translation into narrowly rational procedures of justification. The 'invisible' negative effects of stigmatization, deauthorization, and symbolic violence mean that certain experiences of oppression are better articulated in nonformalized languages such as figurative speech, narrative, testimony, protest, and so on. Habermas's reluctance to acknowledge this gap between the formal demands of his theory and the lived reality of oppression means that, according to a number of his critics, an 'extreme discrepancy' has opened up between discourse ethics and the experiences of those disempowered subjects whom it is supposed to represent (Honneth 2007). With the loss of this foothold in the lived reality of oppression, the radical perspective from which discourse ethics challenges fictitious universals of equality and freedom is undermined and its inclusiveness thereby diminished.

Habermas's discourse ethics has driven a wedge not only between theory and experience but also between reason and imagination, thereby further narrowing the scope of normative reasoning. The elevation of rule-governed processes of justification over other modes of normative expression limits political deliberation to a subset of deontological concerns. While the yes/no logic of validity claims might capture a certain class of social problems to do with injustice, there are other relevant phenomenological and ethical issues to do with oppression and social pathology which it fails to capture. Some of these issues pertain to what Hannah Arendt has described generally as the 'problem of the new', namely, how to safeguard the receptiveness of theory to context such that it is able to identify and respond appropriately to emergent, unthematized experiences and claims that do not fit straightforwardly into established parameters of intelligibility. In respect to unmasking critique, the new is perhaps more appropriately understood not, *pace* Arendt, as the radically new phenomenon or inaugural event but as the 'alienated familiar', a neglected, unthematized substrate of experience the articulation of which unsettles accepted worldviews by presenting the 'old from a new angle' (Mills 1998: 28). Procedural reason is ill-suited to appreciating the distinctive nature of an emergent phenomenon, the newness of the new so to speak, because its assimilative tendencies are likely to efface unfamiliar qualities by absorbing them into preestablished schemata (Arendt 1978: 28ff). Of course, not all 'new' facts and meanings have the potential to dislodge established reasoning processes; some will be found to be assimilable within known parameters. But others—such as hitherto unthematized experiences of marginality and disempowerment—do have potentially destabilizing epistemic implications in so far as they disclose previously unrecognized aspects of social life and thus challenge established ways of seeing and evaluating the world. Such cases are not easily accommodated by the yes/no structure of formal justification, and consequently, the theorist may need to draw on other resources of reasoning resources to formulate an appropriate response or even, at a more basic level, to discern in the first place the relevance of an unfamiliar phenomenon to extant accounts of social justice. Political reasoning in this expanded sense may require the setting aside of procedures that are already up and running and the exercise of qualities such as imagination, empathy, openness to difference, reflective judgement, willingness to be challenged, etc.; all those 'ineffable' qualities, in other words, that Habermas expediently banished from the core activity of democratic reasoning to the peripheral one of world disclosure. As Charles Taylor observes, when the exercise of these qualities is understood to be more central to democratic deliberation and social learning than Habermas allows, then it is possible to conceive of world disclosure not as the 'other' of reason so much as a 'new department' of reason (Taylor 1995: 15).

The untenability of Habermas's stringent separation of rational discourse from disclosive modes of reason and the constraints it imposes on discourse ethics has, of course, been widely noted by other commentators including members of the Frankfurt School such as Honneth (e.g., Honneth 2007: 1–79). Yet, while Habermas's successors have rightly criticized his work for excessive cognitivism and lack of phenomenological reach, their own inclinations towards paradigm-led thinking have meant that, by and large, they have not taken the opportunity to invest the idea of disclosing critique with renewed theoretical significance. It is against this backdrop that the work of the Italian critical theorist Alessandro Ferrara represents an important intellectual departure, for his endeavour to install an idea of disclosure at the heart of political thinking provides a valuable counter to the Habermasian fixation on procedural reason. According to Ferrara, one of the fundamental aims of emancipatory democratic thought is the articulation of new values and needs or what he calls the disclosure of new political worlds. It is through disclosure of previously unarticulated experiences, meanings, and values that sedimented perceptions of the world are shifted and new possibilities for democratic thought and action fostered. At its best, political thinking should have the 'distinctive ability . . . of setting our imagination in motion, inducing the feeling of enhancement, enriching or deepening of the range of possibilities afforded by our life in common . . . it possesses the *potential for disclosing a new political world for us*' (Ferrara 2014: 40). Disclosure of the new is not necessarily a straightforward task in so far as the very unfamiliarity and nebulousness of the new may make it difficult for the theorist to grasp in the first place. This is particularly a problem for mainstream democratic theory, because its fixation on principle governed accounts of justification may blunt sensitivity to the new and close it off from experiences and perspectives not easily articulable within predefined categories. Rule-governed models of reason are of course important for understanding some types of political problem, but their over-extension can lead to 'cognitive solipsism' that immunizes democratic theory against new dimensions of being. At the limit, the solipsistic tendencies of theory render it increasingly rigid and 'perverse' and alienate it from the changing context and real-world problems to which it is supposed to respond. To counter such theoretical closure, the democratic thinker should strive to cultivate a 'passion for openness' defined as an 'ethical receptivity towards "the other"' and a 'cognitive receptivity toward untried paths for the self, untried doctrines, untried theoretical developments' (2014: 214).

While no single conceptual or methodological formula can guarantee such an open ethos, it may be fostered through attempts to pluralize democratic reasoning and, above all, by making greater space therein for the work of the imagination. For, according to Ferrara, the imagination is the only faculty with the crucial capacity 'to make present in the mind what is not [immediately] before the senses' and thereby enable the disclosure of new contexts of meaning and new political worlds (2014: 41). Far from being marginal to democratic deliberation, disclosure is one of its indispensable preconditions in so far as it catalyses the cognitive receptivity to particularity, qua the new and the other, that keeps political reasoning open and inclusive. An ability to see the relevance of the new is crucial to combatting the assimilative and potentially solipsistic tendencies of theoretic reasoning and consequently to maintaining ongoing relevance to the dynamic political context. As well as granting disclosure renewed importance in emancipatory critique, Ferrara also argues, contra Habermas and other proceduralists, that it is not inherently an ineffable process of meaning creation but does in fact have a systematic internal rationale that renders it amenable to democratic validation. In showing how disclosure is inextricably tied to argumentation, Ferrara's ambitious objective is to allay proceduralist fears of its intrinsic irrationalism and, at the same time, expand the scope of justice by hybridizing democratic reason thereby rendering it responsive to unnoticed voices, claims, and experiences.

Exemplary Universalism

Ferrara establishes the centrality of disclosure to normative political reasoning through the idea of exemplarity and associated notion of a universalism without principles. The most notable feature of the exemplary instance is the way it reconciles, in its singular, innovative form, the commonly disconnected realms of is and ought. The exemplar brings together facts and norms not just in a 'passing, occasional and imperfect intertwining' but in a lasting, nearly complete, and 'rare fusion' and in doing so sets the imagination alight (Ferrara 2008: 3). It is a concrete incarnation in the present of how things ought to be in the future, or, in Ferrara's terms, the 'force of *what is as it should be*' (2008: 2–3). Through its very exceptionality, it provides an 'anticipatory prefiguration' of potential change in the world, embodying a tangible sense of 'the rise of new patterns and the opening of new paths' (2008: 3). Usually thought of in the aesthetic terms of an outstanding work of art, exemplarity also occurs in other social realms, epitomized in exceptional cases of authenticity, perfection, integrity, charisma, aura, courage, genius, and so on. Some kinds of exemplarity encapsulate a normativity with which we are already familiar and which confirms an established sense of being. Others, however, have an emphatically innovative character, enlarging horizons of understanding through the opening of 'new vistas on what exists and new dimensions of normativity' (2008: 3). Examples of this in politics include political revolutions, social movements, new religions, inspirational leaders, exceptional acts of courage, and so on. The trail-blazing character of such exemplary instances means that it may be difficult initially to grasp their significance, to fully comprehend the innovative, even radical, implications of their newness. This *sui generis* meaning may only be dimly intuited at first through approximating strategies, such as analogy with past experiences, while its full originality only unfurls completely over time. In short, the challenge that the exemplar presents is one of interpretation itself, for it seems to require 'that we formulate ad hoc the principle of which it constitutes an instantiation' (2008: 3). The normative significance of the newly exemplary instance cannot be fully grasped according to preestablished principles, but nor can it be explained solely as a 'reflection of locally shared and unquestionable preferences' given its impact across contexts. Rather, in so far as it brings forth previously unexpressed aspects of social being, its normative significance derives from its own singularity; it carries within itself its own principle of interpretation so to speak.

Like Arendt, Ferrara sees the potential of this idea of the ground-breaking instance that defies interpretation according to established standards, for expanding established accounts of normativity in politics. He draws on her reading of Kant's idea of reflective judgement to explain the reasoning process that allows us to appreciate the *sui generis* force of the exemplar. According to Kant, the judgement of a work of art as beautiful cannot merely be the expression of idiosyncratic subjective preference ('I like canary wine') because it implies that others ought to agree (regardless of whether they actually do or not) and therefore that a certain type of universality is at stake in the assessment. This implicit universality is not based, however, in externally given norms that all must recognize, because aesthetic judgements cannot compel agreement in the same manner as principle-based, i.e., determinant, ideas of moral judgement. Aesthetic judgement can only solicit or 'woo' agreement on the basis of a shared recognition of the uniqueness of the object itself as an 'outstanding instance of authentic congruency' between the individual and wider, collective sensibility. The universal scope of aesthetic judgement rests then not on compliance with a principle, but on the capturing of a feeling; its normative force flows from the invocation of a transcendent sense of the promotion or furtherance of life. In Kantian terms, reflective judgement is grounded in an appeal to *sensus communis* defined as a 'universal capacity to sense the flourishing of human life and what favours it'

(2008: 31). In so far as the normative force of the exemplar resides in its mobilization of a common sensibility, it embodies what Honneth calls a universalism without principles, i.e., a transcendence that flows from its own singular appeal rather than from the assimilative power of preestablished moral principles.

By recasting central democratic concerns around exemplary universalism, Ferrara claims to extend the normative scope of ideas of justice, obligation, freedom, political justification, and so on which, in mainstream political theories, are often based in Western notions of reason that are implicitly exclusionary. His main claim is that, by tapping deep, commonly held intuitions about human flourishing via the *sensus communis*, the exemplary instance encompasses social and cultural differences more easily than orthodox universals of law, reason, or morality. By activating imagination rather than rationality, its impact is more immediate and potent than abstractly codified ideals, and it therefore has resonance with a wider variety of life-worlds. The vision of better ways of being disclosed by the exemplar galvanizes individuals through an appeal not to reason but to imaginative and emotional convictions about what is means to flourish. Precisely because its normative force is affectual, in the broadest sense, exemplarity appears to resolve a problem that has perennially vexed democratic theory; namely, how to reconcile pluralism with universalism without lapsing into cultural relativism, on the one side, and ethnocentric prescription, on the other. Ferrara illustrates these politically unifying effects by reconstruing human rights as an exemplary universal. A frequently noted problem with the justification of human rights through reference to universal principles is that the latter often take for granted the priority of Western values and norms. Rawls, for example, preempts consideration of the difficulties that human rights as contingent Western constructs may present for a postcolonial world because he assumes a priori their moral independence (2008: 124). Habermas is more successful in bypassing moral foundationalism in so far as he uses a legally derived vindication of human rights as possessing special foundational status ('extra-positive validity') in virtue of their universal scope. Given their democratically enabling capacity, human rights can be justified at the level of international justice in an anticipatory fashion as 'rights on their way to acquiring a full legal status'. But Habermas's thin, proleptic justification also arguably has latent ethnocentric entailments in as much as it rests on acceptance of Western liberal-democratic constitutionalism (2008: 124–7). Ferrara claims to avoid latent cultural bias by relocating the normative force of human rights in their transcultural appeal as exemplars of a certain notion of human fulfilment. This transcendent notion of flourishing or 'superordinate identity' of rights inspires a multitude of concrete struggles precisely because it is a 'noncomprehensive' or 'thin' conception that remains 'impartial with respect to the particularism of the singular contending identities' that it embraces. Exemplary universalism is seemingly consistent then with pluralist intuitions that do not require that 'nonliberal or non-Western individuals and peoples embrace assumptions that are not their own' (2008: 145). At the same time, it has a unifying force in that the 'reconstructible narrative' of flourishing constitutes the shared moral horizon around which diverse political conflicts about rights, equality, nondomination, and so on, are oriented. Indeed, if conflicts did not share this common orientation, they would not be understandable in the first place as specifically political, as struggles over 'something' rather than merely localized difficulties (2008: 137). Moreover, because it is a disclosive rather than regulatory concept, exemplary universalism has counterhegemonic, emancipatory force. As a normatively galvanizing focal point, it makes visible what were previously unnoticed life-worlds and thereby challenges conventional political attitudes; every concrete struggle that it enables potentially contributes to the expansion and enrichment of the democratic imagination.

Priority of Judgement

There is no doubting the prima facie appeal of Ferrara's recasting of democratic ideals as normative exemplars that animate the political imagination and provide a source of inspiration and solidarity for a multiplicity of emancipatory struggles regardless of social and cultural differences. The arid cognitivism of regulative ideals is replaced with an attractive, dynamic vision of ideals as mediated through imaginative figurations or what Sorel terms 'warmly-coloured and clearly-defined images' (Sorel 1975: 164–5). Thus, as well as bypassing the problem of ethnocentric imposition, Ferrara also seems to provide an answer to the question of actor motivation, another common weakness of formal, procedural approaches. For, without imaginative projection and bonds more than those of pure reason, it is not clear how ideals and principles would be able to 'stimulate human agents to engage in transformative social thinking and action' (Cooke 2006: 115). Ferrara's work then stands in line with that of other critical theorists such as Albrecht Wellmer (1991), Iris Marion Young (1996), and Maeve Cooke (2006), all of whom attempt to mitigate the rational proceduralism of Habermas's discourse ethics by introducing various expressive, aesthetic, and disclosive elements into the justificatory process.

Yet, despite undoubted intuitive appeal, Habermasian thinkers would almost certainly remain unconvinced by the idea of exemplary universalism. In their view, the imaginative mechanism of disclosing new political worlds would still seem to be far too haphazard and ineffable a process to be able to bear the normative load that Ferrara wishes to place on it. Moreover, the *sui generis*, self-sustaining act of discernment, namely reflective judgement, which underpins exemplary universalism is insufficiently tethered to the kind of systematic rational argument that is an indispensable feature of assessing the validity of political claims. Without some 'internal relationship to an ability to argue and deliberate well' the normative impact of exemplary disclosure remains 'inexplicable' and rests on a 'mythology of judgement' (Wellmer 2000: 297). This mystification is strongly in evidence in the fetishized idea of individual discernment that informs Arendt's idea of reflective judgement. Unlike the intersubjective logic that drives her idea of action, judgement is, in essence, monological in nature, an individual act of contemplation and perspicacity that obfuscates any clear connection with the wider context of democratic politics (e.g., Fraser 1997b: 166–75).

Ferrara responds to criticisms of obscurantism by demonstrating the inherently inter-subjective character of exemplary judgement and the way that this securely connects it to processes of argumentation and democratic validation. There are two dimensions to the intersubjective nature of judgement. First, it is the necessary communicability of judgement that renders it more than a purely individual and internal act of discernment. The judgement of the spectator about the exemplary status of a certain phenomenon is nonsubjective in that it brings something into view that can only be validated by soliciting the views of others. If this something, this transcending force of exemplarity, was not communicable in any way, it could not be understood by others and it would therefore remain a merely idiosyncratic observation devoid of general relevance. Second, in addition to communicability, the validity of judgement also turns around its inclusivity. A particular object or instance is judged to be exemplary not by assessments of its consistency with the right external principle, but rather by taking the viewpoints of others into account: 'valid...are those judgements that are *as inclusive as possible* of all competing standpoints and are thus as "general" as possible while remaining "closely connected with particulars"'(Ferrara 2008: 46). Here again, however, the inclusivity of enlarged thought is limited by the self-referential terms of the Arendtian formulation which emphasizes the individual's subjective capacity to take account of others by 'visiting' in the imagination. Without reference to wider social relations, this solipsistic formulation lacks an independent way of checking that the internal thought-experiment pays enough heed to 'other' relevant perspectives, especially those that are beyond the individual's direct experience and therefore also possibly beyond their empathetic capacity. Ferrara circumvents this difficulty by replacing individual imagination with collective social imagination, and hence conceiving inclusivity in relation to the shared self-understandings and normative horizons that are the objects of democratic contestation and renewal. Judgement is no longer an arbitrary, self-referential act but can be said to have a certain impartiality by virtue of its communicability and inclusivity.

Thus understood, the intersubjective structure of judgement anchors it in democratic argumentation and validation defined not as hyper-rationalist procedures of justification, *pace* Habermas, but as ongoing, open process of public debate and practical verification. Judgements about our shared world and 'who we are' are not merely arbitrary, incommensurable acts of discernment, since through public argument they can be ordered on a scale of justifiability such that some can be said to be better than others. In this way, Ferrara seeks to circumvent the charges of relativism and radical contextualism that proceduralists frequently level at disclosive modes of reasoning. Some exemplars express ideals more cogently than others and hence are more valuable phronetic guides than others. Such evaluations are based not on conformity with pregiven rules (because this would be to predetermine the criteria that are relevant to the matter at hand) but on the normative allegiance and direction that a given exemplar is capable of commanding from among a multiplicity of conflicting social positions (2008: 39–40).

Ferrara's argument about the inter-subjective structure of judgement extends, in analogous fashion, to disclosing critique and how it might be understood as more than the arbitrary creation of new meanings but as a coherent source of insight amenable to practical verification. By eliding disclosure with aesthetics *tout court*, Habermas fails to appreciate that far from being guided only by the contingency of innovation, disclosure in the context of the critique of power is necessarily subject to the constraints of possessing some kind of correspondence to the main features of the world. In a sociological context, there are better and worse interpretations of the world but there exist a variety of methodological indices, standards of evidence, and conceptual logics with which to explore the explanatory and normative merits of any given act of disclosure. As Axel Honneth puts it: 'whereas in aesthetic representation the opening of new contexts of meaning can transpire without bounds...In social criticism it remains bound to the limits set by the actual constraints of social reproduction' (Honneth 2007: 58). The disclosure of new, hitherto suppressed aspects of social life does not amount to the presentation of a new truth-in-itself, for this would be to fetishize experience as the incontestable ends of critical knowledge. In this respect, Habermas is correct to assert that disclosure does not have a direct relation to the truth because its normative force rests on rhetorically conveyed assertions rather than direct propositional claims. But he is not correct to depict world disclosure as intrinsically unredeemable in rational terms, nor to separate it so sharply from processes of validation thereby denying it systematic sociological and normative coherence. It would be more accurate to say, with thinkers such as Ian Hacking, that disclosure's relation to the truth is indirect; it raises a claim to being a 'candidate for truth or falsehood' (Hacking 2002: 167). The validity of claims to be relevant to the truth, their 'truth content' so to speak, nonetheless still have to be verified through further acts of reflection and deliberation: 'to be critical, the [disclosive] expression must also have this reproducible effect on the audience, as well as simply opening up possibilities and relevances' (Bohman 1994: 93–94). By bringing new or obscured aspects of social experience to the fore, disclosure asks us to see the world differently, to question deeply held assumptions and convictions, to enlarge our understanding of what is considered relevant to the debate at hand and, if necessary, to expand or even radically revise prevailing frameworks.

When disclosure is considered in the light of the newly relevant, it becomes evident that it has effects at a level prior to the content of propositional claims, that is, at the level of the evaluative structures which precede and determine what is regarded as a permissible claim in the first place and what is not. It represents a 'calculated effort to change the preconditions under which a society conducts evaluative discourse on the ends of common action' (Honneth 2007: 58). In this respect, disclosure is necessarily prior to and enabling of deliberation about truth and validity, and Ferrara's argument about the autonomy of judgement helps elucidate the nature of this priority. The autonomy of judgement refers to the way in which, in some sense, it precedes and enables justification. Drawing on Arendt, Ferrara argues that, unlike Habermas, she does believe that judgements can be evaluated from a third-person standpoint (the 'we' of communicative discourse) because this presupposes the existence of a rational consensus that has not yet been formed. For Arendt, it is not possible to take a stance (third person) outside of the actual debate itself, there is only immersion in deliberation. Consequently, deliberation always begins, *in media res*, proceeding from initial acts of judgement about the alternatives at hand. Before the formal process of justification can even begin, a range of preparatory acts of judgement are necessary to kick-start debate; topics have to be selected, appropriate ways of framing issues decided on, the relevance of certain facts and positions to the matter at hand assessed, interlocutors situated in a field debate, and so on. Disclosure plays a fundamental role not only in initially orienting deliberation in a relevant way but also in sustaining ongoing receptivity to changes in the context of debate, to the newly emergent, the other, the unfamiliar. Outdated or reactionary forms of thought often lack receptivity to context, evident in their tendency to assimilate the world to unchanging schemata rather than modify their reasoning processes in accordance with changing circumstances. Cognitive rigidity serves to filter out new, potentially threatening elements by deeming them anomalous, marginal, or irrelevant. In this way, for example, tendentious claims about the inherent inferiority have been instrumental in excluding women, black people, and LGBTQi people from the categories of moral and legal personhood that treat them as democratic equals. Such discounting of the other is not limited to patently reactionary and regressive forms of thought but is evident also, in less pathological form, in everyday, common sensical thinking, and is linked to what social epistemologists regard as a profound cognitive reluctance to have one's worldview disconfirmed (Mills 2017b: 60–1).

Given the exclusionary effects that cognitive bias towards self-confirmation may have, effective emancipatory critique cannot be structured exclusively around the single dimension of procedural reason but must also strive to include other 'styles of reasoning' that work against theoretical closure (Hacking 2002). In contrast to the a-temporal scenarios of theory, deliberation in the world is a dynamic, open process where circumstances and agendas change, and new interlocutors emerge. Were democratic reasoning in actual historical contexts to turn solely around procedural assessments of validity, it would be one-dimensional and deficient. For democratic reasoning also needs to encompass the ability to see the significance of newly emergent factors and to respond to them appropriately; how to identify new interlocutors and include them in debate, how to expand existing frames of reference, how to alter argumentation processes, and so on. As Ian Hacking famously points out, grasping the new or alien often involves deviating from established protocols of reasoning: 'understanding the sufficiently strange is a matter of recognising new possibilities for truth-or-falsehood, and of learning how to conduct other styles of reasoning that bear on those new possibilities' (Hacking 2002: 171). Different styles of reasoning are not fostered by procedural rationality alone because they require more than rule following, springing instead from attunement to the contingencies and changing requirements of the actual debate itself. Formal rules and procedures are not always sufficiently pliable and self-reflexive to be able to ensure sensitivity to context and willingness to question a sedimented modus operandi or fixed discursive habits. *Eo ipso*, procedural reason deals with new phenomena by assimilating them to a predefined rationale, and this subsumptive logic may hinder it from grasping the relevance of that which stands outside established categories, that is, recognizing the new as new, the other as other and, if necessary, changing in response to this. By bringing forward newly emergent experiences not fully understandable under existing frameworks, disclosive reason provide the impetus for critical self-scrutiny and the responsive, open stance to the world that is a necessary feature of emancipatory thought. As Ferrara puts it: 'all the important junctures where something new has emerged in politics and has transformed the world... were junctures where what is new never prevailed by virtue of its following logically from what already existed, but rather by virtue of its conveying a new vista on the world we share in common and highlighting some hitherto unnoticed potentialities of it' (2014: 38). Contra Habermas, then, disclosure is not an unpredictable process of meaning-creation, the intrinsic volatility of which places it outside the core democratic activities of justification and assessment of validity. Rather, it is coextensive with these activities and lies at the very heart of emancipatory political reasoning, enabling the latter to counter its own self-reifying tendencies and maintain openness and relevance to the changing social context.

Sensus Communis

Yet despite the persuasiveness of Ferrara's argument for the centrality of world disclosure to political thought, his decision to ground exemplarity in the questionable abstraction of *sensus communis* undermines its critical promise. Clearly, not all types of world disclosure generate critical insight that enhances progressive democratic understanding. For instance, many critics, Habermas included, have expressed scepticism about the progressive import of Heidegger's monological and ahistorical formulation of world disclosure (e.g., Bohman 1994; Habermas 1985: 131–60). What gives disclosure its emancipatory force is its rootedness not in ontology but in an unmasking critique of power where suffering and other negative experiences are revealed to be indicators of unjust societal relations. On the face of it, Ferrara seems to cleave to such an experientially grounded view of critique when he states that disclosure should be oriented to marginalized life-worlds, or what he terms 'the experience of victims', and should challenge 'sedimented social constructions': 'without ... the ability to see thing with the eyes of another, different from us, nothing can pierce the immunizing armor of our collective representations' (Ferrara 2014: 41). In practice, however, it is precisely this capacity of the exemplar to expand understanding of the world by opening up new vistas and contexts of meaning that is stymied by its foundation in the idea of *sensus communis*. If part of Ferrara's case against procedural reason is that it lacks sufficient sensitivity to social context, then it appears to be a self-undermining move to attach exemplary disclosure to such a tendentious abstraction. For, in so far as this deracinated device directs attention away from the specificities of lived experience and towards a speculative presocial unity, it forecloses critical understanding of hierarchical, social relations and depoliticizes transformative social struggle. Ultimately, then, instead of opening new horizons of understanding, mobilizing the imagination, and fostering a 'passion for openness' and 'ethical receptivity towards "the other"', the effects of exemplary disclosure are limited to the affirmation of an established liberal world view (2014: 214).

Ferrara is aware that his decision to ground disclosing critique in the context-transcending device of *sensus communis* is potentially problematic. On the one hand, he needs to avoid replicating the abstraction of Kantian formulations of *sensus communis* as a free-floating faculty of the mind which, as much as it naturalizes specific socio-cultural characteristics as universal, is potentially exclusionary of difference. On the other hand, he also needs to circumvent the particularism and conventionalism associated with 'thick', phenomenological concepts of *sensus communis* as the taken-for-granted background of practical knowledge that is constitutive of communal life and action. Adopting a path between the two extremes, Ferrara defines *sensus communis* as a 'precultural' yet 'nonnatural' intuitive sense located in a space that is 'topographically after nature but before the differentiation of cultures' and, as such, is 'equi-accessible' from a multiplicity of differing viewpoints (2008: 31–2). *Sensus communis* is, in essence, a matrix of 'denaturalized but not culturally thickened' intuitions about flourishing and the furtherance of life that traverse all cultures and life-worlds. Indeed, this shared intuitive sense of what it means to flourish is so deeply rooted in the human psyche that its bonding force endures even under the intense conditions of 'hyper-pluralism' that characterize the contemporary world (2014: 16–18).

If it is not to be regarded as a speculative and expedient construction, Ferrara needs to specify precisely how to conceive of the hybrid space or dimension in which he imagines *sensus communis* to be located and which he contends is simultaneously presocial and nonnatural. However, the terms in which he defines this enigmatic space are elusive, to say the least and, and the more he attempts to clarify the idea, the more he raises troubling issues that remain unresolved. One possible way to grasp *sensus communis* would be to conceptualize it in a manner similar to what Stephen White (2000) has described as a 'weak ontology', that is, an existential constant that, because of its thinness, nonetheless allows for socio-cultural diversity in its various concrete instantiations. In this sense, flourishing, qua *sensus communis*, could be understood as akin to other weak ontologies such as finitude, vulnerability, or embodiment which have been fruitfully deployed as the postmetaphysical grounds for various ethical theories; for example, Honneth's philosophical anthropology of recognition or Judith Butler's idea of precarious life. Ferrara, however, emphatically rules out any such ontologized interpretation of *sensus communis*, because, as an existential or intuitive substrate, it introduces a 'substantive quality' into the idea that 'disfigures it into one more philosophical anthropology' (2018: 152). This resistance on Ferrara's part to notions of weak ontology is perplexing in so far as elsewhere he frequently makes use of proximate substantive terms, describing exemplarity as mobilizing a 'layer of intuitions' (2008: 34), or as operative '"before" or "underneath"' the differentiation of cultures' (2008: 31), as well as drawing on psychoanalytic theory to reconstruct what 'our notion' of a fulfilled identity might mean.

Even though he leaves hanging the question of how to conceptualize the hybrid nature of *sensus communis*, Ferrara certainly has good reasons to be wary of binding political thought too tightly to ontology because of its depoliticizing entailments. For this reason, he prefers to define *sensus communis* in formal not substantive terms, as expressing relevant 'dimensions of flourishing that can be thought of as formal' (152). Formalism, in his view, avoids the depoliticizing effects of ontology as well as plausibly explaining how *sensus communis* can be topographically after nature but prior to the differentiation of cultures. Yet, formalism is perhaps not as convincing a solution as Ferrara seems to think for, as Adorno puts it, 'there is nothing that can avoid the experience of the situation, nothing counts that purports to have escaped it' (Adorno 1997: 46). In so far as it floats free of any recognizable social location and lacks determinate social content, *sensus communis* seems to be in tension with the supposed attunement of world-disclosing critique to lived experience. Naturalized as an extra-social truth, *sensus communis* is in danger of becoming precisely the type of abstract universal that Ferrara ostensibly rejects as part of his criticism of procedural reason. Certainly his attempt to establish the formal universality of ideas of flourishing using Nozick's thought experiment of the 'intuitive preferability' of life course B over A is not especially persuasive for a thinker concerned with capturing the heterogeneity of experience. The 'simplified and artificially self-contained' thought experiments of the type that Nozick engages in arguably only achieve their supposed moral representativeness through a questionable bracketing of what are held to be tangential experiential and situational detail. But, of course, as critics have repeatedly pointed out, it is these supposed tangential details that are often central to grasping what is actually at stake, and that render real-world normative thinking a more complex, open-ended process (Code 2006: 209). As Stephen Mulhall puts it:

> thought-experiments in ethics presuppose that we can get clearer about what we think on a single, specific moral issue by abstracting it from the complex web of interrelated matters of fact and of valuation within which we usually encounter and respond to it. But what if the issue means what it does to us, has the moral significance it has for us, precisely because of its place in that complex web? If so, to abstract it from that context is to ask us to think about something else altogether—something other than the issue that interested us in the first place; it is, in effect, to change the subject. (Mulhall 2002)

In theory, Ferrara's commitment to maintaining an ethical openness to the other renders him wary of such phenomenological bracketing and reliance on idealizing theoretical devices. But, in practice, it is hard to see how *sensus communis* is anything other than a questionable abstraction that conceals its own social conditions of emergence, and the universality of which is established more by definitional fiat than argumentation.

Poised indeterminately between ontology (culturally unthickened) and formalism (nonnatural), Ferrara's intuitive universalism is a problematic not just because of its ambiguity and under-elaboration, but also because of the way it naturalizes normative consensus and neutralizes political conflict. Ferrara claims that even in cases of deep political conflict, actors necessarily share a common set of intuitions about flourishing that precede and transcend all socio-cultural 'bifurcation'. Indeed, without such a shared reference point, they would not be able to understand themselves as disagreeing in the first place. By virtue of being situated in the same 'division of labour', individuals share a 'common moral space', however thin, and this provides the concrete anchoring point around which otherwise deeply divergent worldviews turn (Ferrara 1999: 183). The idea that 'hyper-pluralism' might lead to deep, potentially unbridgeable discrepancies and conflict between groups is dismissed as making no philosophical sense because it falls into a negative metaphysics of difference as 'total inaccessibility'. But it may be correct, from a narrowly philosophical perspective, for Ferrara to warn against the reification of difference as unbridgeable alterity; it leads to a questionable outcome, from a sociological perspective, in that he markedly understates the extent of entrenched social division, antagonism, and conflict in the world. Put differently, the socially weightless device of *sensus communis* operates as a symbolic denegation of power that forecloses consideration of the relations of domination and subordination around which differences are inevitably organized and which divide groups from each other. In Ferrara's flattened-out vision, hyper-pluralist politics appears to be a version of Rawls's domesticated value pluralism where reasonable persons willingly accept the right of other reasonable persons to hold differing ends. This horizontal dimension of pluralism as a series of homologous differences remains unconnected to a vertical dimension where differences are ordered by hierarchies of power. A result of this flattening is that nothing of any import hangs on differing worldviews, they lack urgency or force, they carry no costs, there are no political stakes at play because they are divorced from the context of power which forms the inevitable backdrop to democratic disagreement and struggle.

This neutralization of politics is compounded by the 'we saying' that shores up *sensus communis* where the first-person plural pronoun is deployed in such a way as to naturalize a shared normative perspective (Code 2006: 215). To whom does the decontextualized 'we' that peppers Ferrara's writing refer? Which groups does the assumed 'communis' in *sensus communis* represent? Who is the 'we' that exists prior to the plurality of cultural perspectives and who so readily assents to the force of Nozick's thought experiment? Who is the 'we' that agrees that the idea of flourishing is the most appropriate guide for political deliberation? Likewise, on what basis are 'liberal' notions of human rights or the 'reasonable' deemed to be politically suitable exemplars when their very embeddedness in particular socio-cultural traditions renders their aptness as neutral, cross-cultural rallying points open to question; when it assumes the status of an extra-social truth and is placed 'beyond the play of power', exemplarity, and its attendant language of flourishing, is naturalized and shifted into what Butler calls a 'new dimension of unquestionability'(Butler 1992: 7). Indeed, it is not clear why the neutralizing language of flourishing is thought by Ferrara to be a particularly compelling way of framing democratic disagreement over competing, politically more apposite ideas of, say, equality or freedom or negativist variants of overcoming exploitation and injustice. In giving such prominence to the discourse of flourishing, Ferrara leaves unquestioned its subtly domesticating effects where political conflict is depicted, in centripetal terms, as polite interpretative divergence around a shared norm rather than as struggle over the control of meaning and resources. In short, the intuitive commonality presupposed by *sensus communis* sanitizes political conflict by detaching it from the determinate context of power and construing it in the anodyne, overly ethicized idea of difference in flourishing.

Politics of Exemplarity

When it is detached from the neutralizing fiction of *sensus communis* and placed in its social context, a different, agonistic and politicized picture of exemplarity emerges. No longer conceived as a supra-social harmonizing force, the meaning, role, and function of exemplarity is indissociably indexed to processes of political struggle themselves. Similarly, conflict is conceived not according to a centripetal model of ethical divergence but as running deeper, as encompassing the rallying point, qua exemplar itself. Political rallying points do not spontaneously emerge from a presupposed intuitive consensus but are themselves part and parcel of political struggle; their significance for different groups and the way they are mobilized are matters of contestation. A politicized account of exemplarity allows issues of inequality, oppression, and disempowerment to come into view along with a conception of politics praxis that is far more fraught, divisive, and fractured than Ferrara's frictionless depiction of hyper-pluralism.

Consider, for instance, that a not uncommon negative experience in hierarchized social conditions is alienation; oppressed groups often feel estranged from privileged social groups and mainstream society more generally (e.g., Honneth 2007: 3–48; Medearis 2015). The lived reality of subordination may mean that these groups feel they have little, if anything, in common with the norms and aspirations of dominant groups. In cases of deep and enduring oppression, they may also feel that dominant groups have no interest in genuinely listening to them or acting in any concretely effective manner to rectify their plight. Numerous historians, sociologists, and theorists of race have documented, for example, the ways in which entrenched racial divisions in the US have left many African-Americans feeling that they live in a world set apart from the social world of whites, despite formal equality[2]—set apart in both the material sense of seemingly unbreakable cycles of poverty, deprivation, violence, and mass incarceration and in the symbolic sense of pervasive racial prejudice which is frequently downplayed and even denied by dominant groups. Du Bois famously captured these experiences of exclusion and alienation in his striking image of the veil that obscures black people from the white gaze, not in a way that renders them completely invisible, but that bestows a false visibility in the form of impoverished and distorting stereotypes (Du Bois 1989). Such estrangement takes the form not just of externally imposed stigmatization but also of an internally lived subjection; a self-alienation arising from the internalization of racial stigma in psychologically

---

[2] The literature is huge but see, for example, Michelle Alexander, *The New Jim Crow: Mass Incarceration in the Age of Colorblindness*. New York: New Press, 2010; Donald Kinder and Lynne Sanders, *Divided by Color: Racial Politics and Democratic Ideals*, Chicago: University of Chicago Press: 1996; Glenn Loury, *Anatomy of Racial Inequality*. Cambridge, MA: Harvard University Press, 2002; Douglas Massey and Nancy Denton, *American Apartheid: Segregation and the Making of the Making of the Underclass*. Cambridge, MA: Harvard University Press, 1993.

injurious and self-destructive ways. Du Bois and Fanon are among the many writers who have shown how difficult it is for the black subject to form an integral, purposive sense of self in a symbolic order that is permeated by racist meanings, 'a world which yields no true self-consciousness, but only lets him see himself through the revelation of the other world' (Du Bois1989: 5). Lacking an affirmative stance of recognition, the black (usually male) subject is often left struggling with negative feelings of self-worth, ennui, rage, despair, and so on (e.g., West 2001). It is the depth and persistence of this self-alienation that, inter alia, has given rise to the long-running and contested debate about the most appropriate terms in which the internal life of Black America might be positively reconstructed (e.g., Kelley 2002; Shelby 2005; West 2001).

Alienation is a phenomenon not limited to a racially divided US; it is a frequent accompaniment of the grossly inegalitarian social relations that seem to be an undiminishing feature of a globalized neoliberal order. Its absence from Ferrara's work is curious given its commonness as a reaction to marginalization and disempowerment and the declared orientation of disclosure to the experience of victims. It is of significance here because the experience of alienated groups complicates what Ferrara unquestioningly takes to be an established consensus around exemplarity. Consider, for instance, how under conditions of racial inequality, pervasive stigmatizing forces routinely cast whiteness as coextensive with humanity, and blackness as 'other', as 'nonpersonhood' and nonhumanity. Racialized symbolic regimes throw into question the supposed neutrality of superordinate notions of flourishing; they are not culturally neutral but unavoidably contingent, socially loaded constructs (Mills 2017a: 244). Ideas of human well-being don't spontaneously emerge from a presocial realm of intuition but are the products of a specific history and social circumstances. As such, their meaning is often coded in a way that, even when not explicitly exclusionary, may tacitly favour certain groups over others; white over black people, men over women, heterosexuals over gay and queer people, and so on. Even in its thinnest, 'culturally unthickened' expressions, meaning is inextricably bound to context, necessarily bearing the traces of the social hierarchies in which it is lodged, and it is for this reason that it a site of contestation and struggle, not quasi-naturalisic consensus. Political debate is not, as Ferrara envisages, an orderly process where subordinated groups insert their own localized content into an overarching exemplary conception of the 'who we are'. Rather, it is likely to involve disagreement, often controversial, antagonistic, and polemical, over the 'who we are', over the latent (white, male) content of the overarching identity or exemplary instance. Such disagreement is not limited to the content of the exemplary instance but extends to the choice of the exemplar itself and the very parameters of political debate. Who selects and defines the superordinate identity? Is it an appropriate rallying point? Is its meaning tacitly skewed to favour some groups over others? Is it amenable to resignification or not? Is it even a relevant way of framing the concrete social issues at stake? The 'Black Lives Matter' movement has become such a potent political exemplar because it exposes the implicitly exclusionary nature of the 'who we are' in advanced democracies. Despite formal equality, such democracies have failed to combat historical legacies of racism and continue to discriminate against black people by excluding them from basic categories of personhood and respect. As Mills puts it: 'Failing to attain the threshold of white humanity, these individuals are not protected by norms of Enlightenment equality, because this supposedly generic norm was never intended to cover them in the first place' (Mills 2017a: 244). What Mills says about enlightenment norms can also be said to hold, *ceteris paribus*, for what Ferrara understands to be shared, uncontroversial instances of exemplarity. Political exemplars do not so much bubble up in a quasi-organic fashion, galvanizing a latent, popular consensus awaiting expression, but rather emerge as rallying points and are consolidated in the process of political strife itself. Indeed, for disempowered groups, the very idea that there exist shared aspirations and expressions of flourishing that transcend deep social differences, holding them in normative unity, seems to be an instance of wishful liberal thinking that focusses on fictitious universals rather than on enduring social inequalities.

In so far as it abstracts from the context of power, the disclosing force of Ferrara's exemplarity is thrown into doubt since it does not so much reveal new horizons of meaning, qua the experiences of subordinated groups, as confirm consensually held, extra-political truths. It does not necessarily follow, however, that the idea of exemplarity should be abandoned; Ferrara's general case about its centrality to an expanded account of political of reason is undoubtedly compelling. It does follow, however, that the disclosing impact of exemplarity is more effectively conceived in relation to the actual dynamics of political struggle than the free-floating universal of *sensus communis*. Understood in sociocentric terms as symbolically significant instances in political conflict, exemplarity takes on an greater interpretative complexity than Ferrara's tranquil, syncretic account. For example, the history of the African-American struggle for equality in the US has many exemplary occurrences that continue to have inspiring effects on the contemporary political imagination: Rosa Parks' defiant act, Martin Luther King's 'I have a Dream' speech, the black power salute at the 1968 Olympics, the Black Lives Matter movement, 'taking the knee' at recent sporting events to name only a few of the most obvious events. To construe the galvanizing effect of these instances in terms of a normativity that proceeds from a shared conception of who we are would be a strangely tangential and apolitical interpretation that ignores how, for many, a deepening racial divide means that 'the discovery of commonality and agreement between the races [is] a dim prospect' (Kinder and Sanders 1996: 33). It is a quietist interpretation that strips such exemplary instances of a political force and urgency that comes not solely from the invocation of a shared humanity but from the need to make visible the brutality and violence of racial domination that has continued in a relatively unbroken, though transfigured line, from slavery to present-day conditions of formal equality.

On this agonistic view, the normativity of the exemplar resides not so much in reaffirming unity around generally held truths, but in the negative impact of making visible experiences that are more usually overlooked, devalued, even denied by mainstream society. Thus, what gives the song '*Strange Fruit*' (and the blues more generally) exemplary political significance in the history of black struggle is the exceptional lyrical expression it gives to the suffering and violence that has blighted the lives of African-Americans.[3] As Ralph Ellison explains, blues is the autobiographical chronicle of personal catastrophe expressed lyrically, it is the 'impulse to keep the painful details and episodes of a brutal experience alive in one's aching consciousness, to finger its jagged grain and to transcend it, not by the consolation of philosophy but by squeezing from it near tragic, near comic lyricism' (Ellison 1953: 78). Ferrara might well argue that in its depiction of the 'radical negativity' of lynching and hanging, *Strange Fruit* reminds us anew of the fundamental right of all human beings to lead a flourishing life. But in so far as this generalized interpretation is detached from a concrete sense of historicity, it obscures other important political functions of the exemplar such as the way it acts as a singularly potent vehicle of protest and black counter-testimony. As Angela Davis reminds us, Billie Holliday's version of the song almost single-handedly rejuvenated the tradition of protest and resistance in African-American popular culture as well as being a frontal challenge to lynching and racism and to 'the policies of a government that implicitly condoned such activities...through its refusal to pass laws against lynching' (Davis 1998a: 196). In this light, it is evident how Ferrara's politically neutralized concept robs exemplarity of its power as an indictment of the established order. The impact of the exemplar flows not from the abstract anticipation of future flourishing but from the shocking reminder of past suffering, suffering that continues into the present day in the form of what Christopher Lebron describes as an invisible moral horror. Speaking of the continuing political resonance of *Strange Fruit*, he writes:

> It is one thing to witness a black corpse hanging from a tree; it is another for black suffering to become less overtly corporeal and increasingly economically, politically, and sociologically systemic. Yet, while we no longer publicly hang blacks by the neck, the fact of systemic racial inequality poses an existential threat all the same for it indicates America's lack of consistency to the ideal of moral equality, which has real costs for black lives. (Lebron 2013: 1–2)

---

[3] As Lebron puts it, the lyrics of *Strange Fruit* 'haunt us aesthetically because the horror of human suffering is depicted in the form of a pastoral ode. Black death in the space normally occupied by verdant life' (2013: 15).

This fierce indictment of US democracy may well be obliquely encompassed in Ferrara's capacious notion of 'horizons of suffering' but his ethically unifying frame of reference cancels out any sense of political urgency and moral outrage. If past injustice is to be adequately acknowledged and present inequality properly understood, then, the 'abstract thought of universality' must be tied to 'the anamnestic power of a remembering that goes beyond the concepts of morality itself' (Habermas, quoted in McCarthy 1993: 214). For many oppressed groups, it is imperative that justice has such retrospective, rectificatory dimensions for, to pass over them, is arguably to indirectly compound oppression in the cognitive form of the historical amnesia that typifies white ignorance (e.g., McCarthy 2004: Mills 2017b: 65).

Ferrara responds to criticisms of political neutralization by maintaining that the exemplary instance always bears within itself a 'genealogical sediment' of previous struggles, that *sensus communis* is 'nourished by the force emanating from... horizons of suffering... these experiences and acts direct our gaze to new dimensions that need to be brought within the circle of justice' (2018a: 154). But here too, political neutralization works through the naturalized 'we' ('our gaze' 'our imagination' p. 154) that substitutes fictional consensus for social division and ever-expanding inclusivity for deepening inequality and stigmatization. In so far as exemplarity reminds us that those who suffer need to be 'bought within the circle of justice', it expresses what Rancière calls 'consensus thinking' which 'conveniently represents what it calls 'exclusion' in the simple relationship between an inside and an outside' (Rancière 1999: 115). Concealed by this inside–outside dynamic is the part played by seemingly inclusive democratic orders themselves in creating the very exclusions that they explicitly condemn. In other words, political exclusion is not, as consensus thinking depicts it, a problem whose cause lies beyond the boundaries of the political order and can be overcome by simply including the previously excluded. Rather exclusion is often a problem internal to the established order itself, one created by its own hierarchies of power, stigmatization, and marginalization where some groups are invariably treated as second-class citizens. When exemplarity is disentangled from consensus thinking, from the 'neutralising magma of ethical politics', its disclosive force takes on a more unsettling and confrontational significance (Vázquez-Arroyo 2016: 5). In the words of Cornel West it 'exemplifies a 'certain sense of urgency, a kind of state of emergency that we find ourselves in with the plight of the most vulnerable' (West 2011: 116–17). As a performative enactment of wider political struggles, the exemplar does not so much shore up wishful liberal thinking about the intrinsic progressivism of democracy but rather attempts to 'shatter the sleepwalking, to awaken, to unnerve, to unhouse people' (pp. 116–17).

The politics of exemplarity and disclosure is, then, more polemical, and fraught than the orderly affirmative process portrayed by Ferrara. Polemical in as much as the rendering visible of suppressed experiences may serve to confront the dominant order with shortcomings it disavows. The force of the exemplar, in this sense, comes not from the assertion of a right to be included in a political order that is 'already up and running and presumed to be reasonably decent' but from the condemnation of that order and implied demand that it be transformed (Allen 2005: 55). This confrontational dynamic is captured in Ellison's description of Richard Wright's autobiography *Black Boy*: 'he [Wright] has converted the American Negro impulse toward self-annihilation and "going-under-ground" into a will to confront the world, to evaluate his experience honestly and throw his findings unashamedly into the guilty conscience of America' (Ellison 1953: 94). As a performative enactment of the divided nature of the social world, the exemplar is likely to be challenging to the established order, its reception contested and potentially divisive. As counter-hegemonic utterance, it does not so much endorse collective norms as engender political dis-identification with the status quo. Nor does it simply 'frame a collective body' but instead disrupts assumed social unities; it produces a 'multiplicity of folds and gaps in the fabric of common experience that change the cartography of the perceptible, the thinkable, and the feasible' (Rancière 2016: 147). For example, the black power salute given by the US athletes (Tommie Smith and John Carlos) in the 1968 Olympics was undeniably an exemplary political gesture, but it was also regarded by many as unnecessarily confrontational and contentious. The athletes were lauded in certain quarters and condemned in others including by the Olympic organizing committee which, using the threat of expelling the whole US team from the games, scapegoated the two men, barring them from further participation. Likewise, taking the knee has now become an iconic gesture against racism but, when first enacted as a statement of solidarity, was a source of political contention and denounced, not only by those on the far Right, as disrespectful, unpatriotic, unsporting.[4]

Polemic, antagonism, and contestability are not limited to a certain genre of political exemplarity but, arguably, are ineliminable characteristics of democratic politics more generally. This conflictual dimension is air-brushed away in Ferrara's sanguine and unified account of disclosure which takes for granted that a commitment to liberal norms is already in place and reaffirmed with every exemplary recurrence. Consider, for example, Ferrara's description of Obama's first election as an expression of the 'exceptionally dynamic property of the whole democratic system, unequalled in any other democratic country' and reminder of the 'extraordinary rapidity with which a constitutional order has proven capable of bringing racial equality from being a contested terrain in the 50's and 60's' ... to a reality fully implemented in the supreme executive institution' (2018b: 398). Certainly, given the nation's history of racial division, the election of Obama was a singular and momentarily hopeful event for many.

---

[4] On the politically 'disorienting' quality of this gesture see: https://www.nytimes.com/2017/09/25/opinion/nfl-football-kaepernick-take-knee.html

Ferrara's glowing interpretation of it as an instance of constitutional exemplarity seems naïve, however, both in its overestimation of the dynamism of US political institutions and disregard of the depth of racial inequality beyond elite political circles. His irenic interpretation presupposes a shared commitment to liberal values and to a progressive understanding of history that downplays actual social dissensus—after all, the election of Obama was not regarded by all groups in the US as an unambiguously good thing. This prior, not fully articulated commitment to liberal norms is problematic because it stands in tension with Ferrara's other contention that exemplars are galvanizing precisely because the ideals they invoke lack cultural and political specificity and appeal to all groups regardless of social situation. In this light, Ferrara's selection of the Rawlsian notion of the 'reasonable' as an 'unthickened' rallying point for transcultural deliberation seems not a little problematic given the ways in which the term has historically been deployed, in exclusionary fashion, to construe women, black people, and other minorities as unreasonable others. This does not mean that such terms are unsalvageable as exemplars; rather it is to warn against what Davis describes as a flattening of history that 'deflects rather than summons more complex efforts at comprehension' (Davis 1998d: 284). Ultimately, then, the univocity of meaning imposed by Ferrara forecloses recognition of the polysemic and contested character of the exemplar, a character that arises from its ineluctable embeddedness in struggles over meaning and symbolic resources. By directing attention away from these patterns of agency and struggle and towards a hypothetical normative commonality, democratic conflict is neutralized and the political significance of the exemplar is reduced to what Gabriel Rockhill describes as the 'magical powers of the talisman' (Rockhill 2014: 5).

Problems of Parochialism

A worry about the rethinking of exemplarity in relation to political context proposed here is that it is an unduly parochial approach that undermines disclosure's transcendent critical-normative impact. The thought is that interpreting exemplary disclosure in relation to the specific circumstances of struggle threatens to downplay its emancipatory bearing on collective self-understanding and the wider social imaginary. Certainly, Ferrara seems to think that parochialism and the undermining of context transcendence are the inevitable consequences of such an approach. He maintains that criticism of *sensus communis* from the perspective of power amounts to the reassertion of radical contextualism that reduces critique to the mere venting of subjective grievance: 'in order for critique to be something more than the venting of a subjective grievance, critique must be validated by, or comport with, something (perhaps not a principle, a value, a standard, but nonetheless something) that is not merely "subjective," parochially or "locally shared"' (Ferrara 2018a: 152). Part of the problem here is that Ferrara does not appreciate sufficiently the ambiguity, considered in the first chapter, inherent in the idea of context transcendence. How far beyond its immediate locale does the impact of the exemplar have to extend to qualify as being not merely a local imaginative projection but a truly context-transcending one? How would we even go about assessing whether this is the case or not? According to what criteria is it possible to establish transcendence? As Richard Rorty notes, the distinction between context transcendence and context dependence is, at best, highly indeterminate, if not, at worst, implausible: 'when I ask myself whether my truth claims "transcend my local cultural context" I have no clear idea whether they do or not, because I cannot see what "transcendence" means' (Rorty 2000: 9). Ferrara ignores these ambivalences and indeterminacies and, in a way typical of paradigm-led thinking, resorts to an exaggerated opposition between transcendence and immanence: if disclosing critique cannot be said to be strongly universalist—in the extra-social sense of *sensus communis*—it must inevitably fall into a parochial contextualism. This all-or-nothing logic, familiar from the work of Forst and Honneth, resurfaces again, forcing ideas of context transcendence into misleading dichotomies. On a pragmatist view, it is not a question so much of choosing between immanence and transcendence as one of avoiding the artificial privilege of one side of the dialectic over the other, and to inhabit the space between experiential disclosure and generalizing critique in a productive and dialogical manner as possible.

To put this dynamic in the left–Hegelian terms of critical theory, the concrete and the universal are inextricably bound up with each other in a multiplicity of ways, and it is within this complex yet unavoidable movement between the two that critique strives to operate. Thus, on this dialectical view, attempts of the radical contextualist to capture pure particularity, the new, and unfamiliar without detour through abstraction would be to lapse back into a conceptually untenable and self-defeating empiricism. Even the most singular and unfamiliar of experiences are only intelligible, albeit in a partial or incomplete fashion, with reference to a matrix of deep-seated normative and conceptual assumptions. Even as newly disclosed particularity may displace and disrupt these frameworks, it is not entirely thinkable outside of them for this would be to hypostatize difference as radical alterity—as Ferrara has rightly observed. Moreover, it is precisely because of the latent presence of the universal in the particular that it is possible for the experience of suffering to be transfigured from mere grievance to a political claim about social wrongs that demand redress. Equally, just as it is not possible to conceptualize the concrete instance in-itself and without detour through abstraction, so too, universals are equally as dependent on particularity for their expression. In the Hegelian tradition, universality cannot be conceived directly—or at least only at the risk of following Kant into groundless abstraction—but only indirectly through social particularity. This co-implication means that, despite assertions of their cultural neutrality or 'un-thickened' nature, universals necessarily rest on selective accounts of social being that highlight certain aspects as 'essential' and normatively significant while passing over others as inessential and insignificant. Historically these insignificant features of being have been associated, explicitly or implicitly, with gendered and racialized dimensions of social existence. When these presuppositions go unexamined and are naturalized as transcendental principles and norms, then the risk is that universals become co-implicated with exclusion and domination. This is attested to by the myriad of criticisms devoted to unpacking universalizing modes of thought, and exposing the unacknowledged racial and gendered premises that often render them less neutral and inclusive than they initially appear. In this context, few would demur from Judith Butler's assessment that 'universality has been used to extend certain colonialist and racist understandings of civilized "man", to exclude certain populations from the domain of the human, and to produce itself as a false and suspect category' (Butler 2000: 38).

It would be simplistic to assume, however, that the inevitable entanglement of the universal within the social terrain of power entails a wholesale rejection of abstracted thought as inescapably distorted, as bad faith impositions of culturally biased norms. It is not a question of permanently eschewing universals in favour of radical contextualism, for even the most particularistic thought depends in some measure for its cogency on capacities of transcendence, abstraction, and generalization. As a necessary condition of thought, the 'craving for generality' cannot be avoided. Given this, the challenge for the theorist is not to relinquish universals so much as to open them up by interrogating their disavowed social content and thus to potentially expand or transform them; to endeavour to be critically alert to the different forms that the universal assumes, to interrogate its all-encompassing rationale from the perspective of social particularity and thereby to problematize its inherent drift to assimilation and normalization. Indeed, it is precisely this treatment of the universal as a site of 'insistent contest and resignification' that, for many thinkers, is a precondition of politically engaged critique (Butler 1992: 7). Thus, contra Ferrara, to criticize *sensus communis* from the perspective of power is not simply to affirm an unmediated contextualism but is rather to question the tendency to present universality as ungrounded and culturally neutral. It is to eschew the false choice of 'narrow particularism' versus 'emaciated universalism' and to endeavour instead to conceive of the universal as 'enriched by all that is particular, a universal enriched by every particular: the deepening and coexistence of all particulars' (Césaire 2010: 152). Accordingly, what Ferrara regards as the inconsequential movement from one subjective grievance to another can be alternately viewed as part of an ongoing attempt to keep universality open to its underlying social conditions of possibility.

The issue, then, is not one of choosing between transcendence and immanence but rather of conceptualizing context transcendence in a way that does not violate critique's wider theoretical and political commitments. As Ferrara helpfully puts it: 'the crux of the matter is not whether context-transcending, and its attendant neutral normative construct, are desirable but *what sort of* context-transcending we should look for, compatibly with our philosophical commitments' (2018a: 152). The problem with *sensus communis* is that, as a way of formulating context transcendence, it is in tension with critique's wider hermeneutic commitments particularly to the situated nature of all thought. To be consistent with this historicizing premise, context transcendence needs to be conceived in intramundane terms, that is, as a principle that while internal to social life is sufficiently general to furnish a wider evaluative perspective. This of course is precisely the move made by various members of the Frankfurt School in their attempts to ground critique in the immanent universals of communicative rationality, recognition, justification, and so on. *Sensus communis* is unlike these other foundational principles, however, in the key respect that it is reconstructed not from practices internal to social life or from the nature of practical reason, but from a supposed intuitive core whose mysterious presocial but nonnatural status serves to place it partially outside of history. Evidently Ferrara has good reasons for wanting to avoid the formalism of discourse ethics and similar proceduralist formulations of 'transcendence within'. But the extra-social status he attributes to the intuitive matrix of *sensus communis* seems to compound rather than overcome potential problems of abstraction and empty universalism. The idea that the free-floating device of *sensus communis* allows us to transcend all determinate positions and assume a definitive critical-normative position seems to be close to what Rorty describes as 'make-believe transcendence' (2000: 9). On this pragmatist view, 'the only thing that can transcend a social practice is another social practice' (2000: 7). Likewise, the validity of critique's diagnoses and insights will always be a matter for argumentation, and the critic must be prepared to justify them 'in a historicist, comparative, open-ended, and concrete way' without resort to a transcendental guarantee (Cooke 2006: 70). Transcendence, as the enlargement of thought, is not the result of assuming a supra-social standpoint but an achievement of dialogical inquiry, one that is ongoing and always open to renewal: 'Real transcendence... occurs when I say "I am prepared to justify this belief not just to people who share the following premises with me, but to lots of other people who do not share those premises but with whom I share certain others"' (Rorty 2000: 11).

To criticize *sensus communis* from the perspective of power is not, then, to fall back into a politics of mere subjective grievance, but to ask for a way of conceiving context transcendence that is more thoroughly historicized and hence more responsive to the particularities of experience than Ferrara's proposal. Even within the ethicized model of politics that Ferrara prefers, it is possible to explain sources of normativity with reference not to an extra-social dimension of intuition but with reference instead to the pragmatic presuppositions built into deliberation and mutual understanding (Baynes 2004: 210). From a pragmatist perspective, it is possible for critical standards to be conceptualized relative to social contexts but for them to still have wider validity, although this may well take the 'weak' form of 'contextualized' or 'internal objectivity' rather than the 'strong' form of intuitive universalism that Ferrara favours (West 2011: 121–2).[5] The context-transcending force of the exemplar could be explained, for instance, through a type of sociolinguistic expressivism or what Ellison calls a 'sociology of sensibility' that addresses the complexities of social context rather than suspending them in favour of a hypothetical commonality (Ellison 1953: 86). On such an expressivist account, an exemplary political act is recognizable beyond its immediate locale in so far as it draws on the norms and values of the wider community and enacts them in a unique and exceptional fashion. Yet although its singular reworking of norms and codes renders the exemplar interpretable as such, it does not follow that individuals need necessarily converge around a single, artificially homogeneous understanding of its wider political or normative significance (e.g., Anderson and Pildes 2000: 1525ff).

Recognizing the contested, polysemic character of the exemplar is not to deny its transcontextual force, but this needs to be explained in terms other than the quasi-naturalized device of *sensus communis*. Its wider resonance could be recast, for instance, around Raymond Williams' idea of a structure of feeling which denotes a dynamic substrate of ideas and experiences—'thought as felt and feeling as thought'—vying to emerge at any one time in history. This social experience 'in solution' may not yet be articulated in a fully worked-out form but nor is it mere flux; it is a structured formation of embodied affects and dispositions that 'exert palpable pressures and set effective limits on experience and action' (Williams 1977: 132). On this view, the normative reach of the exemplar resides in the way it taps into a substrate of inchoate experience, crystallizing fluid, and semi-articulated dynamics into a singular inspirational form. In so far as it gives expression to emergent constellations of experience, the exemplar can be a vehicle of subaltern agency and world-building in the way described, for instance, by Angela Davis in her celebrated study of black women blues singers, *Blues Legacies and Black Feminism*. Emerging as it did, in the decades after the abolition of slavery, the blues gave secular musical expression (as opposed to sacred musical tradition of spirituals and gospel) to 'the new social and sexual realities encountered by African Americans as free women and men' (Davis 1998a: 6). The blues helped to construct a new black consciousness articulated around a different valuation of individual emotional needs and desires: 'the birth of the blues was aesthetic evidence of new psycho-social realities within the black population' (1998a: 5). In particular, in the work of black women musicians, the blues fuelled the formation of an emergent identity for African-American women that, relative

---

[5] On Horkheimer's notion of internal objectivity see F. Rush 2004: 26.

to mainstream norms of femininity, was subversive in that it gave voice to hitherto unexpressed themes of female desire, sexuality, and longing. Moreover, in 'naming' for the first time issues such as male violence that were a threat to the well-being of women, the blues had a consciousness-raising effect. By recasting the isolated experiences of individual women as 'problems shared by the community' it made oppositional stances to male violence culturally possible (1998a: 33). By publicly articulating hitherto unacknowledged social problems, the blues were not merely complaint but powerful political statements about oppressive social conditions. The blues were a historical preparation for political protest: 'they begin to articulate a consciousness that takes into account social conditions of class exploitation, racism and male dominance as seen through the lens of the complex emotional responses of black female subjects. While there may not be a direct line to social activism, activist stances are inconceivable without the consciousness such songs suggest' (p. 119). In short, the disclosive impact of the exemplar as blues came not so much from the affirmation of a 'shared' collective ideal but from politicized expression of an overlooked experiential world—the alienated familiar—which criticized racist and patriarchal social arrangements and pointed towards emerging possibilities for women's social being. The universal is present in this politically reconfigured idea of exemplarity but not, *pace* Ferrara, as a supervening, unifying force, but instead as the expanded horizon of possibility glimpsed in the enactment of a new, determinate subject position. As Davis puts it: 'the blues registered sexuality as a tangible expression of freedom' (1998a: 8). Thinking in this way about exemplarity rooted in social reality avoids the depoliticizing entailments of a free-floating universalism and renders the connection to political agency more visible. Politics is after all a scenario of action; it is a process of resistance, protest, and struggle. In Ferrara's decontextualized account, however, there is little evidence of any such concrete agency. If an agential force can be discerned at all, it appears, in displaced form, in the free-floating abstraction of the exemplar that enigmatically affirms extra-political truths about the human condition.

Conclusion: Priority of the Negative

In the end then, the disclosing force of exemplarity, its imaginative capacity to bring forward possibilities not visible in the present moment, is stymied by its grounding in the fictitious universal of *sensus communis*. Untethered from a determinate social context, exemplarity does not so much disclose new worlds of meaning and possibility as confirm a dominant liberal narrative about the essentially progressive, if unfulfilled nature of democracy. In so far as it sublates the political reality of dissensus, division, and struggle into a supposed intuitive consensus, exemplary disclosure naturalizes the status quo and is more a vehicle of political closure than imaginative openness. The speculative device of *sensus communis* unbalances the dialectic of transcendence and immanence and pushes disclosing critique too far in the direction of abstraction, thus weakening the responsiveness to unfamiliar and marginal experiential worlds that Ferrara regards as essential to democratic thinking at its best.

In so far as this is the case, Ferrara's exemplary universalism can be said to fail in its overarching objective of pluralizing reason, of supplementing rational procedural norms with a mode of democratic thinking guided by the imagination and openness to other ways of being. Exemplary universalism is intended as a version of Arendt's thinking without bannisters that, by eschewing pregiven interpretative principles, enshrines ethical receptivity to the alien, the new, and the other as a crucial element of democratic judgement. But given the abstract, socially weightless terms in which exemplary universalism is construed by Ferrara, it finishes by deploying an assimilative, top-down logic that is not so dissimilar from those formal universals that he ostensibly rejects. In this case, social difference and particularity is negated by being subsumed under the extra-political truth of *sensus communis*. Ferrara's response is that, lacking the transcendent perspective provided by *sensus communis*, disclosing critique is deprived of general relevance and is reduced to the venting of subjective grievance. In making this claim he makes an argumentative move typical of paradigm-led critical theory, that is, to adduce an artificially polarized distinction between universality and particularity, context-transcendence and context-dependence. The politicized idea of exemplarity that I have suggested as an alternative model for disclosing critique does not abandon aspiration to universal relevance—universality is after all a necessary, distinguishing feature of the properly political from the merely social instance. But, at the same time, universality is conceived in thinner terms as inseparable from its always provisional instantiation within the so-called parochial and contingent. This 'polemical configuration of the universal' is one not limited 'to the rules of the game but designates a permanent struggle to enlarge the restricted universal form of universalism (that is the rule of the game)...that make[s] the existing universal confront and supersede its limitations' (Ranicère 2016b: 84).

In sum, exemplarity lacks a firm-enough foothold in lived experience to be able to transcend its own theoretical solipsism and open up new perspectives on social being and new horizons of understanding. It is the paramount importance of grounding emancipatory critique in the experiential reality of oppressed groups that critical theorists refer to when they speak of the conceptual priority of the negative (Wellmer 1991: 202). Priority of the negative denotes a certain methodological orientation where the theorist starts from lived suffering, oppression, and disempowerment and moves outwards from there to formulate a systematic critique of power. From this perspective, the problem for political thinking is not that of reconciling social particularity under harmonizing universals, as Ferrara conceives it, because in so far as the universal can only ever be incompletely conceived through particularity, it can never be fully inclusive. As Butler puts it 'the provisional and parochial versions of universality' can never exhaust 'the possibilities of what might be meant by the universal' (Butler 1997a: 89). What is really at stake, then, is the status of the particular in relation to the universal; how to situate social suffering within a broader critique of society without thereby effacing its lived reality and what this may reveal about the world. Adorno describes this attentiveness to lived suffering as an 'unalleviated consciousness of negativity'. He means by this that it is only through ceaseless attempts to ground and reground itself in concrete experience, that theoretical reason manages to resist its tendency to self-enclosure and to destabilize abstract, frictionless universals by injecting them with new meaning and political relevance. In principle, Ferrara recognizes the priority that the negative, qua 'sedimented social suffering', should hold in democratic political thinking if it is to retain enduring emancipatory relevance. In practice, however, attentiveness to the particularity of experience and hence exemplarity's disclosing force is undermined by his reliance on what might be termed, following Césaire (2010), the 'emaciated' or 'fleshless' universal of *sensus communis*.

5
Critique and the 'Merely Experienced'

Introduction

In the light of what has been argued so far about paradigm-led thinking, it is unsurprising to find that feminists are often justifiably sceptical of the value of Frankfurt School theory to work on gender oppression. Nonetheless, in so far as Frankfurt School thought is more diverse and theoretically richer than current paradigm-led trends suggest, it may be seen to possess resources, nascent but underutilized, that feminist theorists could fruitfully draw upon. Even thinkers such as Wendy Brown, who worry about the depoliticizing effects that Habermasian thought has had on feminist political theory, concede that the Frankfurt School tradition, more broadly conceived, represents a 'wondrously rich constellation of inquiry and ideas' (Brown 2006: 2). These resources comprise of an expanded materialist account of power that extends from structures to the psyche, a method of deriving normative outcomes from social actuality, and the idea of critique as a dialogic and reflexive mode of inquiry. Taking up the threads of the discussion begun in the Introduction, I argue in this and the subsequent two chapters, that it is in the work of prominent feminist thinkers explicitly allied to the Frankfurt School that this promising theoretical potential is most fully realized. Their work is distinguished from that of their male counterparts above all by the way it explicitly eschews paradigm-led theorizing and develops instead contextually sensitive, multidimensional and problem-led ways of analysing gender and other oppressions. This explicitly pragmatic orientation—theorizing with practical intent—obviously comes in large part from their responsiveness to feminist politics more generally and, in particular, its fundamental aim to advance a systematic critique of gender oppression as a global phenomenon while remaining receptive to differences in women's experience across socio-cultural divides. This political impetus has motivated Frankfurt School feminist theorists to pay particular attention to formulating innovative dialogical and inclusive ways of theorizing and talking across perspectives.

The potent, animating connection between feminist critical theory and politics is nowhere embodied more fully than in the work of Nancy Fraser which is the focus of this chapter. Her thought represents a forceful riposte to the androcentric tendencies of other Frankfurt School thinkers, showing that, far from being of marginal significance, the critique of gender oppression is in fact pivotal to understanding capitalist social relations more generally. In moving gender to the heart of critical theory, she develops a ground-breaking analysis of power and oppression and has established an important agenda for feminist research. Fraser's non-monist, multidimensional social critique fruitfully aligns with the ways that black and postcolonial feminist theorists have also rejected single-lens analyses for complex accounts of power capable of grasping intersectional gender oppressions. Likewise, Fraser's 'neopragmatist' model of justice enshrines a contextually indexed approach to normative reasoning comparable with evaluative approaches developed by transnational feminist theorists. In short, Fraser steers critical theory away from the limiting preoccupation with normative foundations, reaffirms its foundations in systematic social criticism, and gives vital new meaning to the Frankfurt School's original, animating intention to proffer an emancipatory critique of power.

Yet, despite the undoubted importance of Fraser's work in integrating gender concerns with critical theory, I argue that there is an aspect of her thought that sits uneasily with her other feminist commitments and this is to do with the status she accords to experience in theoretical inquiry. An unresolved tension runs through her thought between, on the one side, unwavering commitment to placing a materialist account of gender oppression at the heart of critical theory and, on the other, failure to think through certain epistemological dimensions of what theorizing across discrepancies of power might involve. This failure manifests itself in the implicit downgrading of the epistemic value of the experiential perspective to an unmasking critique of power, on the grounds of its inherent unreliability, and corresponding over-assertion of the interpretative authority of the theoretical perspective. This epistemic hierarchy of theory over experience undercuts her contention that the participatory parity model endorses a dialogical, reflexive form of reasoning and is also an incongruous, even alienating, starting position for a political theory explicitly intended to contribute to the emancipation of oppressed groups. It results in an over-emphasis on the adjudicative function of critique in a way that forecloses other contextually indexed, evaluative functions which are potentially more compatible with practical emancipatory aims. Shortcomings in Fraser's attitude to lived experience are particularly evident when compared with the work of black feminist theorists, such as Patricia Hill Collins and Angela Davis, which is rooted in a more acute political awareness of the difficulties of according one-sided privilege to theory over experience in knowledge production. While black feminist theorists share Fraser's materialist concern to avoid essentializing lived experience as the truth of oppression, they are arguably more successful at combining this with ideas of dialogical and reflexive reason based on a genuine methodological equality of the experiential and theoretical perspectives.

Overcoming Monism

If a defining characteristic of Frankfurt School thought is its theoretical openness, its 'aversion to closed philosophical systems' underwritten by '"fallibilistic" and "reconstructive" methodology', then this is most apparent in the work of its feminist theorists (Allen and Mendieta 2018: 5). It is arguably the responsiveness of these feminist theorists to the concerns of feminism as a practical political movement that has induced their deviation from paradigm-led modes of theorizing and development of imaginative, methodologically diverse, and contextually indexed modes of critical inquiry. The animating impulse of the feminist movement in general, namely, to advance a systematic critique of global gender oppression while remaining attentive to differences in women's experience across cultures is the catalyst for this open approach to theorizing. The balancing of critical generality with experiential particularity has meant that feminist theorists have long eschewed falsely unifying universals and analogous homogenizing abstractions and instead have developed modes of critique that combine sensitivity to context with systematic explanatory force. Accordingly, Frankfurt School feminist inquiry is more emphatically pragmatist in nature than that of their male counterparts, embodying an approach that Iris Marion Young has described as 'theorising with practical intent'. By this she means a mode of critique that aims not 'to develop systematic theories that can account for everything in a particular field' but rather follows a line of inquiry 'to solve particular conceptual or normative problems that arise from a practical context' (Young 1997: 5).

Echoing Young's particularly apt description, Nancy Fraser labels her critical approach as 'neopragmatist', as an exercise in 'situated theorizing' led not by fidelity to a specific paradigm but by the diagnosis of concrete social problems (Fraser and Honneth 2003: 45–8; Fraser1989: 7). In an early essay co-authored with Linda Nicholson, she describes feminist critique in similar pragmatist terms as being 'more like a puzzle whose various pieces are being filled in by many different people' rather than a 'construction to be completed by a single grand theoretical stroke' (Fraser and Nicholson 1990: 32). In terms of her own work, what this pragmatism means, first and foremost, is that it starts from real-world dilemmas of power and oppression and not from philosophical questions of normative foundation. Fraser's work reactivates, in other words, a distinguishing aspect of Frankfurt School critique that has been largely forgotten in recent years, namely that as practical emancipatory thought it proceeds from criticism of existing injustices and oppression. For Fraser, this means primarily, but not exclusively, gender inequality and oppression. Over the years, she has repeatedly exposed the tokenism of mainstream Frankfurt School analyses of gender where it is treated as merely epiphenomenal or localized inequity and has shown instead how the critique of women's subordination necessarily entails a critique of the entire social order. Gender inequality is not just a feature of intimate relations between men and women in the domestic sphere but structures all realms of social activity and, via the exploitation of women's reproductive labour, is a crucial precondition of capitalist accumulation. Her early seminal essay 'What's Critical about Critical Theory' remains in many ways unsurpassed as a definitive feminist statement of problems with the Frankfurt School's understanding of gender. Likewise, her recent work on expropriation and the hidden domestic abode brings questions of gender, reproduction, and care to the heart of a social theory of capitalist relations. Indeed, in her view, if critical social theory truly aims towards 'the self-clarification of the struggles and wishes of the age', then one of the most important standards against which it should be assessed is the adequacy of its analysis of gender: 'How well does it theorize the situation and prospects of the feminist movement? To what extent does it serve the self-clarification of the struggles and wishes of contemporary women?' (2013a: 19–20).

It is not just that her pragmatic, power-first approach enables Fraser to give centre stage to hitherto marginalized questions of gender oppression but also that it leads her to reject monist critical theory. While she shares with other Frankfurt School thinkers, such as Honneth, a commitment to grand theory, on which more will be said later, she does not think that analysis of capitalist social totality can be satisfactorily achieved from a 'single variable' or 'monist' perspective. Echoing criticisms of 'single lens' perspectives, made by black feminist theorists such as Collins, Fraser argues that instead of 'uni-categorial' diagnosis, critique needs to advance a multidimensional analysis of power if it is to adequately capture intersectional structures of oppression and the complex social reality to which they give rise. As she puts it: 'Far from generating a single, all-pervasive logic of reification, capitalist society is normatively differentiated, encompassing a determinate plurality of distinct but inter-related social ontologies' (Fraser 2014a: 67). Accordingly, a thread that runs throughout her oeuvre is the attempt to systematically demonstrate the limitations of monist social diagnoses with respect to an account of gender subordination. In 'What's Critical about Critical Theory', Fraser exposes the different ways in which Habermas's unilinear explanation of social injustice caused by the intrusion of money and power into the noninstrumental domains of the life-world serves to simplify the complexity of women's subordination. The one-way model of power implied in his colonization of the life-world thesis effectively naturalizes an androcentric division between public and private realms and ignores the power-mediated character of intimate relations. The depiction of the private realm as a power-free zone not only mystifies women's domestic labour but also serves to obscure the way in which the family, through its interactions with economy, polity, and the welfare state, plays a pivotal role in reproducing cycles of gender subordination. These flaws in Habermas's account of gender can ultimately be traced back to his attempt to harness a comprehensive social theory to the supposedly foundational principle of communication. Against this, Fraser argues that if the complex, nonlinear nature of power relations is to be adequately captured, explanatory frameworks need to be formulated in multidimensional not monist terms; unmasking critique must 'contain no a priori assumptions about the unidirectionality of social motion and casual influence' (2013a: 51).

Similarly, in her well- known exchange with Honneth, Fraser demonstrates how recognition monism results in misdiagnosis of gender inequalities. Honneth's attempt to derive an all-encompassing account of oppression and social wrong from the single underlying source of misrecognition is, in Fraser's view, bad social theory. There are forms of oppression, gender or otherwise, that do not involve processes of misrecognition at all. Many of the economic wrongs of neoliberalism that affect women (and men) in low-paid, precarious jobs have less to do with distorted schemas of cultural esteem than they have with systemic maldistribution of material resources and the relentless drive to maximize corporate profits. Recognition monism simplifies these complex causal logics by collapsing distributive dynamics into evaluative schema and thus underestimating the depth of economic injustice in capitalist societies. Fraser does not deny that there are significant types of recognition injustice, but insists that these are causally distinct from distributive injustices and, as such, their respective dynamics must be independently conceptualized instead of being conflated under the monist rubric of recognition.

In place of monist interpretative paradigms, Fraser proposes a multiperspectival diagnostic framework that presumes neither a fundamental core to social power nor one-way causality and hence can capture the 'full complexity' of structural causation in capitalist society. She initially sketches this out through her well-known 'perspectival dualism' of recognition and redistribution which explains the 'mutual irreducibility' of injustices of maldistribution and misrecognition but also 'their practical entwinement with each other' (Fraser and Honneth 2003: 48). Perspectival dualism enables Fraser to explain gender oppression in a way that markedly differs from other Frankfurt School analyses in that it conceptualizes the entanglement of interpersonal and structural dimensions instead of restricting analysis of gender to the sphere of intimacy and family life only. On Fraser's account, gender is a 'class like' differentiation that structures the division between paid productive labour and unpaid reproductive/domestic labour and as well as divisions within labour markets between high status, male-dominated professions and low status, female-dominated 'pink-collar' and caring jobs. At the same time, gender is also conceived as an entrenched pattern of values that privilege masculinity and devalue femininity, pervading behaviour in virtually all areas of social life. Gender-specific forms of status subordination are codified in many areas of the law, inform policymaking and standard professional practices (Fraser and Honneth 2003: 20–2). They pervade popular culture and everyday interpersonal reactions and are expressed in stereotyping, harassment, the denial of rights, sexual violence, and so on. Gender, in short, is a two-dimensional principle of social differentiation that generates a complex social map of economic disparities and subordinating patterns of value. Analogous to gender, perspectival dualism can be used to explain race and class subordination and, when applied to cross-cutting vectors of oppression, yields an intricate, nonreductive account of social power: 'the need for a perspectival dualism does not just arise endogenously, that is along a single two-dimensional axis of subordination whether that be race, gender or class. It also arises exogenously across intersecting axes of subordination' (Fraser and Honneth 2003: 26). In a nutshell, perspectival dualism overcomes a major failing of monist critical theories, that is, it can conceptualize the intersectional nature of oppression.

The flexibility of Fraser's diagnostic framework can be explained in part by the way that its primary focus on questions of power and social critique, instead of normative foundations, enables it to bypass certain justificatory constraints to which monist analyses are subject. Monist critical theories reconstruct social relations in such a way as to reflect arrangements of power that are not merely contingent but are supposedly constitutive of sociality per se, whether they be relations of communication, justification, or recognition. Explaining societal change then becomes a potential challenge for monist critique because, as relations alter and new, emergent or hitherto under-theorized aspects of power come to the fore, it has to continue to diagnose them according to its foundational logic. To do otherwise, that is to fail to trace the origins of these new forms of power back to a single underlying source, would be to undermine the constitutive status of the monist principle. Precisely because of the importance they attach to foundational structures, monist social theories carry extra 'justificatory burdens' that impose constraints on their ability to analyse heterogeneous dynamics of power. No matter how complex or dissimilar these dynamics might be, they must, in the monist frame, always be traced back in some way to an abstract governing principle. Thus, monist social critique is inherently prone to reductive social analysis because, according to its own foundational logic, it imposes what might be considered a fictitious unity on divergent dynamics of power and social assemblages. In as much as her power-first approach is unconcerned with issues of normative foundation and justifying a transcendental perspective, Fraser's social theory is not subject to such justificatory burdens. For her, the systematicity of critique arises from a differentiated, comprehensive and multilayered theory of structural power and not from identifying the constitutive logic of social being (e.g., Fraser 2014b: 547–9).

The upshot of this rejection of monist foundations is that Fraser seems able more easily than her peers to revise and extend her analytics of power and oppression when it is shown to be lacking in some crucial respect. This responsiveness to changing contexts and emerging problems is reflected in the revisions she has made to her diagnostic matrix over the course of her writings. For instance, she adds the dimension of representation to the original iteration of recognition and redistribution in response to criticisms that perspectival dualism overlooks important political dimensions of oppression. In addition to economic and cultural injustices, representation is intended to capture the phenomenon of political bias; the ways in which the political space is framed that allow democratic orders to implicitly favour some groups over others, accord more weight to some voices over others. By concretely exemplifying how, for instance, third-world women are marginalized as political subjects and gender is rendered invisible as a vector of transnational exploitation, Fraser (2013b) establishes representation as an important, if neglected dimension of democratic struggle. Established democracies operate mainly on principles of state-territoriality but this proves to be ineffective in dealing with problems caused by transnational corporations, such as environmental problems, the exploitation of workers, and so on. The dimension of representation allows Fraser to identify the ways in which, by operating outside of established parameters, globalizing capital has compounded and extended patterns of disadvantage that lead to the marginalization and silencing of vulnerable groups as democratic subjects.

Likewise, Fraser's recent work on Polyani signals an important revision to a materialist account of power by shifting attention from the 'front-story of exploitation' to the 'back-story of expropriation' (2014a: 60). Conceived in relation to the background social conditions necessary for capitalist accumulation, expropriation enables Fraser to update her analysis of the centrality of domestic labour to capitalist reproduction. The category of expropriation also allows her to explain the emergence of the environment as a site of political struggle under neoliberal capitalism and to show how racial domination and exploitation is a crucial precondition of capitalist accumulation. In this way, she overcomes the troubling silence of Frankfurt School critical theory on questions of race, colonialism, and so on. This silence is arguably not just an empirical oversight but also a paradigmatic failing, that is, the effect of using theoretical frameworks that do not permit questions of racism and racial domination to be appropriately formulated in the first place (e.g., Mills 2017a: 244). In sum, although Fraser theorizes at the macro-level of abstract structures of power, her multivalent account of power allows her to develop a diagnostic matrix sufficiently flexible to illuminate a wide variety of social experiences and life-worlds. This explanatory approach resonates with Collins's description of abductive theorizing as an innovative, relational, and fallibilistic mode of social analysis that sheds light on determinate problems by elucidating underlying connections between experiential and structural dimensions of social reality. Abductive theorizing allows her to affirm the importance of a general systematizing critical perspective while avoiding the syncretic universalism of paradigm-led theory and retaining awareness of changing patterns and particularities of lived social reality.

Participatory Parity

Although Fraser decouples unmasking critique from monist foundations, her power-led approach does not mean that she is unconcerned with issues of normativity. From her early essays on Foucault onwards, it is evident that it is precisely because of the neoHegelian interest in eliciting emancipatory values from social practice that Fraser prefers Frankfurt School critique to the normatively *laissez-faire* approach of poststructuralist critique. But, in contrast to the paradigm-led theory of her peers, Fraser embraces a 'neopragmatist' account of normativity that finds multiple emancipatory resources embedded in existing political struggles rather than a single, unchanging emancipatory interest. In contrast to Habermas and Forst, Fraser is adamant that political solutions can't be deduced straight from epistemology or that normatively valid courses of action may be established simply by conforming to monological justificatory procedures. Rather, normative outcomes that are varied and revisable are found in the practical political logic of a given situation: 'legitimation descends to the level of practices and becomes immanent within them...' (Fraser and Nicholson 1990: 23). At the same time, although untroubled by issues of normative foundation, Fraser does not forsake context-transcending judgements for a radically contextualist approach. Instead, she proposes that normative reasoning be guided by the idea of participatory parity which she defines as social arrangements that 'permit all (adult) members of society to interact with one another as peers' (Fraser and Honneth 2003: 36). Participatory parity is a thin universal that encompasses all (adult) partners to interaction and presupposes 'the equal moral worth of human beings'. Unlike the rational universals of other critical theories, it assumes this guiding role not by virtue of its foundational status but rather by virtue of its importance as an existing 'folk paradigm', that is, as a principal idiom of popular deliberation about social justice (Fraser and Honneth 2003: 11). Instead of centring on fundamental dynamics of practical reason or human flourishing, the meaning and content of participatory parity is determined by a primarily negativist focus on overcoming asymmetries of power. It is, in short, an historical rather than ontological reconstruction. Other than its thin presuppositions about equality, the substantive content of justice is determined by the particular dynamics of a given situation: 'For the pragmatist ... everything depends on precisely what currently misrecognized people need in order to be able to participate as peers in social life' (Fraser and Honneth 2003: 47).

According to Fraser, its negativist orientation towards overcoming multifarious asymmetries of power permits the participatory parity model to articulate a fuller account of justice than competing neoKantian critical theories. The proceduralism of the latter often renders them unable to address social wrongs and pathologies that fall outside specific definitions of rational justification and acceptability.

Compare, for example, participatory parity with the idea of justificatory fairness that governs Rainer Forst's account of justice. Both Fraser and Forst deploy a discourse theoretic understanding of justice and share the assumption that its emancipatory ends are best fulfilled when 'it makes the critique of institutionalized injustice its priority'(2008: 336), Fraser claims, however, that the principle of participatory parity will achieve deliberative outcomes that are fairer and more legitimate than the justification principle because of its keen sociological advertence to the power asymmetries that hamper the ability of individuals to participate as equals in political life. In contrast to this materialist orientation, the justification paradigm adopts a primarily linguistic orientation that turns around the successful enactment of principles of argumentation ('generality and reciprocity') that are allegedly immanent within the syntax of justice claims. It thus only ensures egalitarian standing once subjects are already securely situated in the political sphere of justification, but it does not tackle substantive forms of social subordination that exist prior to the justificatory scenario. Many injuries of distribution, recognition, and representation are not straightforwardly reflected in formal argumentation processes because they often manifest in insidious ways that circumvent the stipulated rules of procedural fairness.[1] The linguistic structure of justice as justification is, in short, a 'circuitous route' to underlying issues of power which are in danger of being filtered out of the picture altogether because of the over-concentration on argumentation. By invoking a 'capacious, variegated, and historically open-ended view of social personhood', the participatory parity model tackles power asymmetries, in their full diversity, head on.

On the face of it then, Fraser's power-first approach resonates with the work of nonWestern feminist theorists who are sceptical of reasoning normatively through formal universals, such as the abstract right to justification, because of inadequate consideration given to contexts of power. The abstracted and underdetermined nature of formal universals means that they do relatively little determinate evaluative work compared to 'rich...longitudinal empirical attention to contexts' (Khader 2019: 44). Even in cases where, for instance, it is clear, in an

---

[1] Fraser summarizes the difference between justification and participation models of justice in terms of their respective underlying ontologies of personhood. Fraser shares with Forst a 'political' conception of the person, namely one which highlights features of personhood that a non-sectarian theory of justice must presuppose. Forst, however, deploys a primarily discursive conception of persons as 'givers and receivers of justifications, who participate with one another in the social practice of exchanging public reasons'. Whereas for Fraser, persons are understood in a fuller sense as 'co-participants in an indeterminate multiplicity of social practices' where practices of justification are 'but one of the many social practices in which individuals ought to be able to exercise their free and equal personhood by participating with one another as peers'. Because of this fuller view of social personhood, justice as participatory parity is less vulnerable to the charge of excessive rationalism and posits a close relation between the liberal value of individual autonomy and social belonging, and therefore permits analysis of alienation from one's society and fellow actors. 'Thus the participation-theoretic view manages to recoup within a deontological theory of justice at least one important ethical concern that is usually deemed the exclusive province of teleological theories of self-realization' (2008: 344–5).

abstract sense, what an ideal end-goal might be, it may still be uncertain how it may be concretely brought about in very differing social circumstances. Conversely, some transnational gender harms, such as those associated with militarism or neoliberal exploitation, are difficult to perceive within individualized liberal justice frameworks that fail to 're-emphasize connections between local and universal' (Mohanty 2003: 226. My parenthesis). What Sen terms 'justice enhancing' approaches are better served therefore by adopting a negativist focus on correcting what is wrong, viz. blocked relations of power, in a specific situation rather than downwardly applying an end-goal morality. As Khader puts it 'feminism is mostly a view about the appropriate power relations that should obtain among groups in a society, not a view about which goods make an individual life go well (and so feminism is compatible with a number of different social and cultural forms)' (Khader 2019: 4). In so far as they fail to properly reckon with subtending material inequalities, Fraser concludes that formalist approaches such as Forst's justification critique fall into the error of 'politicism', that is the unwarranted assumption of the political realm's conceptual priority over its social context. Politicism fails to do justice to the 'complexity of structural causation in capitalist society' and cannot therefore conceptualize 'dialectically entwined sources of power asymmetry in contemporary society' (Fraser 2008: 343).

If its negativist emphasis on power allows the participatory parity paradigm to avoid the ungrounded politicism of neoKantian critique, on the one side, it also, on the other, enables it to avoid the troubling tendency of neoHegelian critique to construe socio-economic problems as ethical ones. This propensity to over-ethicize social problems and thereby depoliticize them is exemplified, for Fraser, in Honneth's construal of gender injustices in the family in psychological terms as 'violations of personal identity rooted in a lack of sensitivity to individual need in the sphere of intimacy which is governed by the principal of care' (Fraser and Honneth 2003: 219). On this view, the solution to gendered inequities in the family involves an ethical recalibration of interpersonal dynamics such that women's care-work is more fully recognized as vital to upholding relations of 'social freedom'. Against this, Fraser argues that gender relations in the family are properly conceived not as interpersonal dynamics of care, but as asymmetrical relations that partially reflect wider androcentric values, practices, and structures. By connecting internal familial dynamics to wider socio-economic and legal structures, Fraser conceives the family, in terms suggested by Collins, as a saturated site of power and mechanism for maintaining property accumulation, labour organization, and resource distribution. Reconstruing the family in materialist terms makes apparent that the ethical recalibration of care relations between men and women proposed by Honneth's recognition monism is in key respects tangential to correcting gender subordination. Instead, what might be required are a range of equalizing measures, both redistributive and resignificatory in nature, which reckon more fully with the nexus of intimate injustice and wider social inequalities. Such measures include reducing economic dependence in marriage, realigning the gender division of labour, provision of affordable childcare, rendering work practices more family-friendly, support for domestic violence, and so on (Fraser and Honneth 2003: 19–22). A further problem with Honneth's recognition paradigm in Fraser's view is that, by foregrounding issues of ethical self-realization over those of power, it lacks a principled basis on which to decide whether a claim is genuinely warranted or not. From its nebulous psychological foundation, it seems to follow that anything that enhances the claimant's self-esteem is justified and this can lead to potentially troubling situations where 'racist identities would merit some recognition, as they enable some poor "white" Europeans and Euro-Americans to maintain their sense of self worth ... [whereas] Anti-racist claims would confront an obstacle, in contrast, as they threaten the self-esteem of poor whites' (Fraser and Honneth 2003: 38. My parenthesis). By avoiding the valorization of thick ideas of human flourishing, participatory parity provides a stringent, that is ethically neutral, normative yardstick against which recognition (and redistribution) claims can be assessed: 'the norm of participatory parity serves to evaluate... recognition claims deontologically, without any need for ethical evaluation of the cultural or religious practices' (Fraser and Honneth 2003: 42). This question of adjudicating between genuine and spurious recognition claims is a pressing issue for Fraser and one to which we will return when considering her arguments about the status of lived experience for critique.

For now, it suffices to note that, as well as an expanded sense of justice, the eschewal of normative monism permits Fraser to reconstrue the dialogical aspects of critique in terms more inclusive than those of her peers. Her pragmatist emphasis on the context of power engenders a heightened meta-critical sense of the open and fallibilistic approach to reasoning that is necessary to offset social and epistemic disparities that may exist between theorist and subjects of inquiry, qua oppressed groups. Given that it is usually underwritten by a position of relative social privilege, it is important that emancipatory critique builds into itself as great a responsiveness as possible to the views of the disadvantaged citizens it addresses. Naturally, all critical theorists stress the dialogical nature of their thought; it is, as we have seen, a *sine qua non* of emancipatory inquiry that claims to practically respond to the concerns of oppressed groups. Among its different aspects, dialogism refers to the way that the reasoning process itself should be sufficiently open that it permits all affected citizens, regardless of disparities in social advantage, to contribute to the conversation about justice. A related aspect of dialogism is reflexivity; responsiveness to the 'other' also involves the ability of a given theory to critically scrutinize shortcomings in its own approach and, if need be, modify it, in response to feedback from those it addresses. A difficulty for paradigm-led critical theories is that their ability to operationalize dialogism and reflexivity is compromised by the foundational status accorded to their governing principles. For, as we have seen in previous chapters, the constitutive status bestowed on these principles ultimately places them outside of the hermeneutic circle thereby also placing the interpretative authority of the paradigm beyond question. Thus, a particular paradigm may be dialogical in a thin sense that nominally includes all affected subjects, but the terms of inclusion themselves remain beyond democratic dispute. Debate must be conducted according to the pregiven rationale of, say, discourse ethics, or justification, or recognition which, as rational universals are, *eo ipso*, beyond scrutiny. In so far as it forecloses its own historicity and contestability, paradigm-led theorizing is therefore in key respects monological, not dialogical and irreflexive not reflexive, as Robin Celikates puts it: 'Despite their dialogical spirit and their fallibilistic provisos... [these] approaches are essentially *monological*, since for any constitutive structure it must in principle be the case that it can be revealed independently of (self understanding of the) agents who are subject to this structure' (Celikates 2018a: 140). But, of course, such monologism compromises the fallibilist and corrigible spirit of dialogical and reflexive critique. Everything is open to critical scrutiny except for the paradigm itself—regardless of whether subjects have reservations about the way issues are being framed. Far from being definitive, a given interpretative paradigm can only ever be a 'proposal for a theoretical reconstruction, which competes with alternative proposals that also claim to offer a suitable reconstruction of our practices and self-understandings' (Celikates 2018a: 141). In short, the assertion of the paradigm's constitutive status, qua context-transcending principle, compounds rather than dislodges the problem of 'epistemic authoritarianism' that has dogged Frankfurt School theory since its inception (Cooke 2014: 637).

It seems, then, that to make good on its professed immanent connection to the practical concerns of disempowered subjects, critical theory ought to endorse dialogism and reflexivity in a more emphatic sense where even governing paradigms of inquiry be subject to scrutiny and amendment should it prove necessary. By stressing the historicity of the participatory parity principle, rather than its foundational nature, Fraser is better placed than her peers to mobilize such a developed sense of dialogical reasoning. The principle of participatory parity may provide the yardstick for debate, but its thinness in both substantive and procedural senses means that it is open to revision and amendment according to what may be demanded by the context. The structuring authority of constitutive structures is replaced by a methodological equality between all participants in discussion—theorist and layperson—where none has epistemic priority. By placing theory and experience in a relation of mutual critical scrutiny, Fraser ostensibly refuses the privilege of the former over the latter and hence also the epistemic authoritarianism that this may entail (Fraser and Honneth 2003: 43). Certainly, the theoretical view stands as a corrective to unreflective subjectivism, expressed in psychological models of recognition, where misrecognized subjects, qua claimants, are permitted to determine 'where and how they are adequately recognised' (43). But conversely the experiential stance prohibits the dominance of an 'authoritarian view' where the 'philosophical expert' decides what is needed for human flourishing. In addition, Fraser endorses a pragmatic, open-ended idea of 'good enough deliberation' intended to work against the hermeneutical and testimonial disadvantages that disempowered subjects often experience in formal deliberative scenarios. By allowing participants themselves to decide on how to proceed, rather than requiring them to conform to pregiven justificatory procedures, the participatory parity model works from an account of 'how differently situated agents understand themselves' in order to clarify the 'grammar of social struggle' and possibilities for social change (Fraser and Jaeggi 2018: 123). Importantly, given that 'there are no clearly marked borders separating political theory from the collective reflection of democratic citizens',[2] this presumptive epistemic equality applies not only to interlocutors in the conversation about justice, but also to critique itself and the relationship it has with its addressees and social context (Fraser and Honneth 2003: 71–2). Subjecting 'social practices of critique' to dialogical scrutiny in this way is intended to engender second-order reflexivity, where the theoretical presuppositions informing a given model of democratic interaction—the *frame* of deliberation, not just its content—can be checked for latent status quo bias and other failings (Fraser and Honneth 2003: 45). Knowledge production is therefore not the result of applying the correct theoretical framework, but rather of how subjects use determinate epistemic resources in a concrete situation to expand evaluative and political horizons. In this way, Fraser appears to step beyond the overplayed dichotomies of transcendence versus immanence that hamper Frankfurt School thinking on the evaluative grounds of critique and adopt instead an idea of context-transcending insight as the potential outcome of reasoning across perspectives. Interpretative authority is invested not in the transcendent stance of critique—its 'epistemic super-vision' as Hans-Herbert Kögler describes it—but in the process of perspective-taking itself and the movement between theoretical and experiential stances (Kögler 1997: 159–60).

The 'Merely' Experienced

Yet although Fraser's pragmatic power-first approach allows her to bypass some of the limitations of diagnostic and normative monism, it retains nonetheless certain paradigm-led theoretical tendencies. These are evident in a wariness running throughout her work about the experiential grounds of critique that

---

[2] Ibid., pp. 71–2.

ultimately undercuts its claims to context-sensitivity and dialogism. This wariness arises from a worry about the unreliability of direct subjective experience and hence about its epistemic value to critical theory. In particular, Fraser is concerned to protect the critical distance between theoretical and experiential world-views that safeguards critique's ability to make principled distinctions between legitimate and illegitimate suffering, between anti-racist and racist claims to recognition evinced in her debate with Honneth. There is no doubt that Fraser's concerns are valid but she tends to overstate them, as well as exaggerating the normative representativeness of such 'hard-cases' more generally, and this leads her to presume a priori the unreliability of direct experience. The over-problematization of the experiential stance is paralleled by an under-problematization of the theoretical stance which, in so far as it is associated with objectivism, is accorded ultimate interpretative authority. In making these aprioristic judgements, Fraser fails to substantiate her formal contention that it is the process of dialogical reasoning itself that is the medium for correcting limitations in cross-perspectival reasoning and for validating knowledge. In so far as it rests on a tacit epistemic hierarchy, the dialogism of her justice framework is less open and methodologically egalitarian than it initially appears. In fact, a constrained dialogism is at work where subjects of inquiry, qua disempowered groups, are treated less as interlocutors of equal standing than as the providers of experiential data the validity of which remains to be verified, in the final instance, by the theorist.

The anti-experiential tendencies implicit in Fraser's work need to be considered against its evident shift in focus from the phenomenologically grounded case-studies of her earlier essays to the grand sweep perspective that has more recently been adopted. This grand sweep approach is motivated by what Fraser regards as the politically imperative task of mapping capitalism in its neoliberal phase in order for critique to more effectively challenge marketized dynamics of inequality and oppression (Fraser and Maples 2004: 1108–9). In this respect, she explicitly endorses the grand theoretical ambitions of the Frankfurt School to produce totalizing social critique (Honneth and Fraser 2003: 4). Accordingly, Fraser also urges feminists to 'think big' as an act of intellectual resistance that may prevent their 'best ideas' being instrumentalized by the 'neoliberal onslaught' and that seeks to 'bend the arc of the impending great transformation in the direction of justice' (Fraser 2013c: 226). As her attention has increasingly turned to mapping the contours of neoliberal capitalism, so her work has become correspondingly more broadbrush and lacking in determinate social content. It is, as Richard Bernstein remarks 'extremely vague and abstract' and 'only a prolegomenon' for more detailed critical analysis (Bernstein 2017). Even so, the lack of life-world detail in Fraser's work need not be construed as evidence of a troubling anti-experientialism so much as of the political urgency she feels about contesting the depredations of neoliberalism and of her ambitious, cartographic aims. It is a question of levels of theorizing rather than an explicit disparagement of lived experience. On this view, her strategy is to sketch out a relatively 'empty' evaluative framework which, unlike the monist paradigms of her fellow critical theorists, is flexible enough to capture a range of concrete political problems without effacing their particularity. It is for others engaged in closer empirical work, however, to provide the determinate content missing from her abstract framework.

But there is another more troubling reading of the lack of experiential detail in Fraser's work which places it in tension with her politically radical aims. So, for instance, it leads her to make certain generalizations that are rather high-handed and questionable from the perspective of those with closer involvement. Consider for example, her well-known essay about the unintended complicity that arose between second-wave feminism and neoliberalism in the 1980s and 1990s. Fraser argues that because of an unfortunate confluence of thematic similarities, neoliberal capitalism was able to co-opt feminist discourse and use it to legitimate its own end. What was initially an integrated feminist critique of the androcentric capitalist state was fragmented and deradicalized. Feminist cultural critique of economism became detached from redistributive issues and 'absolutized' as a superficial and 'commodifiable' identity politics. Likewise, feminist critique of androcentrism, which had initially exposed the inequities of a gender-divided labour market, unwittingly came to bolster 'disorganized' capitalism's 'new romance of female advancement and gender justice' (2013c: 220). The entry of women into new 'flexible' jobs, the actuality of which was low-pay, lack of protection and insecurity, was misleadingly repackaged in neoliberal discourse as a new phase of feminist emancipation. Feminist critique of the patriarchal welfare state and its stigmatizing and sexist social policies was used to 'legitimate marketization and state-retrenchment' (2013c: 222) Finally, in becoming entangled with international regulatory bodies such as the UN and European Union, transnational feminist critique of Westphalian globalism lost its connections to grassroots activism, and became bureaucratized and apolitical. Faced with such widespread co-optation, Fraser asks 'was it mere coincidence that second-wave feminism and neo-liberalism prospered in tandem? Or was there some perverse, subterranean elective affinity between them?' (2013c: 218). According to her, the answer lies with the latter and therefore feminism needs to break this 'dangerous liaison' and recover its emancipatory promise. This requires that feminism overcome its internal divisions, reposition itself 'squarely on the Left' and update its integrated critique of capitalism and 'sense of social totality'.

Fraser's analysis has provoked an outcry from several feminists who claim not to recognize themselves in her sweeping claims about neoliberalism's ideological capture of feminism. They insist, in response, that her too-ready dismissal of 'cultural' politics is symptomatic of an unacknowledged economic reductionism that has always pervaded her thought and is evident in the priority it accords to redistributive injustices over what are deemed to be secondary 'merely' cultural aspects of gender domination.[3] They also maintain that Fraser's claim that feminism needs to reposition itself on the left in order to re-radicalize itself rests on a nostalgic vision of class politics that fails to acknowledge that socialism has also been subject to a not dissimilar ideological capture by neoliberal ideas of marketization. Indeed, although Fraser invokes in a talismanic fashion the terms, the 'Left', 'radical', and 'progressivism' etc., they remain, by and large, vague and decontextualized. As Eschle and Maiguashca put it 'socialist feminism is romanticised, presented as an ideal type rather than as a concrete, internally complex, historically specific political project' (2014: 639). Most damagingly for Fraser is the argument that her dismissal of second-wave feminism ignores the large amount of theorizing and activism that was going on in the same period by feminists from the global south, and which addressed precisely those issues of political economy, reproductive labour, care, etc., that she claims were ignored. Her indiscriminate critique seems in fact to be substantially based in her own limited experience of an elite subsection of feminist theory in North America which she misleadingly universalizes as representative of all feminism at the time. She ignores the voices and experiences of feminists working outside of this 'closed community' as if there were 'no dialogue established between them, but above all, as if there was absolutely no conflict or contradiction among different feminist geographies' (Aslan and Gambetti 2011: 132).

The anti-experientialism in Fraser's work runs deeper, however, than a tendency to make unsubstantiated generalizations under the guise of 'thinking big'. For it is also evident in a theoretical mistrust and disparagement of the category of experience itself which is expressed most forcefully in her debate with Honneth on redistribution and recognition. Fraser rightly criticizes Honneth's recognition monism for making the subjective experience of suffering the principal criterion through which instances of misrecognition are identified on the grounds that it is a psychologically reductive, moralizing, and ahistorical approach. Experience is, in her view, too partial and fallible a basis to distinguish between genuine and spurious claims to recognition and therefore to provide secure grounds for systematic social critique. It is not experience per se that Fraser is wary of, for she rightly recognizes that there are different ways of constructing the category, some of which are more 'de-centred' and objective than others. The problem lies specifically with lived suffering or what Honneth calls a 'phenomenology of injustice', that is, direct subjective experience—individuals' perceptions and understanding of the world. Direct subjective experience, Fraser argues, is 'notoriously unreliable' and therefore cannot serve as the foundation for a polycentric and multivalent critical theory. It is too random a social phenomenon to function as a consistent indicator of injustice: not all suffering is indicative of systematically

---

[3] This charge of an economistic suspicion of cultural issues has been levelled at Fraser by several critics including Butler, Phillips, and Young in Olson (2008).

denied recognition and not all injuries of misrecognition are accompanied by suffering: 'it is by no means clear that daily discontent is always a matter of denied recognition' (Fraser and Honneth 2003: 203). It is also too subjective and fallible to be a credible basis on which to decide whether an instance of recognitive injustice is genuine instance or not. Individuals can be mistaken in their understanding of a situation and critical theorists therefore need to deploy independent, nonsubjective criteria to reliably evaluate whether it constitutes an instance of injustice or not. Moreover, to disregard the limitations that a purely experiential standpoint places on a comprehensive account of social power is to fall into the 'myth of the given' and to attribute excessive significance to the perspective of the vulnerable other as incontrovertible indicator of injustice (Fraser and Honneth 2003: 204). Subjective experience is epiphenomenal and therefore of limited use to 'polycentric and multilateral' critical theory that aims at penetrating surface appearances in order to unmask power (2003, 209).

In short, if critique is to have transcontextual normative force, it must do more than simply reflect lived negative experience. It should aim to adopt a 'nonsubjective stance' that does not seek to 'mirror the perspective of any social subject, whether individual or collective, pre-political or political (2003: 207). Given its 'flawed' and 'inchoate' nature, 'inarticulate suffering' or 'impaired subjectivity' (30) must always be put to the 'test' by being run through 'objective, experience distant touchstones...such as structural analyses of social subordination and political sociologies of social movements' (205). Accordingly, Fraser replaces the experientially grounded idea category of suffering with the objective, institutionally anchored one of status subordination. Understood as the denial of participatory parity, misrecognition is a phenomenon that must be verified with reference to empirically observable patterns of institutional and value discrimination. These external indices are empirical but they do not arise directly from subjective experience and provide 'transpersonal' 'nonsubjective' criteria against which to assess the validity of experiential claims or, as Fraser puts it, to 'conceptualize what really merits the title of injustice, as opposed to what is merely experienced as injustice' (2003: 205).

Fraser's concerns about the category of experience are not without grounds but they are exaggerated. Part of the problem is that she seems to take as given a certain mode of moral theorizing that devotes itself to dilemmas and hard cases where 'alternatives are explicit, and the question is which one to choose' (Young 1990: 150). Of course, on occasion it may well be necessary to distinguish, say, between claims to recognition made by racist groups and anti-racist groups but we might question how typical such glaring moral scenarios are of the more complex, ethically nuanced critical work that often needs to be undertaken by emancipatory critique. Indeed, we might ask, with Iris Marion Young, whether such a stark judgement model is adequate for a 'conception of justice that starts from the concept of oppression' (1990: 15). Are decisionist assessments about the validity or not of a given claim all that critique needs to say about justice and oppression? Even in the case of the patently distorted, racist claim, it is arguably necessary to go beyond the explicit content of the speech act itself to consider a host of background issues such as class deprivation, de-industrialization, and demographic shifts as well as the wider context of 'aversive' social meanings and institutional racism that insidiously shore up explicit racism and so on (e.g., Allen 2021: 187–92; Feola 2020).[4] What is required in such difficult cases is not so much adjudication of intentional actions and claims but broader evaluation that takes into account ethical context, social meanings, and background sources of oppression and inequality (Young 1990: 150). Participatory parity is of course meant to bring such wide-ranging, background issues of power into focus; what is more Fraser explicitly espouses an enlarged mode of normative reasoning that avoids over-hasty, dismissive judgements: 'The dismissive response is wrong—and, I would add, *counterproductive*. Right-wing populists *do* have genuine grievances, which deserve to be validated. And reactionary populist movements *are* responding to a real underlying crisis, which also requires acknowledgement' (Fraser and Jaeggi 2018: 199). But her explicit endorsement of nuanced, contextualized evaluative reasoning is undercut by the narrow judgement model of normativity on which Fraser falls back and consequent exaggerated emphasis she places on determining supposedly representative hard-cases.

More will be said about the normativity model of judgement later, but suffice to note here that, precisely because at points in her work she cleaves to it rather too strongly, Fraser is induced to hypostatize direct subjective experience as intrinsically unreliable. She fails to see that there are other ways in which the category of lived experience might be conceived—in the socio-centric, relational terms deployed by black feminist theorists, for instance—that underscore its pivotal importance to an unmasking critique of power; lived experience as a resource rather than a hindrance to the production of knowledge about oppression. It follows from this over-problematization that Fraser also fails to recognize that the flaws she deems to be inherent to the experiential perspective, should, in principle, be addressable and corrigible within the dialogic method of reasoning that she seemingly endorses. In short, there is something ethically troubling about Fraser's construal of subjective experience as 'notoriously unreliable', as inherently in need of verification according to the nonsubjective criteria of the theorist. This presumptive mistrust of subjective experience seems to run counter to one of the animating premises of Frankfurt School critical theory, namely, that as radical emancipatory thought it is immanently connected to those disempowered groups whose condition it addresses. By its own lights, critical theory's account of

---

[4] On this, I am grateful to the insights of Benjamin O'Brien's brilliant reading of recent Frankfurt School work on racism in his unpublished MPhil thesis 'What's Anti-Racist about Critical Theory: The case of Honneth, Jaeggi, Allen and Race'. Oxford University, 2021.

oppression is not an alien, scholastic construct but is supposed to draw on the lived reality of those who suffer precisely in order to help them better understand and resist their circumstances. As the putative addressees of critique as well as its object of inquiry, oppressed groups should in some way be able to recognize themselves in the account of oppression offered by the theorist and hopefully endorse it. For this immanent and dialogical connection to be fully justified, therefore, it would seem both methodologically and ethically important for the theorist to assume, at least as a starting position, that the subjective experiences of oppressed groups have some intrinsic epistemic value to the descriptive and normative aims of the critique of power. To proceed from the contrary assumption of experience's 'notorious unreliability' is to be in danger of tokenism, of making a gesture towards taking seriously the lived reality of oppressed groups while in fact denying them much credibility. It is tantamount to keeping in place the asymmetries of power/knowledge which inevitably characterize the epistemic relation between theorist and disempowered others and which a dialogical reasoning is supposed to try to dislodge.

Fraser's aprioristic down-grading of direct subjective experience is especially problematic given that gender oppression is one of her animating political concerns. As a starting position, the mistrust of the 'merely experienced' seems to be in tension with the analytic centrality that is usually accorded to the category by feminist theorists with pragmatist inclinations. If women's everyday experiences are not somehow taken to be an important guide to theorizing then Fraser's pragmatism is questionable or 'unfinished' in an important sense (Allen 2017). Black feminist, postcolonial, standpoint, and epistemological thinkers are among the many who have shown how the scholastic tendency to attribute automatic credibility deficits to the testimony and experience of subordinated groups is implicated in efforts to keep the conventional hierarchies of knowledge/power intact and unscrutinized. These thinkers have suggested different ways that feminist and other forms of radical critique might combat such epistemological bias and enhance its theoretical responsiveness to the experiential reality of women and other subordinated groups without thereby falling into uncritical subjectivism (e.g., Fricker 2009; Medina 2012). Yet, apart from passing comments on good-enough deliberation, Fraser does not engage with this literature or its entailments for her own theoretical practice, even though the historicizing premises that guide her align with such alternative epistemologies.

Put bluntly, Fraser's use of the term 'merely experienced' shows a lack of the epistemic quality that feminist theorists have variously labelled 'methodological humility' (Narayan 1988) or 'relational humility' (Dalmiya 2016) and that is seemingly an essential requirement of the radical theorist in their engagement with disempowered others. Dalmiya describes relational humility as 'the disposition to acknowledge our own ignorance while acknowledging the knowledge of others'. Likewise, Narayan insists on the importance of methodological humility as a disposition to knowledge production because 'the outsider must always sincerely conduct herself under the assumption that, as an outsider, she may be missing something, and that what appears to her to be a "mistake" on the part of the insider may make more sense if she had a fuller understanding of the context' (1988: 38). In this light, the lack of presumptive generosity displayed by Fraser is problematic because it undermines her declared commitment to inquiry that is sensitive to the context of power. It speaks, inter alia, to an unannounced slippage from the dialogical reasoning she explicitly espouses to a more conventionally hierarchical conception of knowledge where final interpretative authority is reserved for the theorist in determining what really 'merits' the title of injustice.

The untenability of Fraser's assumption of the unreliability of experience can be shown by comparison with black feminist theorists who have similar interests in developing a systematic materialist critique of gender oppression but consider the experiences of subjugated groups to be a 'reliable resource to the theorist' (Collins 2000: 11). Like Fraser, Patricia Collins is worried about essentialism and explicitly states that there is nothing given or incorrigible about experience; it is rather a constructed standpoint that is always 'unfinished' (2000: 290). Unlike Fraser, however, she extends her materialist analysis to the category of experience, conceptualizing it in relation to social location and thereby demonstrating how it may be a 'reliable source of knowledge' and 'central criterion' for theorizing. At some level, people who are oppressed know it and it is precisely the first-hand nature of this knowledge that may render it deeper and more revealing than an external perspective. As Collins puts it, 'those individuals who have lived through the experiences about which they claim to be experts are more believable and credible than those who have merely read or thought about such experiences' (2000: 276; also Narayan 1988: 36). It is especially important to take their lived experience as a 'criterion of credibility' for knowledge claims, given the way which black women have been ignored, discredited, and marginalized in both informal and formal types of thought. This marginalization is the result not just of explicit sexism and racism but also of well-informed, progressive forms of knowledge that mount objections to direct experience on the grounds of its lack of objectivity and inherent particularism. The more sophisticated epistemic logic runs as follows: 'your self-serving identity politics limits your ability to see beyond your own standpoint. Your testimonial authority that is grounded in experience lacks objectivity. How can you support the greater good of equality and fairness using these strategies? Therefore, because you do not play by our epistemic rules, why should we believe you?' (Collins 2019: 142). The 'testimonial smothering' that ensues may well be unintended, but it has practical exclusionary effects that are not so far removed from more explicitly prejudiced arguments. In short, attentiveness to the experiences of subordinate groups is important not only because of the 'new angles of vision' it fosters on oppression but also because it may counter tendencies for the theorist to unconsciously reproduce a dominant world-view through the adoption of certain taken-for-granted conceptual and epistemic devices (Collins 2019: 14).

The Lived Reality of Power

If, rather than disparaging it in advance, we begin by assuming that direct experience is a reliable resource to the theorist, what new angles of vision can it foster? Most obviously, it may reveal modes of soft domination—symbolic violence, to speak with Bourdieu—that, because of the insidiousness of their effects on individuals, are not necessarily noticeable from the theorist's external and often privileged vantage point. Precisely because it operates through disciplinary processes of embodiment and subjective internalization, symbolic violence is often relatively invisible, particularly to groups who occupy positions of social advantage. Absent phenomenological sensitivity to everyday experiences of suffering, critique may be therefore unable to identify diffuse and unarticulated social harms that have not yet crossed a threshold of public visibility. This is one of the points that Honneth raises against Fraser's objective recasting of misrecognition as status subordination, namely that, absent an experiential element, it lacks the disclosive capacity essential to unmask subjective aspects of suffering and oppression. Fraser's reliance on established social movements as indicators of recognitive injustice presupposes that a certain degree of political mobilization has already occurred. They leave unaddressed, however, 'unthematized' and 'embryonic forms of social misery' that, although they do not take an organized political form, speak to no less pressing dimensions of oppression. Moreover, advertence to this prepolitical substrate of suffering is not, as Fraser contentiously claims, to resort to a problematic notion of 'pristine' or unmediated experience. Rather it is to recognize the indirect nature of subordination which is often secured and naturalized through processes of bodily inculcation. It is not sufficient for unmasking critique to focus only on visible struggles and established movements because some societal wrongs are socially submerged and lived as internalized dispositions of quiescence, disempowerment, or resignation.

While the external standpoint of the theorist may well enable them to perceive wider connections that elude those directly involved in a situation, the converse may also hold. Precisely because of their insidiousness, dynamics of stigmatization, de-authorization, hermeneutic marginalization and so on, are often difficult for an external observer to identify. As Narayan observes an 'insider is far more likely than the outsider to know the extent to which a form of oppression permeates a society and affects the lives of its victims and of the very subtle forms in which it can operate' (1988. 3). These insidious dynamics are often unremarked upon because of the credibility deficits under which disadvantage groups are placed and which are the consequence of entrenched dynamics of privilege and prejudice. Society often intensifies indifference to the suffering of oppressed groups by rendering it banal and further occluding it. Christophe Dejours (1988) describes processes of banalization as 'normopathy', a widespread social pathology 'oriented to 'to make the situation look "normal"' at all costs (quoted in Celikates 2018a: 132). By inuring individuals to suffering, normopathy intensifies the emotional costs of oppression for those directly involved in so far as they are forced to confront over and again widespread social denial. When internalized, this denial may be psychologically injurious and expressed by individuals as feelings of resignation, despair, hopelessness, and self-hatred. For instance, the 'black rage' that is such a prominent theme in critical race theory is partly explained as an understandable response to the normopathic indifference of white people to sustained racial oppression (Cornel West 2001). More generally, normopathy blunts the capacity for social criticism on both the part of those who suffer and those who look on: 'when a society gets used to looking away from socially induced suffering, this is bound to damage the capacity to relate reflexively to social conditions and their effects, even in those not directly affected' (Celikates 2018a: 132). It is for this reason of being more attuned to stratagems of disavowal and normalization that render some types of oppression invisible, that the theorist ought to presumptively grant significance to the experiences of those directly affected in an unmasking critique of power. This does not mean that an outside observer is always incapable of independently perceiving such subordinating dynamics but it does imply, as Narayan points out, that they might have to work hard to acquire such insight, a process that might include being willing to scrutinize the unacknowledged epistemic hierarchies underpinning theoretical inquiry itself.

It is not just that Fraser too readily underplays what can be learned from firsthand experience, but also that she fails to recognize how pivotal the category is to the operationalization of her own diagnosis of power. For it is on the basis of the experiences of those directly involved that the theorist may judge how to most appropriately deploy a typology of power. If, for example, the idea of intersectionality is to have explanatory purchase, there cannot just be a theoretically unworkable 'plurality of concepts all the time' (Zack 2005). Rather the theorist must think about how discrete dimensions of power interact in different combinations, some being more predominant than others in certain circumstances. The strength of Fraser's nonfoundational approach is, as we have seen, that she develops a taxonomy of power that is considerably more complex than the monist models of other critical theories. Yet questions of how to apply this taxonomy to everyday life—which categories are appropriate to a concrete scenario, which are not—cannot be answered at the level of theory alone. Answers to such interpretative issues are derived from the practical logic of the situation itself rather than in advance from a general typology. Direct subjective experience can play an important mediating function here, showing which vectors of power might be the most salient in understanding the concrete dynamics at play. For example, Vivian Namaste queries a tendency in Anglo-American feminist theory to explain certain acts of violence against transgender people as automatically motivated by transphobic gender norms. On the basis of her examination of the direct testimony and other contextually relevant details of the cases cited, Namaste found that, at the time of the attacks, the perpetrators were often unaware of the victim's transgendered identity. She also discovered that these acts of violence were committed mainly against transsexual women, not transsexual men, and moreover that most of these women were black and working as prostitutes (as many transsexuals are compelled to do in order to fund the costs of their transition). While not denying at all the horrific reality of transphobic hatred, Namaste argues that in the cases she considered, this was not necessarily the main motivator of the violence so much as misogyny and racial hatred. The outrages were in her words, the 'horrific consequences of a social world that stigmatizes prostitutes such that they are inhuman, "the scum of the earth"' (Namaste 2009, 17). Namaste's general methodological point is that to properly grasp what is going on in instances of violence and hatred, a preconstituted, theoretical explanation may often on its own be insufficient to grasp the variable ways in which intersectional forces are being played out in a specific context. Rather 'in order to adequately understand violence against trans women of color...' abstract, theoretical categories of power need to be accompanied by 'detailed contextual analysis of the different ways social relations of labor, race and gender intersect is required' (2009: 20). Imposing a ready-made theoretical framework on a given situation may give rise to misdiagnosis of what is really going on.

Namaste is not advocating a return to uncritical phenomenalism but rather arguing that, if theoretical explanation aims for accuracy and relevance, it needs to be grounded and regrounded in detailed empirical work that includes those forms of direct subject experience, testimony, and indigenous forms of knowledge that Fraser tends to disparage as unreliable. Theory, as she puts it, is in the details (20). The point, in other words, is not to elevate experience as the end of inquiry itself or to deny that experience is always, in certain respects, fallible, mediated, and theory dependent. It is, however, to think about experience in relation to power and to use it as a resource from which to crystallize an understanding of oppression, particularly with reference to its subjective dimensions that cannot be straightforwardly derived from abstract categories.

The Privilege of Theory

Taking account of direct subjective experience is important for critique not only because it may yield valuable insight into the less blatant workings of power but also because it is a necessary precondition of the dialogical reasoning that is a defining feature of emancipatory theory. Fraser maintains that dialogism is fully embodied in her participatory parity model which accords as much weight to the voice of claimants, that is those who suffer, as it does to experts, that is theorists among others. Yet, this expressed commitment to dialogical reasoning is undercut by the epistemic privilege that she implicitly grants the theoretical perspective over the experiential one. Her tendency to problematize subjective experience as inherently unreliable and cognitively limited while leaving unexplored corresponding problems with the theoretical stance—such as, say excessive detachment from the life-world or intellectual self-referentiality—serves in practice to set up a subtle epistemic hierarchy of the latter over the former. Some time ago, Judith Butler took issue with Fraser's use of the adverb 'merely' as an oblique device of disparagement in the service of orthodox leftist politics. Butler criticizes Fraser for describing certain social movements, particularly those associated with gay and queer politics, as 'merely cultural' and, in so doing, implicitly presenting them as 'factionalizing, identarian, and particularistic' and trivializing their political aims (Butler 2008: 42). A similar downgrading is implied in Fraser's phrase the 'merely experienced' which shores up an unspoken view of direct experience as a drag or shackle on theoretical reasoning, as inherently flawed and epistemically bounded. In this vein, Fraser emphasizes how important it is for the critical theorist to avoid 'mortgaging normative claims to matters of psychological fact' (Fraser and Honneth 2003: 32). It is imperative that 'we' as social theorists, 'are freed to conceptualize types of injustice, their causes and remedies, independently of how they are experienced' (2003: 210). Likewise, as moral theorists, 'we' are able to 'identify norms for adjudicating justice claims, unconstrained by the dictates of a flawed psychology' (210). By eschewing 'psychologization', we are better able to determine what 'really merits the title of injustice', 'to discern the legitimate core of identitarian social protest in order to separate the wheat from the chaff' (Fraser 2008: 330).

Through this subtle hierarchy, dialogism slips imperceptibly into adjudication where the theoretical perspective of the 'expert' is accorded interpretative priority over the experientially bounded one of the 'claimant'. Fraser's 'we saying' compounds this interpretative hierarchy by deploying the first-person plural pronoun in such a way that it takes for granted a shared theoretical perspective and naturalizes its locatedness as one of neutrality and objectivity (Code 2006: 215). Who is it that counts as 'we' when Fraser speaks of the need for us to eschew psychologization and be freed to construct our own sociological and moral principles? Who is the 'we' that distinguishes the 'wheat' from the 'chaff' of experiential claims seemingly independently of those who make those claims? Or the 'we' who has the last word on what really merits the title of injustice? This is not to deny that sometimes, the theorist, by virtue of their external position, may be better placed to discern injustices and causalities that are not so easily identifiable by those subjects directly involved. There are unquestionably instances where social norms violate participatory parity but are not necessarily accompanied by a corresponding experiential harm and do not 'distort the subjectivity of the oppressed' (Fraser and Honneth 2003: 32). In these cases, the theorist may well be better equipped than those directly involved to identify underlying, noncontinuous and indirect dynamics of causality. The capacity of the theoretical perspective to generate distinct and enhanced insights into the workings of power is not in question here. What is in question, however, is the assumption Fraser makes of the categorical epistemic superiority of the theoretical stance relative to the experiential one. Her move to minimize subjective experience as 'merely' subjective is a move that, whether it is intended or not, drives the tendency to conceive of truth, qua the theoretical perspective, as subject-neutral and thus to deny its own dependence on historical experience. The theorist is no longer the participant-observer who has a practical relation with those she studies but rather the neutral onlooker possessed of superior insight. Put differently, Fraser maintains the epistemic authority of theory by eliding its decentred, transpersonal stance with objectivity per se.

In contrast with Fraser's fear that theory becomes clouded by 'flawed psychology', Collins worries more about it becoming unmoored from the lived reality of black women's lives and being 'trapped within [its] own impoverished...feminist universes' (Collins 2000: 45. My parenthesis). Connectedness rather than separation is an essential component of dialogical process of knowledge validation (Collins 2000: 279). In her account of dialogical reasoning, the experiential perspective acts as a necessary anchor for theory and counterbalance to the dangers of scholastic epistemo-centrism. Dialogism for her is built around the premise of a methodological equality between theory and experience. Methodological equality does not deny that there are discrepancies and epistemic asymmetries between the two perspectives, but it does insist that these cannot be presumed in advance nor that they lie only on the side of experience. Rather, blockages and disparities in understanding a particular social scenario may arise in relation to any standpoint involved and need to be dealt with ad hoc as they become evident in cross-perspectival exchange. The dialogical process of knowledge production is built around what Celikates calls 'complex' or 'mixed' asymmetries: 'the (epistemic) relation between...the critic and her addressees is not simply lop-sided, but rather characterised by a variety of "mixed" forms of asymmetry. Some of what the analyst and critic know, the addressees do not, and some of what the latter know, the former do not' (Celikates 2018a: 149). The experiential perspective is not incorrigible, which is precisely why Collins and other standpoint theorists make distinctions between experience and standpoint, between situated knowledge about social location and critical knowledge about potential emancipation (see Wylie 2003). Those who directly experience oppression might misunderstand their situation in some way, their self-interpretation might be cognitively limited or ideologically distorted. Equally, an effect of the scholastic disposition might be that the theorist labours under a misapprehension about the nature of oppression. In the end, such asymmetries and distortions must be substantively demonstrated on a case by case basis and not presumed from the outset to always flow from the self-same myopia of experience.

Differently put, if emancipatory reasoning professes to be dialogic then it needs to place experiential and theoretical knowledge on the same plane instead of in an implicit hierarchy. Dialogism implies that knowledge validation is a cooperative endeavour—what Dalmiya calls 'thinking together'—where the theoretical and experiential perspectives work towards mutual improvement and expansion of thought. Insight emerges in this cooperative enterprise between interlocutors where each side is tacitly asked to approve, or 'practically verify' the interpretation that is being offered or reject it or present a counter-vailing interpretation (Bohman 2001).[5] In so far as Fraser presumes a hierarchy rather than equality of knowledges, the dialogism of her participatory parity model is constrained. While suffering may well be treated as a legitimate object of inquiry, the individuals directly involved are not accorded the status of active subjects in the production of knowledge about oppression. Rather, though lived experience constitutes the raw data of inquiry, it must be fed into a theoretical framework the purpose of which is to assess whether or not it 'merits' the title of injustice. This adjudicative function and the 'appropriate division of labour between theorist and citizenry' (Fraser and Honneth 2003: 71) upon which it rests veers uncomfortably close to what Zurn calls an 'expertocratic' view of critique. In its judgemental mode, critique treats 'social participants as comparatively incapable and undeserving of performing the delicate task of distinguishing between justifiable and unjustifiable social structures' (Zurn 2008: 160).

Epistemic authoritarianism sits uneasily with dialogism and is also inconsistent with the historicizing premise of critical theory that all knowledge, critique included, is situated, perspectival and therefore limited in different ways. Granting epistemic status to the knowledge of oppressed groups need not be a romantic gesture of solidarity on the part of the theorist. It is a way of maximizing knowledge about oppression. Nor is it to slip into a reverse hierarchy that privileges experience over theory as Hekman fears in her 'inversion thesis' (see Wylie 2003). Rather it is an acknowledgement of the possibility that the theoretical or scholastic perspective is inevitably shaped by a particular social location and may itself need expansion or revision in some way. As Mohanty puts it:

---

[5] According to Bohman: 'the interpretive situation is one in which an interpreter is interpreting someone else who in turn can offer an interpretation of his own actions and the interpretation of the other's interpretations. The I who is an interpreter is a you as a participant in communication...I do not simply adopt your point of view or even mine in offering an adequate interpretation. Instead I do something that is much more complicated and dialogical: When I offer an interpretation of your actions or practices, I adopt the point of view that you are an interpreter of me...' (Bohman 2001: 223–4).

when we acknowledge that experiences of victims might be repositories of valuable knowledge, and thus allow that they have epistemic privilege, we are not thereby reduced to sentimental silence. Entailed in our acknowledgment is the need to pay attention to the way our social locations facilitate or inhibit knowledge by predisposing us to register or interpret information in certain ways. (Mohanty 2000: 59–60)

It is this problematization of theory by experience that is surely as an essential part of genuinely dialogical thought as the reverse process that Fraser endorses. Theoretical knowledge is certainly different from knowledge gained from lived experience. It may adopt a transpersonal perspective that, in so far as it draws on wider sources of information, operates as a counter to the inevitable epistemic constraints of agential perspectives. It may take a depersonalized view and it may see more clearly underlying connections between discrete phenomena and structural forces. Nonetheless the theoretical perspective is still a perspective and hence may be liable to suffer from particularism, blindspots, and bias, albeit of a socially weightless scholastic type. As Bourdieu puts it: 'Scholars who do not know what defines them as scholars from the "scholastic point of view" risk putting into the minds of their agents their scholastic view or imputing to their object that which belongs to the manner of approaching it, to the mode of knowledge' (Bourdieu 1998: 130).

Dialogism is, in other words, an essential prompt for the critical self-awareness or reflexivity that critical theorists declare to be an indispensable feature of emancipatory thought. Theoretical interpretation should be as open to critical scrutiny, amendment, even rejection as the experiential one. It might be that the experiential perspective can improve, enrich, expand, even radically challenge the theoretical one, breaking open its rarefied and self-referential logic. As feminist and critical race theory has repeatedly demonstrated, the experiential perspective can deliver an 'ontological shock' to frictionless theoretical paradigms, a shock that arises, in Mills words 'not merely from the simply alien but from the alienated familiar, the presentation of the old from a new angle' (1998: 28). Taking the perspective of experience seriously is crucial therefore not just for an adequate account of oppression but also to enable critical theory to be consistent with its own self-understanding as thought that is dialogical, disclosive, and emancipatory. In attributing interpretative authority to one side only of the dialogue between theory and experience, reflexivity is blocked.

The Priority of Adjudication

A consequence of Fraser's constrained dialogism is that it leads her to give what might be considered an exaggerated significance to adjudication as the central normative function of critique. As we have seen, her discussion of social justice circles mainly around the question of critique's ability to distinguish between genuine and unwarranted claims to justice: 'this interest in distinguishing better from worse recognition claims is indispensable to any critical theory with a practical emancipatory intent' (Fraser 2008: 330). She maintains that the participatory parity principle is particularly well suited to this adjudicative task because of the way it combines sensitivity to determinate content with deontological rigour. Its power-led approach generates an expanded and concrete sense of injustice that avoids the narrowing and desubstantializing effects of neoKantian proceduralism. At the same time, the deontological rigour of the principle enables it to be strictly neutral in relation to culturally specific ideas of the good in a way that ethically thick neoHegelian approaches such as Honneth's find difficult. The declared advantages of her 'thick deontological liberalism' notwithstanding, we might question whether the claim to both deontological rigour and context sensitivity is a case of Fraser having her cake and eating it too. For the primacy of the right over the good that underpins participatory parity's deontological rigour seems on the face of it to run counter to Fraser's avowedly neopragmatist approach to normative reasoning. Far from according an automatic priority to the right over the good, the latter approach would base assessments of putative normative priority in the dynamics specific to a concrete situation.[6] For the pragmatist there is no obvious precedence of the right or just over other normative considerations, rather in cases where this is so, it arises as one point of view within 'the manifold diversity' of orientations to the good (Joas 2000: 173). Fraser arguably fails to see that the normative outcomes that she attributes solely to the deontological bite of the participatory parity principle might equally as well be attributed to the mix of ethical and practical political considerations necessarily made as part of maintaining dialogue across perspectives. In other words, when formulating contextually sensitive evaluations, it is more difficult than she

---

[6] It does not follow that concrete experiential constellations intrinsically lack generalizable normative significance and that they acquire this by being inserted into a formal interpretative paradigm. The pragmatist rejection of the primacy of the right is not to be confused with the rejection of universalizability *tout court*. Certainly, from the actor's practical point of view, the right has no automatic priority over the good. But this is not to say that questions of the right don't arise in determinate problem-solving situations. Certain orientations may require testing through universalization (e.g., for example against ideas of fairness) but this testing (or justification) has no obvious precedence over other normative considerations, rather it arises as one point of view within 'the manifold diversity' of orientations to the good (Joas 2000: 173). Moreover, given that that we do not ever have certain knowledge of what these are, they will always be under pressure of revision according to the exigencies of the concrete action situation. Normative reasoning is in short creative, non-dualist, and open-ended and ineluctably anchored in a situation-specific process of reflection. It is the job of critique to tease out how ideas of the good or the right come into play in a determinate situation. But this specificity does not reduce critique to arbitrary or decisionist reconstruction because, in any situation only certain responses are acceptable and because ethical reasoning always passes through the 'sieve' of general norms and principles albeit in a way that cannot be prescribed in advance (Joas 2000: 173).

acknowledges to stringently bracket off the right from the good. Moreover, while it may no doubt be occasionally necessary to distinguish legitimate from illegitimate claims, one might question the prominence that Fraser gives to this task of adjudication over the other normative tasks that radical emancipatory critique might fulfil such as, say, advocacy, disclosure, attestation, and so on. From the point of view of transnational feminism, the idea that it is the principal role of emancipatory critique to decide what really 'merits' the title of injustice, to separate 'acceptable' from 'unacceptable' experiences might be too closely implicated in a problematic Western mode of normativity that values seemingly definitive judgements over the gradual enhancement of understanding (Fraser and Jaeggi 2018: 122).

Consider, for example, the way in which Fraser demonstrates the deontological force of participatory parity by applying it to the controversial 'affaire foulard', that is, the prohibition by the French government of the wearing of headscarves in schools. Should the ban, she asks, be viewed as a justifiable equalizing educational measure aimed at protecting vulnerable women or an inappropriate use of state power involving the unjust treatment of a religious minority? Fraser claims that the 'correct' way to look at this case is to apply the principle of participatory parity along the two dimensions of inter-group and intra-group equality (Fraser and Honneth 2003: 40). With regard to parity between social groups, she argues that it is relatively straightforward to establish that the headscarf ban exacerbates female subordination since there do not exist analogous prohibitions on articles of clothing and jewellery from other religions, for example, the wearing of Christian crosses. With regard to intra-group subordination, however, she concedes that the issue is more difficult to resolve because strong arguments for participatory parity can be constructed both in support of and against the ban. Thus, French republicans and some feminists have forcefully argued that the ban is justified because the wearing of the foulard is itself an expression of female subordination and therefore should not be recognized by a modern democratic state. On the other side, 'multiculturalists' have argued that the ban is unwarranted because the scarf's meaning varies according to the context in which it is worn and cannot be straightforwardly viewed as a sign of subordination. Fraser acknowledges the impasse but thinks that the multiculturalist stance against the ban is the 'stronger argument'. It is important to note however that the resolution to this contentious issue is based in Fraser's own personal assessment of the relative merits of the relevant arguments but, significantly, not derived from the participatory parity principle which she acknowledges could be applied in an ambiguous fashion.

Despite its claimed stringency, then, the participatory parity principle doesn't in fact help reach a definitive judgement on the legitimacy of the ban. This is significant not because it signals a problem with the participatory parity principle itself, the normative force of which, as a re-rendering of the ideal of equality, can hardly be in dispute.[7] But rather because it points to limitations in the way that Fraser politically frames the matter in the first place, that is, as a deontological issue of justice that avoids a 'premature' turn to ethical evaluations. In fact, other than delineating a baseline of general evaluative standards, the participatory parity principle doesn't seem to do much heavy normative lifting in this case. Like most general orienting principles, it is too thin and undetermined to have much traction in a specific political context. Indeed, in the light of the ambivalent dynamics of neoliberal governmentality, it might even be deployed in a manner that simultaneously legitimates empowering and disciplinary social effects as Fraser herself recognizes in her argument about the cunning of history (Fraser 2013a; cf. Zambrana 2013). Once one concedes, as Fraser does, that contextual considerations are crucial to interpretation in any given situation, it becomes much harder to see how thick ethical, social, and cultural issues can be definitively bracketed off in the way that she also insists is necessary. Besides, as Iris Marion Young points out (ironically using the same phrase that Fraser deploys to downplay lived experience) bracketing the ethical and other particularities of the situation is a 'notoriously unreliable' method for 'how can I and others be confident that I have not carried over assumptions and conclusions derived from my particular standpoint into the supposedly objective general standpoint?' (Young 2000: 113). Put differently, once the issue of the headscarf is seen in thicker, hermeneutical terms as involving divergent life-worlds, practices, and interpretations of cultural values, then the matter is perhaps more effectively dealt with in terms of a model of dialogue rather than adjudication.

On this dialogical reframing, progress comes not so much from reaching a definitive decision based on participatory parity about the wearing of headscarves in public spaces. Indeed, such an adjudicative approach seems inappropriate given the socio-historical complexity of such matters where justice 'cannot be brought about in a single stroke' (Khader 2019: 6). Rather, in so far as progress has been made it can be said to be part of an ongoing, political process of cross-perspectival reasoning, guided not by deontological principles alone but by the aim of opening connections between participants in dialogue. The dialogic reframing is borne out by the way feminists have tried to move beyond addressing the issue of the 'headscarf' in exaggerated dichotomies of freedom and oppression. This movement has been motivated by the pushback from nonWestern feminists against the 'debilitating generality' of the 'object status' that well-intentioned Western feminists apply to Third World women depicting them as in need of 'saving' by enlightened democracies and hence robbing them of their 'historical and political agency' (Mohanty 2003: 39). These counter-arguments have been instrumental in pushing the conversation about veiling and other cross-cultural practice into

---

[7] Fraser states: 'participatory parity simply is the meaning of equal respect for the equal autonomy of human beings qua social actors' (Fraser and Honneth 2003: 231).

terms that are less-dichotomized or zero-sum than the having/not-having of freedom or equality. They have emphatically demonstrated that veiling gains its significance from the particular social and political conditions in which it is worn (e.g., Zakaria 2017).[8] In certain contexts where veiling is imposed by the state (such as Iran), it is clearly part of a wider, often repressive political agenda, which includes the subordination of women. In other contexts, however, the veil has been used strategically as mode of empowerment. In Algeria for example, the wearing of hijab has enabled women to go to work, it has functioned as what Abu-Lughod has called a 'mobile home' that has permitted women to move about society more freely than might otherwise be the case (Abu Lhugod 2013: 40; also Eisenstein 2010: 178; Mohanty 2003, ch. 1). Given the variation in veiling practices across Arab cultures, feminists have come to understand that it is overly simplifying to fixate on it as a definitive symbol of autonomy or victimhood, to reduce 'the diverse situations and attitudes of millions of Muslim women to a single item of clothing' (Lhugod 2013: 40). This understanding has in turn challenged the unthinking association made by some Western feminists of secularism with freedom, which expediently disregards intense pressures in capitalist democracies towards sexualization and commodification, where freedom for some women can mean little more than 'the freedom to undress for men' (quoted in Phipps 2014: 53). In other words, debate has induced some Western feminists to become reflexively aware of the ethnocentric cultural assumptions that tacitly inform the judgements they use to evaluate other cultures. Feminists have also come to realize that adopting an adjudicative logic in such cases borders on 'dynamics of patronage and resentment' where some feminists seem 'to know better than those of (or to) whom they speak' (Hutchings 2013: 22).

Fraser would of course endorse these practical normative outcomes, but she attributes too much significance to abstract deontological principles in bringing them about. If progress has been made on these issues in terms of improving mutual understanding, it has not been achieved primarily through an 'imposition from on high' of the correct abstract principle but from 'a deepening to a more fundamental level of human rapport' (Rosenthal 2002: 216). The feminist nexus of practical and ethical commitments to reasoning across perspectives has helped to break down incompatible positions and opened new avenues for political discussion. Differently put, it is not the correct deployment of a particular theoretical paradigm that does the concrete normative and political work but the process of dialogue itself: 'it is not the theoretical or interpretative framework that is decisive,

---

[8] In some cases, women are forced to wear the veil by their families, but in other cases it is a mode of self-assertion that their families regard as extreme and rebellious. For example, the rise of face veiling in the UK in the early 2000s was regarded with dismay by many older Muslims who cleaved to a cultural Sufi Islam rather than a Sunni conservative variant (Zakaria 2017).

but the practical ability that critics employ in using such frameworks to cross various perspectives in acts of social criticism' (Bohman 2001: 98–9).

This is not to deny that principle-based adjudications are, at times, essential; feminists cannot avoid critically evaluating practices in the light of the deeper social hierarchies that subtend them. It may be that, in some circumstances, it is necessary to decide whether claims from certain groups about experiencing injustice are warranted or not, as in Fraser's paradigm case of distinguishing the white racist's complaint of misrecognition from that of an ethnic or racial minority. Even so, the extent to which this type of hard case represents the essential rationale of practical normative reasoning more generally is questionable. It seems that only a fraction of the practical normative questions arising in relation to injustice and oppression are likely to be reducible to such clear-cut decisions about whether they are warranted or not. In making this kind of decisive adjudication the core of emancipatory critique, Fraser appears to unwittingly replicate a tendency of more conventional types of moral theorizing that limits normativity to 'discussion of dilemmas and hard-cases, where alternatives are explicit, and the question is which one to choose' (Young 1990: 150). Such an adjudicative approach to normativity remains too closely bound up in a decisionist evaluative logic that simplifies the fuzziness of practical reasoning and the historical, ongoing character of evaluations that improve the status of the disempowered over time. As Khader puts it: 'because social change almost always involves long-term negotiation with existing structures of power and systems of meaning, and because such social change often imposes costs on the vulnerable, recommendations about how to achieve it will rarely be articulated as visions of ultimate gender justice' (2019: 6). For these reasons, feminists writing from a nonWestern perspective have problematized, inter alia, Western feminist/liberal proposals of ensuring a 'right to exit' to help cultural minority women to escape from oppressive, particularly violent domestic and cultural arrangements.[9] While motivated by the laudable normative goal of protecting individual freedom, these proposals often underestimate the costs to individual women of exiting cultures or changing practices that are fundamental to their sense of social belonging and recognition. Such proposals also often fail to consider seriously how much the world outside a specific community has to offer these women (Phillips 2009:

---

[9] Khader points out, for instance, that Women living in minority communities often have good reason to distrust interventionist policies even if they are enacted on their behalf because they associate them with repressive state power/imperial domination: 'Aboriginal Australians have reason to distrust the state's incursions in the family because of policies of erasure, such as the stolen generations, that used the family as a fulcrum for cultural domination and destruction. Once this history is in sight, policies that provide only the opportunity to exit rather than helping women live free of violence in their communities, can be seen ... as the continuation of generations of harm to indigenous women' (2019: 57). This contextual historical character of real-world oppression might actually give rise, in the short term, to actions that seem contrary to feminist principle. Like the right to exit, participatory parity is a laudable regulative ideal but might, *ceteris paribus*, be subject to the same type of resistance from vulnerable women.

133–58). This doesn't mean that, as a regulative ideal, the right to exit isn't worthwhile but, in the short to medium term, it might well be counterproductive given that it is so far removed from the existential realities of women who are highly socially vulnerable. In the pursuit of emancipatory ends, then, it would seem important to give more detailed consideration to particularities of context and experience other than generalized assessments of validity:

> knowing... the desired end state is different from knowing how to get there, as well as to recognise that the latter is likely to be context specific. Knowledge about which political strategies would work is likely to require first-personal information from the people affected and attention to the fact that women have interests besides gender interests... such as interests in not being victims of imperialist domination. (Khader 2019: 11–12)

Certainly, Fraser's sociologically grounded critique is more sensitive to contextual detail than comparable procedural approaches. Nonetheless, there remains a question about the extent to which the felt realities of injustice and suffering can be reduced to questions of justification or, even if they can be, whether this is always most appropriate way of dealing with such matters. For example, Fraser's seemingly noncontentious statement that 'claimants have to show how the social changes that they seek will in fact promote parity of participation', may be experienced by vulnerable and disempowered groups as an onerous and alienating demand (Fraser and Honneth 2003: 38). Given circumstances of dispossession, the requirement to justify oneself according to fixed normative criteria may be felt to be inappropriate, misjudged, even insulting, in that it places an additional epistemic burden on already vulnerable groups (Ackerly 2008: 54). Some theorists have argued that it might be fairer to register circumstances of structured social advantage by adjusting the burden of the conversation about justice so that it falls more heavily on privileged interlocutors learning to listen than disempowered groups having to justify themselves. For, as Young points out, 'asking the oppressed to reverse perspectives with the privileged in adjudicating a conflict may itself be an injustice and an insult' (1997: 48). Likewise, instead of focusing one-sidedly on the vindication of the claimant's experience and, consequently, tacitly limiting how they can appear to others, it may be more equalizing to require privileged interlocutors to cultivate an ethos of 'epistemic responsibility' for others (Fricker 2009; Medina 2012). There is, in short, an unresolved tension in Fraser's thought between her radical political commitments and her endorsement of what is, in key respects, an essentially liberal justice model of judgement and justification.

What normative roles could unmasking critique fulfil other than determining the relative merits of claims to justice? A list, gleaned from other radical political theories, might include advocacy, building coalitions and solidarity, disclosure of marginalized life-worlds, making sense of painful and inchoate experiences of oppression, expansion of evaluative horizons, and enrichment of the radical political imagination so on. Because of their attunement to the practical concerns of disempowered groups, postcolonial and black feminist theorists often have a sense of the normative aims of critique that goes beyond scholastic theoretical concerns. Collins, for example, argues that one of the main aims of dialogical reasoning is to recover and give public voice to the 'resistant knowledge projects' of disempowered groups. Often passed over or trivialized as mere activism, these knowledge projects offer an alternative normative resource, 'an expanded repertoire of critical ideas', that may challenge and enrich received theoretical truths and established academic approaches (Collins 2019: 116–20). For theorists engaged in unmasking critique, the normative role of advocacy—giving 'voice to positions of subordination'—may also be important given that the groups they are concerned with are often unheard (Urbinati 2000: 778). As a way of enacting epistemic responsibility, advocacy involves replacing the supposedly neutral role of theorist as adjudicator with the partisan, proactive one of rendering visible the lifeworlds of subjugated groups, pressing for their claims to be heard and mobilizing for political action on their behalf. Advocacy is a type of experientially led theorizing that enables the theorist to go beyond what Honneth terms 'shortsighted presentism' and 'to advocatorially thematize and make claims about socially unjust states of affairs that have so far been deprived of public attention' (Fraser and Honneth 2003: 115–16). It belongs to what might be described as an 'orientational normativity', that is a practical wisdom that, in being responsive to the patterns and particularities of experience, strives to orient ourselves vis-à-vis others (Azamova 2012: 131). Fraser would no doubt endorse such an expanded idea of normativity; it is certainly implied in her idea of good-enough deliberation and acknowledgement that all decisions in her deliberative process are fallible and revisitable. But it is undercut by her repeated insistence on the primacy of adjudication and the need for critique to test the validity of the 'merely' experienced.

Conclusion

In the end, there are weak and strong readings of my interpretation of Fraser's work. The weak interpretation is that the kind of experientially rooted theorizing that is advocated here is entirely compatible with the general thrust of her thought. In this case, my argument might be understood as simply continuing the type of practical, problem-based theorizing that her earlier work so fruitfully exemplifies. Although theorizing from experience doesn't take up Fraser's later challenge to feminists to 'think big', it is continuous with her critical agenda in that it explores the embodied, lived realities alluded to in her magisterial outline of oppression and injustice.

On a stronger reading of my comments, however, there is a more pronounced tension between the idea of theorizing from experience and Fraser's grand-sweep conception of emancipatory critical theory. There are costs to thinking big, some of which evidently relate to the dangers of over-generalization. In the context of reasoning across socio-cultural differences, thinking big can often mean inattentiveness to the situations and views of nonWestern women and disempowered groups more generally. As the work of black feminists and other radical thinkers remind us, paying attention to the experiences of those who suffer is vital for the critical theorist concerned with unmasking oppression because, inter alia, it may reveal a lot about the assumptions that drive their own reasoning practice. The experiences of subjugated groups often are the primary prompt for the dialogic and reflexive mode of reasoning that critical theorists regard as indispensable to genuinely emancipatory thought. It is by engaging with and attempting to respond appropriately to the unfamiliar and unsettling experiences of others that the theorist may come to realize limitations in their own explanatory frameworks and hopefully revise them to be more inclusive. Fraser endorses such situated and dialogical theorizing, in principle, but, in practice, she undermines this by adopting a judgement model of normativity that grants an automatic epistemic authority to the theoretical world-view, and critique more generally, over the experiential one. Intended or not, this position reproduces an elitist strand in Frankfurt School theory where critique is regarded as the sole bearer of radical political insight. In this respect, Fraser's grandiose mode of theorizing is not only at odds with the pragmatic, dialogical method she claims to adopt but also with a general understanding of critique as emancipatory inquiry that speaks directly to the practical political concerns of oppressed groups.

6
The Incompatibility of Formalism and Negativism

Introduction

While it is commonplace for members of the Frankfurt School to highlight affinities between their thought and pragmatism, it is probably in the work of its feminist theorists that it is possible to find the most systematic working through of what this means for critical theory. Pragmatism's experiential and agent-centred approach lends itself to the Frankfurt School contention that critique is of practical emancipatory use to oppressed groups and also the feminist interest in the recovery and exploration of women's lived experience as part of its analysis of gender inequality. This nexus of pragmatist and critical theoretical concerns is also evident in the work of Rahel Jaeggi and in the pivotal place she accords to everyday ethical experiences in an unmasking critique of power. By analysing the lived reality of ethical experience, particularly those experiences that are blocked and regressive in some way, she breaks with Habermasian orthodoxies and paradigm-led theory and initiates fruitful new lines of pragmatist inquiry for Frankfurt School critique. Although, unlike critical theorists such as Fraser and Young, her work does not explicitly concern itself with issues of gender, it nonetheless has interesting, if indirect, implications for feminism which turn largely around her negativist, contextually indexed methodology. As well as suggesting innovative intellectual directions for unmasking critique, Jaeggi's methodology fruitfully intersects with the idea proposed here of experience-led theorizing.

A striking feature of Jaeggi's work is the way it circumvents the preoccupation of other Frankfurt School theorists with normative foundations and instead roots unmasking critique in social criticism. By reaffirming the Frankfurt School's original insistence on the inherence of fact and norm, Jaeggi aims to enlarge the normative scope of critique to include within it everyday ethical experiences and particularly those that might be deemed regressive or blocked in some sense. In her view, the proceduralism of Habermasian discourse ethics has led to an unwarranted neglect of ethical matters in general and, in particular, to an under-theorization of 'bad' or unliveable forms of life which ought to be of central concern to a theory of social justice broadly construed. For Habermasian thinkers, ethical matters are matters of purely personal choice and, precisely because they lack generalizable moral relevance, they necessarily fall beyond the scope of evaluative criticism. Jaeggi challenges Habermas's depiction of ethical life as individualized value pluralism and reconceives it, in collective terms, as constellations of practice that have transpersonal significance and are therefore legitimate objects of scrutiny for normative critique. Bypassing Habermas's ethical parsimony, she thus overcomes proceduralism's much remarked upon blindspot regarding injurious ethical practices. Even though such regressive practices may not be captured within formal definitions of injustice, they ought to be targets of moral criticism because of their deeply distorting and harmful effects on the life chances of individuals.

Jaeggi's anti-procedural approach to normativity redefines the main purpose of emancipatory critique as problem-oriented world-disclosure rather than, *pace* neoKantian critical theorists, as judgement. Open-ended ideas of disclosure and problematization are more closely aligned with the explicitly transformative agenda of feminist and other radical forms of critique. Furthermore, in so far as the process of problematization includes critique itself, Jaeggi's work is better equipped to enact the reflexivity that Frankfurt School thinkers claim is a defining feature of emancipatory critical theory. Finally, the negativist focus of Jaeggi's work on the contradictions and failures of forms of life permits her to tie normativity more strongly to the context of power than the monist paradigms of other Frankfurt School theorists. In many ways her negativist, 'crisis-oriented' approach resembles Honneth's method of grounding critique in a phenomenology of social suffering. But whereas Honneth thinks that negativism is a parasitical critical strategy, Jaeggi shows how it contains sufficient resources to guide evaluative critique by drawing on Adorno's idea of the normativity of the actual. Negativism is not simply lack of possibility but akin to determinate negation, that is, effectual normative responses are gleaned directly from attending to the specific ways in which regressive experiences are materialized in any given situation. Jaeggi's radical construal of negativism avoids the conventionalism that limits Honneth's recognition monism and is also more responsive to the context of power and the multiplicity of forms that oppressive social experiences assume. The critique of forms of life takes forward an insight, also held by feminist theorists, that oppression may be more effectively combatted through a range of contextually indexed practices of empowerment rather than through a single grand theory of emancipation.

In the end, however, the methodological promise of Jaeggi's experientially grounded critique is curtailed by her reliance on a 'formal' account of progress as rational continuity derived from Hegel. For all that she maintains her version of progress to be deflated, open and multifactorial, it is ultimately incompatible with the negativist emphasis she places on historicity and the context of power. Specifically, the functionalist language of problem-solving and learning, through which the idea of progress is thematized, obfuscates and neutralizes issues of power by framing structural inequalities as localized or situationally specific blockages. This neutralization of power is compounded by the criteria Jaeggi uses to evaluate progress as rational continuity whose highly formalist nature insinuates a sanitized and quietist model of social transformation, emptied of concrete agents and conflict. It is ultimately questionable whether the formal idea of progress does in fact have the evaluative bite that Jaeggi claims for it in so far as its abstracting tendencies run counter to the attentiveness to social context that supposedly galvanizes negativist ethical critique. In short, an unresolved methodological tension runs through Jaeggi's thought between the assertion that context-transcending insight is secured through a formal idea of progress and the counter-vailing insistence on critique's historicity and embeddedness within the context of power. It would be possible for Jaeggi to mitigate this tension by conceiving of context transcendence differently, in terms more compatible with the idea of immanent negativist critique. Context transcendence on this view comes not come from the attempt to measure life-worlds against the yardstick of progress but rather is enabled by the way actors utilize the various resources—norms, meanings and practices—that are present within a given form of life to expand existing horizons of understanding. But, in the end, cleaving like other Frankfurt School theorists to an exaggerated dichotomy of immanence and transcendence, Jaeggi fears that construing context transcendence as anything less than a free-standing idea of progress would plunge critique into relativism and arbitrary partisanship. This contradicts her pragmatist intellectual leanings and undermines the critical force of ethical critique.

Critique of Forms of Life

In keeping with their understanding of critique as historically situated inquiry, critical theorists often highlight the intellectual affinities between their thinking and the tradition of pragmatist philosophy. Certainly, Habermas has often emphasized the many ways his endeavour to detranscendentalize Kant and ground normative reason in the intra-mundane universal of communication is indebted to the thought of Pierce, Mead, and other pragmatists: 'After the pragmatist deflation of Kantian conceptuality, "transcendental analysis" refers to the search for presumably universal but only de facto unavoidable conditions that must be fulfilled in order for fundamental practices or achievements to emerge (Habermas 2003: 10–11). Despite these declared affinities, critics have questioned the extent to which Habermas's thought could be characterized as pragmatist in anything other than a weak sense given the formal proceduralism of communicative ethics. One aspect of Habermas's thought that is especially well known for troubling pragmatists is the sharp separation he makes between morality and ethics, construing them respectively as the realms of universal and particularistic normativity (e.g., Bernstein 2010: ch. 8; Joas 2000; Warnke 2001). In Habermas's view, this distinction is justified because it enables discourse ethics to focus exclusively on the generalizable moral issues that are associated with justice claims and to abstain from evaluating thick issues of identity and self-realization that are matters of personal ethical choice. Justice must bear only on matters of general social significance, that is, claims that are amenable to rational reconstruction and can generate universal moral assent. In contrast, ethical questions about what might constitute a worthwhile life are matters of purely personal choice, have an inherently non-generalizable nature, and therefore lie outside the scope of justice. This stringent partitioning of morality from ethics, as Habermas explains it, 'casts a bright but narrow cone of light that sets apart from the mass of evaluative questions those practical conflicts that can be solved with reference to a generalizable interest. These are questions of justice' (Habermas 1993: 151). Pragmatists are among the many commentators who have questioned this aprioristic separation of morality from ethics on the grounds that it rules out *ab initio* the consideration of certain social wrongs that ought to be included in a broad understanding of justice. Moreover, they also doubt the feasibility of isolating morality so rigorously from ethics when, in practice, norms and values appear to be closely interwoven and better conceived not as separate spheres of value but as a 'dynamic shifting continuum such that some are more particularistic and some more universalistic' (Bernstein 2010: 196). Acknowledgment of this inextricable imbrication necessitates, in their view, the development of evaluative frameworks that are less formalistic and procedural than discourse ethics and more responsive to ethical context and variation in practical normative reasoning (e.g., Bernstein 2010: 193–9; McCarthy 1993).[1]

It is just such a pragmatist concern to enhance critical theory's ability to grasp the complexity of life-world experience and shed light on the 'extra-philosophical darkness' into which ethical questions have been relegated by Habermas that

---

[1] In terms of the overall aims of normative theory, the costs of drawing an excessively sharp line between morality and ethics are arguably higher for a critical theorist such as Habermas than they are for other neoKantian thinkers who make a similar distinction, most obviously political liberals such as Rawls. This is because, in contrast to the hypothetical foundations of political liberalism, critical theory regards itself as practical political thought that addresses issues of justice and emancipation from the perspective of oppressed groups. Habermas explicitly rejects the artificial devices of the original position and the veil of ignorance because of their tacitly exclusionary effects. The a priori separation of the just from the good which they serve to install inevitably rules out from the very start the consideration of certain social wrongs and matters of democratic practice. In contrast, discourse ethics claims to start from the everyday realities and experiences of citizens and, through rational deliberation, help them clarify what is at stake in terms of the right and the good. In other words, the distinction between justice and ethics is an a posteriori achievement of the public use of reason rather than an a priori imposition. In this way, Habermas claims that discourse ethics speaks directly to the disparate life-worlds of all democratic subjects, including the most vulnerable and disempowered, rather than just to the stylized concerns of a fictional reasonable citizen. Critics cast doubt, however, on the claimed inclusiveness of discourse ethics and its receptivity to the real-world concerns of citizens.

motivates the work of Rahel Jaeggi (2018: 9). In her view, sequestering issues of identity and self-realization to the particularistic realm of value pluralism is misconceived and the ensuing doctrine of ethical abstinence yields a worryingly attenuated account of justice. Even though they may not fall within the strict remit of rationally generalizable claims, there are nonetheless background forms of life that are sufficiently injurious and damaging to individuals to merit public condemnation as collective social wrongs. In advancing this line of ethical critique, Jaeggi pursues the Hegelian criticism initiated by Honneth who maintains that Habermas's hyper-rationalist account of validity effectively imposes an 'extreme discrepancy' between discourse ethics and the experiential reality of those subjects whom it is intended to address. There are widespread forms of social suffering that, though they can't be easily aligned with formal procedures of validation, nonetheless speak to deep-seated social wrongs and pathologies. A society could be fully vindicated on Habermas's justificatory measures and yet still exhibit deep experiential deficits that would lead us to question the nature of the justice that supposedly prevails. In a similar vein, Jaeggi maintains that evaluative choices about the way we live are imbricated in general moral concerns, to such complex and inseparable degree, that to artificially separate one from the other risks creating a normative stance that is discontinuous and inconsistent. By way of example, she points to the seeming inconsistency between societal willingness to condemn the corporal punishment of children on general moral grounds of cruelty but simultaneous reluctance to object to harsh and humiliating non-physical forms of parental discipline on the grounds of their being a matter of private choice (2018: 17). Given the inextricable entanglement of these behaviours, that practices of parental control constitute the background matrix of values ('proto-values') that sustain the environment for corporal punishment, it seems somewhat arbitrary to draw a moral line between the two, permitting condemnation of one but not the other. As Jaeggi puts it: 'where does the domain of universally binding moral issues end and that of ineluctable ethical value judgements begin?' (2018: 17). In the light of this normative discontinuity, Jaeggi believes that critical theory needs to pivot away from its neoKantian influences and enhance its capacity to criticize background frameworks of meaning and ethical forms of life that might be considered socially harmful or regressive in some way.

Whereas Honneth uses the idea of social suffering to break open the narrowness of Habermasian deontology, Jaeggi adopts the strategy of a revised social ontology the aim of which is to establish the trans-personal rather than merely individual significance of ethical practice. Habermas's insistence that ethical forms of life are beyond the remit of justice rests on the seemingly unscrutinized assumption that they are essentially matters of private individual concern. The manner in which, in spite of his left–Hegelian inheritance, Habermas takes this individualized depiction of ethical practice as a given brings him close to the

Rawlsian vision of value pluralism where ethical life is naturalized as constitutive particularity, as 'something given and ineluctable that resists rational questioning'(Jaeggi 2018: 23). The schismatic separation of the just from the good arising from the assumption of irredeemable ethical particularity also serves to arbitrarily split rationality from the wider context of social meaning. Jaeggi counters, however, that ethical behaviour takes on renewed significance in an understanding of social justice when it is conceptualized not as arbitrary individual choice but, in collective terms, as 'transpersonal forms of expression that possess public relevance' (2018: 4). Obscured in Habermas's individualizing social ontology is the background infra-structure of meanings and practices or 'forms of life' in which ethical beliefs are embedded and which create the matrix of possible lifestyle choices in the first place. As reservoirs of collective meaning and value, ethical forms of life constitute the fundamental bedrock of just society and, given this primary importance, should be subject to critical scrutiny.

Drawing widely on pragmatist and communitarian thought, including that of MacIntyre, Dewey, and Hegel, Jaeggi defines forms of life as sedimented bundles of practices, attitudes, and interpretative schema which harmonize collective co-existence in spheres of action. The distinctive logic of any form of life manifests itself not as explicitly codified rules and procedures but as habitual and regularized attitudes and practices—akin to the practical sense that Bourdieu calls 'feel for the game' or knowing how to go on. As enduring, quasi-inert constellations of behaviour, forms of life are generative of stable patterns of social action. They are not so sedimented, however, that they can't alter in response to emerging new modes of social praxis or problems emanating from the wider social context; every act of reproduction is simultaneously also a potential act of production or innovation as Giddens' idea of structuration would explain it. Changes and dysfunctions in wider, 'real' social conditions place forms of life under corresponding pressure to adapt in some way or another, that is, they are compelled to deploy problem-solving capacities. Problem-solving and adaption is simultaneously a functional and ethical process. Problems may initially appear as technical issues that pertain to the effective or coherent functioning of a form of life, but these inevitably also have evaluative implications for existing collective belief and self-understanding. Fundamental questions are posed about societal self-definition, about the shared common world, about the character of the relations in which a particular problem arises, and about the most appropriate way to respond or change: 'functional and ethical dimensions are constitutively interrelated...in the domain of human activities, there is no such thing as functioning *per se* but only always more or less *good* functioning' (2018: 112). Reconfiguring ethical life in collective interpretative-functional terms allows Jaeggi to argue that it is legitimate to subject it to critical evaluation from the perspective of its problem-solving capacities. The extent to which a form of life can be considered successful or not can be judged on the measure that it deals with problems in an efficacious and coherent fashion that does not hinder human flourishing. A good or 'progressive' form of life is that which solves problems in a way that is consistent with its internal functional/ethical logic and allows individuals to continue to flourish and develop. A bad or 'regressive' form of life is that which deals with problems in an incoherent or contradictory manner, that is, in a manner that is inconsistent with its inherent normativity, and thereby creates 'blockages' of experience for individuals.

To illustrate what she means by progressive and regressive problem-solving, Jaeggi takes from Hegel the example of the way in which the family, as a form of life, has evolved to cope with the fundamental tension between individualization and integration that is characteristic of modernity. On the Hegelian view, the core rationale of the modern family is to establish the ethical grounds of social freedom by holding in productive tension the counter-vailing dynamics of mutual dependency and self-realization. On the one hand, the family fosters bonds of duty, intimacy, care, and so forth, that tie its members to each other in relations of mutual dependence. On the other, it also nurtures the capacities for autonomous self-realization that enable each individual member to eventually break free of familial intimacy and assert themselves as independent beings in the wider world. Hegel regarded the bourgeois civil family as demonstrably superior in reconciling these counter-vailing ethical dynamics than other, contemporaneous ways of arranging intimacy, that is, patriarchal contract or unions of free love. The problem-solving efficacy of the bourgeois family resides in the distinctive way that it combines affect and law, stabilizing fragile relations of love and care within a protected legal form. In contrast, marriage as patriarchally imposed alliances amounts to an empty contractual arrangement devoid of motivating affect. Free-love arrangements are equally as unsatisfactory in so far as they represent evanescent emotional unions that lack the protective carapace of recognition in law. Extending this Hegelian logic to contemporary society, Jaeggi argues that the evolution of the family structure to encompass a broader 'psychosexual and social constellation' of intimacy including patchwork, same-sex, and polyamorous relationships may be seen as a progressive adaption to this continuing ethical dilemma (2018: 129). In response to growing social equality and individual freedom in wider society, the family continues to successfully reconcile autonomy and dependence by democratizing its internal structure. Groups that were previously excluded from legally sanctioned intimate relations are now included and the expressive possibilities of its members enhanced by levelling down traditional gendered divisions of labour. In comparison to these flexible families, traditional nuclear or 'hermetic' families that continue to enshrine conventional heteronormative values might be said to be less successful at resolving this dilemma of care and autonomy. For, on the side of mutual care and dependence, traditional arrangements continue to exclude certain people (same-sex and queer couples) from formal participation in family life. While, on the side of autonomy, they constrain opportunities for independent self-realization on the part of its socially less powerful members (e.g., women) in wider social life. A regressive form of life is, in short, one that is unable to confront problems and deal with them coherently and, because of this failure, distorts or truncates the expressive possibilities of its members in violation of its societal ethical purpose. Persistent failure to solve problems successfully and adapt to change ultimately renders forms of life regressive, 'not liveable' or 'uninhabitable' (2018: 153).

Ethics in the Family

Jaeggi's analysis of the family as an ethical form of life encapsulates her general critical approach which takes its cue from Adorno's normativity of the actual. The criteria against which any specific form of life or constellation of experience is judged to be progressive or regressive are drawn internally from the values and norms implicit within the form of life itself. Evaluations are made not on the basis of independent standards situated above social practice—of a 'free-floating "value-heaven"' (113)—but on the basis of the implicit validity claims a form of life raises in relation to its problem-solving capacity: 'the reference point of immanent criticism is ... not so much a set of values shared by all as the *implicit normativity of social practices*.. it is not just a matter of something that we *believe* but of something that we .... already *do* when we participate in certain social practices' (2018: 199). In keeping with the normativity of the actual, Jaeggi also situates ethical critique itself within the field of inquiry; there is a dynamic feedback loop between theoretical practice and social context such that critique is an 'experiential and learning process'. Attentiveness to experiences of failure and deficiency not only indicates how they might eventually be overcome but also serves to suggest ways in which critique itself might be improved and enlarged in a 'movement of differentiating enrichment' (2018: 204). In short, Jaeggi's idea of societal progress as problem-solving reformulates a pragmatist agent-centred approach to normativity. Ethical critique is less a matter of downwardly applying general rules and principles to a situation than it is of evaluating forms of life according to the implicit normative standards immanent within social practice: 'Forms of life can be understood as historically developing learning processes endowed with normative claims to validity that is the key to their evaluation' (2018a: xiii).

Even on such a preliminary discussion, the decisiveness with which Jaeggi's idea of ethical critique breaks with the monist normative paradigms of other Frankfurt School thinkers should be apparent. By grounding normativity in the pluralized dynamics of social practice rather than a single underlying principle, she is able to introduce greater ethical nuance into a diagnosis of key life-world institutions. Compare, for example, her analysis of the family with that of Habermas, the rather conservative nature of which flows from the dichotomizing (system-life-world, instrumental-communicative reason) and unidirectional assumptions about power built into his social criticism. In his view, the family, as a life-world institution, is in danger of being eroded from the outside (nonrenewably dismantled) by the intrusions of the 'systems media' of money and power. On this colonization thesis, power is external to the family, an exogeneous instrumentalizing force that penetrates and corrodes intimate internal bonds of solidarity and affection. Missing from his one-sided and nostalgic vision is an account of power not just as external force but also as internal to familial relations and manifested, inter alia, in the gendered division of labour, sexualized dynamics of masculine power, domestic violence, parental discipline, and so on (e.g., Fraser 2013a). By disregarding relations of power endogenous to the family, Habermas finishes by naturalizing it as a prelapsarian haven of intimacy and care, one which is under threat from hostile external social forces. This propensity to sentimentalize the family is not unconnected, moreover, to his strategy of ethical abstinence which automatically places intimate-domestic relations beyond the scope of justice in virtue of their inherent particularism. In so doing, Habermas's analysis of the family fails to reckon with the ways in which intimacy is a site of inequality and domination, and therefore a legitimate target of critical scrutiny for an unmasking critique of power. By attending to dynamics internal to the family, Jaeggi draws a more intricate normative picture than Habermas that identifies discrepancies in the way that possibilities for self-expression are differentially realized for its members. By being alert to the complex admixture of progressive and regressive dynamics in intimate life, ethical critique arrives at a less monolithic account of the family and more differentiated understanding of potential strategies of empowerment and emancipatory change.

Unsurprisingly, given their shared Hegelian influences, Jaeggi's account of the family as an ethical form of life is closer in key respects to Honneth's interpretation of it as the grounds of social freedom. But, here too, attentiveness to the dynamics internal to the form of life help her avoid the mystifying tendencies that afflict Honneth's recognition monist account of the family. As we saw in Chapter 3, Honneth's interpretation of the family through the lens of recognition leads him to overemphasize patterns of mutuality and care at the expense of negative, gendered asymmetries of power. The eschewal of mono-categorial interpretation and negativist orientation to problem-solving allows Jaeggi to be more alert to the power-laden, potentially regressive aspects of family life and thus avoid naïve ethical endorsement of the institution. For example, where Honneth underplays those regressive aspects of family life that relate to the reproduction of heteronormativity and soft masculine domination, Jaeggi explicitly criticizes these features as limiting of expressive possibilities and therefore as an unliveable ethical state of affairs. In short, situating forms of life in the context of ethical and functional problem-solving processes means that questions of power do not recede from view as much as they do in the monist, over-ethicized analyses of other Frankfurt School theorists.

Negativism and Experience

Despite the advantages that Jaeggi's pluralized social analysis has over the paradigm-led analyses of her peers with regard to an explanatory account of power, there still remain questions to be answered concerning the normativity of the actual. If it is not to lapse into a simplifying communitarian stance, then it follows that any form of life must be understood as itself internally hierarchized and divided according to wider social divisions. Divisions internal to forms of life raise, in turn, issues about the interpretative perspective of ethical critique. For instance, what are the decisive indicators of normativity in the context of disagreement about norms and values within a specific form of life? From whose perspective is a particular experiential constellation judged to be problematic or regressive? Conversely, which group's perspective is of importance in determining whether progress has been made, whether a problem has been successfully solved? After all, something that is deemed to be a pressing problem by one particular group need not be so deemed by others. Even in cases of agreement over the appropriate criteria to be used in evaluating a problem, there are no guarantees that conflicting, incommensurable views would not arise. Moreover, there is a risk that, because ethical critique is explicitly pitched at the 'practice-theoretic' level, it produces a merely epiphenomenal or dissipated assessment of social problems relative to a deeper structural account of power. In this light, Jaeggi's analysis might be vulnerable to the criticism commonly levelled at pragmatist philosophy, that, by concentrating on inter-subjective dynamics and group practices, it too readily disregards the determining force of underlying social structures. The foreclosure of power is evidently a more serious problem for Jaeggi than it is for mainstream pragmatist philosophers given critical theory's stated commitment to anchoring normativity in sociological criticism.

Jaeggi keeps such issues of power at the forefront of ethical critique in two ways. First, in analysing a given constellation, critique focusses not on the level of immediate appearances—what is explicitly said and done—but on the deeper level of its underlying social conditions of possibility. Following Adorno, Jaeggi contends that ethical critique is first and foremost materialist critique in that it concentrates on social conditions of possibility, on explaining the subtending relations of power that are constitutive of behaviours and practices: As she puts it, in her discussion of *Minima Moralia*: 'attention...is directed not only... toward the question of "how should we *act*?" or "what should we do?" It also asks what *lets* or *makes* us act? It thus thematizes how the world in which we act is concretely and "materially" organized and structured and how this *organization* influences our actions and life possibilities within it' (Jaeggi 2005: 66). Second, attentiveness to material relations of power is further accentuated by critique's explicitly negativist method or 'crisis' orientation. In evaluating a form of life, reference is made not to substantive notions of the right or good but to its internal points of contradiction and failure, to its regressions, lapses, and 'crisis experiences' (2018a: 296).

The idea that critique starts from the negative, that it is 'compelled by the experiences of a failure or a deficiency' is of course one that Jaeggi shares with other thinkers of the Frankfurt school. 'Social theoretical negativism', as Honneth describes it, is the fundamental starting place of critique. It is by attending to negative experiences, that the critical theorist is first alerted to underlying systematic sources of inequality and subordination that render a given social order deficient (Honneth 2004: 338). However, Honneth also captures the qualified attitude to negativism that prevails among Frankfurt School thinkers when he says that although it may tell us what is wrong with the world, it is ultimately a 'parasitical critical procedure' that fails to provide enough normative resources to help decide how to intervene in the world or justify a particular course of action. His solution to this normative insufficiency, a solution typical of paradigm-led theory, is to install a transhistorical principle as the evaluative grounds of critique. A tension exists, however, between the context-transcending perspective and negativist social critique such that the latter is rendered virtually inoperative by the former. Negativism requires a theoretical flexibility and openness to the details of socially injurious experiences that is effectively curtailed by the stylizing and abstracting tendencies of the monist interpretative principle. In contrast, because she does not hold negativism to be a normatively insufficient procedure, Jaeggi's contextually indexed ethical critique is less circumscribed than the monist variants of her peers. It is precisely because it tries to grasp the nature of the bad or wrong situation, in its particularity, that it succeeds in articulating a sense of how to proceed normatively: as Adorno famously put it: 'the false, once determinately known and precisely expressed, is already an index of what is right and better' (1988: 288). Negativism then is not simply a lack of possibility or unalleviated social negativity but what Jaeggi calls 'free standing determinate negation' (von Redecker 2018: 176). It is inventive and creative and 'animates a new set of positions for the subject' (Butler 2009: 792). Knowing what to do next emerges from the details of the situation itself: 'the deficiency of a particular situation can be shown only by its failure: however, the possibility of resolving it follows from criticism of the deficient state itself' (Jaeggi 2018: 209).

From the idea of determinate negation, Jaeggi outlines a different normative path for unmasking critique than the paradigm-led one it has been following since Habermas. Departing from the neoKantian prioritization of issues of validity and justification, Jaeggi argues that critique's main normative concern ought to be one of problem-solving rather than adjudication. This problem-solving focus aligns itself with the inherent logic of societal development, qua progress and regress. In her view, a judgement model of normativity whose main role is the articulation of 'binding and objectifiable standards for evaluating social relations and institutions' has assumed over-inflated importance in critical theory (2018: 26). As well as pushing it closer to liberal political philosophy—a cause of lament for commentators who emphasize critical theory's radical left–Hegelian credentials—this judgement model has de facto marginalized other possible normative functions for critique. Jaeggi resists this corralling of critical theory into a narrow subset of justice-theoretic concerns. Instead of 'clarifying and demonstrating arguments and counterarguments' it needs to embrace a broader evaluative remit focussed on improved understanding of the regressive and alienated aspects of forms of life and what this might reveal about society more generally (2018: 27). Echoing Foucault and Dewey, she describes this interpretative task as one of problematization—that is, to redescribe the world in such a way as to bring certain problems or regressive dimensions to the fore, thus prompting a more general critical reassessment of attendant social relations. Inquiry frames or 'sets' the problem as problem in the first place; it recognizes that a certain situation requires definition (or further definition), and gives coherence and visibility to a previously inchoate or misunderstood situation. This concretization of a certain problem space in turn suggests determinate ways of proceeding; the very act of framing problems is itself a contribution to their overcoming: 'if identifying the problem is already the first step toward solving it, it is because this makes it possible to work one's way out of the indeterminateness and to achieve the first intimations of orientation, identification, and hence indeterminacy' (2018: 142).

The suggestion that critique's role is one of problematization comes under the broader category of ideas about world disclosure: 'immanent criticism...involves a moment of disclosure that renders aspects of this reality visible in new ways' (2018: 208). By redescribing the world in such a way as to render it unfamiliar, critique aims to establish new connections and insights and thereby enlarge a sense of political possibility. Jaeggi regards disclosure as more consistent than a judgement model of normativity with historicized, immanent critique because it explicitly situates the critic in the horizon of enquiry in a way that is obscured by the latter's emphasis on impersonal procedures and justificatory principles: 'the immanent critic is also involved in what is criticized. He, too, does not judge in an abstract way from an external point of view; instead he takes his orientation from the concrete deficits and the actually existing potential for overcoming these deficiencies' (2018: 209). While for Honneth, critique is also an essentially disclosive, its transformative force is limited by the substantialism and conventionalism that afflict recognition monism. His view that negativism is a parasitical critical procedure that needs to be supplemented by an unchanging emancipatory interest, entails the burden of having to substantiate the claim that positive recognition is a vital precondition for healthy individual self-realization. What does it mean to be positively recognized? Fleshing out the meaning of recognition in such constitutive terms, exposes him, in turn, to the risk of generalizing as a supposedly universal need what are in fact culturally specific conceptions of flourishing. Jaeggi's negativist method avoids the problem of substantialism by focussing on overcoming the bad rather than realizing the good. It may well be that notions of the bad presuppose some conception of the good but, this need only be a very thin notion of flourishing rather than a fully fledged philosophical anthropology of recognition. Moreover, from the point of view of critique's real-world political efficacity, it may be more productive to focus on overcoming the bad than trying to specify a 'necessary and sufficient' conception of the good which is likely, as Jo Woolf points out, to be 'narrow, dogmatic or unconvincing' (Woolf 2015: 23).

Recognition monism is also prone to conventionalism because of its coupling to an essentially sanguine account of the progress of modernity. The integrative account of progress as the unfolding and expansion of recognition orders locks Honneth's theory into a path-dependent account of emancipatory change skewing it towards known, institutionalized routes of change, such as the extending recognition through legal and political rights, rather than more radical routes. What is insufficiently acknowledged in this organic vision of progress is that future struggles for emancipation may fundamentally challenge currently established modes of political practice and recognition, taking forms more disruptive, polemical, and radical than can be imagined at present. Jaeggi avoids such conventionalist bias by negatively deriving emancipatory strategies from crises and regressive experiences, rather than from already established political routes. This negativist orientation heightens critique's alertness to society's others, to alterity and nonidentity, thus rendering it politically open-ended and experimental in nature (280). By replacing Honneth's substantive question about the 'content of successful forms of life' with the more 'formal question' of 'how forms of life unfold', critique becomes explicitly transformative rather than merely reconstructive (2018a: 216). Critique aims not so much to reaffirm established ethical practices but, in response to its encounter with alterity and negative experience, to change the way in which reality is normatively framed and contribute thereby to wider processes of societal transformation. Critique represents a theoretical contribution to wider, world-building processes, it 'does not restore a prior harmony between norm and reality...but instead seeks to transform a contradictory and crisis-riven situation into something new'. This transformative process works both on reality and thought about reality, i.e., the critique of critique or reflexivity: 'reality and its concept, the "object" and its "yardstick" have undergone change' (2018: 203). Here again, then, Jaeggi breaks with the paradigm-led tendencies of Frankfurt School theory which, even as it insists that reflexivity is an indispensable feature of emancipatory critique, fails to operationalize it with regard to scrutinizing its context-transcending grounds.

In summary, the strong interpretation Jaeggi gives to negativism allows the critique of forms of life to move along a different normative path to the one Frankfurt School theory has been following since Habermas. By complicating the overly dichotomous distinction, deployed by other Frankfurt School theorists, between enabling normative foundations and negative social criticism, critique works within an altered understanding of the structure of normativity as a gradual, open-ended movement towards overcoming the bad. Negativism doesn't foreclose normative responses to injurious states of affairs, rather it does not think these can be discovered from a monist, quasi-transcendent perspective but instead from one that is attentive to the repressed particularity of oppression and domination. Instead of a unified grand theory of emancipation, critique as determinate negation elicits a plurality of strategies of empowerment that directly confront the manifold forms of subordination. Yet, despite breaking so emphatically with some of the schematizing, grand-theoretical aspects of the Frankfurt School project, Jaeggi's thinking is of a piece with it in other aspects especially her approach to the issue of context transcendence. Context transcendence is conceived by her as the evaluative perspective supplied by the 'formal' idea of progress as learning. Jaeggi justifies this formal construal of progress on the grounds that, unlike other monist principles, it is thin enough to encompass a sense of historicity but, at the same time, provides robust evaluative criteria for assessing the quality of social dynamics of transformation. However, as I show in the coming sections, this is not the case. In fact, formalism is incompatible with negativism in so far as it undermines the attentiveness to historicity and unliveable forms of life that are ostensibly ethical critique's main theoretical virtues.

Context Transcendence as Learning

For many members of the Frankfurt School, Jaeggi's redirection of critical theory towards what Adorno describes as unalleviated consciousness of negativity would do little to allay worries about context-transcending foundations. The critique of forms of life may well yield valuable insight into discrete constellations of experience but it lacks the grounding in a transcontextual evaluative principle that prevents it from lapsing into particularism. One possible way for Jaeggi to respond to such concerns, a way that would be consistent with the pragmatist and negativist inflection of her thought, would be to unpack the exaggerated oppositions between universality and particularity, transcendence versus immanence that drive such worries. As we saw in the first chapter, taking a critical stance towards certain types of abstract universalism need not be tantamount to plunging critique into irremediably particularistic and relativist analysis. Indeed, relativism and particularism may well themselves be problems created by the desire for absolute foundations, by an insufficiently interrogated craving for generality that is not compatible with immanent critique. When false antitheses of immanence and transcendence are problematized, therefore, a space is opened for exploring the ways in which, although critique always speaks from a certain situation, it may nonetheless aspire to coherence, systematicity and transcontextual relevance. In this pragmatist vein, Jaeggi might conceive of context-transcending critique not in terms of a grand theory or paradigm that encompasses all particularity, but as problem-led thought that attempts to systematically trace connections between regressive ethical constellations and underlying structures of power.

Jaeggi, however, does not pursue this pragmatist option, instead she chooses to locate the context-transcending foundations of critique in a 'formal' account of successful learning or progress. Instead of the 'all-too-strong focus on normative justification' that prevails in Habermasian critical theory, the idea of progress provides alternative, historicizing foundations that bring issues of power and social transformation squarely into view. By virtue of its 'thinness', that 'it doesn't say anything substantial about the content of "progress"' formalism is compatible with a negativist sense of historicity (Jaeggi 2018c: 37). Equally, however, this foothold in historicity does not collapse into mere contextualist analysis because the idea's formal core highlights certain fixed and recurrent patterns of change as indicators of progress and learning. In Jaeggi's view, then, a formal account of progress resolves the apparent tension between immanence and transcendence, between historical sensitivity and normative rigour: 'for a critical theory that wants neither to build on a freestanding normativity nor to be in some way contextualistic and relativistic with respect to its normative foundations, some notion of progressive social change seems indispensable' (Jaeggi 2018b: 189).

What does Jaeggi mean by a formal account of learning and progress? On her definition, it comprises a set of 'robust' evaluative criteria against which it is possible to identify fixed and recurrent features of change and therefore evaluate how successful a form of life has been as an instance of problem-solving. These criteria are guidelines for assessing the 'very quality of social dynamics of transformation', whether ethical progress has been made in a specific realm of practice or whether it has stalled (2018b: 193). As formal rather than substantive criteria, the focus is not on thick ethical content, 'what' is required for a good life, but rather on 'how' a life-form is lived: 'the substantive question about the *content* of successful forms of life is replaced by the...more formal question concerning how forms of life unfold and the dynamics of their development' (2018a: 216) The main criterion for evaluating successful learning is that of rational continuity and is derived from Hegel's idea of progress as dialectically cumulative, that is, as continuity in discontinuity; as Jaeggi puts it: 'In order to be able to say of a form of life that it has *learned* something, it must have undergone change and at the same time remained the same; it must exhibit identity in difference' (2018a: 273). Ways of dealing with problems that radically break with a previous state of affairs do not count as progress because 'a result without any connection with the initial situation...would be so radically discontinuous that it could not be easily recognised as the result of a learning process' (273). In addition to the criterion of rational continuity, successful learning can be assessed on two further accounts. First, in solving a problem successfully, a form of life needs to have provided individual members with a noticeably expanded or differentiated array of expressive possibilities in accordance with its internal ethical logic. Second, collective self-understanding must be demonstrably enriched and enlarged, that is, a form of life must demonstrate awareness of its own past failings and what it has done to surmount them. Progress and learning can be said to have occurred when there is evidence of a 'differentiating enrichment through experience' (2018a: 311).

Conversely, a form of life can be said to have failed, is 'bad, irrational or inappropriate' (2018a: 216) when it manifests systematic blockages of experience, that is when it fails to deal adequately with internal problems and conflicts such that individuals suffer in some way. The most fundamental or serious of these problems are those which stem from underlying social contradictions. Problems as contradictions are localized, life-world manifestations of deeper socio-structural faultlines (2018a: 270). Although the idea of problems as contradictions is sociologically underspecified, Jaeggi presumably means to capture inequalities of race, class, and gender that subtend realms of ethical practice but appear as localized distortions of social praxis. She may also intend to denote abstract forms of domination such as macro-social tendencies towards exploitation, reification, and so on. Persistent failure to deal with problems as contradictions, qua enduring injustice, calls into question not only our 'factual reference to the world' but also the form of life itself as a 'self-reflexive formation' (2018a: 254). A form of life becomes crisis-prone or unliveable when it becomes a reified, inert formation that no longer has capacity to deal successfully with problems—it becomes 'trapped' within a learning blockage: 'the specific blockages to learning in which forms of life can become trapped typically involve forms of collective self-deception or ideology' (2018a: 285).

According to Jaeggi, then, this formal account of progress as successful learning provides emancipatory critique with a transcontextual vantage point which retains an acute sense of historicity. It facilitates a rebalancing of critical theory that counters the restricting preoccupation with normative foundations and prompts it to pick up again questions of 'how material, social and normative developments interact in order to provoke social change' (2018a: 190). Naturally, Jaeggi, is mindful of problems that stem from reliance on a Hegelian idea of progress and accordingly, like Honneth, she argues that her version is open, nonteleological, and pragmatically deflated. Progress by her lights is guided not by an external, metaphysical goal as by changing societal dynamics of varying complexity and magnitude. In place of a uniform macro-narrative, her idea of progress is nonsynchronous, uneven, ongoing, and anticipatory in nature. Even in this deflated version, however, the formal idea of progress allows us to normatively distinguish better from worse social developments: 'Progressive processes can thus be identified in a free-floating way: better solutions to problems can be distinguished from worse counterparts without any need to justify progress in metaphysical terms or to situate the goal of the development in a fixed point outside of the process itself' (2018a: 240).

A formalistically conceived idea of progress may not, however, be as compatible with materialist, negative critique as Jaeggi seems to think. In fact, arguably a considerable tension exists between, on the one side, the historical attunement to the particularities of regressive forms of life that negativist critique requires, and, on the other, the decontextualizing and homogenizing tendencies of a formal notion of progress on the other. This tension manifests itself in three main ways which will be examined below. First, Jaeggi's pluralized social ontology and practice-theoretic vocabulary of problem-solving combine to obfuscate and neutralize an account of power. By framing structural inequalities and abstract forms of domination as situationally specific blockages, Jaeggi fails to capture their primacy in determining hierarchical social relations across all fields of social practice. This piecemeal approach to power in turn engenders a mode of ethical critique, that in as much as it is sociologically underspecified and generic, underestimates the ways in which life-world experiences of certain groups are inescapably shaped by subtending forces of race and class. Second, Jaeggi's functionalist vocabulary of problem-solving and learning lacks social grounding and therefore has depoliticizing effects on critique. Its socially deracinated perspective forecloses questions of interpretation and contestability that are fundamental to the idea of problem-solving—from whose perspective is a problem defined and judgements made about whether it has been successfully overcome or not—but left unanswered. By presenting learning and problem-solving as impersonal social tendencies it also obscures the context of struggle in which these processes are ineluctably embedded. Third, the correlate of this neutralization of power is a more general negation of agency and experience. The formal idea of progress conceives of societal change as an essentially abstract rather than historical process and sublates concrete agents and real-world conflict into the dubious Hegelian devices of the world historical individual and contradiction. In the end it is questionable whether Jaeggi's formal criteria of rational continuity and expressive enrichment are adequate for evaluating progress, or whether in fact such assessments can only ever be made drawing on the particular constellation of resources immanent within a particular life-world context. Given the sanitized and quietist account of social transformation to which they give rise, it is doubtful whether such criteria are ultimately appropriate for critique that has radical transformative aims.

Neutralization of Power

Doubts about the diagnostic bite of negativist critique arise in the first instance in relation to the obfuscating effects that Jaeggi's pluralized social ontology and practice-theoretic vocabulary of problem-solving have on an account of power. The problem, in a nutshell, is one of a conceptual levelling out of different forms of life and different modes of power. To describe all regressive power dynamics in the same terms as blockages and problems to be solved is to erase qualitative differences between them and to minimize the impact of enduring structural inequalities in shaping constellations of experience. It is not that the vocabulary of problem-solving, learning, and so forth entirely overlooks power; negativist critique explicitly intends to examine the material conditions of possibility of ethical of life and particularly its failures and crises, qua oppression: 'the specific ways in which forms of life can fail, on the crises to which they succumb, and on the problems they may encounter' (xiii). Yet regardless, there is a sense in which the practice-theoretic discourse of problem-solving and learning (or failing to learn), while appropriate for framing difficulties at local or mezzo levels of action, does not adequately capture the pervasive and entrenched effects of structural inequalities. To call enduring inequalities of race, gender, or class failed instances of learning is not so much an erroneous description as a tangential one that neutralizes material relations by sublimating them into epistemic ones. The reason that racial, gendered, and class oppressions persist as problems is arguably not because learning processes have stalled, but because they are key to the extraction of surplus value and profit from labour; they are, as Nancy Fraser (2014a) puts it, necessary preconditions of capitalist accumulation. The dissipated vocabulary of problem-solving, etc., fails to sufficiently capture the material reality of these structural inequalities as mechanisms of expropriation and exploitation that are functionally indispensable to the reproduction of capitalism. As Celikates puts it: 'are these structures, their resilience, their tendency to develop a logic of their own, their path dependency, and their ability to shape and enlist practices in top-down ways not pointing beyond the practice-theoretical vocabulary that conceives of the emergence and reproduction of structures exclusively in terms of practices' (Celikates 2018b: 140–1). In sum the cognitivist sublimation of power into problem-solving sanitizes questions of exploitation and oppression—viz., Jaeggi's insistence that apartheid and slavery are instances of problem-solving (2018b: 202)—and has depoliticizing effects on critique.

The failure to distinguish structural imperatives from contingent, localized arrangements of power is compounded by the relatively indiscriminate fashion in which Jaeggi uses the term 'form of life'. It denotes a range of heterogenous social constellations from the most general of systemic imperatives, for example, 'capitalism as a distinct form of life', to far more localized, institutionally specific practices such as the professional conduct of medics, academia, gender norms in marriage, and so on. This undiscriminating usage leaves hanging the question of whether it is appropriate to treat all forms of life as homologous and formally equivalent, or whether some might not be regarded as more fundamental than others in determining the overall direction of social practice. As Celikates says: 'from the point of view of a critical theory of society, not all forms of life seem to be located on the same ontological or explanatory level; some appear as more basic, in ontological or explanatory terms, because they structure and format the conditions under which other forms of life are functioning and reproduced, criticized and transformed' (2018b: 139). It seems curious, for example, to describe the totality of capitalist relations in precisely the same terms as more localized fields of action (e.g., the family) given that the former encompasses the latter and constitutes their material horizon of their possibility. The commodifying logic of capitalism is not formally equivalent to field-specific ethical practices in that it has the capacity to penetrate and shape localized behaviours in pervasive and insidious ways.

Consider, for example, Michael Thompson's (2017) argument that commodity fetishism continues to be a major source of abstract domination and dysfunction in capitalist societies, distorting all levels of social practice from economic production to the socialization of the individual psyche. Indeed, it is at the pre-rational level of ego-formation that the commodifying logic is fully secured, shaping 'value-orientations and emotional investment' (2017: 135). Organizing the psyche around the commodity form naturalizes the capitalist order and ensures compliance in so far as genuinely critical attitudes to society are disabled and pathologized as deviant. In so far as epistemological processes are 'dialectically linked' to such distorted socialization, they are also 'infected by rationalized value-orientations rooted in the logic of capital agglomeration' (2017: 23). On this view, social learning is not about processes of functional/ethical problem-solving, *pace* Jaeggi, but about inculcating conformity and ensuring the compliance of individuals with the structural-functional imperative of commodified self-realization. Although, like Althusser, Thompson's account of ideological interpellation is rather monolithic, his general point stands, namely, that certain formations of power, viz.s commodity fetishism, are far more powerful in determining the shape and orientation of social action than others. To fail to recognize this determining force is to fall into what he calls the neoIdealist fallacy where consciousness and social action are severed from 'the structural-functional logics of social systems' (2017: 22). It is also to fail to recognize that transformative strategies derived from localized processes of problem-solving may, on their own, be relatively ineffective in bringing about progressive social change.

What can be said about the pervasiveness of the commodity fetish as an abstract mode of domination can be said, *ceteris paribus*, about structural oppressions. Jaeggi's practice-theoretic emphasis on ethical diversity underplays those vertical hierarchies of race, class, and gender that routinely position women, working-class, and black people in relatively subordinate positions in any given form of life. Indeed, as involuntary, imposed forms of identity and social positioning, it might be more appropriate to describe gender, class, or race as 'a form of life' since their subordinating effects are materialized in a relatively predictable fashion across all realms of practice and with equally as predictable impacts upon the life-chances of the poor, women, and black people. Certainly, Jaeggi attempts to conceptualize these structural dimensions of power through the Hegelian formulation of problem as contradiction. It is, however, too abstract and diluting a device to capture either the inexorable impact of certain compulsory social identities on the lives of individuals or the ways in which, despite superficial appearance of diversity, constellations of experience are traversed, at a deep structural level, by homologous subordinating forces.

Ultimately Jaeggi's dissipated language of problem-solving and learning results in ungrounded social critique conducted largely through generic archetypes. Indeed, in general, for all the emphasis placed on ethical critique's attentiveness to the context of power, there is a striking paucity of relevant concrete examples in Jaeggi's work. Given her declared intention to reaffirm the grounds of Frankfurt School critique in social criticism, this lack of determinate sociological content is troubling. Most of the 'concrete' examples adduced by Jaeggi are taken from Hegel—for instance problem-solving in the family—and, by virtue of their rather anachronistic nature, are of questionable sociological relevance for contemporary critique. So, for example, it is not clear how much is to be gained in terms of a diagnosis of power, from treating the family as a 'form of life' per se since families, and the life-chances and obstacles that its members will experience, vary according to their gendered, racial, and class composition. A generic ethical-functional vocabulary tends to abstract away from the specificities of experience that are in themselves crucial to understanding the precise nature of problems in the first place. For instance, it makes a considerable difference in the diagnosis of 'experiential blockages' if the family is conceived as an ethical form of life or, as Patricia Collins suggests, as the site of saturated power relations—that is, as a pivotal, 'hyper-visible' site of intersecting social forces. On the latter view, families are interpreted neither in isolation from other social institutions—as through the refracting lens of forms of life—nor according to generalized inconsistencies in internal validity claims, but instead as transfer points for power and the reproduction of wider cycles of gender subordination. As Collins describes it: 'families underpin important social functions of gaining citizenship rights, regulating sexualities, and intergenerationally transferring wealth and debt. Family rhetoric and practices organize social inequalities of gender, sexuality, race, ethnicity, religion, class and citizenship, yet they normalize social inequalities by naturalizing social processes' (Collins 2019: 236). In the next section, we will see the difference that interpreting the family in the context of power rather than in the deracinated language of problem-solving makes to understanding its sociological significance as a form of life.

Problem-solving and Disagreement

Such questions of power are bound up with questions of perspective. It is not just that the focus on localized problem-solving dissipates a structural account of power, but also that the impersonal terms in which it is thematized foreclose accompanying issues of disagreement and struggle. As Jaeggi acknowledges, problematization is always a potentially contested process; problems can look considerably different depending on the perspective from which they are viewed— 'a problem first becomes a problem through interpretation' (143). Whether a problem is recognized as such in the first place, how it is construed, how seriously it is taken, what type of effort is deemed necessary to overcome it, these are all matters of dispute and struggle. Furthermore, such interpretative disagreement is likely to be more pronounced in divided societies where, all too often, it is the perspective of dominant groups that prevail in the setting and solving of problems, as Celikates points out: 'In societies rife with conflicts not only about first order problems but also about the procedures and agencies tackling problems, how questions such as who gets to determine what solutions to which problems are to be assessed in which ways and from which perspective are to be answered is far from evident' (2018b: 143). Even when a problem has been recognized generally by society, it may nonetheless remain a matter of deep ongoing ideological division. The racialized nature of poverty in the US is a widely acknowledge social 'fact' that few would dispute, but there exist deep ideological divergences and conflicts around its significance and interpretation. For many, black poverty is the continuing effect of entrenched structures of racial expropriation and exploitation the historical origins of which lie in slavery and segregation. For others, however, black poverty is amenable to racist interpretation as a symptom of the supposed inherent weaknesses of the African-American character. Interpretative conflicts such as these are not merely the relatively benign disagreements that accompany value pluralism but speak to deep ideological schisms and enduring social division and injustice.

Yet despite acknowledging interpretative disagreement, Jaeggi proceeds to disregard it by discussing life-world problems in terms so socially ungrounded that they naturalize precisely the type of unsituated critical perspective that immanent critique rejects. She often deploys a free-floating 'we' stance whose neutrality is taken as given, where it is not clear which groups and interests it represents nor on whose behalf it supposedly speaks. Reliance on this view from nowhere ultimately throws into question the salience of the critique of forms of life in terms of exposing and combatting regressive constellations of experience.

Consider, for example, Jaeggi's discussion of problem-solving in the family. Her claim is that, as society modernizes and norms of gender and sexuality become more permissive, so the traditional family structure become dysfunctional, in her terms, unliveable as a form of life that blocks the self-realization of some of its members: 'it cannot function as a family, because it does not actualize the idea of autonomy constitutive for the modern family (which requires that its members be allowed to become self-sufficient), but instead remains trapped within a psychologically and socially regressive, traditionalist model' (2018a: 158). These blockages are particularly acute for women in so far as traditional ideas of motherhood and domesticity conflict with their wider social roles as workers and so on. They can be progressively resolved as families take on a more democratic internal structure and extend equally to its members possibilities for autonomous self-realization. A question arises, however, about the representativeness of this 'normatively guided' transformation in interaction with 'reality', namely whose reality does this particular Hegelian narrative represent? For what Jaeggi presents as an ethical problem common to all families is arguably actually reflective of the experiential reality of a specific group, namely, white, middle-class women. It is not that this specific experiential reality is not sociologically significant in some respects, but rather that it cannot stand in for the experiences of all other social groups and is therefore not straightforwardly generalizable as a free-standing ethical critique of the family. In naturalizing a subset of social experience as the norm, Jaeggi overlooks the lived reality of women who are situated differently with respect to the family. Black feminist theorists have frequently argued, for instance, that feminist critiques of the family conducted in terms of an overriding concern with patriarchal power often overlook racialized and class dimensions of oppression, and therefore do not adequately capture the experience of black women. For black women (and, to a lesser degree, poor white women) problems with the family have not historically pivoted on the clash that Jaeggi identifies between conventional accounts of domesticity and motherhood, on the one side, and wider social and economic possibilities for autonomous self-realization on the other. This particular dilemma has, by and large, not been pertinent to their lives, mainly because historically black women have always had to work outside the family to survive and therefore, have rarely occupied conventionally defined positions of femininity and domesticity. Their role in rural, domestic, and industrial labour has meant that, unlike white women, black and poor women have not usually been regarded as fitting feminine subjects, as dependent, fragile, nurturing beings. This orthogonal position vis-à-vis conventional notions of femininity persists in that nowadays, black women are still more likely than white women to be heads of household and are often not financially dependent on men because of a labour economy that allows for high unemployment among black men. Traditional gender norms have also had less effect on the internal workings of black families because, unlike their white counterparts, they have been persistently subjected to pathologizing forms of social regulation. As thinkers such as Hazel Carby and Shatema Threadcraft show us, there has been little social concern in the US and British contexts to 'protect or preserve the black family'; instead the state has been instrumental in reproducing 'common sense notions of its inherent pathology: black women were seen to fail as mothers precisely because of their position as workers' (Carby 1982: 116). In the US context Threadcraft (2016) describes similar pathologizing processes where children from female-headed black families are far more likely to be taken into care for neglect than their white counterparts. Single black mothers are punished rather than assisted for their efforts to combine paid labour with care for their families.

These divergent social realities cannot be dismissed as incidental experiential details for they influence the very way in which we understand the family as a form of life, the ways in which it fails or protects its members. Arguably for black women, blockages turn not so much around internal ethical tensions between conventional gender norms and opportunities for wider self-actualization, *pace* Jaeggi, but around the pressures that wider gendered and racialized dynamics of exploitation in the informal and formal labour markets place on the family in the form of poverty, discrimination, and marginalization. These effects are particularly acute given that many black women in Europe and the US work in the care economy and are subject to low wages, vulnerable working conditions, and low social esteem. Against this backdrop, the family is often experienced not as a site of ethical tension so much as a refuge and source of cultural and political resistance to a hostile social world (Carby 1982: 112; Collins 2000: 52). In this light, Jaeggi's generic critique appears skewed because it is not clear that what she views as a pivotal 'ethical' problem is really that salient in pinpointing the key problems and pressures that afflict family life relative to other factors such as material disadvantage and discrimination. Regressive patterns of practice in the family of course play a part in perpetuating 'cycles of gendered vulnerability' but it is questionable how much explanatory weight such a personalist, over-ethicized diagnosis can bear on its own.

Negation of Agency

Ultimately, then, the decontextualized standpoint from which Jaeggi conducts ethical critique, qua problem-solving, underestimates the presence of sectional interests, antagonism, and conflict in wider process of social reproduction and change (e.g., Giddens 1976: 360–1). In so doing, it negates agency. Identifiable agents and concrete political struggles are replaced by impersonal, free-standing dynamics of social change. The negation of agency is at odds with Jaeggi's own negativist, practice-theoretic account of critique which would seemingly requires a determinate account of 'historically developing learning processes' and change.

Which groups precisely are the concrete bearers of social learning processes? To what extent are these developing processes contested and resisted? How deeply embedded in societal attitudes and practices are normatively guided transformations of the social order? What kind of backlash, if any, do they provoke? And so on. In place of such specificity, however, Jaeggi depends on a supra-agential and formal account of problem-solving as 'continuity in discontinuity'. This socially ungrounded account of learning floats free from concrete agents along with any related sense of the concrete costs and stakes of particular struggles, or, for that matter, from any concrete indicator of what might plausibly be taken as evidence of successful learning in a divided social context. For instance, dominant groups who benefit from exploitative dynamics and who, ostensibly, ought to be the subjects of progressive learning processes, often steadfastly choose not to recognize certain problems as problems in the first place (in the sense of a willed ignorance) because they stand to lose too much materially. Social learning is therefore blocked by powerful sectional interests.

Jaeggi acknowledges in passing some questions of ideological recalcitrance and willed ignorance but the cognitivist and ungrounded nature of her analysis forecloses a developed sense of the conflictual societal context in which societal learning always takes place. So, for example, on Jaeggi's account, the expansion of marriage to include same-sex couples represents successful learning in the sphere of intimacy and family life. But learning on whose part exactly? There is no doubt that same-sex marriage represents an emancipatory achievement from certain political perspectives. But to what extent it can be taken as indicative of wider processes of social learning is moot. For the progressive expansion of rights along one dimension needs to be squared with the simultaneous rise in the last few years in UK and Europe of levels of anti-LGBT hate crime and abuse. This abuse is expressed in explicit acts of violence and hate as much as in insidious micro-aggressions and forms of poor treatment against LGBT people as they go about their daily lives.[2] This suggests that the expanded societal values and successful social learning of which same-sex marriage is an ostensible signifier are in fact far from being firmly secured throughout society. In the context of such a fractured and divisive social landscape, it would seem premature, politically naïve, even self-congratulatory to speak of successful ethical learning processes.

Insufficiently tethered to a sense of social agency, of the historical actors who drive or resist processes of change, Jaeggi's ungrounded account of social learning fails to reckon with the fragile, fraught, and uncertain nature of social transformation. On the few occasions where Jaeggi explicitly addresses questions of agency, she equivocates and fails to shed light on matters such as which groups are the

---

[2] Stonewall report (2017) *LGBT in Britain: Hate Crime*. https://www.stonewall.org.uk/lgbt-britain-hate-crime-and-discrimination, Also see European Union Agency for Fundamental Rights: https://fra.europa.eu/en/theme/lgbti

subjects of learning and what might be concrete indices of successful problem-solving. According to her, social learning, on the one hand, does not take place at the voluntarist level of individual or group action: 'rarely are the changes in... forms of life as a whole, intended, consciously directed, desired, and made in awareness' (2018a: 227). Nor, on the other hand, does learning occur, at an impersonal societal level, 'behind the backs of individuals', as a quasi-evolutionary shift in collective social consciousness. Searching for some intermediate agential category to resolve this dilemma, Jaeggi alights on the rather enigmatic Hegelian idea of the world-historical individual. In their 'regulating response' to a situation, the world historical individual succeeds in realizing possibilities latent in a given situation that might not have otherwise been realized: 'it is the world historical individual who has in fact done the right thing at the right time, who has comprehended and channelled the trends of his time in appropriate ways' (2018a: 309) Certainly, an account of social change needs to steer a path between voluntarism and determinism in order to grasp the complex web of interactions between individuals, institutional processes, and *longue durée* shifts in social and economic structures. Whether such interconnections are adequately addressed through the dubious abstraction of the world historical individual is moot since it raises far more questions than it answers. Who/what groups does this hypothetical figure represent and does it not border uncomfortably close on an orthodox view of history and change written from the victor's perspective? From whose perspective is the 'right thing at the right time' being defined? Is it even feasible to speak about social learning without reference to identifiable social agents, collective or individual? Indeed, the main effect that this questionable device has on Jaeggi's critique is to further simplify multidimensional dynamics of change by distilling them into the 'actions' of a mystical super-agent.

Granted, Jaeggi's aim is not to produce a multilevel account of change so much as delineate the formal criteria by which it is possible to judge whether problem-solving has been successful or not. It is questionable, however, whether, like the figure of the world historical individual, Jaeggi's formal criteria are as compatible with a developed sense of historicity as she seems to think. Far from allowing an assessment of the nature and extent of progress, the criteria of rational continuity, enrichment, and expanded self-understanding are arguably instrumental in installing a sanitized, top-down account of societal transformation that effaces historical realities of conflict and struggle. For instance, following Jaeggi's criteria, it would be possible to interpret the 1964 Civil Rights Act as an example of successful problem-solving that is rationally continuous with the preceding historical struggles for racial equality in the US during the nineteenth and twentieth centuries. The granting of formal legal equality could be described, in her terms, as a 'differentiating enrichment through experience' in that it marks the gradual expansion of the concrete rights, liberties, and opportunities that have been historically withheld from African-Americans. It could also be seen to confirm her third criterion of enhanced collective self-understanding, viz. a progressive shift in US societal consciousness towards anti-racism. There are, however, several counts upon which this unifying, sanitized narrative could be questioned, not least that it effaces the long, often violent history of African-American struggle for equality by retrospectively sublating it into a story about the inevitable unfolding of progressive liberal reason. By abstracting away from the reality of struggle, formal criteria of learning lend themselves too easily to a self-congratulatory narrative that understates the formative role that the 'politics of exclusion' has played in shaping American democracy (e.g., Stears 2007). It also deflects attention from the ways in which, despite the undoubted political and symbolic significance of the Civil Rights Act, it has been ineffective in dislodging the material conditions of oppression, deprivation, and discrimination that many African-Americans continue to live under. Questionable too is the idea, entailed in Jaeggi's abstract account of progress, that collective self-understanding has expanded in terms of the steady growth of anti-racist sentiment. The resurgence of racist populism under Trump—which according to some commentators has set civil rights and anti-racist struggles back by thirty years—is but one manifestation of the uneven and divisive social reality that renders progress a more fraught and uncertain achievement than the formal criteria allow. It is not just blatant racism that throws into doubt the extent of societal learning but also the persistence of insidiously racialized common-sense beliefs and white ignorance, such as colour-blind neutrality, which ultimately, in Le Bron's view (2013), represent a collective failure of moral character.

Historical situations are, in short, more messy, violent, and divisive than the deracinated range of learning options staked out by Jaeggi's evaluative criteria. This is not to abandon the possibility of being able to say that something represents progress, albeit in a more qualified sense than Jaeggi, but it is to question whether this can be done on a purely formal basis. It is to ask what is to be taken as 'evidence' of successful learning and to insist on the importance of being explicit about the perspective from which judgements about progress are made. It is to argue moreover, that formal criteria do not provide sufficient normative resources for such evaluations, rather they must draw on resources immanent within a form of life and take the form of contextually indexed judgements. Consider for instance the resemblance between Jaeggi's measure of progress as the expansion of expressive possibilities and the way that capitalism maximizes profits through the proliferation of commodified differences. Formal criteria give us no way of effectively distinguishing between expressive possibilities that are genuinely emancipatory and those that are lifestyle choices engineered to secure consumer acquiescence and social conformity. Indeed, formal criteria also don't allow the possibility that there may well be no clear-cut answer to such questions, that empowerment and constraint are inextricably intertwined in a repertoire of regulated liberties. In such cases, it is probably more relevant for unmasking critique not to engage in summary assessments of progress or regress so much as to trace precise distributions of power and the matrix of agential possibilities to which they give rise.

In the end, then, formalism works against a negativist critique of power and effectively endorses a naïve liberal progressivism, or, as Celikates bluntly puts it, a 'pacifying and one-sided reinterpretation' of social transformation as learning that verges on a 'self-congratulatory form of Whig history' (2018b: 144–145). Societal transformation is emptied of existential content and seems to have more to do with the unfurling of a formulaic logic than with real-world dynamics of power, suffering, and agency. Through an epistemic reduction upwards, the 'quasi-evolutionary' logic of problem-solving irons out negative historical forces such as catastrophe, violence, domination, contingency, and suffering. Detached from concrete agency, formalist analysis also renders invisible the part played by confrontation, strategy, rebellion, uprising, conflict, struggle, and so on in forcing social change. Devoid of phenomenal content, negativism is little more than an abstract moment of contradiction or crisis which is fetishized as the driver of impersonal learning processes. This abstract negativism lacks a sense of why individuals might decide to engage in political action even when they know that the costs will be high, of the suffering, anger, and moral outrage that motivates them to act in conditions that are felt to no longer be tolerable. Equally, it fails to shed much light on very different historical circumstances where, in seemingly intolerable conditions, individuals opt not to resist or rebel (Gaventa1982). In such cases, it may be that, for those who suffer, quiescence is the only viable possible response in so far as they internalize objective harms as a habitus of disempowerment and resignation. Likewise, lacking experiential content, abstract negativism has little to say about forms of life which, even though clearly 'blocked' in some respects, may simultaneously be sites of subversion, the locus of 'resistant knowledge projects', and counter-hegemonic agency on the part of dominated groups (e.g., Collins 2019: 87–154; Scott 1990). Even though it would seem necessary for critique to take account of such reservoirs of subaltern agency in evaluating the degree to which a form of life is regressive or not, there seems to be no way of incorporating such thick considerations under formal criteria which seem to only admit either–or alternatives. Indeed, the very idea that a form of life is blocked or uninhabitable is a one-dimensional abstraction—a gross theoretical concept as Shapiro would have it—unaccompanied by appreciation of what this might entail at the level of lived suffering, of the harms and anguish that individuals endure as part of being subject to regressive social relations. As Max Pensky puts it: 'to translate *unlivability* into an occasion for *problem solving* seems... to retain its plausibility only by downplaying... the dimension of the unlivability of crisis-ridden forms of life as the *experience of negation*. Unlivability is the *loss* of meaning, of the validity of existentially significant norms' (Pensky 2018: 91–2).

In an exchange with Amy Allen, Jaeggi concedes that her 'very narrow or thin' formulation of negativist critique might not be sufficiently informed by an account of suffering: 'it seems to be such an impoverished account of progress to say that it's just some way of accumulating experiences' (Von Redecker 2018: 182). Yet the implications that this concession of impoverishment has for Jaeggi's overall approach might be more destabilizing than she realizes, for it might ultimately involve abandoning the attempt to ground critique in a formal idea of progress. For it is hard to see how she can bear out the claim that the idea of progress is 'deflated' and 'open' to history when its origins in Hegelian abstraction have such sanitizing and depoliticizing effects on an understanding of social reality.

Negation of Actuality

In the tradition of left-Hegelianism dialectics that Jaeggi follows, there is evidently no possibility of definitively reconciling opposing theoretical tendencies of formalism and negativism. Rather the challenge is one of ongoing adaption; critique endeavours to move between the two poles in as productive a manner as possible, trying to avoid the artificial privilege of the one over the other. The space of critique is one of a 'continual negotiation and adjustment of thought to experience and experience to thought' (Oksala 2016: 45). When she describes her task as a 'dialectical analysis of regression', Jaeggi appears to recognize the importance of this ceaseless process of adjustment, of balancing attentiveness to the particularities of a given form of life with application of formal evaluative criteria (von Redecker 2018: 167). In order to offset the formalist tendencies of her idea of progress, she insists on the necessity of studying the 'untidy situations' in which change comes about and on the precedence that 'events, circumstances, innovations' and 'new experiences' must take over impersonal historical dynamics (von Redecker 2018: 174). In practice though, she doesn't so much move between formalism and negativism, theory and experience, as unfailingly prioritize the former over the latter, the 'freestanding' principle of progress over 'fine grained analysis' of constellations of experience (Von Redecker 2018: 167). This lop-sidedness is driven partly by the way that, like other Frankfurt School theorists, she resorts to an overly strong interpretation of context-transcending critique which construes experience as pure particularism and immanence. She maintains that, unsupported by a formal account of progressive learning, critique is left in a 'contextualist or relativistic' position with respect to normative foundations (2018b: 189). Attentiveness to particularity is elided with mere particularism and the critique of power with a 'partisanship for social struggles' that can be justified only 'in a decisionistic or merely standpoint-theoretical way' (2018b: 198).

Jaeggi's dismissal of the experiential perspective as pure particularism is not only tendentious but at odds with the avowedly pragmatist and dialectical tenets of her thought. With regard to the diagnosis of power, it is not the case that all marginalized experiences represent an inherently limited epistemic standpoint given the causal connections between particular social locations and capitalist structures. Some marginalized locations yield crucial knowledge about power and inequity and make visible certain connections and transfer points that are not visible from privileged locations. Far from being a 'merely' localized standpoint, an 'experiential and analytic anchor in the lives of marginalized communities... provides the most inclusive paradigm for thinking about social justice... particularize viewing allows for a more concrete and expansive vision of universal justice' (Mohanty 2003: 231). Likewise, from a normative perspective, it is not the case that, unsupported by a freestanding principle of change, critique's attentiveness to the context of power condemns it to arbitrary and relativist judgement? In assuming this to be the case, Jaeggi elides contextualism with relativism and thereby undermines her own Adornian notion of the normativity of the actual which pivots around responsiveness to the circumstances of power. On a pragmatist view, sensitivity to context does not lead automatically to an inability to hold systematic normative commitments or to take in the position of the universal at all. As Amy Allen reminds us, contextualism is not the same as relativism. Contextualism operates at the second-order level of meta-normativity whereas relativism operates at the first-order level of substantive normative commitments. It is possible therefore to hold strong first-order normative commitments (i.e., not be relativist), commitments that may even be universal in the scope of their application, while at the same time accepting that these commitments are not absolute but in need of historically indexed justification. As Allen puts it: 'our normative principles can be justified relative to a set of basic normative commitments that stand fast in relation to them, but because there is no context-transcendent point of view from which we can determine which contexts are superior to which others, these basic normative commitments must be understood as contingent foundations' (Allen2016: 215). Moreover, the process of meta-normative justification is never arbitrary or decisionist, *pace* Jaeggi, because, in any historical situation, there are always specific contextual criteria of coherence, systematicity, and veracity that enable us to distinguish better from worse claims. Contextualism may well entail fallibilism but not inevitably relativism. Indeed, as pragmatist thinkers observe, relativism is only a problem for those who cleave to absolutized values and ideas of transcendence which hang, as Adorno memorably puts it 'like herrings from the ceiling' (quoted in Allen 2016: 216).

Teasing apart contextualism from relativism in this way raises the possibility of conceptualizing context transcendence in a fashion more compatible than Jaeggi's formalist stance with critique's responsiveness to lived experience. Context-transcending insight is enabled not by adopting a purely disengaged or objectifying stance, qua a formal account of progress, but rather by the resources—norms, meanings, and practices—that are present within a given form of life. It does not amount to the ability to stand outside a form of life, rather it is a critical-reflective attitude is enabled by the reasoning capacities and resources inherent within the form of life itself. Forms of life 'provide resources for, and not just obstacles to, surpassing their limitations... the renewal and correction of traditions looks to be co-extensive with self-renewal and self-correction' (Kompridis 2006: 7–8). Put differently, context-transcending insight is a dialogical achievement—it comes from within the situation itself, from inclusive, cross-perspectival deliberation on the part of actors involved about the most appropriate way to respond to problems in their shared world. A critical perspective on this world, one that overcomes limitations in existing knowledge, is generated precisely by the estranging, and potentially enlightening, effects that arise from bringing alien perspectives to bear on one another. Such a dialogically reformulated idea of context transcendence as the critical potential immanent within the resources and perspectives of a given life-form is moreover implicit in Jaeggi's own insistence on the situated nature of critique and involvement of the theorist within the horizon of inquiry. Yet, in as much as she fails to follow through on this implication preferring to solve the issue of context transcendence through a formalized account of progress, so her explicit commitment to negativist critique is undermined.

It is Jaeggi's view, as we have seen, that, by virtue of its 'thinness'—that 'it doesn't say anything substantial about the content of "progress"'—that formalism is compatible with a negativist sense of historicity (Jaeggi 2018c: 37). The claim is that formal evaluative criteria are sufficiently neutral and open that they can be filled with any manner of determinate content so to speak. But to sever form from content in this simplistic fashion is inconsistent with an Adornian emphasis on their inevitable imbrication and especially to overlook the latent framing that form has on content; the way, despite the appearance of neutrality, it implicitly directs attention towards some kinds of social content and facticity and away from other kinds. In other words, formalism is not quite as impartial a framing device as Jaeggi assumes since it implicitly shapes the conditions of intelligibility itself—what is taken to be a significant object of critical inquiry and what isn't.

These indirect framing effects are evident for example in Jaeggi's earlier work on alienation which preempts many of the themes and theoretical concerns of her subsequent critique of regressive forms of life. As with the idea of progress, Jaeggi maintains that alienation ought to be conceived in formal terms, as a 'relation of relationlessness', in order to avoid invoking the essentialist ideas of human nature that, in her view, hamper other versions of the concept. The formal criteria according to which alienation can be identified include those of rigidification (reification) and appropriation. An alienated state is one where circumstances appear to have become so inflexible, i.e., 'rigidified', that individuals feel that they lack control over them. Not all such situations are alienating; they only become so when they prevent individuals from responding to their surroundings in an 'affirmative' way: 'with respect to rigidification... what is alienating is the halting of experimentation' (2016: 66). To be alienated is to be unable to establish meaningful relations with other individuals and the world in general. A paradigm case of alienation proposed by Jaeggi is that of the young academic who, having moved to the suburbs, feels discontented because his metropolitan life has somehow slipped away and been replaced by a routine existence (2016: 52). Living in the suburbs is not alienating per se, what renders it so in this instance is that the academic experiences his circumstances as so unalterable that he feels he has no choice but to conform to conventional norms and expectations. He is alienated because he loses the capacity to create a meaningful relationship with his social environment.

What is immediately striking about Jaeggi's exemplar of alienation is the way it differs from other usages of the concept where it commonly denotes the estranging psycho-subjective effects of exploitative and degrading material circumstances. Although her academic may well be suffering from a psychic malaise of some sort, the implied equivalence between the relatively privileged circumstances of suburban living and the patently oppressive social conditions highlighted in these other usages seems rather strained. The focus in these latter formulations of alienation on structural causation and the way in which objective injustices are internalized as subjective injury is replaced by a focus on individual self-realization. Indeed, the primacy Jaeggi's model places on the abstract capacity for self- realization over material circumstances seems in many ways more compatible with liberal accounts of the autonomous self than with radical social critique. Differently put, defining alienation in the abstract terms of the 'subjectless subject' is less of a neutral framing device than Jaeggi assumes, in so far as its voluntaristic emphasis pushes into the background highly salient considerations about subtending structures of power. Similar criticisms can be made of the 'formal' account of progress, the apparent emptiness of which is belied by its implicit framing effects. Given its predisposition towards rational continuity, the idea of progress will tend inevitably to discount apparently singular or anomalous 'facts' that are not assimilable to its syncretic Hegelian logic. In this way, the interpretation of progress is tacitly biased towards reformist, conventional outcomes that fit in with known patterns of behaviour and against more radical and uncertain processes of social transformation. Formalism then is not simply a 'theoretical vacuum' into which 'one can simply place the content of their choosing' for in so far as it tacitly preselects suitable content, it is danger of obscuring the very thing—negativist historicity—that it was meant to bring into view (Froese 2015: 244).

The paradox of formalism is that while, on the one hand, it is not as thin as it appears, vis-á-vis the diagnosis of power, on the other hand its lack of determinate content undercuts the capacity of critique to normatively evaluate forms of life. So, the lack of determinate content in Jaeggi's formalist rendering of alienation weakens its analytical purchase such that it is difficult to see how it differs from adjacent concepts such as anomie, meaninglessness, or even an existentialist account of bad faith. Its formalistic lineaments are not sufficiently 'fine-grained' to be able to capture the patterns and particularities of real-world experiences of alienation in comparison with other regressive experiences. In fact, if such distinctions are to be made, they are done so using contextual considerations and knowledge of the determinate social circumstances rather than abstract criteria. Relatively little can be learnt from Jaeggi's thought experiment of the 'alienated' young academic precisely because it lacks specificity; beyond his highlighted inner frustration, not enough is known about his socio-economic context. So, for example, as Foesne points out, it would make a difference to evaluations of the case, qua alienation, if it occurred in some regions of the US rather than others. In areas such as Detroit, movement to the suburbs is often part of a wider exodus of white people from inner cities because of urban riots and racial tension. This exodus in turn compounds racial inequality and, especially, the widely documented 'implosion of urban ghettos' and eventual transformation into 'dilapidated hyperghettoes', that is, derelict, virtually uninhabitable zones of urban relegation (Wacquant 2010). Were these to be the background conditions of Jaeggi's hypothetical academic, then the labelling of his suburban condition as alienation would seem to be misplaced given what one presumes are his circumstances of relative privilege. But on Jaeggi's formal account such contextual detail is deemed incidental and hence it is not possible to distinguish in anything other than vague, ungrounded terms between the plight of the academic and those stranded in inner cities who might well desire to move to the safety of the suburbs but are unable to because of lack of material resources. In these circumstances, to call the academic's state one of alienation might be stretching the concept too far (e.g., Christman 2018: 46). It is, in short, judgements about the context of power and subtending structural constraints that assist in making the type of discriminations that are pivotal to assessing whether a given state is alienating or not and not ungrounded, formalistic criteria. Moreover, the generic emptiness of a formal account of alienation cannot simply be amended by importing the relevant empirical data because of the way those self-same criteria implicitly act as interpretative filters rendering certain facts visible while occluding others. The normative burden of negativist critique is carried therefore not by formalism but by sensitivity to the context of power and exploration of how to eliminate the bad. It is this attentiveness to the lived reality of injurious experiences that that critical theorists refer to when they speak of the conceptual priority of the negative (Wellmer 1991: 202). For all that Jaeggi's negativist critique takes its cue from the priority of the negative, it undercuts itself by its reliance on formalist understanding of context transcendence.

While it is vital that unmasking critique strives to systematically identify the ways in which a form of life might be damaging to individuals and how this might be rectified, it is not clear that broadbrush appraisals of progress are particularly helpful to this endeavour. In so far as appraisals about whether a form of life is demonstrably superior to that which came before, or whether it is blocked and regressive in some way, lack nuance, they are of questionable normative use to critique (Woolf 2019). In place of generic assessments of progress, it might be more productive to concentrate attention on analysing specific distributions of power in a given constellation and the ways that these enable some groups and practices while marginalizing and constraining others. As Foucault puts it 'critique is not a matter of saying that things are not right as they are. It is a matter of pointing out on what kinds of assumptions, what kinds of familiar, unchallenged, unconsidered modes of thought the practices that we accept rest' (Foucault 1990: 154). Normative judgements of this kind will inevitably need to be nuanced and open to revision partly because the object or practices under consideration may themselves be Janus-faced, both constraining and enabling, depending on the perspective from which it/they are viewed. So, as commentators have noted, practices of autonomous self-realization in a neoliberal society have a double-edged significance. They might, on the side, enable marginalized groups to forge the kind of positive social identity and sense of social worth that has hitherto been denied them. On the other side, they might also serve to bind those same groups more closely into commodifying social dynamics (e.g., McRobbie 2008). The important thing is to analyse such cases in their particularity, to trace how these ambivalent dynamics play out in the social field rather than formulate simplifying judgements about whether they represent progress or not. This is after all the intended meaning of Jaeggi's negativism, that emancipatory critique is politically more effective by keeping a vigilant focus on understanding and overcoming the bad in its particularity. This negativist disposition is echoed in Foucault's famous statement that 'everything is dangerous', a warning about the perils of conceiving of emancipation as an end state rather than as a practice of ongoing critical vigilance.[3] It means that foregoing broadbrush and self-congratulatory analyses of learning and progress need not inevitably plunge critique into the piecemeal contextualism that Jaeggi fears, so much as enhance its responsiveness to the oppressed groups it ostensibly addresses.

---

[3] 'My point is not that everything is bad, but that **everything is dangerous**, which is not exactly the same as bad. If everything is dangerous, then we always have something to do. So my position leads not to apathy but to a hyper- and pessimistic activism. I think that the ethico-political choice we have to make every day is to determine which is the main danger.' 'On the Genealogy of Ethics: An Overview of Work in Progress.' Afterword, in Hubert L. Dreyfus and Paul Rabinow, *Michel Foucault: Beyond Structuralism and Hermeneutics*, 2nd edn. Chicago: University of Chicago Press (1983).

Concluding Remarks

Ultimately then, the contradiction in Jaeggi's work between her formalist method and negativist understanding of immanent critique remains unresolved. The emphasis she places on the negative character of critique is intended to reaffirm the original connection posited by Frankfurt School thinkers between normativity and social criticism, a connection that their subsequent turn to foundations has downplayed. In renewing this connection, Jaeggi's negativism underscores how important it is for emancipatory critique to attend to both the object of inquiry, that is, cultivating alertness to the patterns and particularities of negative experience, and the practice of inquiry, that is, awareness of the critic's involvement in the field of study. Jaeggi explicitly rejects the idea that the role of the theorist is one of judgement 'in an abstract way from an external point of view' and instead stresses the idea of world disclosure that finds political possibilities immanent in the concrete deficits of the real world. In these respects, Jaeggi's negativism breaks productively with established lines of thought about the context-transcending grounds of critique set in train by Habermas.

Yet, by resorting to the formal idea of progress as an independent yardstick for evaluating forms of life, Jaeggi ends up replicating other problematic features of paradigm-led theory which effectively cancel out the negativist import of her thought. Despite claims of being open and deflated, the idea of progress as learning imposes on social reality a tendentious, homogenizing template of change that effaces the real-world experiences of suffering and struggle that it is supposed to highlight. Its governing principle of rational continuity replaces social agents with ahistorical schemata and the contingency of struggle with the abstract logic of dialectics. Far from being implicated in the field of inquiry, the critic, qua situated arbiter of progress, is screened behind a quasi-functionalist, socially ungrounded vocabulary of problem-solving and learning. This lack of self-reflexivity fuels the illusory objectivism of progress as an evaluative principle and suppresses pivotal issues of power and interpretation such as the perspective from which a problem is defined and judgements about learning and progress are made. There is another way for Jaeggi to conceive of the context-transcending grounds of critique which, moreover, would be more consistent than formalism with her explicit endorsement of negativist historicity. Context-transcending insight in this sense is generated not by the adoption of a 'free-standing' principle of progress but by situated and dialogical reasoning that moves between the experiential and theoretical perspectives and uses each to interrogate and transcend the limitations of the other.

Conclusion
Theorizing from Experience

If Frankfurt School theory is to realize its aspiration to be a radical political critique of capitalist society then it may need to pay more heed than it arguably has done up till now to the experiences of oppressed groups and what these tell us about the way the world is organized. That these experiences should be of pivotal importance in guiding theory is a direct implication of the claim that unmasking critique makes a practical contribution to real-world struggles against oppression. It would be mere tokenism for critical theorists to assert such practical emancipatory aims without trying to connect their attempts to conceptualize oppression to the lived reality of those groups whom they purportedly address. Yet, because of their propensity to a certain style of grand-sweep theorizing—what I have called here paradigm-led theory—it is precisely such a tokenistic and self-undermining position that Frankfurt School theorists find themselves inadvertently assuming at least with regard to the part that direct experience plays in their work.

Certainly, it is understandable why Frankfurt School theorists have concentrated their efforts on developing totalizing interpretative paradigms as a way of capturing the distinctively global dimensions of injustice and oppression under neoliberal capitalism. If transnational care chains, flows of migrant labour, volatile economies, exploited and precaritized work forces, ecological depredation, and so forth are to be properly grasped, it would seem necessary to develop correspondingly capacious interpretative frameworks capable of grasping large objects of enquiry and analysing neoliberal society in its totality. The importance of large-scale, systematic explanation for a critical theory of oppression is not in question here. Rather, what is in question is the specific way that this task has been undertaken by Frankfurt School thinkers through the deployment of single-lens paradigms and the degree to which this approach is compatible with the historicizing tenets of immanent critique. My contention is that the construal of critique in such monist and normativized terms has all but effaced one of the defining features of the Frankfurt School approach, namely its starting place in sociological criticism and advertence to negative experience. If oppression in a neoliberal order is complex and intersectional, it follows that, diagnostic theories ought to be similarly differentiated and multidimensional in both explanatory and normative senses. But instead of developing flexible frameworks capable of analysing complex distributions of power, paradigm-led critical theory diagnoses social relations according to a single foundational principle with correspondingly stymying effects on its account of oppression. If anything, these problems are exacerbated when interpretative paradigms are scaled up to explain transnational dynamics of oppression, because the receptivity to context and experience that is necessary for thinking across cultures is replaced by socially ungrounded generalization. Ensuing accounts of oppression are so vague and schematic that it is hard to see how they bear upon the lived reality of oppressed groups or represent a practical-theoretic contribution to their ongoing political struggles.

In sum, for all that critical theorists insist on the radical democratic import of their unmasking critique of power, it is hard to find much concrete evidence in their work that bears this out, as is betokened by their superficial treatment of gender oppression. Instead of stretching monist frameworks ever more thinly to ensure global reach, it seems that what unmasking critique may in fact require is anchoring more securely in experientially led social analysis. To stress the centrality of lived experience to an account of oppression is not to parochialize critique and strip it of transcontextual relevance, as Frankfurt School theorists fear, but rather to enable it to trace the ways in which gender intersects with other vectors of power and work out more effectively what might be done to rectify enduring dynamics of oppression. In this regard, lived experience is not antithetical to systematic critique but enabling of it. It is to affirm with Mohanty the insight that universal justice is best thought through particularity rather through what is deemed to be a single, all-encompassing emancipatory interest: 'particularized viewing allows for a more concrete and expansive vision of universal justice' (Mohanty 2003: 231).

Driving problems with the paradigm-led approach is the strong interpretation that Frankfurt School thinkers give to the context-transcending grounds of critique, an interpretation which arguably stands in tension with their hermeneutic understanding of the situated nature of thought. Naturally, Frankfurt School thinkers dispute that such a tension exists and maintain that their construal of critique's foundations in intra-mundane or 'quasi-transcendent' terms explicitly aims to incorporate a sense of historicity and overcome false binaries of transcendence versus immanence, universality versus particularity. In practice, however, grounding critique in a monistic and invariant emancipatory interest has subtly dehistoricizing effects that reinforce rather than dislodge these binaries, blunts critique's sensitivity to the context of power, and facilitates a too-ready dismissal of direct subjective experience as mere immanence or particularism. Doubt about the value of lived experience to an unmasking critique of power has dogged Frankfurt School thought since its inception and has been accompanied by the presumption of critique's vanguard role, that is, of the superiority of its insights relative to other perspectives when it comes to emancipatory knowledge. In Adorno, intellectual vanguardism is part and parcel of his despairing social theory where ordinary individuals have been so successfully co-opted by mass consumerism that they are apparently oblivious to the exploitative and regressive reality of capitalist society. Only the critic (and his proxy of the high art form) can penetrate this ideological smokescreen and see society for what it truly is. While subsequent generations of the Frankfurt School have explicitly distanced themselves from this elitist and politically untenable vision of mass deception, the vestiges of intellectual vanguardism remain in the way their monist paradigms implicitly assume the epistemic superiority of the generalizing theoretical stance relative to the particularistic experiential one for an unmasking critique of power. While not wanting to undermine the distinctive and invaluable nature of theoretical insight, I have argued that the presumption of an uncontested epistemic superiority warrants scrutiny on several fronts especially as it seems to contradict basic premises of immanent critique as an exercise in dialogical and reflexive thinking. By positioning the theorist/critical framework as validating authority vis-à-vis the veracity of direct experiential understanding, paradigm-led theory undermines dialogical reasoning, replacing it instead with a tacit hierarchy. The nonreciprocal dynamic where theory improves on or verifies experience, but not the other way round, not only undercuts dialogism but also stymies reflexivity by shielding the interpretative paradigm from the critical self-scrutiny that is supposedly another hallmark of Frankfurt School critique. As a result, paradigm-led theory is self-confirming rather than, as it declares, self-critical. In the end, then, despite asserting its foothold in social reality and alertness to issues of oppression and suffering, paradigm-led theorizing suffers from the kind of imperviousness to the context of power more commonly associated with idealizing types of normative thought (e.g., Woolf 2019). Indeed, disregard of lived experience is actually more of an acute problem for critical theory than it is for other sorts of normative theory precisely because, unlike the latter, it declares its political-ethical alliance with oppressed groups and its aim to contribute in a practically effective manner to their struggles for societal transformation.

Accordingly, at the heart of the idea of theorizing from experience lies a different notion of context transcendence, one which is dialogically construed and therefore arguably more compatible than paradigm-led theory with the idea that unmasking critique should be guided by the experiences and practical concerns of oppressed groups. This reconfigured understanding of context transcendence does not represent a radical break with the Frankfurt School approach—as some of its proponents claim—but a continuation, albeit one that is emphatically pragmatist in nature and draws on nascent but under-utilized resources in the tradition. It is underpinned by the assumption that lived experience is an indispensable resource for critique, and that the knowledge that oppressed groups have of the world is central to the production of unmasking critical theory. It also assumes that according equal epistemic status to disempowered subjects as knowers is a fundamental ethical entailment of theory that professes practical emancipatory aims. Context-transcending insight is accordingly reconstrued as the outcome not just of using the correct interpretative paradigm or foundational diagnostic principle, but of thought's movement to and fro between theoretical and experiential perspectives. It is by utilizing the hermeneutic resources present in the life-world and reasoning across perspectives in as inclusive and open-ended manner as possible that immanent worldviews are potentially expanded and enriched. By virtue of their mutual estrangement, each perspective acts as a vehicle of potential criticism and self-improvement for the other.

This dialogical view of context transcendence is more consistent than a paradigm-led approach with the hermeneutic premises of immanent critique because, by being conceived of as an element within a larger critical exchange, the theoretical perspective or paradigm itself is brought into the field of historical inquiry rather than removed from it. The paradigm is not taken as given nor is it unproblematically aligned with a non-partisan and totalizing stance, objectivity per se so to speak, but is regarded as itself in need of ongoing verification by others included within the process of inquiry. Immanent critique necessarily begins *in media res* with initial judgements pertaining to the setting and framing of a particular problem space; how a problem is best construed, its scope and content, what kind of evidence should be considered, whose interests are relevant and which groups should be consulted, and so on. The theorist may well have a carefully considered, well-informed idea of how to proceed, but this still does not obviate the importance of checking this initial starting point with the subjects of inquiry to ensure its validity and continuing relevance to dynamic and changing social circumstances. This equalizing methodology doesn't deny the distinctive contribution that theoretical perspective brings to the process of knowledge production, particularly with regard to exposing structures and tendencies that may not be readily apparent at the level of immediate embodied experience. But nor does it one-sidedly associate the transpersonal perspective with objectivity per se or endow it, in vanguardist manner, with the sole capacity to penetrate cognitive-ideological distortions and other epistemic blindspots that seemingly go unrecognized by those directly effected. It acknowledges that the theoretical perspective may suffer from its own unconscious biases and shortcomings, some of which come from the projection of scholastic dispositions onto the subjects of enquiry thereby distorting their lived reality. In this regard, the experiential perspective has as much of a corrective role to play vis-à-vis theoretical inquiry as the more commonly assumed reverse dynamic.

Conceiving of context transcendence in these dialogical terms overcomes the imbalance, typical of paradigm-led theory, where the theoretical perspective is under-problematized and the experiential one over-problematized. All positions, the theorist's included, are partial in relation to inquiry and this necessitates sustained vigilance about the ways in which certain scholastic assumptions may naturalize social privilege as general, uncontroversial norms. In this regard, paradigm-led critical theory is only dialogical in a weak, first-order sense, that is, once democratic debate is already up and running and interlocutors have always-already accepted the pregiven terms of interaction, qua principles of justification, recognition, communication, and so forth. Paradigms are not dialogical, however, in the deeper second-order sense that the governing interpretative principle or rational universal is also an object of scrutiny. Such scrutiny is preemptively shut down through the contention that the principle represents a definitive expression of emancipatory interests. In this way, monological foundations foreclose a fundamental dimension of political disagreement, namely the controversy that arises when subjects don't accept the basic rules of the game or the way debate has been set up. It matters a lot that the criteria for inquiry and debate are not removed from the space of disputation, that they are dialogically agreed on rather than imposed. For there is an important difference, as Lugones and Spelman remind us, between 'developing ideas together, in a "pre-theoretical" stage, engaged as equals in joint enquiry' and 'one group developing, on the basis of their own experience, a set of criteria for good change [for women]—and then reluctantly making revisions in the criteria at the insistence of women to whom such criteria seem ethnocentric and arrogant. The deck is stacked when one group takes it upon itself to develop the theory and then have others criticize it' (Lugones and Spelman 1983: 579).

Dialogical method assumes then, that just as theory cannot be reduced to experience, so too experience should not be overridden by theory. For, as Catherine Mackinnon reminds us, 'We know things with our lives, and live that knowledge, beyond anything any theory has yet theorized' (MacKinnon 1991: 14) Keeping this mutual irreducibility in mind serves to focus attention on divergences between perspectives, divergences that require probing rather than ignoring or reconciling for they may offer opportunities for improving understanding. Divergences between, for example, philosophical and practical-political worldviews where activists and those with direct experience of oppression may reject accepted theoretical diagnoses of existing struggles and also, implicitly, the underlying intellectual division of labour which endows the theorist/philosopher—as secular priest—with unquestioned insight into political matters. It is not always the case that distance from a political situation equates to enhanced insight for it may also result in misleading scholastic projection and abstraction. Why, for example, should we consider a putative universal right to justification to be a politically compelling way of responding to injustice and oppression given the epistemic barriers encountered by disadvantaged groups when the normative space of reasons is organized around certain notions of validity? Or, for example, how is the critique of oppression furthered by framing intimate relations between men and women as dynamics of recognition–misrecognition when this occludes entrenched gendered asymmetries of power? Likewise, what, from an activist perspective, is to be gained by diagnosing societal oppression in the language of problem-solving and learning when it drastically understates the extent to which capitalist societies are functionally dependent on racial expropriation and exploitation? And so on. Paradigm-led theory's intellectual vanguardism and relative lack of methodological self-awareness means that it rarely seems willing to question the aptness of its normative insights vis-à-vis those of activists or why, when they are articulated from a place of privilege and detachment, its monist interpretations are endowed with more explanatory weight than those of individuals with direct experience of political struggle. As Celikates remarks, it is all too frequent that 'critical theorists underestimate the reflexive and self-critical potential of existing struggles at their own disadvantage' (Celikates 2017: 852). Reconstruing context transcendence in dialogical terms as reasoning across perspectives—where the theoretical frame is itself included as one of the perspectives open to scrutiny—creates a space for a deeper level of contestation than paradigm-led theory allows. For, on this dialogical account, it is the theoretical rules of the game itself that are open to disputation and alteration as much as the concrete ways that actors go about playing a particular political game. Such thoroughgoing contestation is moreover not inherently inimical to systematic critique, as somehow destructive of stable foundations and therefore parochializing, but is necessarily part and parcel of the expansion of epistemic and political horizons. Expanded understanding or context-transcending knowledge in this sense is not equated, *tout court*, with a totalizing interpretative perspective but with how subjects use the resources immanent within a given situation to gradually improve their grasp of problems that confront them—theorizing, that is, with practical intent.

Inevitably, there are a few provisos that need to be made about the dialogical aspects of this reconfigured understanding of context-transcending critique. First, an institutional objection must be considered, namely that given the elite, specialized conditions under which academic knowledge production occurs nowadays, there are significant, if not insuperable, barriers to the establishment of genuine cross-perspectival reasoning. The chasm that exists between the worlds of political activism and formal political theory renders the idea of dialogical knowledge production quixotic at best. Certainly, these barriers should not be underestimated and ultimately can probably only be effectively overcome—as radical theorists and activists have been saying for years—through a drastic overhaul of universities and academic institutions that aims for demographic representativeness at all levels. Nonetheless, even in the current inegalitarian institutional context, there are types of theory, usually rooted in what is often dismissively termed identity politics, that have stronger links to activist movements and, as a result, have been more successful at dialogically incorporating everyday political concerns and experiences into formal knowledge production. In this regard, an important lesson for Frankfurt School critique is the way in which black feminist theory, decolonial feminist theory, and others have reversed the uni-directional, scholastic problematization of experience to show how empty and politically redundant theory can be when it loses its anchor in the lived reality of disempowered groups. One of the things that a theorist can do therefore to try to correct for the absence of a direct connection with political activism, is to work in a methodologically open and interdisciplinary manner, striving to ground normative reflection in sociologically informed inquiry. To explicitly embrace a bottom-up, interdisciplinary approach which begins, not from abstract philosophical questions, but from concrete social problems and 'people in forgotten places' and endeavours to ground and reground theory in these lived realities (Gilmore 2008). Although, on the face of it, this seems a fairly minimal requirement for dialogical knowledge production, it may in fact signal quite a shift in intellectual practice given the self-referential and socially weightless nature of some types of radical political theory (see McNay 2014).

The second proviso is that dialogism should not be taken to mean an anodyne, frictionless process of mutual understanding and empathy. This again is an important lesson from black feminist theory, and the work of Iris Marion Young, that, given its inseparability from political struggle, the dialogical encounter is always asymmetrical, fraught, and liable to fail. Overcoming differences and barriers to understanding can never be a purely epistemic matter because it inevitably involves, at the same time, challenging the status quo and confronting background asymmetries of power and privilege. The demand that oppressed groups be allowed to express themselves in their own terms is as much as a demand for the dominant groups to divest themselves of assumed privilege and status as it is a demand for linguistic self-determination. Even if the conversation is uncomfortable and agreement seems perpetually unattainable, there is nonetheless intrinsic value, in inegalitarian social orders, in revealing structural conflicts of interests that would otherwise remain suppressed under deliberative assumptions of overlapping consensus, shared reasons, and so on (e.g., Young 2000: 119). Given these considerable political stakes, the outcome of dialogical knowledge production, qua enhanced understanding, can never be assured; it is always a discomfiting and conflictual process. Nonetheless, short of retreating to a monological model of knowledge, there is no alternative; it is necessary to attempt to work through 'fierce disagreement', mutual incomprehension, and hostility if understanding and solidarity are to be eventually reached. As hooks reminds us: 'expression of hostility as an end in itself is a useless activity, but when it is the catalyst pushing us on to greater clarity and understanding, it serves a meaningful function' (hooks 2000: 66).

The third proviso about dialogism pertains to its thematization by some theorists through analogy with psychoanalysis and therapeutically acquired understanding. Taking their cue from arguments put forward by Habermas in *Knowledge and Human Interests* but subsequently abandoned, theorists such as Celikates (2018a) and Allen (2021) regard the psychoanalytic encounter as a valuable way of thinking about the production of knowledge in critical theory. Allen sees it primarily as an effective corrective to the problematic drift towards rationalism, cognitivism, and normative idealism that has crept into Frankfurt School theory mainly through Habermas's subsequent work on discourse ethics. In her view, the realistic, non-progressive account of personhood and societal development found in psychoanalysis, particularly Kleinian drive theory, furnishes critical theory with tools to explain unsettling political phenomena such as the rise of the alt-right and resurgence of authoritarian populist and racist political movements in the last decade or so. Rather than pathologizing these movements as backward and regressive—a balkanizing move that is ultimately politically counterproductive—psychoanalysis enables critique to reckon with the 'deep irrationality of our politics and the possibilities for moving beyond our current impasse' (2021: 191). Understanding the 'paranoid-schizoid' impulses that drive aggressive and persecutory politics enhances the capacity to accept the inevitability of conflict—the Kleinian 'depressive mode'—and to sustain democratic dialogue in difficult circumstances. Celikates focuses more on the methodological parallels between psychoanalysis and critical theory, how the therapeutic encounter provides a dialogical alternative to vanguardist conceptions of critique and the hierarchical accounts of expert knowledge production that they rest upon. Emancipatory insight is likened to the self-knowledge that is produced by analyst and analysand, working together and confronting difficulties of transference and countertransference, to overcome a particular psychological blockage. Improved self-understanding cannot be foisted on the analysand by the analyst at the risk of alienation, rather it must be constructed gradually through a process of mutual engagement which draws on 'agents competences, attitudes and standards if for no other reason than that it is a dialogue with them, in which it cannot simply assume a substantive conception of a successful life' (Celikates 2018a: 153). The learning process is moreover mutual not one-sided since, because by virtue of their own implication within the therapeutic encounter, the analyst is presented with opportunities for self-reflection and critique as much as the analysand.

The comparison of critical theory and psychoanalysis provides valuable insight into a dialogical method of knowledge production, particularly the idea that context-transcending insight is generated by reasoning across theoretical and experiential perspectives rather than by downwardly applying the correct monist paradigm. But there is reason to be wary of pushing the analogy too far because of its potentially depoliticizing entailments. A risk of interpreting societal relations in terms of individual or collective psychic dynamics is that it weakens a sense of historicity and, particularly, the contingent specificity of structures and modalities of power. Defenders of psychoanalytic theory would dispute this, pointing to the way it highlights the ever-changing motivations for action and failure to comply with societal norms straightforwardly. But what is at stake here is where the burden of causality is placed. Reliance on archetypal psychic dynamics inevitably implies that social relations are, in some sense, exteriorizations of prior, interior drives rather than specific ways of organizing and exploiting human labour power under capitalism. As Fanon's sociogenic method teaches us, the primary roots of suffering lie in exploitative and distorting social arrangements—introjected as psychological malaise—not in ontogenetic blockages and resistances. Relations between social groups should not be too readily assimilated to intra-psychic dynamics, lest explanation of oppression in its historical variability is simplified and distorted. It is undoubtedly helpful to understand the psychic origins of the alt-right's anti-immigrant persecution complex but this cannot substitute for a developed sociological account of the ways in which neoliberal capital has disempowered and precaritized all members of the working class while simultaneously exacerbating racial divisions between them. Also lost in the psychoanalytic register is a sense of the materiality of political struggle and demand which is replaced with accommodationist ideas of psychological adaptation to conflict. Arguably, many types of social suffering are more directly alleviated not by conducting democratic politics in a realistic 'depressive' mode but by redistributing economic and other social resources more equitably. In so far as it places emphasis less on the socio-material context and more on psychological states, critique in this psychoanalytic vein seems prone to reformist if not political quietist outcomes. In short, dialogical critique is better construed in social and political terms rather than psychoanalytical ones if the priority that a materialist account of power should occupy in a diagnosis of oppression is to be maintained.

The revised understanding of context transcendence as an achievement of dialogical reasoning across perspectives is underpinned by a relational account of experience. Conceptualizing experience in relation to power and social location is a way of overcoming its dismissal as an irremediably particularistic and parochial standpoint. All knowledge proceeds from a particular location, and a relational account of experience makes clear how some locations, by virtue of their exposure to subordinating dynamics, afford general insight into inegalitarian social orders. Interpreting experience in relation to power and social location is hardly a new theoretical strategy; it is one of the animating premises of black feminist theory, postcolonial and critical race theory, social epistemology, and so on. These theorists all regard the conflation of lived experience with insurmountable particularism as a subtle way of invalidating the experiences and views of oppressed groups while, at the same time, naturalizing a dominant worldview as an uncontroversial norm. By relativizing experience to power, they show how the standpoint of subordinated groups may give access to a wider understanding of the operations of power. In principle, Frankfurt School theorists endorse such relational social analysis, in practice, however, they make little attempt to treat lived experience in this way but instead reify it as inherently particularistic. Unable to transcend its own limited epistemic horizons, their treatment of lived experience stands in stark contrast to the all-encompassing viewpoint they attribute to the theorist. Iris Marion Young is one of the few Frankfurt School theorists to demur from this tendentious dismissal of lived experience as mere particularism. She does so by redefining group difference in relation to social position and, as a consequence, is able to specify the various sorts of knowledge that oppressed groups may have of their situation:

> (1) an understanding of their position and how it stands in relation to other positions; (2) a social map of other salient positions, how they are defined, and the relation in which they stand to this position; (3) a point of view on the history of the society; (4) an interpretation of how the relations and processes of the whole society operate, especially as they affect one's own position; (5) a position-specific experience and point of view on the natural and physical environment.
> (2000: 117).

By disengaging group difference from a logic of identity or substance, Young shows how situated knowledges are not purely self-interested claims but a valuable resource to democratic theory because of what they reveal about unequal distributions of power: 'it allows us to notice structural relations of domination and subordination among groups that raise important issues of justice for individuals' (2000: 102). Echoing other feminist theorists, she is careful to emphasize that the type of knowledge generated from first-hand experience is not unmediated, or incontestable but is the product of political labour, achieved through critical reflection, consciousness raising, and politicization within groups. Nonetheless, precisely because of their position within the societal order, certain groups have experience of the workings of power, qua social totality, that may not be generated from other, usually more privileged, social locations. This, as we have seen, is Crenshaw's point about intersectionality, namely that black women's experience of the cross-cutting effects of race, class, and gender reveal dynamics of subordination and exclusion that had hitherto been unrecognized by other political theorists. Other Frankfurt school theorists are seemingly oblivious to this valuable corpus of work because, when called upon to justify monist social critique, they do so in ways that invariably replay simplifying oppositions between theoretical transcendence and experiential immanence. They fail to appreciate how those who directly experience oppression may be able to offer insights into power that do not just confirm and enrich preestablished theoretical paradigms but may also destabilize and challenge them.

A relational account of lived experience has not only an important disclosive role vis-à-vis an unmasking critique of power but also a pivotal methodological one in helping the theorist decide how best to deploy their interpretative toolkit in studying a given situation. Not every concept and idea in the theorist's toolkit will be relevant to all situations. The theorist may well hold in advance a fully elaborated theory of gender intersectionality, for instance, but it is through advertence to the lived reality of particular situations that it becomes clear which dimensions of their abstract typology of power have most explanatory salience. Lacking such focus on the particularities of experience, monist critical theory is unable to capture the varying ways in which intersectional oppression is realized, and instead interprets social reality through invariant and simplifying interpretative spectacles. Theorizing from experience goes hand-in-hand therefore, with an inductive, problem-led mode of inquiry. It concentrates on building up constellations of knowledge around determinate social problems arising from the study of oppression, rather than on formulating totalizing paradigms that can account for everything in the social realm. A problem-led approach does not equate to naïve empiricism; there is evidently no theory-independent way of characterizing problems. Problems do not simply bubble up spontaneously from the social context but are brought into view and fixed as 'problems' by evaluative frameworks. But even while acknowledging that observation is inescapably theory-laden, it is nonetheless possible to distinguish between modes of political theorizing that are more or less open to the social context, more or less amenable to reappraisal in the light of diverging phenomena and competing ways of grasping a situation. According to Shapiro, 'theory-drivenness kicks in when the pursuit of generality comes at the expense of the pursuit of empirical validity' (Shapiro 2005: 189). The self-referential construction of problems that occurs in paradigm-led theory—which often seem to be more about vindicating the theory's outlook and conceptual integrity than developing an adequate account of power—contrasts with a more open, problem-led approach where there is greater interplay between theoretical method and the problem under study. For all that Frankfurt School theorists highlight their reconstructive and hence implicitly inductive method, paradigm-led theory is, in key respects, deductive in method in that it 'starts from the preferred theory or model and then opts for the type of description that will vindicate the general claims implied by the model' rather than 'trying to account for particular phenomena or groups of phenomena, and then [seeing] under what conditions, if any, such accounts might apply more generally' (Shapiro 2005: 188. My parenthesis). Advertence to the ways in which individuals directly subject to oppressive relations of power practically deal with their situation—what they might think, say and do about it—is vital to breaking out of the self-confirmatory cycle of paradigm-led theory where the problems under study are often the rather contrived artefacts of the preoccupation with monist foundations. This alternate inductive approach is evident, for example, in the way that feminist theories of race cast doubt on constructions of the family in the monist frame of recognition because of the way that its disregard of forces of race and class effectively renders the experiences of black women invisible. Similarly, sociological underspecification of the intersections of poverty, race, and gender means that the specific types and levels of violence to which black women in marginalized communities are subject is minimized, if not ignored altogether (Ritchie 2012;

Threadcraft 2017). Such critical feminist analysis which exposes the implicit bias and exclusionary effects of what are taken to be uncontroversial ways of framing the world and suggest alternative conceptualizations—the family as a saturated site of power for instance—exemplifies the 'two-step venture' of problem-led theory. It begins by showing 'that the accepted way of characterizing a piece of political reality fails to capture an important feature of what stands in need of explanation or justification'; in this case, how the absence of an intersectional account of power effectively renders the lived reality of certain oppressed groups (black women) invisible. It 'then offers a recharacterization that speaks to the inadequacies in the prior account', that is, proposes alternative ways of conceptualizing the family in terms of subtending dynamics of gender, race, and class (Shapiro 2005: 202). Precisely because of its attentiveness to contextual particularity, theorizing from experience seems to give rise to a mode of analysis that is methodologically more open and imaginative in establishing connections between micro and macro levels of social reality than a monological, paradigm-led one. It gives rise to critique that eschews the urge to affirm a particular theoretical end in favour of conceptual and methodological heterogeneity better suited to examining the divergent life-worlds created by intersectional structures of power. In so far as it is open to the reappraisal of its working assumptions in the light of what lived experiences reveals about the world, critique in this sense is also more consistent than paradigm-led theory with reflexivity or the willingness to subject theoretical models to critical scrutiny, a feature that Frankfurt School thinkers take to be the hallmark of critical theory but fail to implement.

Critical theorists would no doubt object that this problem-led, dialogical mode of inquiry is still too particularistic and nonsystematic to vouchsafe the transcontextual viewpoint necessary for critique's wider emancipatory impact. But this objection is itself generated by a questionable adherence to exaggerated binaries of immanence and transcendence and absolutized notions of generality and universality. Although theorizing from experience aims towards a general account of power and oppression, it does not equate generality with monist, grand theory but instead regards its transcontextual relevance as contingent, as open to question, disconfirmation, and reappraisal. In this respect, theorizing from experience takes its cue from historical, pragmatist, standpoint, and genealogical modes of inquiry, and embraces a different understanding of objectivity, one that is situated, multiperspectival, and dialogical but nonetheless retains the aspiration to systematicity and generality vis-à-vis the critique of power. Critical insight comes not from the adoption of a single, transcendent theoretical perspective that somehow manages to escape the parochialism afflicting all other perspectives, but from reasoning across perspectives *within* the contradictions, discontinuities, ruptures, and constraints constitutive of a determinate socio-historical horizon. It does not follow from this rejection of strongly conceived ideas of context transcendence, that critique lacks explanatory rigour and wider normative relevance; it means rather that these latter qualities are organized around a different intellectual goal, one that starts from lived suffering and the generalizes outwards to an unmasking account of power via the integration of insights from both experiential and theoretical worldviews.

A final feature of theorizing from experience is its negativist orientation. Social theoretical negativism is widely endorsed by Frankfurt School thinkers in as much as they hold that the critique of power is motivated by suffering and other negative experiences. Epistemic negativism, in a weak sense, also partially defines the Frankfurt School approach to normativity in so far as emancipatory critique ought to refrain from stipulating in advance—that is predemocratically— determinate ideas of the right, the just, or the good. In place of thick, action-guiding values and norms, critique proposes thin second-order principles and procedures by which citizens might decide for themselves the determinate content of justice and emancipation. Negativism in this sense of a weak orientation towards societal wrongs is regarded as a critically enabling strategy that enhances critique's responsive to context and particularly the experiences and voices of disempowered groups. However, it is this very sensitivity to the context of power, supposedly called forth by negativism, that is undermined by Frankfurt School theorists' subsequent resort to monist foundations. As a parasitic critical procedure, negativism needs to be supplemented, in their view, by a grounding emancipatory interest but, as I have argued, this results in schematic and incomplete social critique. Codifying critique with reference to a single emancipatory principle not only blunts responsiveness to context but may engender inappropriate normative responses to determinate wrongs, exemplified in Adorno's well-known argument that Auschwitz renders moral justification redundant. Even were it possible to define this overriding emancipatory interest in a sufficiently nonexclusionary way, its practical real-world force is questionable since it is, of necessity, so capacious as to be unlikely to produce specific, targeted normative responses to concrete injustices. Theorizing from experience then adopts a stronger negativist stance—typical of thinkers influenced by Adorno—one that assumes its normative sufficiency for emancipatory critique and gives priority to the object of inquiry, that is social suffering. It is through concrete knowledge of suffering and negative experience, through attending to the suppressed particularities of oppression, that a sense of how to proceed normatively is acquired. This stronger negativist stance doesn't entirely preclude ideas of the good, they are present as weak background assumptions (e.g., flourishing) that orient diagnosis of the wrong, but its focus is primarily on grasping negative experience in its particularity and the normative work that this does in terms of yielding determinate outcomes. Moreover, contra criticisms that it amounts to little more than localized complaint, negativist critique need not preclude commitment to universal values. It certainly rejects universalism in the paradigm-led form of intellectual vanguardism that claims to identify in advance a guiding emancipatory interest, but thereby risks being perceived, by vulnerable interlocutors, as epistemically authoritarian and alien to their practical concerns. But negativist critique does not reject universalism in self-reflexive form, that is, of being committed to the belief, on a first-order level, that certain standards and norms ought to be universally applied while at the same time accepting that, at a second-order level, this belief can only ever be justified in a contextually indexed and recursive fashion, i.e., not through the assertion of monist foundations. Such meta-contextual awareness involves therefore being alert to the different forms the universal assumes, distinguishing between its meanings and problematizing its inherent drift to assimilation and normalization from the perspective of social particularity. For, as Young reminds us: 'universality in the sense of participation and inclusion of everyone in moral and social life does not imply universality in the sense of the adoption of a general point of view that leaves behind particular affiliations, feelings, commitments and desires' (Young 1990: 105). In short, theorizing from experience does not abandon universals so much as endeavour to interrogate them from the perspective of their disavowed social content with a view to potentially transforming the restricted form they inevitably assume.

Despite the undoubted importance of Adorno's negativism for efforts to stake out alternatives to paradigm-led normativity, especially strong interpretations of his thought often forget the primary importance he accorded to suffering as the anchor point of negative critique. In these cases, 'unalleviated consciousness of negativity' borders on being a theoretical reflex primarily concerned with upholding critique's rigorous scepticism vis-à-vis normative-ethical orientation. Displaced by this solipsistic theoretical concern, however, is the practical political one with critique's world-disclosing function vis-à-vis suffering and other negative experiences (e.g., Allen, 2017b; Celikates 2017). By weakening the connection to lived social reality, abstract negativism obscures the way in which critique may have a constructive-disclosing as well as negative-disclosing dimension. By shining a light on suffering, negative critique aims not only to expose what is wrong with the world but also to reveal how individuals resist societal wrongs by creating other ways of living and alternative bodies of knowledge and practice. These suppressed modes of agency—that form part of what I have called the alienated-familiar—are both a vital corrective to the narrowly theoretical worldview and an alternate source of normativity in that they bring forth underappreciated ways of resisting inegalitarian social organization. Conditions that an externally positioned observer may regard as intolerable or unliveable may, when viewed from the perspective of those directly involved, turn out to be meaningful and politically purposive social practice. Negativist social critique in this experientially grounded sense shows that vulnerability ought not to be automatically elided with passivity, that suffering may engender not only quiescence but resistance and subversion. Consider for instance the way that feminist theorists of race and postcoloniality have repeatedly challenged assumptions of mainstream, 'white' theory by reconstruing situations of vulnerability and submission as sites of solidarity and political resistance (e.g., Abu-Lughod 2013; Mahmood 2011). Or, as Butler's work on performative assembly demonstrates, the way in which public enactments of vulnerability can be potent expressions of political agency and protest, iconically exemplified in nurse Iesha Barnes taking a stand in the BLM protest at Baton Rouge. As Butler describes it: 'even as public resistance leads to vulnerability, and vulnerability (the sense of "exposure" implied by precarity) leads to resistance, vulnerability is not exactly overcome by resistance, but becomes a potentially effective mobilizing force in political mobilizations' (Butler 2016: 14). Dynamics of vulnerability and resistance overlap in complex ways which it is important to grasp if, on the one hand, naïve celebration of subaltern agency is to be avoided, and, on the other, paternalist overemphasis on victimhood and passivity. When negativism loses connection to lived experience and becomes an abstract theoretical position, these complexities of oppression and agency, vulnerability and resistance are effaced. This is evident in the way that a certain type of negativist critical theory persistently underestimates the critical and agential capacities of oppressed groups and, correspondingly, overestimates the authority of critique as the sole locus of insight into power. By attending to these marginalized ways of being and acting—often deplored or discounted—and exploring their wider implications for an understanding of oppression, negativist critical orientation becomes more than a theoretical fetish and acquires politically disclosive force, i.e., it becomes determinate negation, not mere nay-saying.[1] Differently put, negativism denotes the priority of experience not as an uncritical privileging of the insight of oppressed groups but as the animating impulse of critique. It is lived experiences of suffering and negativity that motivate unmasking critique in the first place, and which are the touchstone around which critique must continually orient and reorient itself.

Finally, theorizing from experience enables critique to venture beyond evaluative monism and embrace a broader, pluralist normative repertoire. The problem with monist critique is not only that it effaces social complexity by subsuming heterogenous practices under a unifying rationale but also that it narrows normativity to a subset of issues to do with justification and validity. For all that Frankfurt School theorists insist on their radical democratic agenda, the prevalence of the judgement model in their work suggests that they have allowed their normative thinking to be defined by the problem space of liberal political philosophy. Even a bold thinker like Nancy Fraser, prepared to buck many paradigm-led trends in Frankfurt School thinking, nonetheless still identifies justification and validity as the normative core of radical critique. It is not that such matters are unimportant or that they shouldn't assume central place in critical political theory

---

[1] I am grateful to Maeve Cooke for suggesting to me that there is a tendency among some Frankfurt School theorists to fetishize negativist critique.

where necessary but, when they completely delimit critique's normative problem space, other equally as vital emancipatory functions are overlooked. Moreover, as we have seen, the priority accorded to this judgement model of normativity often seems to go along with a blinkeredness on the part of Frankfurt School theorists to recurring criticisms that their way of construing the space of reasons may disadvantage already disempowered interlocutors. The preoccupation with justification keeps Frankfurt School thinkers wedded to an overly 'expertocratic' and tamed account of political disagreement and struggle—as the regulated confrontation of words—that implicitly accords a privileged place to critique/the theorist in evaluating the merits of justice claims made by ordinary citizens. For good reasons, then, experientially grounded critique resists giving overriding significance to justification as the culmination of normativity and follows other radical theorists in endeavouring to stake out a wider range of normative functions for critique. Exemplified in the work of feminist theorists, these functions include bearing witness, giving voice to pain, advocacy, world-building, disclosure of forgotten life-worlds, facilitation of dialogue and thinking across perspectives, the forging of solidaristic bonds, the expansion of horizons of understanding, and so forth. In so far as they are motivated by the political concerns of disempowered groups and articulate values and norms that are part of their self-understanding, these other functions are more consistent with critique's claim to be of practical emancipatory value than imposed monist paradigms.

While these normative functions undoubtedly have a philosophical facet, they cannot be exclusively comprehended as such because they relate above all to political praxis and represent ways in which theory might concretely contribute to existing struggles. One would have thought that such practical political concerns might be of paramount interest to Frankfurt School theorists given their emancipatory objectives. But far from allowing these first-order political concerns to guide their normative thinking, Frankfurt School theorists put them aside in favour of what they regard as the imperative, second-order problematic of monist foundations and context transcendence. There is, however, a mismatch between this philosophical view and a political one for what, on the former, are pressing, ground-clearing matters that must be resolved to enable effective engagement with the world are, on the latter, likely to be fairly orthogonal to practical action. From a political perspective, questions of context transcendence and justification, especially in the absolutized terms that Frankfurt School thinkers pose them, may well appear to be abstruse philosophical conundrums—gross concepts as Shapiro might put it—that have little bearing on the complexities of concrete struggles. Practical debate and action proceed regardless of being securely grounded in an invariant emancipatory interest or procedure that guarantees the force of the better argument. This does not mean that political actors don't strive to improve the quality of argumentation or to make judgements in as systematic and rational way as possible, but these things are always done *in media res*, imperfectly, and without resort to any final warrant. Their propensity to sublimate political into philosophical concerns would of course not be so troubling if Frankfurt School thinkers understood themselves as engaged in conventional normative inquiry. But as we know, they conceive their intellectual practice in more radical terms and, given this, it is difficult to see where the practical emancipatory import of unmasking critique lies given the cluster of rarefied issues that currently preoccupy it. My argument for the experiential grounds of critique is an attempt to redirect critical theory back to precisely the type of practical political inquiry that it claims to be undertaking. By drawing on nascent but under-utilized resources in the tradition of Frankfurt School thought, I hope to have shown that paying attention to the experiences of oppressed groups enhances the transcontextual force of critique rather than compromises it. In doing so, I hope also to reopen an unfinished conversation with feminist theorists about gender oppression.

Bibliography

Aboulafia, M. (2002) 'Introduction' in M. Aboulafia (ed.). *Habermas and Pragmatism*. London: Routledge.
Abu-Lughod, L. (2013) *Do Muslim Women Need Saving?* Cambridge, MA: Harvard University Press.
Ackerly, B. (2008) *Universal Human Rights in a World of Difference*. Cambridge: Cambridge University Press.
Adorno, T. (1974) *Minima Moralia: Reflections on a Damaged Life*. London: Verso.
Adorno, T. (1997) *Aesthetic Theory*. London: Bloomsbury.
Adorno, T. (1998) 'Critique' in *Critical Models: Interventions and Catchwords* (trans H. Pickford). New York: Columbia University Press.
Akin, A. (2019) 'Race, racism and social policy' in A. Lever and A. Poama (eds). *The Routledge Handbook for Ethics and Public Policy*. London: Routledge.
Allen, A. (2008) *The Politics of Ourselves: Power, Autonomy and Gender in Contemporary Critical Theory*. New York: Columbia University Press.
Allen, A. (2014) 'The power of justification' in R. Forst, *Justice, Democracy and the Right to Justification: Rainer Forst in Dialogue*. London: Bloomsbury.
Allen, A. (2016) *The End of Progress: Decolonising the Normative Foundations of Critical Theory*. Columbia University Press.
Allen, A. (2017a) 'Beyond Kant Versus Hegel: An Alternative Strategy for Grounding the Normativity of Critique' in B. Bargu and C. Bottici (eds). *Feminism, Capitalism and Critique: Essays in Honour of Nancy Fraser*. London: Palgrave Macmillan.
Allen, A. (2017b) 'Comments on Fabian Freyenhagen's Adorno's Practical Philosophy'. *European Journal of Philosophy*, 25: 840–45.
Allen, A. (2021) *Critique on the Couch: Why Critical Theory Needs Psychoanalysis*. New York: Columbia University Press.
Allen, A., Forst, Rainer, and Haugaard, Mark (2014) 'Power and Reason, Justice and Domination: A Conversation'. *Journal of Political Power*, 7 (1): 7–33.
Allen, A. and Mendieta, E. (eds) (2018) 'Introduction' in *From Alienation to Forms of Life: The Critical Theory of Rahel Jaeggi*. University Park, PA: Penn State University Press.
Allen, D. (2005) 'Invisible Citizens: Political Exclusion and Domination in Arendt and Ellison' in S. Macedo and M. Williams (eds). *Political Exclusion and Domination*. New York: New York University Press.
Anderson, E. (2009) 'Toward a Non-Ideal, Relational Methodology for Political Philosophy: Comments on Schwartzman's *Challenging Liberalism*', Hypatia, 24(4): 130–45.
Anderson, E. and Pildes, R. (2000) 'Expressive Theories of Law: A General Restatement', *University of Pennsylvania Law Review*, 148: 1503–1575.
Anderson, J. and Honneth, A. (2005) 'Autonomy, Vulnerability, Recognition, and Justice' in J. Christman and J. Anderson (eds). *Autonomy and the Challenges to Liberalism: New Essays*. Cambridge: Cambridge University Press.
Arendt, H. (1978) *The Life of the Mind:V2 Willing*. New York: Harcourt Publishing.

Arruzza, C., Bhattacharya, T., and Fraser, N. (2019) *Feminism for the 99%: A Manifesto*. London: Verso.

Aslan, O. and Gambetti, Z. (2011) 'Provincializing Fraser's History: Feminism and Neoliberalism Revisited', *History of the Present*, 1(1): 130–47.

Azamova, A. (2012) *The Scandal of Reason: A Critical Theory of Political Judgement*. New York: Columbia University Press.

Bajaj, S. and Rossi, E. (2020) 'Noumenal Power, Reasons and Justifications: A Critique of Forst' in E. Herlin-Karnell and M. Klatt (eds). *Constitutionalism Justified: Rainer Forst in Discourse*. Oxford: Oxford University Press.

Baynes, K. (2004) 'The Transcendental Turn' in F. Rush (ed.). *The Cambridge Companion to Critical Theory*. Cambridge: Cambridge University Press, pp. 194–218.

Baxter, J., Hewitt, B., and Western, M. (2005) 'Post-familial families and the domestic division of labour' *Journal of Comparative Family Studies*, 36 (4): 583–600.

Beaujot, R. and Liu, J. (2005) 'Models of time use in paid and unpaid work'. *Journal of Family Issues*, 26: 924–46.

Bell, M. (2009) 'Anger, Oppression and Virtue' in L. Tessman (ed.). *Feminist Ethics and Social and Political Philosophy: Theorizing the Non-Ideal*. New York: Springer.

Benhabib, S. (1992) *Situating the Self: Gender, Community and Postmodernism in Contemporary Ethics*. London: Routledge.

Benhabib, S. (2015) 'The Uses and Abuses of Kantian Rigorism: On Rainer Forst's Moral and Political Philosophy'. *Political Theory* (Review Symposium on The Right to Justification), 43(6): 777–90.

Berk, S. (1985) *The Gender Factory: The Apportionment of Work in American Households*. New York: Plenum Press.

Berenstain, N. (2016) 'Epistemic Exploitation'. *Ergo*, 3(22): 569–90.

Bernstein, R. J. (2010) *The Pragmatic Turn*. Cambridge: Polity Press.

Bernstein, R. J. (2017) 'From Socialist Feminism to the Critique of Global Capitalism' in B. Bargu and C. Bottici (eds). *Feminism, Capitalism and Critique: Essays in Honour of Nancy Fraser*. London: Palgrave Macmillan.

Bhavani, K. and Davis, A. Y. (1989) 'Complexity, Activism, Optimism: An Interview with Angela Y. Davis'. *Feminist Review*, 31: 66–81.

Bohman, J. (1994) 'World Disclosure and Radical Criticism'. *Thesis Eleven*, 37: 82–97.

Bohman, J. (2001) 'Participants, Observers and Critics: Practical Knowledge, Social Perspectives, and Critical Pluralism' in W. Rehg and J. Bohman (eds). *Pluralism and The Pragmatic Turn: The Transformation of Critical Theory*. Cambridge, MA: MIT Press.

Bohman, J. (2021) 'Critical Theory' in Edward N. Zalta (ed.). *The Stanford Encyclopedia of Philosophy* (Spring 2021 Edition). <https://plato.stanford.edu/archives/spr2021/entries/critical-theory/>.

Bohman, J. and Richardson, H. (2009) 'Liberalism, Deliberative Democracy, and "Reasons that All Can Accept"'. *The Journal of Political Philosophy*, 17 (3): 253–74.

Bourdieu, P. (1990a) *The Logic of Practice*. Cambridge: Polity Press.

Bourdieu, P. (1990b) *In Other Words: Essays Toward Reflexive Sociology*. Cambridge: Polity Press.

Bourdieu, P. (1998) *Practical Reason: On the Theory of Action*. Cambridge: Polity Press.

Bourdieu, P. (2000) *Pascalian Meditations*. Cambridge: Polity Press.

Bourdieu, P. (2001) *Masculine Domination*. Cambridge: Polity Press.

Bourdieu, P. and Wacquant, L. (1992) *An Invitation to Reflexive Sociology*. Cambridge: Polity Press.

Brown, W. (2006) 'Feminist Theory and the Frankfurt School: Introduction'. *differences*, 17 (1): 1–5.
Bubeck, D. (1995) *Care, Gender and Justice*. Oxford: Clarendon Press.
Butler, J. (1992) 'Contingent Foundations: Feminism and the Question of Postmodernism' in J. Butler and J. Scott (eds). *Feminists Theorize the Political*. London: Routledge.
Butler, J. (1997a) *Excitable Speech*. London: Routledge.
Butler, J. (1997b) *The Psychic Life of Power*. Stanford: Stanford University Press.
Butler, J. (2000) 'Restaging the Universal: Hegemony and the Limits of Formalism' in J. Butler, E. Laclau, and S. Žižek (eds). *Contingency, Hegemony, Universality: Contemporary Dialogues on the Left*. London: Verso.
Butler, J. (2008) 'Merely Cultural' in K. Olson (ed.). *Adding Insult to Injury: Nancy Fraser Debates her Critics*. London: Verso.
Butler, J. (2009) 'Critique, Dissent, Disciplinarity'. *Critical Inquiry*, 35(4): 773–97.
Butler, J. (2016) 'Rethinking Vulnerability and Resistance' in J. Butler, Z. Gambetti, and L. Sabsay (eds). *Vulnerability in Resistance*. Durham: Duke University Press.
Caney, S. (2014) 'Justice and the basic right to justification' in R. Forst, *Justice, Democracy and the Right to Justification: Rainer Forst in Dialogue*. London: Bloomsbury.
Carby, H. (1982) 'White Woman Listen!: Black Feminism and the Boundaries of Sisterhood' in Centre for Contemporary Cultural Studies, *The Empire Strikes Back: Race and Racism in 70s Britain*. London: Routledge.
Cavell, S. (1990) *Conditions Handsome and Unhandsome: The Constitution of Emersonian Perfectionism*. Chicago: University of Chicago Press.
Celikates, R. (2017) 'Critique and Resistance: Ethical, Social-Theoretical, Political? On Fabian Freyenhagen's *Adorno's Practical Philosophy*'. *European Journal of Philosophy*, 25: 846–53.
Celikates, R. (2018a) *Critique as Social Practice: Critical Theory and Social Self-Understanding*. London: Rowman and Littlefield.
Celikates, R. (2018b) 'Forms of Life, Progress and Social Struggle: On Rahel Jaeggi's Critical Theory' in A. Allen and E. Mendieta (eds). *From Alienation to Forms of Life: The Critical Theory of Rahel Jaeggi*. UniversityPark, PA: Penn State University Press.
Césaire, A. (2010). 'Letter to Maurice Thorez'. *Social Text 103*, 28(2): 145–52.
Chakrabarty, D. (2000) *Provincializing Europe: Postcolonial Thought and Historical Difference*. Princeton University Press.
Child Poverty Action Group (2021). *Child Poverty Facts and Figures*.
Christman, J. (2018) 'Decentred Social Selves: Interrogating Alienation in Conversation with Rahel Jaeggi' in A. Allen and E. Mendieta (eds). *From Alienation to Forms of Life: The Critical Theory of Rahel Jaeggi*. University Park, PA: Penn State University Press.
Code, L. (2006) *Ecological Thinking: The Politics of Epistemic Location*. Oxford University Press.
Collins, P. (1986) 'Learning from the Outsider Within: The Sociological Significance of Black Feminist Thought'. *Social Problems*, 33(6): 14–32.
Collins, P. (2019) *Intersectionality as Critical Social Theory*. Durham: Duke University Press.
Collins, P. (2000) *Black Feminist Thought: Knowledge, Consciousness and the Politics of Empowerment*. London: Routledge.
Connolly, W. E. (2004) 'The Ethos of Democratization' in S. Critchley and O. Marchart (eds). *Laclau: A Critical Reader*. London: Routledge.
Cooke, M. (2006) *Re-presenting the Good Society*. Cambridge, MA: MIT Press.
Cooke, M. (2014) 'Truth in Normative Fiction'. *Philosophy and Social Criticism*, 40 (7): 629–43.

Crenshaw, K. (1989) 'Demarginalizing the Intersection of Race and Sex: A Black Feminist Critique of Antidiscrimination Doctrine, Feminist Theory and Antiracist Politics'. *University of Chicago Legal Forum*, 1(8): 139–67.

Crenshaw, K. (1991) 'Mapping the Margins: Intersectionality, Identity Politics, and Violence against Women of Colour'. *Stanford Law Review*, 43(6): 1241–99.

Cudd, A. (2006) *Analyzing Oppression*. Oxford: Oxford University Press.

Dalmiya, V. (2016) *Caring to Know: Comparative Care Ethics, Feminist Epistemology and the Mahabharata*. Oxford: Oxford University Press.

Davis, A. Y. (1981) *Women, Race and Class*. New York: Vintage Books.

Davis, A. Y. (1998a) *Blues Legacies and Black Feminism: Gertrude "Ma" Rainey, Bessie Smith and Billie Holiday*, New York: Vintage Books.

Davis, A. Y. (1998b) 'Reflections on the Black Woman's Role in the Community of Slaves' in J. James (ed.). *The Angela Y Davis Reader*. Oxford: Blackwell.

Davis, A. Y. (1998c) 'Afro-images: Politics, Fashion and Nostalgia' in J. James (ed.). *The Angela Y Davis Reader*. Oxford: Blackwell.

Davis, A. Y. (1998d) 'Meditations on the Legacy of Malcolm X' in J. James (ed.). *The Angela Y Davis Reader*. Oxford: Blackwell.

Davis, A. Y. (1998d) 'Race and Criminalization: Black Americans and the Punishment Industry' in J. James (ed.). *The Angela Y Davis Reader*. Oxford: Blackwell.

Davis, A. Y. (2012) *The Meaning of Freedom: And Other Difficult Dialogues*. San Francisco: City Lights Publisher.

Dawson, M. (2006) 'After the Deluge: Publics and Publicity in Katrina's Wake'. *Du Bois Review*, 3(1): 239–49.

Dejours, C. (1998) *Souffrance en France: La banalisation de l'injustice sociale*. Paris: Seuil.

Dotson, K. (2011) 'Tracking Epistemic Violence, Tracking Practices of Silencing'. *Hypatia*, 26(2): 236–57.

Dotson, K. (2012) 'How is this Paper Philosophy?' *Comparative Philosophy*, 3(1): 3–29.

Du Bois, W. E. (1989) *The Souls of Black Folk*. London: Penguin.

Eisenstein, H. (2010) *Feminism Seduced: How Global Elites Use Women's Labour and Ideas to Exploit the World*. London: Routledge.

Ellison, R. (1953) *Shadow and Act*. New York: Vintage Books.

Eschle, C. and Maiguashca, B. (2014) 'Reclaiming Feminist Futures: Co-opted and Progressive Politics in a Neo-Liberal Age'. *Political Studies*, 62: 634–51.

Farr, A. (2018) 'Adorno, Marcuse and Angela Davis' in P. Taylor, L. M. Alcoff, and L. Anderson (eds). *The Routledge Companion to the Philosophy of Race*. London: Routledge.

Fazio, G. and Ferrara, A. (2019) 'Introduction'. *Philosophy and Social Criticism*, 45(6): 627–34.

Feola, M. (2020) '"You Will Not Replace Us": The Melancholic Nationalism of Whiteness'. *Political Theory*. Online December 11. https://doi.org/10.1177%2F0090591720972745.

Ferguson, A. (1997) 'On Conceiving Motherhood and Sexuality: A Feminist Materialist Approach' in D. Tietjens Meyers (ed.). *Feminist Social Thought: A Reader*. London: Routledge, pp. 39–63.

Ferrara, A. (1999) *Justice and Judgement: The Rise and the Prospect of the Judgement Model in Contemporary Political Philosophy*. London: Sage Publications.

Ferrara, A. (2008) *The Force of the Example: Explorations in the Paradigm of Judgement*. New York: Columbia University Press.

Ferrara, A. (2014) *The Democratic Horizon: Hyperpluralism and the Renewal of Political Liberalism*. Cambridge: Cambridge University Press.

Ferrara, A. (2018a) 'Debating Exemplarity: The "Communis" in Sensus Communis'. *Philosophy and Social Criticism*, 45(2): 146–58.
Ferrara, A. (2018b) 'Exemplarity in the Public Realm'. *Law and Literature*, 30(3) 387–99.
Ferrara, A. (2019) 'Social Freedom and Reasonable Pluralism: Reflections on *Freedom's Right*'. *Philosophy and Social Criticism*, 45(6): 635–42.
Flynn, J. (2015) 'On the nature and status of the right to justification'. *Political Theory*, 43(6): 793–804.
Folbre, N. (1994) *Who Pays for the Kids?: Gender and the Structures of Constraint*. London: Routledge.
Forst, R. (1997) 'Situations of the Self: Reflections of Seyla Benhabib's version of Critical Theory'. *Philosophy and Social Criticism*, 23(5): 79–96.
Forst, R. (1999) 'Justice, reason and critique: basic concepts of critical theory' in D. Rasmussen (ed.). *The Handbook of Critical Theory*. Oxford: Blackwell.
Forst, R. (2007) *The Right to Justification: Elements of a Constructivist Theory of Justice*. New York: Columbia University Press.
Forst, R. (2011) *Justification and Critique: Toward a Critical Theory of Politics*. Cambridge: Polity Press.
Forst, R. (2014) *Justice, Democracy and the Right to Justification: Rainer Forst in Dialogue*. London: Bloomsbury.
Forst, R. (2015) 'Noumenal Power'. *The Journal of Political Philosophy*, 23(2): 1–17.
Forst, R. (2018) 'Noumenal Power Revisited: Reply to my Critics'. *Journal of Political Power*, 11(3): 294–321.
Forst, R. (2020) 'The Constitution of Justification: Replies and Comments' in E. Herlin-Karnell and M. Klatt (eds). *Constitutionalism Justified: Rainer Forst in Discourse*. Oxford: Oxford University Press.
Foucault, M. (1984) 'What is Englightenment?' in P. Rabinow (ed.). *The Foucault Reader*. London: Penguin.
Foucault, M. (1990) 'Practicing criticism' in L. Kritzman (ed.). *Politics, Philosophy, Culture: Interviews and Other Writings 1977–84*. London: Routledge.
Fraser, N. (1989) *Unruly Practices: Power, Discourse and Gender in Contemporary Social Theory*. Cambridge: Polity Press.
Fraser, N. (1997a) 'After the Family Wage: A Post-Industrial Thought Experiment' in *Justice Interruptus: Critical Reflections on the Post-Socialist Condition*. London: Routledge.
Fraser, N. (1997b) 'Communication, Transformation and Consciousness Raising' in C. Calhoun and J.McGowan (eds). *Hannah Arendt and the Meaning of Politics*. Minneapolis: University of Minnesota Press.
Fraser, N. (2008) 'Prioritizing Justice as Participatory Parity: A Reply to Kompridis and Forst' in K. Olson (ed.). *Adding Insult to Injury: Nancy Fraser Debates her Critics*. London: Verso.
Fraser, N. (2013a) 'What's Critical about Critical theory? The Case of Habermas and Gender' in her *Fortunes of Feminism: From State-Managed Capitalism to Neoliberal Crisis*. London: Verso.
Fraser, N. (2013b) 'Reframing Justice in a Globalizing World' in her *Fortunes of Feminism: From State-Managed Capitalism to Neoliberal Crisis*. London: Verso.
Fraser, N. (2013c) 'Feminism, Capitalism and the Cunning of History' in her *Fortunes of Feminism: From State-Managed Capitalism to Neoliberal Crisis*. London: Verso.
Fraser, N. (2013d) 'Struggle over Needs: Outline of a Socialist-Feminist Critical Theory of Late-Capitalist Political Culture' in her *Fortunes of Feminism: From State-Managed Capitalism to Neoliberal Crisis*. London: Verso.

Fraser, N. (2014a) 'Behind Marx's Hidden Abode: For an Expanded Conception of Capitalism'. *New Left Review*, 86: 55–72.
Fraser, N. (2014b) 'Can Society be Commodities all the Way Down? Post-Polanyian Reflections on Capitalist Crisis'. *Economy and Society*, 43(4): 541–58.
Fraser, N. (2015) 'Legitimation Crisis? On the political contradictions of financialized capitalism'. *Critical Historical Studies*, 2(2): 157–89.
Fraser, N. and Honneth, A. (2003) *Redistribution or Recognition: A Political-Philosophical Exchange*. London: Verso.
Fraser, N. and Jaeggi, R. (2018) *Capitalism: A Conversation in Critical Theory*. Cambridge: Polity Press.
Fraser, N. and Maples, N. (2004) 'To Interpret the World and To Change It: An Interview with Nancy Fraser'. *Signs*, 29(4): 1103–24.
Fraser, N. and Nicholson, L. (1990) 'Social Criticism Without Philosophy: An Encounter between Feminism and Postmodernism' in L. Nicholson (ed.). *Feminism/Postmodernism*. London: Routledge.
Freyenhagen, F. (2013) *Adorno's Practical Philosophy: Living Less Wrongly*. Cambridge: Cambridge University Press.
Fricker, M. (2009) *Epistemic Injustice: Power and the Ethics of Knowing*. Oxford: Oxford University Press.
Friedman, M. (2005) 'Autonomy and Male Dominance' in J. Christman and J. Anderson (eds). *Autonomy and the Challenges to Liberalism: New Essays*. Cambridge: Cambridge University Press.
Fritsch, M. (2015) 'Rational Justification and Vulnerability: On the "All-Affected" Principle in Rainer Forst's Right to Justification'. *Political Theory*, 43(6): 805–21.
Froese, R (2015) 'Review of Alienation by Rahel Jaeggi'. *Studies in Social and Political Thought*, 25: 244–53.
Frye, M. (1983a) 'A Note on Anger' in her *The Politics of Reality: Essays in Feminist Theory*. New York: Crossing Press.
Frye, M (1983b) 'Oppression' in her *The Politics of Reality: Essays in Feminist Theory*. New York: Crossing Press.
Gaventa, J. (1982) *Power and Powerlessness: Quiescence and Rebellion in an Appalachian Valley*. Oxford: Clarendon Press.
Geras, N. (1999) *The Contract of Mutual Indifference: Political Philosophy After the Holocaust*. London: Verso.
Geuss, R. (1981) *The Idea of a Critical Theory: Habermas and the Frankfurt School*. Cambridge University Press.
Giddens, A. (1976) 'Functionalism: Apres la Lutte', *Social Research*, 43(2): 325–66.
Gilmore, R. W. (2008) 'Forgotten places and the Seeds of Grassroot Planning' in C. R. Hale (ed.). *Engaging Contradictions: Theory, Politics, and Methods of Activist Scholarship*. Berkeley: University of California Press.
Griffin-Cohen, M. and Brodie, J. (eds) (2007) *Remapping Gender in the New Global Order*. London: Routledge.
Guidroz, K. and Berger, M. (2009) 'A Conversation with Founding Scholars of Intersectionality: Kimberlé Crenshaw, Nira Yuval-Davis, and Michelle Fine' in K. Guidroz and M. Berger (eds). *The Intersectional Approach: Transforming the Academy Through Race, Class and Gender*. Chapel Hill: University of North Carolina Press.
Habermas, J. (1971) *Knowledge and Human Interests*. Boston: Beacon Press.
Habermas, J. (1973) *Theory and Practice*. Boston: Beacon Press.

Habermas, J. (1985) *The Philosophical Discourse of Modernity: Twelve Lectures*. Cambridge: Polity Press.
Habermas, J. (1993) *Justification and Application: Remarks on Discourse Ethics*. Cambridge, MA: MIT Press.
Habermas, J. (2003) *Truth and Justification*. Cambridge: Polity Press.
Habermas, J. (2011) 'Reply to my Critics,' in J. G. Finlayson and F. Freyenhagen (eds). *Habermas and Rawls: Disputing the Political*. New York and London: Routledge.
Hacking, I. (2002) 'Language, Truth and Reason' in his *Historical Ontology*. Harvard University Press.
Harding, S. (1992). 'Rethinking Standpoint Epistemology: What is Strong Objectivity?' *The Centennial Review*, 36(3): 437–70. Reproduced in *The Feminist Standpoint Reader* ed. S. Harding (2003) and *Feminist Epistemologies*, L. Alcoff and E. Potter (eds). Routledge, 1993: 49–82.
Hartmann, M. and Honneth, A. (2006) 'Paradoxes of capitalism'. *Constellations* 13(1):. 41–58.
Haraway, D. (1988) 'Situated Knowledges: The Science Question in Feminism and the Privilege of Partial Perspective'. *Feminist Studies*, 14(3): 575–99.
Herzog, L. and Zacka, B. (2019) 'Fieldwork in Political Theory: Five Arguments for an Ethnographic Sensibility'. *British Journal of Political Science*, 49(2): 763–84.
Hirschmann, N. (2002) *The Subject of Liberty: Towards a Feminist Theory of Freedom*. Princeton: Princeton University Press.
Hochschild, A. (1989) *The Second Shift*. New York: Avon Books.
Hochschild, A. (2012) *The Outsourced Self: Intimate Life in Market Times*. New York: Metropolitan Books.
Hochschild, A. R. (2000) 'Global Care Chains and Emotional Surplus Value' in W. Hutton and A. Giddens (eds). *On the Edge: Living with Global Capitalism*. London: Jonathan Cape.
Honneth, A. (1995) *The Struggle for Recognition: The Moral Grammar of Social Conflicts*. Cambridge: Polity Press.
Honneth, A. (2002) 'Grounding Recognition: A Rejoinder to Critical Questions'. *Inquiry*, 45(4): 499–519.
Honneth, A. (2004) 'A Social Pathology of Reason: On the intellectual legacy of Critical Theory' in F. Rush (ed.). *The Cambridge Companion to Critical Theory*. Cambridge: Cambridge University Press.
Honneth, A. (2007) *Disrespect: The Normative Foundations of Critical Theory*. Cambridge: Polity Press.
Honneth, A. (2009) *Pathologies of Reason: On the Legacy of Critical Theory*. New York: Columbia University Press.
Honneth, A. (2011) 'Rejoinder' in Danielle Petherbridge (ed.). *Axel Honneth: Critical Essays*. Leiden: Brill, pp. 391–421.
Honneth, A. (2014a) *Freedom's Right: The Social Foundations of Democratic Life*. Cambridge: Polity.
Honneth, A. (2014b) 'The Normativity of Ethical Life', *Philosophy and Social Criticism*. 40 (8): 817–26.
Honneth, A. (2015) 'Rejoinder'. *Critical Horizons*, 16(2): 204–26.
Honneth, A. (1995) *The Struggle for Recognition: The Moral Grammar of Social Conflicts*. Cambridge: Polity Press.
Honneth, A. (2002) 'Grounding Recognition: A Rejoinder to Critical Questions'. *Inquiry*, 45(4): 499–519.

Honneth, A. and Margalit, A. (2001) 'Recognition'. *Proceedings of the Aristotelean Society, Supplementary Volumes*, 75: 111–39.
hooks, b (1991) 'Essentialism and Experience'. *American Literary History*, 3(1): 172–83.
hooks, b (2000) *Feminist Theory: From Margin to Centre*. London: Pluto Press.
Horkheimer, M. (1975) 'Traditional and Critical Theory' in his *Critical Theory: Selected Essays*. Continuum, pp. 188–243.
Hutchings, K. (2013) 'Choosers or Losers? Feminist Ethical and Political Agency in a Plural and Unequal World' in S. Madhok, A. Phillips, and K. Wilson (eds). *Gender, Agency and Coercion*. London: Palgrave Macmillan.
Jaeggi, R. (2005) '"No Individual Can Resist": *Minima Moralia* as Critique of Forms of Life'. *Constellations* 12(1): 65–82.
Jaeggi, R. (2016) *Alienation*. New York: Columbia University Press.
Jaeggi, R. (2018a) Critique of Forms of Life. Cambridge, MA: Harvard University Press.
Jaeggi, R (2018b) 'Reply to My Critics' in A. Allen and E. Mendieta (eds). *From Alienation to Forms of Life: The Critical Theory of Rahel Jaeggi*. University Park, PA: Penn State University Press.
Jaeggi, R. (2018c) '"Resistance to the Perpetual Danger of Relapse": Moral Progress and Social Change' in A. Allen and E. Mendieta (eds). *From Alienation to Forms of Life: The Critical Theory of Rahel Jaeggi*. University Park, PA: Penn State University Press.
Jaggar, A. (ed.) (2014) *Gender and Global Justice*. Cambridge: Polity Press.
Jaggar, A. and Tobin, T. (2013) 'Situating Moral Justification: Rethinking the Mission of Moral Epistemology'. *Metaphilosophy*, 44(4): 383–408.
James, J. (ed.) (1989) *The Angela Y Davis Reader*. Oxford: Blackwell.
James, J. (2013) 'Teaching Theory, Talking Community' in her *Seeking the Beloved Community: A Feminist Reader*. Albany: State University of New York Press.
Joas, H. (2000) *The Genesis of Values*. Cambridge: Polity Press.
Joseph Rowntree Trust (2021) *UK Poverty 2020/21*.
Kelley, R. (2002) *Freedom Dreams: The Black Radical Imagination*. Boston: Beacon Press.
Kempf, V. (2019) 'The Subjects of Socialism: Politicizing Honneth's Idea of Socialism'. *Critical Horizons*, 20(3): 262–81.
Khader, S. (2019) *Decolonizing Universalism: A Transnational Feminist Ethic*. Oxford: Oxford University Press.
Kinder, D. and Sanders, L. (1996) *Divided by Color: Racial Politics and Democratic Ideals*. Chicago: University of Chicago Press.
Kittay, E. F. (.1999) *Love's Labour*. New York: Routledge.
Kogler, H. (1997) 'Alienation as Epistemological Source: Reflexivity and Social Background After Mannheim and Bourdieu'. *Social Epistemology*, 11(2): 141–64.
Kogler, H. (1996) *The Power of Dialogue: Critical Hermeneutics After Gadamer and Foucault*. Cambridge, MA: MIT Press.
Kompridis, N. (2006) *Critique and Disclosure: Critical Theory Between Past and Future*. MIT Press.
Kompridis, N. (2008) 'Struggling Over the Meaning of Recognition' in K. Olson (ed.). *Adding Insult to Injury: Nancy Fraser Debates her Critics*. London: Verso.
Kompridis, N. (2012) 'Critical Theory as Disclosing Critique: A Response to Kompridis'. *Critical Horizons*, 19(3): 369–81.
Lebron, C. (2013) *The Colour of our Shame: Race and Justice in Our Time*. Oxford: Oxford University Press.
Lee, Y.-S. and Waite, L. (2005) 'Husbands' and Wives' time spend in housework: A comparison of measure'. *Journal of Marriage and Family*, 67: 328–36.

Leonard, S. (1990) *Critical Theory in Political Practice*. Princeton, NJ: Princeton University Press.
Lorde, A. (1981) 'The Uses of Anger'. *Women's Studies Quarterly*, 9(3): 7-10.
Lugones, M. and Spelman, E. (1983) 'Have we got a theory for you! Feminist theory, Cultural Imperialism and the demand for "the woman's voice"'. *Women's Studies International Forum*, 6(6): 573-81.
Lynch, K., et al. (eds). (2009) *Affective Equality: Love, Care and Injustice*. Basingstoke: Palgrave Macmillan.
Mackenzie, C. and Stoljar, N. (eds). (2000) *Relational Autonomy: Feminist Perspectives on Autonomy, Agency, and the Social Self.* Oxford: Oxford University Press.
Mackinnon, C. (1991) 'From Practice to Theory or What is a White Woman Anyway?' *Yale Journal of Law and Feminism* 4(1): 13-22.
Mahmood, S. (2011) *The Politics of Piety: The Islamic Revival and the Feminist Subject*. Princeton, NJ: Princeton University Press.
McCarthy, T. (1990) 'Private Irony and Public Decency: Richard Rorty's New Pragmatism'. *Critical Inquiry*, 16: 355-70.
McCarthy, T. (1993) *Ideals and Illusions: On Reconstruction and Deconstruction in Critical Theory*. Cambridge MA: MIT Press.
McCarthy, T. (2004) 'Coming to Terms with Our Past: On the Morality and Politics of Reparations for Slavery. Part Two'. *Political Theory* 32(6), 750-72.
McCarthy, T. (2009) *Race, Empire and the Idea of Human Development*. Cambridge: Cambridge University Press.
McGuire, J. (2016) 'Two Rawls Don't Make a Right: On Rainer Forst and the New Normativity'. *Constellations*, 23(1): 110-21.
McNay, L. (2009) *Against Recognition*. Cambridge: Polity Press.
McNay, L. (2014) *The Misguided Search for the Political: Social Weightlessness in Radical Democratic Theory*. Cambridge: Polity Press.
McNay, L (2016) 'Agency' in L. Disch and M. Hawkesworth (eds). *The Oxford Handbook of Feminist Theory*. Oxford: Oxford University Press.
McNay, L. (2021) 'The Politics of Welfare'. *European Journal of Political Theory*, 22 April. https://doi.org/10.1177%2F14748851211008002.
McRobbie, A. (2008) *The Aftermath of Feminism: Gender, Culture and Social Change*. London: Sage.
Medearis, J. (2004) 'Social Movements and Deliberative Democratic Theory'. *British Journal of Political Science*, 35: 53-75.
Medearis, J. (2015) *Why Democracy is Oppositional*, Cambridge, MA: Harvard University Press.
Medina, J. (2012) *The Epistemology of Resistance: Gender and Racial Oppression, Epistemic Injustice, and Resistant Imaginations*. Oxford: Oxford University Press.
Merleau-Ponty, M. (1964) 'From Mauss to Claude Levi-Strauss' in his *Signs*. Evanston, IL: Northwestern University Press.
Mills, C. (1998) *Blackness Visible: Essays on Philosophy and Race*. Cornell University Press.
Mills, C. (2005) 'Ideal Theory as Ideology'. *Hypatia* 20(3): 165-83, 173-5.
Mills, C. (2017a) 'Criticizing Critical Theory' in P. Deutscher and C. Lafont (eds). *Critical Theory in Critical Times: Transforming the Global Political and Economic Order*. New York: Columbia University Press.
Mills, C. (2017b) 'White Ignorance' in his *Black Rights/White Wrongs: The Critique of Racial Liberalism*. Oxford: Oxford University Press.
Mohanty, C. Talpade (2003) *Feminism Without Borders: Decolonizing Theory, Practising Solidarity*. Durham, NC: Duke University Press.

Mohanty, S. P. (2000) 'The Epistemic Status of Cultural Identity: On Beloved and the Postcolonial Condition' in P. Moya and M. Hames-Garcia (eds). *Reclaiming Identity: Realist Theory and the Predicament of Postmodernism*. Berkeley: University California Press.

Mulhall, S. (2002) 'Fearful Thoughts'. *London Review of Books*, 24(16): 22 August.

Müller, F. Suárez (2013) 'Justifying the Right to Justification: An analysis of Rainer Forst's constructivist theory of justice'. *Philosophy and Social Criticism*, 39(10): 1049–68.

Namaste, V. (2009) 'Undoing Theory: The "Transgender Question" and The Epistemic Violence of Anglo-American Feminist Theory'. *Hypatia*, 24(3): 11–32.

Narayan, U. (1988) 'Working Together Across Difference: Some Considerations on Emotions and Political Practice'. *Hypatia*, 3(2): 31–47.

Narayan, U. (2000) 'Essence of Culture and a Sense of History: A Feminist Critique of Cultural Essentialism' in U. Narayan and S. Harding (eds). *Decentring the Centre: Philosophy for a Multicultural, Feminist and Postcolonial World*. Bloomington: Indiana University Press.

National Women's Law Center (2020) 'National Snapshot: Poverty Among Women and Families, 2020' https://nwlc.org/wp-content/uploads/2020/12/PovertySnapshot2020.pdf.

Okin, S. (1989) *Justice, Gender and the Family*. New York: Basic Books.

Oksala, J. (2016) *Feminist Experiences: Foucauldian and Phenomenological Investigations*. Evanston, IL: Northwestern University Press.

Olson, K. (ed.) (2008) *Adding Insult to Injury: Nancy Fraser Debates her Critics*. London: Verso.

Olson, K. (2014) 'Complexities of Political Discourse: Class, Power and the Linguistic Turn' in R. Forst. *Justice, Democracy and the Right to Justification: Rainer Forst in Dialogue*. London: Bloomsbury.

Outlaw, L. (2005) *Critical Social Theory in the Interest of Black Folk*. London: Rowman and Littlefield.

Owen, D. and Van Den Brink, B. (eds) (2007) *Recognition and Power: Axel Honneth and the Tradition of Critical Social Theory*. Cambridge: Cambridge University Press.

Pensky, M. (2018) 'In Search of the Negative in Rahel Jaeggi's *Kritik von Lebensformen*' in A. Allen and E. Mendieta (eds). *From Alienation to Forms of Life: The Critical Theory of Rahel Jaeggi*. University Park, PA: Penn State University Press.

Phillips, A. (2009) *Multiculturalism Without Culture*. Princeton, NJ: Princeton University Press.

Phipps, A. (2014) *The Politics of the Body: Gender in a Neoliberal and Neoconservative Age*. Cambridge: Polity Press.

Rancière, J. (1999) *Disagreement: Politics and Philosophy*. Minneapolis: University of Minnesota Press.

Rancière, J. (2016a) 'The Method of Equality: Politics and Poetics' in K. Genel and J-P. Deranty (eds). A. Honneth and J. Rancière. *Recognition or Disagreement: A Critical Encounter on the Politics of Freedom, Equality and Identity*. New York: Columbia University Press.

Rancière, J. (2016b) 'Critical Questions on the Theory of Recognition' in K. Genel and J-P. Deranty (eds). A. Honneth and J. Rancière. *Recognition or Disagreement: A Critical Encounter on the Politics of Freedom, Equality and Identity*. New York: Columbia University Press.

Ransby, B. (2015) 'The Class Politics of Black Lives Matter'. *Dissent*, 62(4): 31–4.

Ritchie, B. E (2012) *Arrested Justice: Black Women, Violence and America's Prison Nation*. New York: New York University Press.

Rockhill, G. (2014) *Radical History and the Politics of Art*. New York: Columbia University Press.
Rorty, R. (2000) 'Universality and Truth' in R. Brandom (ed.). *Rorty and His Critics*. Oxford: Basil Blackwell.
Rosenthal, S. (2002) 'Habermas, Dewey, and the Democratic Self' in M. Aboulafia, M. Bookman, and C. Kemp (eds). *Habermas and Pragmatism*. London: Routledge.
Rush, F. (2004) 'Conceptual Foundations of Early Critical Theory' in F. Rush (ed.). *The Cambridge Companion to Critical Theory*. Cambridge: Cambridge University Press, pp. 6-39.
Salamon, G. (2009) 'Justification and Queer Method, Or Leaving Philosophy'. *Hypatia*, 24(1): 225-30.
Scheuerman, W. (1999) 'Between Radicalism and Resignation: Democratic Theory in Habermas's *Between Facts and Norms*' in P. Dews (ed.). *Habermas: A Critical Reader*. Oxford: Blackwell.
Schwartz, J. (2009) *The Future of Democratic Equality: Rebuilding Social Solidarity in a Fragmented America*. London: Routledge.
Schwartzman, L (2006) *Challenging Liberalism: Feminism as Political Critique*. University Park, PA: Penn State University Press.
Scott, J. (1990) *Domination and the Arts of Resistance: Hidden Transcripts*. New Haven: Yale University Press.
Shapiro, I. (2005) *The Flight from Reality in the Human Sciences*. Princeton, NJ: Princeton University Press.
Shelby, T. (2005) *We Who Are Dark: The Philosophical Foundations of Black Solidarity*. Cambridge, MA: Harvard University Press.
Sklar, J. (1990) *The Faces of Injustice*. New Haven: Yale University Press.
Smith, B. (1999) *Home Girls: A Black Feminist Anthology*. New York: Rutgers University Press.
Sorel, G. (1975) *Reflections on Violence*. New York: AMS Press.
Stears, M. (2007) The liberal tradition and the politics of exclusion'. *Annual Review of Political Science*, 10: 85-101.
Stears, M. (2010) *Demanding Democracy: American Radicals in Search of a New Politics*. Oxford: Princeton University Press.
Strydom, Piet (2011) *Contemporary Critical Theory and Methodology*. London: Routledge.
Taylor, C. (1995) *Philosophical Arguments*. Cambridge, MA: Harvard University Press.
Thomas, L. (1998) 'Moral Deference' in C. Willett (ed.). *Multiculturalism: A Guide to the Current Debate*. Oxford: Blackwell.
Thompson, M. (2017) *The Domestication of Critical Theory*. London: Rowman and Littlefield.
Threadcraft, S. (2016) 'Intimate Injustice, Political Obligation and the Dark Ghetto' in her *Intimate Justice: The Black Female Body and the Body Politic*. Oxford: Oxford University Press.
Threadcraft, S. (2017) 'North American Necropolitics and Gender: On #BlackLivesMatter and Black Femicide'. *South Atlantic Quarterly*, 116(3): 553-79.
Threadcraft, S. (2019) 'Black Feminism and the Dilemma of Agonism'. *Contemporary Political Theory*, 18(4): 650-55.
Tobin, T. and Jaggar, A. (2013) 'Naturalizing Moral Justification: Rethinking the Method of Moral Epistemology'. *Metaphilosophy*, 44(4): 409-39.
Tronto, J. (2012) 'Democratic Care Politics in an Age of Limits' in S. Razavi and S. Staab (eds). *Global Variations in the Political and Social Economy of Care: Worlds Apart*. London: Routledge.

Tully, J. (2011) 'Dialogue'. *Political Theory* 39(1): 145–60.
Urban Walker, M. (1992) 'Feminism, Ethics and the Question of Theory', *Hypatia*, 7(3): 23–38.
Urbinati, N. (2000) 'Representation as Advocacy: A Study of Democratic Deliberation'. *Political Theory*, 28(6): 758–86.
Vázquez-Arroyo, A. (2016) *Political Responsibility: Responding to Predicaments of Power*. New York: Columbia University Press.
Von Redecker, E. (2018) 'Progress, Normativity and the Dynamics of Social Change: An Exchange Between Rahel Jaeggi and Amy Allen' in A. Allen and E. Mendieta (eds). *From Alienation to Forms of Life: The Critical Theory of Rahel Jaeggi*. University Park, PA: Penn State University Press.
Wacquant, L. (2010) 'Class, Race and Hyperincarceration in Revanchist America'. *Daedalus*, 39(3): 74–90.
Walzer, M. (1987) *Interpretation and Social Criticism*. Harvard University Press.
Warner, M. (1999) *The Trouble with Normal: Sex, Politics and the Ethics of Queer Life*. Cambridge, MA: Harvard University Press.
Warnke, G. (2001) 'Taking Ethical Debate Seriously' in W. Rehg and J. Bohman (eds). *Pluralism and the Pragmatic Turn: The Transformation of Critical Theory (Essays in Honour of Thomas McCarthy)*. Cambridge, MA: MIT Press.
Wellmer, A. (1991) *The Persistence of Modernity: Essays on Aesthetics, Ethics, and Postmodernism*. Cambridge, MA: MIT Press.
Wellmer, A. (2000) *Endgames: The Irreconcilable Nature of Modernity Essays and Lectures*, Cambridge, MA: MIT Press.
West, C. (2001) 'Malcolm X and Black Rage' in his *Race Matters*, Boston: Beacon Press.
West, C. (2011) 'A Prisoner of Hope in the Night of the American Empire: Dialogue with Gabriel Rockhill' in G. Rockhill and A. Gomez-Muller (eds). *Politics of Culture and the Spirit of Critique*. New York: Columbia University Press.
White, S. K. (2000) *Sustaining Affirmation: The Strengths of Weak Ontology in Political Theory*. Princeton, NJ: Princeton University Press.
Wiggershaus, R. (1994) *The Frankfurt School: Its History, Theories and Political Significance*. Cambridge: Polity Press.
Williams, R. (1977) *Marxism and Literature*. Oxford: Oxford University Press.
Woolf, J. (2015) 'Social Equality, Relative Poverty and Marginalized Groups' in G. Hull (ed.). *The Equal Society: Essays on Equality in Theory and Practice*. Lexington Books.
Woolf, J. (2019) 'Method in Philosophy and Public Policy' in A. Lever and A. Poama (eds). *The Routledge Handbook of Ethics and Public Policy*. London: Routledge.
Wylie, A. (2003) 'Why Standpoint Matters' in R. Figueroa and S. Harding (eds). *Science and Other Cultures: Issues in Philosophies of Science and Technology*. London: Routledge.
Young, I. M. (1990) *Justice and the Politics of Difference*. Princeton, NJ: Princeton University Press.
Young, I. M. (1996) 'Communication and the Other: Beyond Deliberative Democracy' in S. Benhabib (ed.). *Democracy and Difference: Contesting the Boundaries of the Political*. Princeton, NJ: Princeton University Press.
Young, I. M. (1997) *Intersecting Voices: Dilemmas of Gender, Political Philosophy and Policy*. Princeton, NJ: Princeton University Press.
Young, I.M. (2000) *Inclusion and Democracy*. Oxford: Oxford University Press.
Young, I. M. (2005) *On Female Body Experience: Throwing Like a Girl and Other Essays*. Oxford: Oxford University Press.

Young, I. M. (2007) 'Recognition of Love's Labour: Considering Axel Honneth's Feminism' in B. Van den Brink and D. Owen (eds). *Recognition and Power: Axel Honneth and the Tradition of Critical Social Theory*. Cambridge: Cambridge University Press.

Young, I. M. (2009) 'The Gendered Cycle of Vulnerability in the Less Developed World' in Debra Satz and Rob Reich (eds). *Toward a Humanist Justice: The Political Philosophy of Susan Moller Okin*. Oxford: Oxford University Press, pp. 223–37.

Zack, N. (2005) *Inclusive Feminism: A Third Wave Theory of Women's Commonality*. London: Rowman and Littlefield.

Zakaria, R. (2017) *Veil*. London: Bloomsbury.

Zambrana, R. (2013) 'Paradoxes of Neoliberalism and the Tasks of Critical Theory'. *Critical Horizons*, 14(1): 93–119.

Zambrana, R. (2018) 'What's Critical About Critical Theory-Redux' in A. Allen and E. Mendieta (eds). *From Alienation to Forms of Life: The Critical Theory of Rahel Jaeggi*. University Park, PA: Penn State University Press.

Zurn, C. (2008) 'Arguing Over Participatory Parity: On Nancy Fraser's Conception of Social Justice' in Olson, K. (ed.). *Adding Insult to Injury: Nancy Fraser Debates her Critics*. London: Verso.

Index

For the benefit of digital users, indexed terms that span two pages (e.g., 52–53) may, on occasion, appear on only one of those pages.

abductive analysis 7–8, 49–53, 162
Abu-Lughod, L. 185–6
action-guiding principles 30–1
actuality, negation of 218–23
adjudication, priority of *see* priority of adjudication
Adorno, T. 15–17, 27–8, 34–5, 46–7, 54–5, 121–2, 154–5
  Dialectic of Enlightenment 40
  formalism and negativism 192, 219
  intellectual vanguardism 226–7
  and Jaeggi 200–1, 204–5
  justification critique 69, 83–4, 90
  theorizing from experience 237–9
advocacy 188–9
affectability 82–3
African-American women 49–51, 74–5
  see also black feminist thought; black women
agency
  negation of 213–18
  and progress 116–22
  subaltern 238–9
alienation 4–5, 26–7, 31–3, 40, 55–6, 188, 231–2
  alienated familiar 18, 59–60, 128–9, 152–3, 182, 238–9
  disclosure 129–30, 135, 143–4
  effects 55–6
  Jaeggi on 201–2, 221–2
  negation of actuality 220–2
  self-alienation 142–3
Allen, A. 9–11, 72–3, 119–20, 218–19, 231–2
Althusser, L. P. 209
Anderson, E. 94–5
anger, expressing 31–2
antecedent justification 67–8
anti-essentialism 14–15, 45–6
Arab cultures 184–6
Arendt, H. 73–4, 128–9, 131–2
  priority of judgement 133–4, 136
asymmetries of power 1, 29–30, 78–9, 164–5, 231
  and the family 93–4, 105, 107–8
  noumenal power 70–3
  participatory parity 163–4

asymmetry, mixed forms 180–1
Auschwitz 83, 237–8
autonomous self-realization 99–100, 107, 197–8, 211–13
autonomy
  and care 197–8
  deliberative 105–6
  and dependence 197–8
  equality 184–5
  and family 100–2, 113–14, 197–8
  individual 101–2, 106–7
  of judgement 136
  justification critique 65–6, 90
  legal 102
  moral 102
  and social freedom 102
  value of 100–1
  veiling practice 185–6
  of women 105–6
Azamova, A. 86

banalization 176–7
Barnes, I. 238–9
Bell, Macalaster 31–2
Benhabib, S. 9–13
Berenstain, N. 79–80
Bernstein, R. 169–70
black feminist thought 24–5, 31–2, 49, 59, 157, 159–60, 190, 211–13, 231
  and 'merely' experienced 173–6
  theorizing from experience 46–9
'Black Lives Matter' movement 143–4
black women 24–5, 30–2, 47, 180–1
  African-American 49–51
  and the family 211–13
  female slaves 50–1
  identity 152–3
  and justification critique 79–80
  power and abductive theorizing 51–2
  rape of 50–1
  and white women 211–13
Bohman, J. 40, 81–2, 181
bottom-up analysis, preference over top-down method 1, 25–7, 49

Bourdieu, P. 26–7, 33, 70–1, 176, 182, 196–7
  and context transcendence 38–9, 41–2
Brown, W. 11–13, 156
Bubeck, D. 104–5
Butler, J. 139, 141, 178–9, 238–9
  on 'passionate attachments' 70–1, 105–6
  on universality 149–50, 154–5

capitalism 11, 26–7, 111, 118–19, 185–6, 208–9
  see also neoliberalism
  agglomeration 209
  capitalist accumulation 50–1, 114–15, 118–19, 158–9, 162, 208
  capitalist societies 1–4, 25–6, 28–9, 122–3, 126, 159–61, 164–5, 209, 226–7, 229–30
  critique 170, 225
  'disorganized' 170
  exploitative nature 26–7, 118–19, 232–3
  global 15–17, 161–2
  neoliberalism 102, 162, 169–70, 225–6
  profit maximization 216–17
  reproduction 162, 208
  social relations 112–13, 156–9
  social structures 15–17, 161–2
Carby, H. 211–13
care
  care work, gendered 4, 93–4
  and duty 103
  gap in literature 104–5
  lack of 104–5
  and mutual responsibility 94–5
  and social freedom 103, 115–16
  and social justice 112–16
Cavell, S. 76
Celikates, R. 180–1, 208–9, 211, 217, 231–2
Cesaire, A. 154–5
child poverty 53–4, 110–11
Child Poverty Action Group 110–11
Civil Rights Act (1964), US 215–16
Collins, P.H. 15, 47, 157, 162, 165–6, 175–6, 180–1, 188–9
  on the family 210–11
  feminist theorizing 48–9
colour blindness 119–20, 215–16
commodity fetishism 209–10
communicative ethics 8, 64–5, 77–8, 193–4
  see also discourse ethics (Habermas); ethics; Habermas, J.
constitutionalism, liberal-democratic 132–3
constructivism
  discursive 67–8, 78
  moral 65–6, 94–5, 107–8
  political 66
  and practical reason 65–6

context transcendence 19, 23–4, 85–6, 201, 219–20
  see also Frankfurt School critical theory; Habermas, J.; paradigm-led theorizing
  dialogical view 219–20, 228–34
  and feminism 15
  foundations of critique 6–7, 205
  Frankfurt School on 2–4, 6–8
  Habermas on 2–3, 36–8, 43, 224
  insight 219–20, 224
  as learning 204–7
  monism 37–9, 240–1
  and paradigm-led theorizing 37–9, 45–6
  political theories 35–6, 41
  reconfiguring 43–6
  and retreat from experience 2–3, 35–43
  and validity 45–6
contextualism
  meta-normative 56–8
  parochial 148–9
  piecemeal 223
  radical 37–8, 45, 134–5, 148–50
  and relativism 219–20
  unmediated 150
contingent conflict situation 43, 55–6
conventionalism
  bias 203
  and particularism 138
  and recognition monism 192, 202–3
Cooke, M. 39, 56–8, 133
Covid-19 pandemic 105–6, 108–11
Crenshaw, K. 49–50, 74–5, 234
critical race theory 125–6
critical theory
  emancipatory orientation 23
  explanatory features 29
  and feminism 9–13, 24–5
    General Other and Concrete Other 11–13
    importance of feminist theory 9
    paradigm-led theorizing 9–13
  see also feminism
  first-generation 2–3, 40
  Frankfurt School see Frankfurt School critical theory
  goal of unmasking of oppression 23
  Habermas on 34–5, 53–4, 194–5
  importance of interpretative understanding of experience for 29
  and injustice 25–6, 90
  legitimacy of 4–5
  and liberal democratic theory 25–6
  methodological features 29
  and morality 25–6
  multivalent 7–8, 13, 38–9, 162, 171–2

normative features 25-6, 29
  see also normative theory/normativity
  paradigm-led see paradigm-led theorizing
  and psychoanalysis 231-3
  self-understanding 34-5
critique
  black feminist thought see black feminist thought
  capitalism 170, 225
  context transcendence
    reconfiguring 43-6
    and retreat from experience 2-3, 23-4, 35-43
    of critique 68-9
  as determinate negation 204
  dialogical see dialogism
  disclosive function 17-18
  emancipatory see emancipatory critique
  and experience 28-9
    downplaying of lived experience by Frankfurt School 1
    experience-led theorizing as alternative to paradigm-led theories 11, 24-5
    feminist theorizing from 46-9
    as starting point of 27-8
  expertocratic view 181, 239-40
  of forms of life 193-8
  and Frankfurt School 157
  Fraser on 156-90
  ideology 26-7
  immanent 11-13, 30-1, 37-8, 41, 43
  importance for oppressed groups 28-9
  justification see justification
  'merely' experienced 168-76
  monism, overcoming 158-62
  negativist approach to 21-2
  nonsubjective stance 172
  normativity 53-8
  participatory parity 536 163-8, 172-3, 182-4
  and power 49-53, 219
  practical emancipatory status of 6, 23-4, 26-7, 44-5, 62
  priority of adjudication 182-9
  problematization role 202-3
  reconstructive 98-9
  reflexive see reflexivity
  role of suffering in 27-8, 34-5
  situated nature of 99-100
  'super-vision' 41
  thinking across perspectives 58-60
  transcontextual normative force 172
  validity of 9-11, 35-6, 41, 45, 90-1

Dalmiya, V. 174-5, 181
DAU (deductive application of a universal moral standard) 55-8

Davis, A. 9-11, 15-17, 20, 50-1, 145, 147-8, 157
  Blues Legacies and Black Feminism 152-3
  theorizing 47, 59-60
Dejours, C. 176-7
democratization
  disclosure and democratic politics 124
  families and gender inequality 108-10
  freedom 101-2
  liberal democratic theory 25-6
  of love 93-4, 103, 117-18
  modern family 103-4
  predemocratic modes of normative reasoning 56-8
  shortcomings in narrative 113-14
  sovereignty 67-8
  state-territoriality 161-2
  thought 124-5, 129-30
  validation 130, 134-5
  virtues 94-5
determinate negation 121-2, 192, 230-1
  see also negation
  critique as 204
  free-standing 201
  Jaeggi on 201-2
Dewey, J. 196-7, 201-2
dialogism/dialogical reasoning 5-7, 23-4, 32-3, 35, 167-9, 179-81, 188-9, 224, 226-7, 233-4
  see also normative reasoning
  constrained dialogism 41-2, 182-4
  context transcendence 219-20, 228, 230-4
  and epistemic authoritarianism 181
  hierarchized dialogism 41
  and 'merely' experienced 168-9, 173-5
  and paradigm-led theorizing 40-1, 166-7
  privilege of theory 178-81
  and reflexivity 4-5, 13, 166-7, 182
  theorizing across perspectives 58-60
disagreement 211-13
disciplinary embodiment (Foucault) 71
disclosure 17-18, 59-60
  see also exemplarity
  'alienated familiar' 18, 59-60
  emancipatory force 137-8
  exemplarity
    exemplary universalism 130-3
    politics of 142-8
  experiential 35-6
  Jaeggi on 202-3
  negative, priority of 153-4
  open-ended ideas 191-2
  parochialism, problems of 148-53
  politics of 124-55
  priority of judgement 133-7

disclosure (*cont.*)
   and reflexivity 66–9
   rethinking 126–30
   sensus communis 20, 137–41
   world 126–9, 135, 137–8, 192, 202–3, 224
discourse ethics (Habermas) 9, 17–18, 77–8, 166–7
   see also communicative ethics; ethics; Habermas, J.
   and experiences of disempowered subjects 127–8, 194–5
   formalism 150–1, 193–4
   modified 11–13
   morality–ethics relationship 193–4
   proceduralism of 191–2
   rational justification procedures 127–8
   rational proceduralism 133
   and reason 128–30
   thought-experiments 140
division of labour
   domestic 71–2, 113–14
   gendered *see* gendered division of labour
   reordered 115–16
domestic violence 53–4, 105–10, 119–20, 165–6
domination 9, 15–17, 106–7, 126, 140–1, 149–50, 234
   abstract 206–7, 209–10
   critique 63–4
   gender 170–1
   imperialist 188
   interpersonal 103–4
   male 55–6, 71–4, 105–6, 111–12, 199–200
   and progress 119–22
   racial 144–5, 162
   racialized modes 50–1
   soft 105–6, 111–12, 176, 199–200
   theories 54–5
Dotson, K. 79–80
Du Bois, W. E. 142–3
Durkheim, É 98–9

economism, feminist critique 170
egalitarianism 15, 107–10
   see also inegalitarian social order
   methodological 168–9
   values 72–3
EIRE (empirically informed reflective equilibrium) 55–8
Ellison, R. 145
emancipatory critique
   justification 19
   participatory parity 166–7
   practical emancipatory status 6, 23–4, 26–7, 44–5, 62

reflexivity 5–6
   situated 23–4
empathy 84
epistemic authoritarianism 43, 166–7, 181
epistemic equality 6, 15, 58–9, 167–8
epistemic exploitation 79–80
epistemic prison 40
epistemic value
   intrinsic 41–2, 173–4
   of lived experience 5–6, 157, 168–9
epistemo-centrism 180–1
equality *see also* gender inequality; inequality
   affective 115–16
   African-American struggle for 144–5, 215–16
   autonomy 184–5
   democratic 115
   discursive 76–7
   Enlightenment 143–4
   epistemic 6, 15, 58–9, 167–8
   formal 19, 73–4, 142–5
   and freedom 115–16, 127–8
   gender 53–4
   ideal 184–5
   inter-group/intra-group 184
   between interlocutors 53–4, 58–9
   and justice 94–5
   of knowledge 181
   legal 215–16
   in marriage 82
   methodological 7–8, 24–5, 45–6, 58–9, 157, 167–8
   moral 145
   of opportunity 119–20
   paradox of equal treatment 84
   racial 119–20, 147–8, 215–16
   reflexive 115
   social 115
   between theory and experience 180–1
Eschle, C. 170–1
essentialism 48, 104–5, 175–6
ethics *see also* discourse ethics (Habermas)
   of care 104–5
   communicative 8, 64–5, 77–8, 193–4
   contextually indexed critique 201
   ethical praxis 102
   ethical progress 111–12
   ethics-first approach 11–13, 66–7
   in the family 111–12, 115–16, 198–200
   and justice 193–4
   liberal political thought 11–13
   and morality 193–4
   negativist 21–2, 200–1
   and power 200–1
ethnocentrism 53, 78

Eurocentrism 1–2
exemplarity *see also* exemplary universalism
   and disclosure 124–5
   Ferrara on 20, 124–5
   imaginative force 124–5
   politics of 142–8
exemplary universalism 20, 124–6, 130–4, 154
experiential perspective 25–35
   see also Frankfurt School critical theory;
      theorizing from experience
   anti-essentialism 45–6
   and critique 1–2, 28–9
      experience-led theorizing 24–5
      feminist theorizing 46–9
      as starting point of 27–8
   de-essentialization 6–7
   difficulty in explaining to others 29–30
   disclosure, experiential 35–6
   downplaying by Frankfurt School critical
      theory in unmasking critique *see*
      Frankfurt School critical theory
   epistemic value 5–6, 157, 168–9
   everyday experience 191–2
   feminist theorizing 46–9
   hierarchy of theory over experience 40–1
   interpretative account of 23–61
   and knowledge production 5–6
   limited and fallible nature 28–9
   at limits of justification 62–92
   'merely' experienced 168–76
   negativism and experience 27–8, 200–4
   normative foundations, Frankfurt School
      preoccupation with 23, 191–2, 206–7
   oppressed groups directly affected,
      significance 6, 23, 27–9, 32–3
   over-problematization 5–7, 15, 40–2, 168–9,
      173–4, 182, 228–9
   paradigm-led theorizing insufficiently
      responsive to *see* paradigm-led theorizing
   and particularism 44–5, 47–9
   relational account of lived experience 234–6
   retreat from 2–3, 23–4, 35–43
   as starting point of critique 27–8
   unreliability, assumed *see* unreliability of
      subjective experience, assumed

fact and norm 4, 38–9, 122–3
   inherence between 53, 191–2
fairness 163–4, 175–6, 182–4
family 93–123
   archetypes 4
   asymmetries of power 93–4, 105, 107–8
   and autonomy/individual freedom 100–2
   black women in 211–13

   bourgeois 197–8
   care and duty 103
   care and social justice 112–16
   democratization of modern family 103–4
   ethics in 111–12, 115–16, 198–200
   feminist critiques 106–7
   foundational role 19–20
   and gender inequality 108–12
   Habermas on 111, 198–9
   Hegel on 197–8
   heteronormativity 107
   heterosexual family unit 103
   Honneth on 93–4, 104–12, 199–200
   Jaeggi on 198–200
   modern family life 103–4
   nurturing, feminized nature 107
   'patchwork' families 103
   poverty 108–11
   and power 103–4, 106–7
   problem-solving in 211–13
   progress and agency 116–22
   purification 104–8
   recognition of gender 94–100
   self-sacrificing role of mother 107
   sentimentalizing 198–9
   sex-affective triangle of father–mother–
      child 107
   shifting of conventional patterns of
      parenting 103
   single-parent 108–10
   social theory of 93–5
Fanon, F. 142–3, 232–3
Fazio, G. 118–19
female genital cutting (FGC), Maasai
   communities (Kenya) 55–8
femininity
   conventional notions 211–13
   devaluing 160–1
   mainstream norms 152–3
   male-defined 51–2
feminism *see also* black feminist thought
   Anglo-American theory 9, 177–8
   anti-essentialism 14–15
   black feminist thought *see* black feminist
      thought
   and context transcendence 15
   and critical theory 9–13, 24–5
      General Other and Concrete Other 11–13
      importance of feminist theory for 9
      paradigm-led theorizing 9–13
   cultural critique of economism 170
   family life, critique 106–7
   and ideas of Honneth 93–5, 104–5
   non-ideal standpoint methodology 94–5

feminism (*cont.*)
  and normativity 56–8
  outside Frankfurt School 14–17
  and postcolonialism 50–1
  and race 50–1
  second-wave 170–1
  theorizing from experience 46–9
  theory 24–5
Ferrara, A. 20, 118–19
  on disclosure 124–5
  on equality and freedom 115
  exemplary universalism 130–3
  and Habermas 124–5
  parochialism, problems of 148–51
  politics of exemplarity 143–7
  priority of judgement 134–7
  sensus communis 137–41
first-generation critical theory 2–3, 40
Flynn, J. 88–9
formal equality 19, 73–4, 142–5
formalism
  discourse ethics 150–1, 193–4
  negation of actuality 219–20
  and negation of agency 217
  and negativism 21–2, 191–224
  and negativist historicity 220
  and ontology 140–1
  paradox of 221–2
  progress 205
  and relativism 64–5
  sensus communis 139–40
forms of life (Jaeggi) 196–8, 204, 223
  bad or 'regressive' 196–8, 217
  blocked 217
  critique of 193–8, 204–5
  ethical progress 195–6
  failure of 206
  good or 'progressive' 196–8
  and Habermas 195–6
  and Honneth 203
  problem-solving 196–7
  successful 194–5, 203, 205–6
  terminology 208–9
Forst, R. 2–3, 19, 33, 51–4, 148–9
  and Fraser 163
  on justice 25–6, 82–3, 88, 163–4
  justification critique 43, 62–92, 164–5
  on normative foundations 63–4, 66
  practical transcendentalism 63
Foucault, M. 70–2, 120–1, 201–2, 223
foundations
  abstract questions, normative foundations 9–11
  context-transcending 2–3, 6–7

family, foundational role 19–20
foundational principles 2–6
foundational turn 2–3, 9–11, 15–17, 19, 23–4, 36–7, 126
immanent and transcendent 63–6
monist 21–2, 161–3, 234–8, 240–1
monological 228–9
normative *see* normative foundations
problem, post-metaphysical solution to 2–3
quasi-transcendental status of *see* quasi-transcendental status
recasting as 'intra-mundane transcendence' 2–3, 62–3
and social praxis 2–3
transcendental 36–7
Frankfurt School critical theory 5–7, 28–9
  aims, epistemic 43
  context transcendence *see* context transcendence
  contributions of 9–11
  decontextualized accounts of gender 4
  definition of itself as unmasking critique 6
  definition of theoretical inquiry 32–5
  downplaying lived experience in unmasking critique of oppression 1–15, 157
  ambivalence about epistemic value 5–6
  and context transcendence 2–4, 6–8, 35–7
  and Fraser 168–77
  minimizing status of suffering and misery 1–2
  over-problematization 5–7, 40–1, 168–9, 173–4, 182
  retreat from experience 2–3, 23–4, 35–43
  tokenistic treatment 93
  epistemic authoritarianism, alleged 43, 166–7, 181
  failure to thoroughly address oppression 1–2
  on the family 94–5
  and feminism 9, 14–17
  and gender oppression 1–2, 11–13, 23, 156
  hermeneutical requirement defining 4–5, 58–9
  ideology critique 26–7, 35–6
  intersectionality, failure to theorize 4
  left-Hegelian roots 13, 25–6, 149–50, 195–6, 218
  Marxist roots 1–2, 25–6
  monism of *see* monism
  negativism 201
  normative theory 1–4, 53
  normative turn 2
  paradigm-led theorizing *see* paradigm-led theorizing
  on power 66–7

practical emancipatory status of critique 6, 23–4, 26–7, 44–5
and pragmatism 158, 191, 227–8
racial inequality, failure to consider 51–2
rejection of metaphysical notions 36–7
situated rationality 43–4, 91–2
on suffering and critique 1, 27–9
thought 3–4, 9–11, 156, 158, 191, 226–7, 240–1
value, reconstructive approach to 11–13
value of for gender oppression 156
Fraser, N. 9–11, 13–17, 20–1, 27–8, 30–1, 34–5, 43–4, 46–7, 87, 119–20, 156–7, 181, 188–9
anti-experiential tendencies 168–77
notorious unreliability 168–9, 171–4, 184–5
on capitalism 208
constrained dialogism 41–2, 182–4
on the family 107–8, 114–16
grand sweep perspective 169–70, 190
and Honneth 160, 165–6, 168–9
interpretation of work 189
on justification and validity 239–40
and monism 160–2
power-first approach 164–5, 168–9
Redistribution or Recognition? 122–3
sociologically grounded critique 188
'What's Critical about Critical Theory' 158–60
freedom
defining 102
democratic debate 101–2
and equality 115–16, 127–8
formal and substantive 119–20
individual 100–2, 106–7, 187–8, 197–8
metavalue 115
negative theories 101–2
positive theories 101–2
reflexive theories 101–2
social *see* social freedom
Frye, Marilyn 31–2
fundamentum inconcussum 65–6

gay marriage 82, 103–4, 117–18
gender *see also* gendered division of labour; gender inequality; gender justice; gender norms; gender oppression; gender subordination
gendered violence 50–1, 55–8
recognition of 94–100
gendered division of labour 72–3, 140–1, 165–6, 181, 198–9, 229–30
care and social justice 113–16
and family 93, 103, 105–6, 108–10, 113–16
gender inequality 11, 20–1, 26–7, 114–15, 158–9, 169–70, 191
see also inequality
entrenched 110–11
and the family 108–12
and gender subordination 108–10
household duties and employment 108–10
and modernity 111–12
noumenal power 71–3
persistent nature of 105
and social freedom 111–12
gender justice 53–5, 170
gender norms 70–1
conventional/traditional 211–13
hegemonic 71
transphobic 177–8
gender oppression 9–13, 19–21, 63, 69, 93, 112–13, 174
accounts 9–11, 19–20, 93–4, 157
critique 9, 156–7
materialist 175–6
systematic 9–11, 156
diagnosis of 19–20, 60–1
and Frankfurt School 1–2, 11–13, 23, 156
global 158
and monism 19–20
normative responses to 11–13
power and abductive theorizing 51–2
recognition of gender 99–100
structural-functionalist dimensions 122–3
unmasking critique of oppression 48–9, 53–4, 56–9
gender subordination 9–11, 71–2, 93–4, 158–9, 165–6
black women 59–60
care and social justice 112–15
cycles of 159–60, 210–11
and inequality 108–10
noumenal power 71–4
and 'passionate attachments' 105–6
priority of adjudication 185–6, 188–9
recognition of gender 95–6, 99–100
generality
craving for 150, 204–5
critical 158
debilitating 185–6
and monism 236–7
and reciprocity 65–6, 80, 88, 163–4
and validity 234–6
Geras, N. 111
Geuss, R. 28–9, 36–7
Giddens, A. 196–7
globalism
Westphalian 170
grand theory 24–5, 39, 122–3

Habermas, J. 20, 27–8, 36–7, 53–4, 110–11, 159–60, 163
  communicative ethics *see* communicative ethics
  context transcendence 2–3, 8, 36–8, 43, 224
  critical theory 34–5, 53–4, 194–5
  critique of forms of life 193–6
  disclosure 124–5, 132–3, 137–8, 146
    priority of judgement 135–7
    rethinking 126–30
    world 137–8
  discourse ethics *see* discourse ethics (Habermas)
  exemplary universalism 132–3
  on family 111, 198–9
  and Ferrara 124–5
  and Forst 82
  and Frankfurt School /paradigm-led theory 2–3, 23–6, 201–2, 204
  and Fraser 163
  fundamentum inconcussum 65–6
  and Jaeggi 191–2, 195–6
  on justice 126–7
  justification critique 63–6, 82
  Knowledge and Human Interests 25–6, 231–2
  on morality-ethics distinction 193–4
  priority of judgement 135
  social ontology 195–6
  and unmasking critique 28–9, 32–3
  on validity 194–5
  on world disclosure 126–7
Hacking, I. 135
Haraway, D. 44–5
Harding, S. 44–5
headscarves, prohibition on wearing 184–5
Hegel, G.W.F. 98–9, 101–2, 108, 149–50, 196–8
  see also left-Hegelianism
  anachronistic social theory 112–13
  formalism of 192–3
  'Logic of the concept' 117
  on progress 205–7
Hekman, S. 181
hermeneutics 28–9, 82–3
heteronormativity 107
hijab, wearing of 185–6
historical immanentism 62–3, 75–6
historical relativism 85–6
holism, theoretical 48–9
Holliday, B. 145
Holocaust 83–4, 237–8
Honneth, A. *see also* recognition; recognition monism
  on contemporary culture 103–4
  on context transcendence 43
  on ethical purification 107
  on the family 104–12, 199–200
    recognition and progress 93–123
    social theory of the family 93–5, 104–5
  and feminism 93–5, 104–5
  and Fraser 160, 165–6, 168–9
  Freedom's Right 100–2, 118–19
  fundamentum inconcussum 65–6
  'gentle stylization' of accounts of 105
  and Habermas 195–6
  Hegelianism of 103, 108, 182–4
  and Jaeggi 192
  justification critique 64–6, 88–9
  method of normative reconstruction 107–8
  on negativism 201
  personalist model of gender and power 114–15
  phenomenology of misrecognition 27–8, 171–2
  politics of exemplarity 148–9
  on progress 93–123
  on recognition 19–20, 64–5
  reconstructive method 99–100, 111–12
  Redistribution or Recognition? 122–3
hooks, b. 29–31
horizons of understanding, expanding 6–7, 44–5
Horkheimer, M. 25–6
  Dialectic of Enlightenment 40
humility 174–5
hyper-pluralism 124–5, 138, 140–2
hyper-rationalism 17–18, 75, 134–5, 194–5

ideal theory 66–8
identity
  counterhegemonic formation 15–17
  and difference 205–6
  female black 152–3
  fulfilled 139
  imposed forms 209–10
  logic of 234
  overarching 143–4
  personal 165–6
  and self-realization 193–5
  social 223
  superordinate 132–3, 143–4
  transgendered 177–8
identity politics 230–1
  commodifiable 170
  movements 46–7
  self-serving 175–6
ideology critique 26–7, 35–6
imagination
  collective 124–5, 134
  democratic 20, 132–3

individual 134
political 133, 144–5, 188–9
and rationality 132–3
and reason 128–9
social 134
immanence and transcendence 23–5, 63–6, 90–1, 192–3
immanent critique 9–13, 30–3, 54–5, 66–7, 202–5, 211–13, 224–8
context transcendence 37–8, 41, 43–4
and family 93–4, 98–9, 120–1
and Frankfurt School critical theory 62–3, 123
hermeneutical premises of 37–8, 228
historical immanentism 41, 62–3, 75–6
historicized premises of 41, 43, 202–3
immanence and transcendence 192–3
and justification 68–9
radical 62–3
impartiality 25–6, 86–7, 132–4, 221
of General Other 11–13
ideal of 11–13, 90–1
immanent and transcendent foundations 63–5
rules and principles 30–1
inegalitarian social order 126, 231, 233–4, 238–9
experiences of suffering 27–8
gendered division of labour 72–3, 122–3
institutions 230–1
social relations 143–4
inequality 26–7, 121–2, 198–9, 201
economic 111
gender *see* gender inequality
and justification 78–9
material 111
politics of exemplarity 146
of power 4, 25–6, 87
and purification of family 105–6
racial 51–2
structural 207–8
injustice 13, 41, 76, 165–6
adjudication, priority of 182–4, 187–8
and critical theory 25–6, 90
cultural 161–2
direct experience 35–6, 62, 66–7, 77–8, 80–1
real-world circumstances/concrete instances of 62, 82, 85–7, 89–90, 237–8
distributive/redistributive 160–1, 170–1
economic 160–2
enduring 206
epistemic 63, 76–7
existing injustices 25–6, 76, 158–9
formal definitions 191–2
gender 165–6
global 225–6

hermeneutical 82–3
institutionalized 163–4
justification 79–81, 83, 86–7, 229–30
meriting title of 172, 178–84, 187–8
'metablindness'/'metainsensitivity to' 86–7
and normativity/normative theory 25–6, 83–4
objective 221
oppressed groups 31–2
original 82–3
past 146
phenomenology 34–5, 93–5, 171–2
political struggle against 45, 60–1
and progress 121–2
recognitive 123, 160, 171–2, 176
reconciliation or vacillation between critical and ideal perspectives 87
right not to suffer 88–9
sensus communis 141
severe 82–3
social 63–4, 73–4, 127–9, 159–60, 211
'as a surprising abnormality' from norm of justice 25–6, 85–6
testimonial 82–3
and theory 178–9
unmasking 66–7
validity of claims 20–1
interpretative account of direct subjective experience 23–61
importance for critical theory 29
importance for Frankfurt School theory 29
monist 38–9
validity 34
intersectionality 4, 38–9, 234
power and abductive theorizing 7–8, 49–52
intersubjectivity 11–13, 65–6, 89–90, 101–2, 133–4
intersubjective turn 40
judgement 134–5
nature of judgement 134–5
practical reason 89–90
validation 20, 124–5
intra-mundane transcendence 2–3, 62–3
inversion thesis 181
Islam, patriarchy in 88–9

Jaeggi, R. 13–14, 21–2
see also forms of life (Jaeggi); problem-solving (Jaeggi)
and Adorno 200–1, 204–5
on alienation 201–2, 221–2
anti-procedural approach to normativity 191–2
on context transcendence 192–3
contradictions in 224
on critique 34–5

Jaeggi, R. (*cont.*)
  defining forms of life 196–7
  on disclosure 202–3
  on everyday experience 191–3
  on the family 198–200
  on formalism and negativism 191–224
  and Habermas 195–6
  and Honneth 192
  on learning 214–15
  on negativism 192
  on progress 43, 198, 206–7, 216–18, 220–1, 224
  on social justice 195–6, 219
Jaggar, A. 55–8, 78–9
James, Joy 46–7
Jeffries, S. 9
Joseph Rowntree Trust 110–11
judgement
  autonomy of 136
  dismissive 172–3
  exemplary 134
  intersubjective 134
  nature of 134–5
  normative 173–4, 223
  priority of 133–7
  reflective 124–5, 133–4
  validity 134
justice 2–3, 11, 19, 66–7, 80–2, 89–90, 146, 163–4, 166–70, 188
  see also injustice
  binding theory 64–6
  and care, gap in literature 104–5
  claims 66, 80–1, 163–4, 178–9, 193–4, 239–40
  critical theory 34–5
  defining in relation to injustice 13
  and equality 94–5, 115, 167–8
  and ethics 193–4
  expanding scope of 130, 198–9
  'first question' of 2–3, 62, 66–7
  Forst on 25–6, 82–3, 88, 163–4
  and freedom 100–2, 106–7
  gender 53–5, 170
  Habermas on 126–7
  injustice as a 'surprising abnormality from norm of' 25–6, 85–6
  international 132–3
  justification and participation models 163–4
  justification criteria 76–8, 80–1, 163–4
  liberal agenda 124, 164–5
  maximally and minimally just society 66
  merits of claims to 188–9
  negative definition 13
  neopragmatist model 156–7

  normative 15–17, 25–6, 67–8, 74–5, 107–8, 121–2
  norm of 25–6
  and oppressed groups 172–3
  as participatory parity 20–1
  political theories 64–5
  and power 25–6, 63, 69–70, 73–4
  principle-interpreting or principle-generating accounts 67–8
  and progress 121–2
  sensus communis 146
  separation of the just from the good 193–6
  social *see* social justice
  as social freedom 106–7
  substantive content 163
  supporting within the family 103–5
  theory of 64–6, 91–2
justification 19, 62–92
  see also injustice; justice; justification monism
  acceptability, general and reciprocal 80
  Adorno on 69, 83–4, 90
  antecedent 67–8, 82
  basic structure, guaranteeing 66
  burdens 82–7
  construing as 'progressive and mutual moral accounting' 86
  and context transcendence 85–6
  contextually sensitive and an ahistorical principle 68–9
  detranscendentalized 86–7
  disclosure and reflexivity 66–9
  discourse ethics 127–8
  duty to justify 65–6
  Forst on 62–92
  Honneth on 64–6, 88–9
  hyper-rationalist procedures 134–5
  ideal and actual 76–82, 87
  immanent and transcendent foundations 63–6
  and inequality 78–9
  justificatory fairness 163–4
  latent status quo bias 77–8
  meta-normative 219
  neutrality, questioning 74–5, 78–82
  normatively justifiable and unjustifiable claims 80
  normative relevance 63
  noumenal power 69–76
  one-dimensional formulation 87
  principle 43, 62–3, 65–9, 85–6, 88–91, 163–4
  procedural 124–5
  rational 53–4
  reasonable 78–80

reconciliation or vacillation between critical
    and ideal perspectives 87–91
  and reflexivity 63, 68–9
  right to 65–6, 89–90, 164–5
  and social justice 66–7
  and teleology 86
  thinness of 78–9, 88
justification monism 63, 67–9, 74–5, 78, 85–6,
    90–2
  see also justification; monism

Kant, Immanuel/Kantism 25–6, 68, 118–19
  exemplary universalism 131–2
  'groundless circularity' of Kantianism 93
  neoKantian critical theories 53–4, 60–1, 93,
    165–6, 193–5
  rejection of Kantian ideas 30–1, 45
Kempf, V. 117
Khader, S. 11–13, 164–5, 187–8
King, M. L. 144–5
Kittay, E. 104–5
knowledge production
  dialogical 32–3
  disempowered groups, insufficient account
    of 23
  and experiential understanding 29–30, 36–7
  hierarchy of theory over experience 41, 43
  oppression 34–5, 173–4
  participatory parity 167–8
  and value of lived experience 5–6
Kogler, H. 29, 41
Kompridis, N. 17–18

learning
  context transcendence as 204–7
  Jaeggi on 214–15
  and negativism 217
  and progress 205–6
  social 128–9, 209, 213–15
Lebron, C. 145
left-Hegelianism 13, 25–6, 149–50, 195–6, 218
Leonard, S. 53
Levinas, E. 84
LGBT people, hate crime against 214
life-world 11–13, 15, 19–20, 51–2, 107–8,
    159–60, 169–70, 178–9, 194–5, 211–13,
    227–8
  context transcendence 206–7
  recognition of gender 94–9
  system-life-world 198–9
lived experience *see* experiential perspective
Lorde, Audre 31–2
Lugones, M. 228–9
Lynch, K. 115–16

Maasai communities, Kenya
  female genital cutting (FGC) 55–8
McCarthy, T. 37–8
MacIntyre, A. 196–7
Mackinnon, C. 229–30
Maiguashca, B. 170–1
male privilege 105–8, 160–1
Marcuse, H. 15–17
Margalit, A. 121–2
marriage 82, 113–14
  and democratization 103–4
  gay 82, 103–4, 117–18
  gender norms 208–9
  noumenal power 71–3
  patriarchal 197–8
Marx, K. 30–1
Marxist roots of Frankfurt School critical
    theory 1–2, 25–6
'merely' experienced 168–76
Merleau-Ponty, M. 6–7
Merton, CV 48
methodological equality 7–8, 24–5, 45–6, 58–9,
    157, 167–8
Mills, C. 18, 25–6, 29–30, 59–60, 119–20,
    143–4
minority communities, women in 187–8
misrecognition
  phenomenology of 27–8, 171–2
  as status subordination 176
  of women's social role 51–2
modernity 1–2, 197–8, 203
  contemporary 106–7
  democratization of love 100–1, 103
  and gender inequality 111–12
  neoliberal 103
  and progress 117–18, 203
Mohanty, S. P. 181–2, 226
money, material power of 71
monism 6, 23–4
  see also justification monism; paradigm-led
    theorizing; recognition monism
  and care 53–4
  context transcendence 37–9, 240–1
  diagnostic 15–17, 168–9
  elision with systemacity 52
  and gender oppression 19–20
  and generality 236–7
  limitations of 4
  monist foundations 21–4, 161–3, 234–8,
    240–1
  normative 11–13, 168–9, 198
  overcoming 158–62
  paradigm-led theorizing 3–4, 6, 11–13, 38–9
  social theory 95–6

mono-causal/mono-categorical diagnostic frameworks *see* single-lens diagnostic frameworks, rejecting
moral constructivism 65–6, 94–5, 107–8
moral equality 145
morality 132–3, 146
  autonomy of 90
  'covering-law' models 25–6
  end-goal 164–5
  and ethics 193–4
  justification critique 83, 85–6, 90
  socially practised 102
moral law 84
Mulhall, S. 139–40
Muller, F. 89–90
multivalent critical theory 7–8, 13, 38–9, 162, 171–2
mutual indifference, contract of 111
mutual responsibility 94–5

Namaste, V. 177–8
Narayan, U. 52–3, 174–7
needs interpretation 11
negation 21–2
  see also negativism
  of actuality 218–23
  of agency 213–18
  determinate *see* determinate negation
  experience of 217
  and negativism 121–2
  priority of the negative 153–4
  and unmasking critique 201–2
negativism 21–2, 192
  see also negation
  abstract 217, 238–9
  and context transcendence 201
  and experience 200–4
  and formalism 191–224
  Frankfurt School critical theory 201
  Honneth on 201
  Jaeggi on 200–4
  and justification 83–4
  and learning 217
  narrow formulation of critique 218, 220
  and negation 121–2
  and progress 121–2
  social theoretical 201, 237–8
neoliberalism 15–17, 102, 119–20, 162, 232–3
  see also capitalism
  capitalism 102, 162, 169–70, 225–6
  and family 111–14
  globalized neoliberal order 143–4
  'merely' experienced 169–70
  and second-wave feminism 170–1

neopragmatics 9–11, 20–1, 156–9, 163
  see also pragmatism/pragmatics
  normative reasoning 20–1, 182–4
neutralization of power 74–5, 207–11
normative foundations 2–3, 9–11, 19, 60–1
  see also foundations; normative reasoning; normative theory/normativity
  and context transcendence 19, 35–7, 161, 205, 218
  Forst on 63–4, 66
  Frankfurt School preoccupation with 23, 191–2, 206–7
  and intra-mundane transcendence 62–3
  limitations of 156–7, 161
  and negative social criticism 204
  and participatory parity 163
  philosophical questions 158–9
  thin 93–4
normative monism 168–9
normative reasoning 67–8, 94–5, 128–9, 193–4
  contextually indexed modes 55–6, 156–7
  conventional 63–4
  enlarged mode 172–3
  immanent 56–8
  inductive approach to 54–5
  multivariant 13
  neopragmatist model 20–1, 182–4
  participatory parity 163
  political 66–7
  power-first approach to 66–7
  practical 187–8, 193–4
  'predemocratic' modes 56–8
normative theory/normativity 53–8
  see also foundations; normative reasoning
  and critical theory 25–6
  deontological models, rejecting 93
  and feminism 56–8
  and Frankfurt School critical theory 1–3, 53
  implicit normativity of social practices 198
  limitations in normative response 4
  monism 11–13, 168–9, 198
  neopragmatatist account 163
  normative grammar 30–1, 66
  normativity of the actual 192
  and paradigm-led theorizing 11–13, 38–9, 238–9
  responses to oppression 30–1
  thought 1, 63–4, 85–6, 94–5, 121–2, 226–7
  validity 63–6, 85–6, 122–3
  white normativity 30–1, 33, 150–1
normopathy 176–7
noumenal power 19, 63, 69–76
  see also power
  defining 71–2
  expansive and restricted ideas of 75

explanatory limitations of 75–6
gender subordination 71–4
Nussbaum, M. 31–2

Obama, B. 147–8
objectification of the subject 33
objectivity 27–8, 151–2, 175–6, 179–80, 228, 236–7
  and context transcendence 41, 43–4
  positioned 44–5
  strong 44–5
O'Brien, B. 172–3
Okin, Susan 71–2
Oksala, J. 34
ontology 137–40
  of recognition 95–6, 99–100
  social 64–5, 195–6, 207–8
  weak 139
opportunity
  equality of 119–20
  lack of 72–3
oppression *see also* experiential perspective; justice
  class 1–2
  cycles of 71–2
  epistemic insight into 47–8
  gender *see* gender oppression
  in global South 9–11
  importance of critique for oppressed groups 28–9
  justice and injustice 31–2, 172–3
  normative responses 30–1
  racial 1–2, 30–1
  real-world dynamics 1–2, 29–30, 217
  significance of direct experience of oppressed groups 6, 23, 27–9, 32–3
  structural 59, 63, 71–2, 126, 209–10
  and suffering *see* suffering
  underlying structures 1
  unmasking critique of 1–15, 23–61
  see also critique

paradigm-led theorizing 3–11, 13, 19, 23–4, 40–1, 44–5, 52, 60–1, 63, 156, 225–6
  see also context transcendence; Frankfurt School critical theory; monism
  and context transcendence 37–9, 45–6
  and dialogism 40–1, 166–7
  experience-led as alternative to 11, 24–5
  features 38–43
  and grand theory 39
  hierarchy of theory over experience 40–1
  incompatible with practical and dialogical inquiry 35

insufficiently responsive to lived experience 3–4
insufficient reflexivity 41–2
Jaeggi's break with 203
monist 3–4, 6, 11–13, 38–9
and negation 201–2
and normativity 11–13, 38–9, 238–9
origins in Habermas 8
rationale 3–4
and recognition monism 99–100
syncretic universalism of 162
and theorizing from experience 6, 60–1
totalizing 3–4, 6–7, 23–4, 39
Parks, R. 144–5
parochialism, problems of 148–53
Parsons, T. 101–2
participatory parity 15–17, 163–8, 172–3, 181
  asymmetries of power 163–4
  deontology 182–4
  headscarves, prohibition on wearing 184–5
  justice as 20–1
  knowledge production 163
  pragmatism 163, 167–8
  social justice 163
particularism 35–6, 132–3, 182, 233–4
  and conventionalism 138
  and experience 44–5, 47–9
  first-hand experiences seen as particularistic and unreliable 23–5, 28–9
  inherent 175–6, 198–9
  intellectual 41–2
  mere 218, 226–7, 233–4
  pure 218–19
  and relativism 204–5
  and universalism 43–4, 150
  and value pluralism 194–5
patriarchal narratives 59, 63, 71–3
Pensky, M. 217
perspectival dualism 160–1
phenomenology
  case studies (Fraser) 169–70
  injustice 34–5, 93–5, 171–2
  of misrecognition 27–8
pluralism 132–3, 191–2
  evaluative 78
  hyper-pluralism 124–5, 138, 140–2
  value-pluralism 140–1, 191–2, 194–6, 211
political constructivism 66
political praxis 9–11
political theories 6–7, 31–3, 124–5, 132–3, 157, 167–8, 188–9, 234–6
  binding 64–5
  context transcendence 35–6, 41
  critical 9–11, 27–8, 239–40

political theories (*cont.*)
    feminist 156
    formal 230–1
    idealizing 25–6, 94–5
    of justice 64–5
    liberal 11–13
    mainstream 18, 93, 132–3
    normative 9
    objectifying modes 23
    radical 188–9, 230–1
politicism 164–5
postcolonialism 24–5
poststructuralism 163
poverty 71–2, 108–10
    black 117
    child 53–4, 110–11
    family 108–11, 213
    gender 108–10
    migration of female workers from poorer countries 114–15
    rising levels 108–11
    in the UK 110–11
    in the US 117
    in-work 110–11
power
    and abductive analysis 49–53
    asymmetries of *see* asymmetries of power
    bottom-up perspective 26–7
    cognitivist construal 69–74, 208
    deep inequalities of 25–6
    disciplinary bio-power 71
    embodied 70–1
    entrenched relations of 38–9
    and the family 103–4, 106–7
    feminist critical theorists on 11
    hierarchized relations of 125–6
    inequalities 4, 25–6, 87
    insufficiently differentiated account of 51–2
    and justice 25–6, 63, 69–70, 73–4
    lived reality 176–8
    localized arrangements of 208–9
    material 71–2
    multivalent/intersectional account 7–8
    neutralization of 74–5, 207–11
    non-coercive 103–4
    noumenal 19, 63, 69–76
    occlusion of 25–6
    origins 4
    and problem-solving 208
    and reason 63
    and recognition 106–7
    social 11
    socio-structural configurations of 4, 47

    systemic 79
    undifferentiated other 73–4
practical reason 43, 150–1, 163
    and constructivism 65–6
    fuzziness of 187–8
    justification 62–3, 65–6, 68–9, 76–7, 88–92
    and normative reasoning 187–8, 193–4
pragmatism/pragmatics 11–14, 43–4, 64–5, 156, 159–60, 190
    and context transcendence 24–5, 44–5, 204–5
    criticism of 200
    critique of forms of life 193–7
    and disclosure 126, 148–52
    and ethics of family 198
    experiential and agent-centred approach 191
    and feminist theorists 174
    and Frankfurt School critical theory 158, 191, 227–8
    neopragmatics 9–11, 20–1, 156–9, 163, 182–4
    and normativity 53–4
    participatory parity 163, 167–8
    philosophy 9–11
    and power 166–9
    thought 227–8
    tradition 193–4
    universal 36–7
priority of adjudication 182–9
    principle-based adjudications 186–8
priority of judgement 133–7
privilege
    artificial 148–9, 218
    asymmetries of 231
    epistemic 14–15, 32–3, 47, 178–9
    invisible 34
    male/masculine 105–8, 160–1
    managerial 85–6
    masking 79–80
    position of 31–2, 229–30
    relative 221–2
    social 33, 166–7, 228–9
    tacit 7–8, 24–5
    of theoretical perspective 41–2, 157, 167–8, 178–82
problematization of experience *see also* Frankfurt School critical theory; monism; paradigm-led theorizing
    context transcendence 40–1
    over-problematization in experiential perspective 5–7, 15, 40–2, 168–9, 173–4, 182, 228–9
    in paradigm-led theorizing 40–2
    preemptive, avoiding 15

under-problematization in theoretical
     perspective 5–7, 40–1, 168–9, 173–4,
     182, 228–9
problem-solving (Jaeggi) 196–8, 201–2, 208
   and disagreement 211–13
   in the family 211–13
   functionalist vocabulary of 207, 210–11
   problems as contradictions 206
   progressive and regressive 197–8
   quasi-evolutionary logic 217
   successful 197–8, 200, 205–6
proceduralism 17–18, 64–5, 200
   discourse ethics 191–2
   formal 53–4, 193–4
   neoKantian 182–4
   rational 133
procedural universalism 20
progress 43, 119–20
   and agency 116–22
   ethical 111–12
   and family 103–4
   formal account of 192–3, 207
   Hegel on 205–7
   Honneth on 93–4, 98–9
   inevitability of 98–9, 103–4, 107–8, 117–18,
     121–2
   Jaeggi on 192–3, 198, 206–7, 216–18,
     220–1, 224
   and justice 121–2
   and learning 205–6
   metanarrative 123
   and modernity 117–18, 203
   quasi-organic model 111–12
   reason as 98–9
   and recognition 19–20
psychoanalysis 231–3
purification of family 104–8

quasi-transcendental status 2–3, 5–6, 62–3
   context transcendence 36–7, 42
   vs metaphysical notions 44–5
Qur'an 88–9

RACAs (reasons that we can all accept) 81–2
racial equality 119–20, 147–8, 215–16
racial inequality 51–2
racial oppression 1–2, 30–1
racial violence 31–2, 73–4, 144–5
Ranciere, J. 88–9
Ransby, Barbara 31–2
Rawls, J. 66–8, 76, 79, 195–6
reality 30–1
   see also experiential perspective
   alienated 40

   of capitalist society 226–7
   care dynamics 95–6
   corporeal 71
   emotional 107
   lived, of oppressed/disempowered groups
     2–5, 8, 19, 27–8, 30–2, 52
     black women 180–1
     disclosure 124–5, 127–8, 154–5
     ethical experiences 191
     experiential 28–9, 154–5, 174, 194–5,
        211–13
     formalism and negativism 211–13,
        221–2
     struggle 15–17, 118–19, 215–16
     subjective 29–30
     subordination 142–3
     suffering 2, 83–4, 173–4
     theorizing from experience 225–6, 228,
        230–1, 234–6
     unmediated 47–8
   material 208
   models 38–9, 69
   normative, of marginalized groups 78–9, 203
   political 153–4, 234–6
   practical 30–1, 54–5, 107
   social 7–8, 28–9, 43, 46–7, 53–4, 60–1, 97–8,
        111–12, 117, 126, 152–3
     context transcendence 15–17
     critique 159–60, 162
     formalism and negativism 215–16, 224
     power and abductive theorizing 49–50, 52
     theorizing from experience 226–7, 234–6,
        238–9
   social and experiential 96–7
reason 18
   see also practical reason
   communicative 11–13
   democratic 130
   disclosure 136–7
   and discourse ethics 128–30
   and imagination 128–9
   instrumental-communicative 198–9
   liberal 215–16
   monological conception 11–13
   normative 193–4
   pluralizing 154
   political 136–7
   and power 63
   procedural 128–30, 136–40
   as progress 98–9
   pure 11–13, 30–1, 133
   reflexive 157
   separation of rational discourse from modes
     of 129–30

reason (*cont.*)
　theoretical 154-5
　unity of 17-18
reciprocity
　and generality 65-6, 80, 88, 163-4
　and mutuality 115-16
　reciprocal self-subjection 107
　temporal expansion of 103
recognition *see also* Honneth, A.; misrecognition
　ahistorical psychology of recognition 99-100
　claims to by racist/anti-racist groups 172-3
　and feminism 94-6
　gender/gendered care work 4, 94-100
　Honneth on 19-20, 64-5
　institutionalized forms of social
　　recognition 101-2
　neoHegelian recognition model 19-20, 93
　ontology of 95-6, 99-100
　ontology of recognition 95-6
　philosophical anthropology of 202-3
　and power 106-7
　and progress 19-20
　recognition of gender and social freedom
　　94-5, 98-9
　recognition-theoretic model 112-13
　recognitive injustice 123, 160, 171-2, 176
　sociology of recognition 93-4
　trans-historical anthropology of
　　recognition 95-6
　unfolding and expanding 203
recognition monism 19-20, 160, 165-6, 171-2, 192
　see also Honneth, A.; monism
　and conventionalism 192, 202-3
　and paradigm-led theorizing 99-100
　and recognition 93-6, 115, 122-3
　recognition of gender 99-100
reflexivity 5-6, 32-4
　and dialogism 4-5, 13, 166-7, 182
　and disclosure 66-9
　epistemic features 23-4
　freedom, reflexive theories 101-2
　insufficient, in paradigm-led theorizing 41-2
　and justification 63, 68-9
　reflective judgement 124-5
　self-scrutiny 42, 88-90
regimes of truth (Foucault) 71
relativism 35-6, 43-4
　and constructivist abstraction 98-9
　and contextualism 219-20
　parochial 88-9
　and particularism 204-5
　priority of judgement 134-5
　progress and agency 119-20
　and universalism 55-6, 93-4, 123

Richardson, H. 81-2
Rockhill, G. 147-8
Rorty, R. 37-8, 43-4, 148-9

Salamon, G. 79-80
same-sex relationships 82, 103
Schwartz, J. 111
second-wave feminism 170-1
self-awareness, critical *see* reflexivity
self-confirmation, bias towards 136-7
self-realization 64-5, 93-4, 101-2, 221
　autonomous 99-100, 107, 197-8, 211-13
　blocking 97-8, 211-13
　commodified 209
　ethical 165-6
　and identity 193-5
　independent 197-8
　and obligation 107
　organized 110-11
　successful 93-4, 202-3
　teleological theories 163-4
self-scrutiny
　critical 33, 68-9, 136-7, 226-7
　reflexive 42, 88-90
Sen, A. 164-5
sensus communis 20, 132-3, 137-41, 146
　and human flourishing 125-6
　parochialism, problems of 150-3
　phenomenological concepts 138
　priority of the negative 153-4
Shapiro, I. 217, 234-6
Shklar, Judith 25-6
Simmel, G. 48
single-lens diagnostic frameworks, rejecting 4,
　　39, 44-5, 225-6
　power and abductive theorizing 49, 51-2
single-parent families 108-10
slavery 50-1
social freedom 93, 118-19, 165-6, 197-200
　autonomy as 102
　and care 103, 115-16
　conditions 101-2
　and gender inequality 111-12
　justice as 106-7
　market as a sphere of 118-19
　material conditions necessary 115-16
　and recognition of gender 94-5, 98-9
social justice 19-20, 25-6, 64-7, 85-6, 91-2,
　　128-9
　see also injustice; justice
　and adjudication, priority of 182-4
　'black rage' as weapon of 31-2
　and care 112-16
　corrective account of 115

and Frankfurt School critical theory 191–2
Jaeggi on 195–6, 219
and participatory parity 163
recognition of gender 94–5, 99–100
reconciliation or vacillation between critical and ideal perspectives 88–91
reconstructive account of 115–16
social learning
  conformity 209
  Habermas on 128–9
  negation of agency 213–15
socially reconstructive method 65–6, 94–5
social ontology 64–5, 195–6
  pluralized 207–8
social praxis 2–3, 102, 196–7, 206
social suffering 26–7, 34–5, 93, 120–1, 124, 154–5, 192, 232–3, 237–8
  see also suffering
  critique of forms of life 194–6
  justification critique 76, 83
sociogenic method 232–3
Spelman, E. 228–9
standpoint theorists 14–15, 21–2, 180–1, 218
status subordination 160–1, 172, 176
structural oppression 59, 63, 71–2, 126, 209–10
subjectivism 35–6, 43–4
subordination
  axes of 160–1
  class 160–1
  dynamics 234
  forms 204
  gender *see* gender subordination
  group/intra-group 184, 234
  indirect nature 176
  race 160–1
  social 172
  status 160–1, 172, 176
suffering
  Adorno on 27–8
  downplaying by Frankfurt School theorists 1–2, 28–9
  horizons of 146
  and justification 83–4
  'lived' 26–7
  reactions to 83
  role in critique 27–8, 34–5
  seen as a 'symptom' 28–9
  social *see* social suffering
  and status subordination 172
symbolic violence 29–30, 73–4, 127–8, 176

Taylor, C. 128–9
teleology 86, 163–4

theorizing from experience 14, 19, 225–41
  see also experiential perspective; theory/theoretical inquiry
  advantages of 6
  experience-led theorizing as alternative to paradigm-led theories 11, 24–5
  feminist 46–9
  and paradigm-led theorizing 6, 60–1
  particularistic 23–5
  problem-led mode of inquiry 234–7
theory/theoretical inquiry *see also* critical theory; first-generation critical theory; normative theory
  abductive 49–53
  and context 128–9
  epistemic authority of 179–80
  experience-led theorizing *see* theorizing from experience
  feminist 46–9
  Frankfurt School definition 32–5
  Frankfurt School's commitment to 4–5
  hierarchy of theory over experience 40–1
  ideal theory 66–8
  paradigm-led *see* paradigm-led theorizing
  a priori theories 83
  privilege of 41–2, 157, 167–8, 178–82
  under-problematization 5–7, 40–1, 168–9, 173–4, 182, 228–9
  problem-led, inductive theorizing 11
  theoretical-juridical model 85–6
thick description 35–6
Thomas, L. 83–4
Thompson, M. 209
thought *see also* context transcendence; Frankfurt School critical theory; normative theory/normativity; paradigm-led theorizing; pragmatism/pragmatics
  abstract 146, 150
  autonomous 40
  communitarian 196–7
  context transcendence 37–8, 44–5
  contextually indexed modes 43
  democratic 124–5, 129–30
  disclosive 18, 60–1, 124
  emancipatory 182, 190
    political 66–7
    practical 19, 23–4, 158–9
    racial 173–4
  'estranging enigmas' 46–7
  everyday modes 46–7
  and feeling 152–3
  feminist 14–15, 52
    see also black feminist thought

thought *(cont.)*
  Frankfurt School 3–4, 9–11, 156, 158, 191, 226–7, 240–1
  liberal political 11–13
  mainstream 18
  normative 1, 63–4, 85–6, 94–5, 121–2, 226–7
  normative political 62, 68
  "outsider" 46–7
  paradigm-led 6–7, 13, 19, 24–5, 44–5, 60–1
  particularistic 150
  political 20, 26–7, 35–6, 95–6, 137–40
  pragmatic 196–7
  preconditions 68
  situated nature of 39, 43–4, 150–1
  social 35–6, 95–6
thought-experiments 141, 221–2
  counterfactual 82
  discourse ethics 140
  internal 134
  simplified and artificially contained 139–40
Threadcraft, S. 211–13
Tobin, T. 55–8, 78–9
tokenism 19–21, 23, 34, 93–5, 158–9, 173–4
top-down analysis, limitations 1, 25–7, 32–3, 49
totalizing paradigm-led theorizing 3–4, 6–7, 23–4, 37–8, 169–70
transcendence/transcendentalism *see also* context transcendence; quasi-transcendental status
  critical 23–4
  and immanence 23–5, 63–6, 90–1, 192–3
  intra-mundane 2–3, 62–3, 111–12
  justification, immanent and transcendent foundations 63–6
  metaphysical notions 36–7, 44–5
  practical 63, 68–9
  and pure reason 30–1
transphobic violence 73–4, 177–8
Tronto, J. 104–5
truth 7–8, 18, 34–5, 49–50, 59–60, 75, 126–7, 136–7, 145, 157, 179–80
  authentic 34
  extra-political 144–5, 152–4
  extra-social 139–41
  higher truths 65–6
  moral 31–2
  new truth-in-itself 135
  regimes of 71
  theoretical 188–9

United Kingdom
  domestic abuse 105–6, 108–10
  face veiling 185–6
  hate crime 214
  poverty 110–11
  single-parent families 108–10
United States
  African-American struggle for equality 144–5
  African-American women 49–51
  athletes 146–7
  black families, treatment of 211–13
  care economy 213
  Civil Rights Act (1964) 215–16
  colour blindness 119–20
  and election of Obama 147–8
  feminist theory, North America 170–1
  neoliberalism 111–12
  penal system 59
  problem-solving 211–13
  racial divisions 142–3
  racial equality 215–16
  racialized nature of poverty in 211
universalism
  abstract 11–13, 204–5
  discursive 77–8
  empty/'emaciated' 150
  exemplary 20, 124–6, 130–3, 154
  free-floating 66–7, 152–3
  and historicism 120–1
  intuitive 140–1, 151–2
  moral 11–13
  and particularism 43–4, 150
  procedural 20
  'rational universal' 64–5
  rejecting 237–8
  and relativism 55–6, 93–4, 123
  strong 44–5, 90–1
  syncretic 162
  without principles 124–5, 130–2
unmasking critique 1–15, 23–61, 67–8, 93–4, 226
  see also critique; experiential perspective; Frankfurt School critical theory; monism; oppression; paradigm-led theorizing
  Frankfurt School on own role in 6
  validity 4–5, 14–15
unreliability of subjective experience, assumed 5–6, 23–5, 28–9, 35–6, 46–7, 175–6
  notorious, Fraser on 168–9, 171–4, 184–5

validation *see also* truth; validity; verification
  authority 59
  democratic 130, 134–5
  Habermasian 77–8
  intersubjective 20, 124–5
  knowledge 180–1
  procedures 194–5
  processes 135

self-validation 47–8
universally acceptable 86
validity 80, 126–7
   see also validation; verification
   and adjudication 15–17
   context-independent 37–8
   and context transcendence 45–6
   of critique 9–11, 35–6, 41, 45, 90–1
   extra-positive 132–3
   and generality 234–6
   generalized 120–1
   hyper-rationalist 194–5
   of injustice claims 20–1
   interpretive paradigm 11–13
   judgement 134
   and justification 2–3, 11–13, 53–4, 65–6,
      69–70, 124, 134–5
   logic 127–8
   norms/normative validity 63–6, 85–6, 122–3
   of political claims 133–4
   surplus 105, 116–17
   trans-contextual 37–8
   universal 37–8
   of unmasking critique 4–5, 14–15
   yes/no logic 128–9
value-pluralism 140–1, 191–2, 194–6, 211
verification 4–5, 28–9, 43, 173–4, 228
   see also truth; validation; validity
   practical 32–3, 45, 86, 127–8, 134–5
violence 1–2, 74–6, 234–6
   domestic 53–4, 105–10, 119–20, 165–6
   and erase of agency 73–4
   gendered 50–1, 55–8
   male 73–4, 105–6, 152–3
   racial 31–2, 73–4, 144–5
   sexual 73–4
   symbolic 29–30, 73–4, 127–8, 176
   systematic 55–6, 73–4
   transphobic 73–4, 177–8
   unacknowledged 50–1
volunteerism 214–15

Wacquant, L. 42
Walsh, J. 115–16
welfare state, patriarchal 170
Wellmer, Albrecht 43–4, 133
West, C. 146
White, S. 139
white normativity 30–1, 33, 150–1
Williams, B. 66–7
Williams, R. 152–3
women's subordination *see* gender
   subordination
Woolf, J. 202–3
world disclosure 126–9, 135, 137–8, 202–3, 224
   problem-oriented 192
Wright, R.
   Black Boy 146–7

Young, I. M. 1, 9–11, 13, 34–5, 80–1, 113–14,
   133, 172–3, 231, 234, 237–8
   monism, overcoming 158–9
   and priority of adjudication 184–5, 188

Zakaria, R. 185–6
Zurn, C. 181